I0820146

Insurgent Politics in the Lone Star State

Remembering the Antiwar Movement in Austin, Texas, 1967–1973

Martin J. Murray

University of North Texas Press
Denton, Texas

Printed in the United States of America.

10 9 8 7 6 5 4 3 2 1

Permissions:
University of North Texas Press
1155 Union Circle #311336
Denton, TX 76203-5017

The paper used in this book meets the minimum requirements of the American National Standard for Permanence of Paper for Printed Library Materials, z39.48.1984. Binding materials have been chosen for durability.

Library of Congress Cataloging-in-Publication Data is available from the Library of Congress.

ISBN 978-1-57441-981-8 (cloth)
ISBN 978-1-57441-989-4 (ebook)

UNT Press acknowledges the generous subvention for publication from the Research Catalyst and Innovation (RCI) Program, funded by the Office of Vice President for Research, University of Michigan, with funding from Taubman College (University of Michigan). Seed Grant and matching funding from Department of Afroamerican and African Studies (DAAS), University of Michigan.

The electronic edition of this book was made possible by the support of the Vick Family Foundation.

Cover photograph: Unauthorized march following Kent State shootings, 5 May 1970. Johnny B. Jenkins, photographer. Courtesy of Prints and Photographs Collection, e_ppc_0022, Dolph Briscoe Center for American History, University of Texas at Austin.
Author at the far, far left of the image.

Typeset by vPrompt eServices.

Contents

Dedication

The Greek philosopher Heraclitus purportedly said, "You never step into the same river twice." Even the slightest passage of time transforms the original river into an entirely new one. The same holds for people. I am now no longer the same person as I was in 1967–1973 when I was living in Austin. The person who participated in the antiwar movement at that time is no more. I miss that person. I wish I remembered more about him. This book is dedicated to the person, now no more, that I once was a long time ago.

This book is also dedicated to my lost friends and comrades David MacBryde, Martin Wiginton, Greg Calvert, Cam Cunningham, Judy Smith, Beth Livezey, Richard Minus, John Kniffin (a Vietnam veteran who passed away due to complications from exposure to Agent Orange), Steve Russell, Terry DuBose, Sam Jones, John Miur, Doyle Niemann, and Gary Fitzgerald. I also wish to acknowledge fallen Irish Republicans Dolours Price and her sister, Marian, but especially Mairead Farrell. We all shared a vision for a better future. Alas, it did not come to pass in the ways we hoped it would. Finally, this book is especially dedicated to my younger brother Dennis, a dear friend and a loving person. He was a veteran of the US Army. When he left the military in 1969, he organized antiwar demonstrations at Diablo Valley Junior College. He would have read and loved every word of this book.

I am going to donate all the materials regarding the antiwar movement in Austin that I have in my possession to the Dolph Briscoe Center for American History at the University of Texas at Austin.

List of Acronyms

AABL	African Americans for Black Liberation
AMDT	Armadillo May Day Tribe
APD	Austin Police Department
CUF	Community United Front
CO	conscientious objector
COINTELPRO	Counter Intelligence Program
CPUSA	Communist Party, USA
DRV	Democratic Republic of Vietnam
DPS	Department of Public Safety
FBI	Federal Bureau of Investigation
FOIA	Freedom of Information Act
GWMC	Gerard Winstanley Memorial Caucus
HUAC	House Un-American Activities Committee
IRS	Internal Revenue Service
IWW	Industrial Workers of the World
LBJ	Lyndon Baines Johnson
MDC	May Day Committee
MDS	Movement for a Democratic Society
NAM	New American Movement
NARA	National Archives Records Administration
NISO	National Intelligence Security Organization
NLF	National Liberation Front
NPAC	National Peace Action Coalition
NLEP	New Left Education Project
OSI	Office of Special Investigations
PCPJ	People's Coalition for Peace and Justice
PL	Progressive Labor
ROTC	Reserve Officer Training Corps
SAC	special agent in charge [FBI]
SWP	Socialist Workers Party

SDS	Students for a Democratic Society
SMC	Student Mobilization Committee
SNCC	Student Nonviolent Coordinating Committee
SOA	School of Architecture (University of Texas)
SSOC	Southern Student Organizing Committee
TI	Texas Instruments
TEI	Transportation Enterprises Inc.
TRO	temporary restraining orders
USF	University of San Francisco
UTCEWV	University of Texas Committee to End the war in Vietnam
UT Austin	University of Texas at Austin
VVAW	Vietnam Veterans Against the War
WITCH	Women's International Terrorist Conspiracy from Hell
YSA	Young Socialist Alliance

Preface

> History has rhythms, tunes and even harmonies, but the sound of the past is an agonistic multiplicity. Chance decides what is obliterated and what survives if only to be distorted and misheard.
> —Tim Robinson, *Listening to the Wind*

From the time I arrived in Austin in September 1967 until I departed in June 1973, I was involved in the antiwar movement, both as a member of a variety of different political organizations committed to end the war in Vietnam and combat racism and sexism at home, and as an organizer of mass marches, rallies, demonstrations, sit-ins, and building occupations. These protest activities sometimes led to direct confrontations with university security officers and with the Austin law enforcement. These years were a concentrated period of intense social, cultural, and political turmoil. While I was a PhD student (first in the Department of Philosophy and then in the Department of Sociology at University of Texas at Austin), my primary focus was participation in the insurgent politics of the day. My political activism overshadowed my life as a diligent student. At the very beginning, I played a largely supportive role in the antiwar movement, following the lead of those veteran forerunners who provided direction. Eventually, as I gained experience and confidence, I assumed a shared leadership role in direct action political campaigns.

At first glance, to select the political ferment in Austin, Texas, in the 1960s and 1970s as a site for the investigation of the antiwar movement and the state of play of the state security surveillance and political repression aligned against popular protest might seem a bit odd. After all, the organizational core of political opposition to the war in Vietnam and support for the Black liberation movement and women's rights was centered in the major urban centers of the East and West Coasts, along with Upper Midwest cities like Chicago. Despite the widespread perception in movement circles that Austin was a bit of a backwater where if anything happened it was merely copied from the "real movement" located in New York, Boston, Los Angeles, Chicago, and the San Francisco Bay Area, the political opposition that emerged and developed in Austin assumed its own historically specific characteristics with a distinctiveness not found anywhere else.

In the 1960s Austin had a population of around 240,000 residents. It was the state capital and home to the flagship University of Texas campus, with an estimated thirty to thirty-five thousand students. Texas has a long history of populism that ebbed and flowed from the mid-nineteenth century until today. In the 1960s the University of Texas administration poured a lot of money into building academic programs in the hard sciences (particularly oil and chemical engineering), social sciences, and humanities, and into luring well-known professors from elite Ivy League universities. This effort paid dividends, bolstering the prestige of its faculty and attracting PhD students from around the country. Out-of-state tuition was $400 per year, and in-state tuition was a paltry $100—due in part to windfall profits and revenues from oil extraction from the Permian Basin of West Texas.

The last vestiges of formally segregated commercial establishments in Austin—like movie theaters, restaurants, and hotels—remained in place in the mid-1960s. The student body at University of Texas was highly segregated, with African Americans and Chicanos making up only about 2 percent of total enrollment. In 1970 University of Texas and University of Arkansas became the last Southwest Conference football teams to fully integrate, some four years after Southern Methodist University fielded its first African American players. Statutes of Confederate generals and key Texas segregationist figures lined the prominent mall in the shadow of the university tower. These statues remained in place until their unannounced removal in 2017. Social life at the university centered on fraternities and sororities, enclaved bastions of white privilege and stepping-stones for the anticipated postcollege world of business, family, and social status. With the exception of small pockets of dissatisfaction and the embryonic stirrings of alienated youth, students and faculty hewed to the straight and narrow under the seemingly benign but ever watchful eye of the university administration. The university administration adhered to an "in loco parentis" approach to student life on campus, and this attitude reigned supreme.

What might be loosely called "the movement" in Austin originated in the early to mid-1960s (with populist roots in earlier times) and fell into disrepair by the late 1970s. During the decade of high-velocity politics and resistance, those in the movement intermingled and intersected, diverged and converged, often in strange alliances. We all came to the same dance but gathered in different circles and then left to go our own separate ways. The goals—end the war in Vietnam, combat entrenched racism and discrimination, expose misogyny and promote the liberation of women, support gay rights, and promote a clean environment—were not shared equally and pursued with the same vigor by all the participants in the New Left and the Austin antiwar movement. That is not surprising. What distinguished the New Left and the movement in Austin from other leftist traditions across the United States was their deep roots in a kind of populist, anarcho-syndicalist vision that eschewed the top-down command-and-control structure of Old Left Marxist–Leninist parties with their "one way" formulas for revolution. Unlike the growth of the New Left in East and West Coastal cities with their long traditions of liberal middle-class values, the movement in Austin came into existence under very different conditions. We had no thick and enduring liberal veneer to shield us from exposure to the elements of condemnation and repression. The antiwar movement was born under circumstances that brought us face-to-face—without any protective buffers—with a deeply conservative popular culture nurtured under the long shadow of the Confederacy, racial segregation, and the omnipresent Ku Klux Klan.

In Austin the fledgling efforts in the early 1960s of small groups to hasten racial desegregation and the first embryonic expressions of antiwar sentiment proceeded in tandem with stepped-up police surveillance and the monitoring of so-called anti-American activities. In this sense what was being born in Austin was not particularly distinguishable from what was happening at other university campuses around the country. Yet what was different was that the University of Texas was one of the first college campuses away from the West and the East Coasts and the Upper Midwest to have a vibrant local Students for a Democratic Society (SDS) chapter. From the start the underlying sensibilities in Austin that defined the movement was a loose designation called "prairie power," a visceral commitment to the independence of ideas and autonomy of action. SDS in Austin always adopted an irreverent posture with a strong dose of anarchism (and anarcho-syndicalism).[1] While organized left-wing groups—like the Communist Party, USA (CPUSA), the Socialist Workers Party (SWP), and the Progressive Labor (PL) Party—carved out places for themselves in the political movement in big cities of the West and East Coasts, these groups never established much of a foothold in Austin. They maintained an organized presence but neither led the antiwar movement nor strongly influenced its direction. To differentiate ourselves from the Old Left clustered around the Marxist-Leninist parties that defined oppositional politics in earlier decades, we embraced the idea that we were part of a New Left.

My Autobiographical Self

This is my story about those turbulent times when the world seemed literally turned upside down. I am both the main character and the principal narrator. My story is a blend of history and memory, speculation and reasoned conjecture. What I offer is largely an autobiographical account of my experiences and participation in alternative politics and popular protest during this compressed time of great upheaval. There are many stories to tell, and mine is only one of them. In the wide arc of historical time, I form but a single thread in a much more complex and nuanced tapestry of dissenting politics. I helped to shape the movement, but I was also fundamentally shaped by it.

My autobiographic recollections of the rise and decline of the antiwar movement in Austin share much in common with other accounts that also work from a participant-observer perspective (such as Todd Gitlin, Robert Pardun, and Alice Embree).[2] The reason that I hold on to the autobiographical tone of this book, and try not to let it be swamped by secondary historiographical accounts, is to preserve the first-person voice: I was the one who experienced the antiwar movement, and I am the one who shall remain as the principal narrator of what happened.

My story is not framed within an overarching narrative that I can rely on to magically pull events and people into some sort of coherent and unfolding order, or to confidently predict when and why things would fall apart. Writing about this personal journey over fifty years after the events in question took place, I am bound to be mistaken some of the time. Let me say at the outset, there are no true heroes or ignoble villains in my story. My account is not intended to be a romantic tale of high-minded, faultless people confronting the evil war machine. Collectively speaking, we were ordinary persons responding to unusual circumstances in extraordinary times.

We in the antiwar movement were motivated by noble goals, but we also carried our prejudices, biases, and preconceptions into our political activism. We often mistreated each other and made hurtful, reckless, and even thoughtless decisions. Those of us who participated in the antiwar movement experienced a common predicament: We were part of a shared story, but one in which the direction was open-ended and the ultimate goals were not clear at all. It would be misleading to present the politics of the time as explicit, self-evident, and consistent. The antiwar movement and the accompanying countercultural experience emerged out of turbulence and crisis, and we often arrived at political decisions in a visceral way rather than rooted in intellectual or philosophical core beliefs. Yet one can detect a defining vision: Ending the war in Southeast Asia, confronting the war makers, and challenging the institutional apparatuses that kept the war machine going were interwoven with a broader assault on the sociocultural underpinnings of the

Cold War ideology that defined Communism as the enemy of the American way of life.

Confrontational politics became the appropriate mode of dissent when conventional liberal politics of periodic elections and appeals to moral reason failed to budge those in power. We grew weary of patiently waiting for the redress of grievances as it became clear that the state security apparatuses were bent on the extralegal use of force to violently suppress political opposition. Our understanding of the misguided imperialist adventure in Southeast Asia blended with the sense of social injustice stemming from institutional racism and sexism and provided a platform that sustained the movement. Yet without a shared commitment to a common future rooted in the continuity of popular struggle in America, it was impossible to sustain the momentum.

During my protest years in Austin, I can say that the events I participated in, the friends I kept, and the organizations I joined established the framework within which I arrive at judgments of the past. Our collective goal was to end the war in Vietnam; challenge the racism, sexism, misogyny, and homophobia that permeated American culture; and build a better world around social justice. Our goals were admirable objectives, approached only asymptotically. We advanced in the direction of the line but never quite reached it. In a sense, our intentions were rooted in an existential belief that our collective actions were morally legitimate, our aims were laudatory, and the ends we set our sights upon justified the means we chose to reach them.

The antiwar movement in Austin originated out of the rapid escalation of the war in Southwest Asia and disappeared into the fog of historical time. It is an impossible task to truly reconstruct what happened and why. I have not tried to construct a single, coherent narrative with a clear beginning, middle, and end, but rather to weave together disparate storylines that sometimes overlap and sometimes conflict. I do not seek to identify universal insights and timeless lessons that help to explain the place and the relevance of the Austin antiwar movement in the broad arc of insurgent politics during the 1960s and 1970s. It is understandable that when I began this journey of self-discovery I hoped, and perhaps even expected, that the events that I cared deeply about could be, at least to a certain extent, pulled together and understood objectively. In short, we *know* something happened in those unsettling times, and it is reasonable to expect that we should be able to discover what it was and what it meant in the larger scheme of history. Yet whatever certainty we have with what we *know* about what happened is always offset by the *unknown* and *unknowable*. The full story remains in a permanent state of contradiction. A more sanguine engagement with the historical past reminds us that for complex social and political events and processes, the questions and answers to "what happened and why"—and how it really mattered in the long run—are always understood differently by whomever is asking the questions.

History and Memory

Writing an autobiographical account starts in the present and looks retrospectively back in time. Looking backward is like summoning ghosts from the past—fleeting, spectral images, never fully formed and never willing to remain in one place. Relying on one's own memory alone is a flawed method for the recovery of the past. Subject to the corrosive ravages of time, memory is not always a dependable companion or the most reliable repository or archive for storing information. The goal of piecing together the shards and fragments of the past into a coherent whole is as elusive as it is frustrating. "Historians are left forever chasing shadows, painfully aware of their inability ever to reconstruct a dead world in its completeness," Simon Schama once wrote. "We are doomed to be forever hailing someone who has just gone around the corner and out of earshot."[3] I feel that it is my younger self, nearly fifty years ago, who has just gone around the corner, disappearing into the fog of tear gas and followed by the loud shouts of protest. So I am forced to write against forgetting, pursuing ghosts, seeking the spectral presence of my self as it dissipates over time and disappears into nothingness.

In trying to make sense of my involvement in the antiwar movement, there are gaps and silences in the story. Elisions are, of course, inevitable. By itself memory is an untrustworthy partner in the search for genuine accuracy, often overlooking uncomfortable events because they are unpleasant or just discarding them altogether because they seem unimportant to me. Recalling the past can sometimes fill in the missing links with unseemly doses of fantasy and make-believe. The temptation is always to select from the past what one wants to remember. It is easy to substitute "it *must* have happened that way" for "it *did* happen that way." In retelling a story from the past, sometimes we are so sure we remember exactly what happened and when, only to discover through cross-checking documents that what we remembered might not be precisely accurate or factually true.

In order to ensure that the excavation of my memories was not just a kind of magical wishful thinking, determined as much by what I wanted to have happened as an accurate recollection of what actually happened, I have relied upon a combination of aide-mémoire, including police/security records, newspaper accounts, available secondary sources, old photographs, and personal communications and conversations with fellow political activists who participated in the events that I describe here. I am seeking to offer a story of people enmeshed in concatenated events that defined a particular time and place in American history. It is also an exploration of my memories of these tumultuous times, the relationship between the person I am now and my younger self, and the tenuous connection between my personal recollections and a verifiable historical account.

Researching Myself

My story is autobiographical. By definition autobiographical accounts are introspective, where one's own interpretation often crowds out a more balanced, objective reconstruction of the past. In this sense I admit that I suffer from experience bias; I make no apologies for recounting events as I recall them through the subjective lens of hindsight. Remembering events and people from the past is not only about "getting the facts straight" but also about deciding on the best way to make sense what happened and why. After all, like in the famous 1950 Japanese film *Rashoman* (directed by Akira Kurosawa), participants in the same events always remember what took place from their own point of view and offer sometimes wildly different interpretations of their shared past experiences. Yet in telling my story, I do not just construct events out of thin air, and I do not attest to their unchallenged factual accuracy. When I was unsure of dates for events, I cross-checked using newspaper accounts, the recollections of friends, and other source materials. This triangulated approach enabled me to reconstruct an accurate sequential order to events, but it does not really help in accurately conveying the meaning of what took place and the connections between events. My personal experience establishes the vantage point from which I venture forth to tell my own story.

In a real sense, a revelatory story is built into every confessional autobiography: The one telling the story purports to be the one who remembers, who experienced what happened, who responded in distinct ways, and who felt the full range of emotions. Yet the one telling the story is no longer that person who took part in those events of fifty years ago. That person who existed so long ago is no longer real, only a fading memory. In writing the storyteller can, metaphorically speaking, be reborn. In laying claim to recounting authentic experience through self-exposure, the storyteller paradoxically declares independence or distance from the past. I am that storyteller, trying to recall my thoughts, my feelings, and my actions from a half century ago.

Let me say, at the outset, that this book is not intended to be a definitive and comprehensive account of political activism and the antiwar movement in Austin. My aim is to construct a work of narrative nonfiction. I cannot vouch that everything I say in this book is unassailably true, backed with mountains of corroborating evidence. I have tried to the best of my ability to tap into memories of events, persons, and organizations and to reconstruct how I fit into each. I started this project with a narrow focus on researching myself, trying to discover in the records of security agencies how they constructed me not as a person but as a deviant social category—"militant subversive." Because I never thought of myself in these terms, I was extremely curious how the FBI and other law enforcement / security agencies could arrive at such a dismissive designation.

What I am offering here is a retrospective journey into the past, a time-travel odyssey that tentatively ventures backward in time with the aim of reconstructing an earlier time and place. What I want to stress is that my story is not a conventional historiographical account tied to the search for reliable and valid evidence. Hence, it is not subject to the same rules of evidence as "fact-based" historiographical accounts. My memories can be incomplete, distorted, or even factually inaccurate. I understand these obstacles as not only an impediment to a full and accurate accounting of the past but also an opportunity to look backward through the vantage point of the present.

Writing an autobiographical account requires a certain distance before I can claim perspective. This mode of storytelling involves reorganizing my recollections of past experiences so that the larger meanings of the story are revealed, rather than merely trying to recall what happened with as much detail as possible. I have had to select, omit, and reshape from the great mass of available information so that a coherent view of the past as I remember it can emerge.

No single story can provide a definitive account of the intricate connections between events, people, and organizations that gave substance to the many iterations and twists and turns of alternative politics and popular protest. Grounded in opposition to imperialism and the war in Vietnam and animated by the desire to combat racism, sexism, and other forms of oppression, the broad-based movement at the center of the political maelstrom never constituted a coherent entity easily captured in simple catch phrases or slogans.

Dead Certainties

What is known with a high degree of certitude is the unfolding sequence of visible events that accompanied the upsurge of popular protest in Austin in the 1960s and 1970s. What is clear is that the lack of surviving evidence (whether in the form of oral histories, written documents, or newspaper accounts) makes it almost impossible to fully reconstruct what happened and why. I am sometimes left with guesswork and speculation, filling in the gaps as best I can from memory, scraps of evidence, and conjecture.

Both the emergence and growth of the antiwar movement and the strategies designed to monitor and crush it were collaborative efforts, with both political activists and police/security agencies cooperating among themselves, without fully understanding it, to keep the other side off balance.

Even though the evidence is fragmentary and often ambiguous, it is possible to piece together a narrative account that approximates some degree of accuracy.[4]

At the end of the day, the unknown and unknowable past has largely evaporated into a kind of spectral collection of partial memories. The passage of time brings different ways of seeing. It would have been impossible for me to know the significance of events at the historical moment that they took place. Events are always part of a pattern, and their impact only becomes apparent after they become part of the past. By establishing myself as an object of inquiry in its own right, I am seeking to make sense of the turbulent politics of Austin in the 1960s and 1970s.

So in the end, I have constructed a sort of multicolored tapestry—something less than an accurate story but certainly more than make-believe fiction. Often regarded as works of art, tapestries can fill the gaps left open by fading memory and lack of facts by allowing one's own personal lived experience of a time and place—what might be called "structures of feeling"—to take center stage.

I write this account with the sad realization and the grim acknowledgment that the world as I had lived it, and understood it, no longer exists except as a fleeting memory no one really cares about as much as I do. I cling to those evaporating memories not for some nostalgic longing for something irretrievably lost or to seek to relive the past as something akin to youthful glory days. Instead, I return to these memories as markers or signs of a fleeting moment in time, allowing me to glimpse into who I was at the time and what I have become. This undertaking is a bit surreal and strange. Looking backward on these police reports requires a certain kind of mental gymnastics—to experience myself in objective terms, as a separate and detached being that was once me.

In recounting these events that took place a long time ago, I dispense with the standard modernist technique of the use of a free-floating narrator. I am intricately imbricated in my own story. The form of knowing that I employ is not, as it might seem at first glance, my own personal experience but my recent reflections on that experience. It is not myself that I write about, but my reflections of who I was once upon a time.

Origins

Writing this autobiographical account originated out a curiosity on my part to explore my own experiences in the antiwar movement in Austin. The immediate inspiration behind this book began to take shape after my twin brother Mark used the Freedom of Information Act (FOIA) in mid-2017 to obtain three separate caches of FBI files (numbering around seventy pages in all) related to his periodic trips to visit me in Austin. He came to stay with me for several few weeks at a time on three separate occasions in the spring of 1969, 1970, and 1971. Mark would arrive to participate in the annual spring festival of protest rallies, marches, and events that far surpassed anything happening in the political backwater of Omaha, where he lived. He blended in well with my friends. He enjoyed the warm weather, the friendly Austin atmosphere, and his freedom from the Midwest dreariness of Nebraska and its famed Cornhuskers. He became one of us in the Austin antiwar movement. Despite his limited participation in antiwar activities, he amassed an impressive set of FBI files reporting on his activities.

Perhaps not so surprisingly, my name appears alongside his with uncanny regularity. While the reports begin with my brother Mark, they always end with discussions of the two of us—like bookends holding up something subversive in the middle. It took me a number of years before I let my curiosity get the better of me. I became intrigued about my own FBI files. If law enforcement agencies collected all this information on my brother who came to Austin for six weeks over the course of the six years when I lived there, what kind of surveillance did they conduct on me? I then began a three-and-a-half year, tortuous quest to obtain my own FBI files via the assistance of a lawyer (Peter Sorenson) who specializes in FOIA requests.

At the start this journey yielded disappointing results. In back-and-forth correspondence with Pete Sorenson, FBI officials stalled and dissembled, claiming that the files that I requested either could not be found, had been destroyed, or had been transferred to the National Archives Records Administration (NARA). My lawyer reached an impasse when the US assistant district attorney in Washington, DC, the government official who handled the case, accepted the FBI version of events. She concluded that the FBI had made a good faith effort to locate my files and agreed with the

FBI that some of the files I requested were sufficiently sensitive that I had no legal right to obtain them. My long journey into the legal labyrinth of FBI files seemed to have stalled.

My lawyer then turned to NARA to break out of the cul-de-sac. This pathway yielded some results. Persistence paid off. After a yearlong effort, NARA archivists were able to find some records that were of interest to me. Finally, following a last-ditch effort that involved a Zoom meeting in late 2023 with the head of NARA, three on-staff lawyers, and two archivists, we hit pay dirt. After some renewed digging, archivists first uncovered 1,521 more pages of FBI files either directly or indirectly related to me that somehow had eluded their earlier efforts. As they searched, they were able to discover 461 more pages. All in all, these files related to me, Martin Wiginton, Greg Calvert, Bobby Nelson, the Armadillo May Day Tribe, and the protests at the LBJ Library dedication. It had taken close to four years from start to finish, but I finally received these files in March 2025. In the meantime, with the assistance of the Sorenson Law Firm, I sued the FBI for violations of the Freedom of Information Act (FOIA) on the grounds that they had improperly withheld files from me. As part of this case, we asked the court to order the FBI to pay me reasonable attorney fees and costs. Eventually, the FBI agreed to a payment of $10,000 to settle the issue.

As I began to write about my own experiences in the antiwar movement from memory, I learned that the Dolph Briscoe Center for American History at the University of Texas at Austin had obtained these separate collections of materials from three local law enforcement figures. The Burt Gerding Papers consist of a treasure trove of memorabilia from the former head of the Criminal Intelligence Division, Austin Police Department (APD). The Allen Hamilton Papers contain photographic images and memorandum from the former head of campus security at UT Austin. Finally, the George Carlson Papers consist of police reports, photographs, and newspaper clippings from the former head of security for the University of Texas System.

I embarked on a personal journey to find out what these conjoined state security agencies—the FBI, the Criminal Intelligence Division of the APD, University of Texas campus security, and the University of Texas System Security—had learned about me and how they reported it. What I wanted to know was the extent to which the policing/security agencies aligned against the antiwar movement paid attention to me. I was most intrigued to learn how they constructed me through their security lens in their language of subversion and threat. I know what I did and I know what I thought during those heady days of political turmoil. How can I reconcile what I know about myself in counter-distinction to how the security agencies constructed me in the image of a subversive radical and a threat to national security?

What began as an intensely personal journey of discovery directed at locating my younger self in official security records gradually blossomed into a broader exploration of the trajectory of the antiwar movement in Austin during the crucial years between 1967 and 1973. Once I began looking through the security files, I broadened my inquiry into understanding the relationship between the political protest movement and the various security agencies aligned against it. In moving in this broadened direction, I expanded my sources beyond personal recollections to include collaborating evidence derived from FBI memos, undercover informant reports, newspaper accounts, recollections of fellow antiwar activists, and various pamphlets and leaflets distributed at the time.

What I came to realize is that the antiwar movement—with all its internal contradictions, faults, indecisiveness, and wrong turns—cannot be understood without grasping its symbiotic relationship with the array of security agencies that were aligned against it. This connection was, of course, toxic: Political activists both feared and despised the forces of law and order. We knew that the security agencies were both able and willing to go outside the law to undermine our efforts. On the other side, security agencies began with the assumption that political activists held naive anti-American ideas and that those who participated in the antiwar movement were dupes, unduly influenced by Communists bent on overthrowing the US government. In this narrow worldview, participation in antiwar marches, rallies, and demonstrations was only the slippery slope toward embracing views in opposition to free enterprise and private property and mainstream American cultural values. From the vantage point of the security agencies, the conventional tenets of the American way of life were under threat.

As the war in Vietnam raged on, millions of people—idealists, pacifists, and draft resisters mixed in with those who wanted to "Give Peace a Chance" by making moral appeals to elected leaders and those who tried to bring the war home with trashing and bombing—took part in trying to change the course of history.[5] I felt a part of a mass movement to stop the war in Vietnam. We all got swept up into a swirling cauldron of unrest not of our own making. Yes, of course, we all sort of blended together, inadvertently (and perhaps consciously) learning from each other, copying and mimicking styles of attire, mannerisms, and shared language. We identified with a cause and collective purpose, and we acted and dressed the part. To our detractors we were long-haired, pot-smoking hippies—"freaks"—who were irresponsible, irreverent, and disrespectful of the American flag and traditional values. Frank Erwin, the chair of the Board of Regents at the University of Texas, a Texas "good ole boy" and a real bully, gained lasting infamy when he referred to protesters as a "bunch of dirty nothins" at a birthday party event held for Lyndon Baines Johnson (LBJ) on the UT campus in 1967. We were actually quite proud of this disparaging label and wore pins that attested to our notoriety. Putting us all in the same category made us much larger than we were as individuals.

We were Leninists before we were Marxists. The earliest and strongest currents in the late 1960s were anti-imperialism and antiracism. We interpreted US entanglements in Vietnam and elsewhere in the "third world" as instances of imperialism. This idea borrowed directly from Lenin's *Imperialism: The Highest Stage of Capitalism*. The focus on antiracism derives from the shifting currents epitomized by the turn from the Civil Rights Movement (meaning some sort of integration into an existentially flawed system) to the Black Power movements (emphasizing the failure of the system to fulfill its promises and the need to go it alone). Including questions of inequality and class in our analysis only came later, along with a sensitivity to male chauvinism, sexism, misogyny, and an awareness of homophobia.

Organization of the Book

I have divided my account of the antiwar movement into two distinct sections, each with two parts. The first section consists of my account of my experiences in the antiwar movement. The second section focuses on how the state security forces that were aligned against us tried to monitor us and disrupt our plans and actions. I argue that the antiwar movement developed and grew under the dark shadow of state repression. The origins and evolution of insurgent politics—and particularly the strategies and tactics of the antiwar movement—cannot be properly understood without unpacking the actions of the layered security apparatuses aligned against us. As they sought to contain and disrupt our actions, we sought to outmaneuver their efforts. In parts 1 and 2, I trace my early political awakening ("Chapter 1: Formative Years: Learning to Take Chances and Make Unpopular Choices, 1965–1967") in the years before I arrived in Austin before I explore how I found my own place in the antiwar movement ("Chapter 2: Gaining Traction in the Lone Star State, 1967–1969"). Following a chronological order, in part 2 I then turn to an examination of the growth and development of the Austin antiwar movement in the post-SDS era ("Chapter 3: Cut Loose from Our Original Birthplace"). I explore the antiwar movement through the lens of the shift from protest politics to more deliberate and provocative direct action and disruption ("Chapter 4: Direct Action and Disruption: Establishing a Public Presence for Popular Protest, 1970–1971"), followed by expanding the terrain of confrontation ("Chapter 5: Expanding the Terrain of Confrontational Politics, 1971–1972").

In part 3 I use three angles of vision to try to make sense of the efforts of the state security apparatuses to watch us. I look first to the broad contours of police surveillance ("Chapter 6: The State Security Apparatuses and Policing"). I then provide a granular account of the activities of Lt. Burt Gerding, head of the Criminal Intelligence Division, APD ("Chapter 7: Merry Prankster, Pied Piper, and Rogue Cop: Lt. Burt Gerding and His Fantasy World of Espionage"). What is striking here is that Lieutenant Gerding, captured in his own words in a transcribed interview, reveals his enthusiastic willingness to engage in extralegal tactics to accomplish his goals. Finally, I delve deeply into the correspondence of FBI agents (attached to several different field offices) who shared information about their spying efforts targeting my twin brother ("Chapter 8: My Twin and I and the FBI"). What I found most intriguing about these FBI reports is how these security agents frequently treated us as a single person and occasionally confused us. In part 4 I return to the Austin antiwar movement, where I seek to shed light on its decline and eventual disappearance ("Postscript: Denouement: The Demise of Popular Protest and the Eclipse of the Antiwar Movement").

Introduction

In *The Sociological Imagination* (1959), C. Wright Mills distinguished between biography and history.[1] In his view the *sociological imagination* enables us to grasp the intersection of one's own specific experiences with the broad historical stream of evolving events that surround us. Mills suggests that the trajectories of individuals are shaped by the historical period in which they live, and that personal troubles cannot be separated from societal problems. I found this way of thinking to be helpful. "I didn't get political," as Tom Hayden, an early founder of SDS reportedly said. "Things got political."[2] Put in another way, I did not make history, but history made me. In writing this memoir, I have tried to stick to this advice, stepping back from my own personal recollections of my own experiences to investigate how my surroundings and circumstances shaped my understandings and my actions. In so many ways, I was, and remain, a product of my place in historical time.

My account is an effort to conjoin the personal and the political, coupling my own experiences with the long arc of history. My story opens a window into the life of the person I was a long time ago. This task involves looking for the person I no longer am, someone I do not fully recognize or even remember.

This excursion is an effort to recover, and hence to rediscover, my younger self through my own memory and through the eyes of law enforcement officials and undercover informants. Security agents and undercover informants actually knew very little about me as a person, nor did they care. They were simply doing the job of monitoring and surveillance, watching over those they deemed as potential enemies of the state.

My generation faced all sorts of choices about how to forge one's place in the world. While some sleepwalked through the ongoing turbulence, preferring to find safe passage through the uncertainties by focusing on their careers and their futures, I participated in the outward politics of protest and rebellion. I chose the path of critical engagement with the insurgent politics of the day.

Understanding the New Left in Austin and Its Historical Time

In trying to understand my "autobiographical self" in relation to the Austin New Left, I situate my story through the lens of particular events, social organizations, and the structural circumstances of the historical moment. For me, I cannot make sense of my own biography without understanding the broader socio-structural histories of the time and place of the antiwar movement in Austin. What is required is a multidimensional approach to the fissures, gaps, tensions, and contradictions of the period. I suggest that this multidimensional approach can enable me to view the Austin antiwar movement along several axes. First, there was a distinction between public organizations and movements that contributed to the visible manifestations of protest, like picketing, leafleting, distribution of printed materials, mass demonstrations, rallies, and marches. In contrast, there were the less visible, more personalized organizational formats, which often took shape, for example, as women's consciousness raising groups, political study groups, and experimental forays into alternative lifestyles. Whereas the former spread our message with the aim of confronting power and winning over new recruits, the latter deepened our understanding of ourselves, built solidarities, and strengthened our resolve. These twin faces of building the movement operated in tandem.

Second, there was a division between the action-oriented militants and the institution-building activists. The action-oriented ones were the most visible and public, calling for demonstrations, marches, leafleting, and public displays of protest. In contrast, the institution builders were usually less visible. These efforts consisted of creating alternative institutions like food cooperatives, underground newspapers (like *The Rag*), free health clinics, printing and popular media operations, draft-counseling centers, and alternative schools. These efforts created the foundational pillars that sustained militant protest activities.

Third, there was the tension between organized political movements and the so-called counterculture.[3] In Austin these mostly blended together, but not always. At the extremes, hard-core political radicals regarded the countercultural mantra of "do your own thing" as hopelessly naive and self-serving. For their part, the countercultural hippies regarded political engagement as a waste of time. Sex, drugs, and rock-and-roll became the most important elements of personal expression.

Fourth, and finally, there was the liberal versus radical divide. The liberal orientation believed that the system was flawed but not fundamentally broken. Liberals were committed to the idea of gradual reform through reasoned debate and electoral participation. In contrast, the radical orientation identified capitalist imperialism as source of oppression and exploitation, and argued that it was necessary to replace the basic structures of capitalist democracy with different economic institutions and with alternative modes of political decision-making.

I was tossed willy-nilly into this ever-changing mix. It was a whirling, twirling, topsy-turvy world of personal reflection and growth, along with collective action and shared values, born out of a firm conviction that something was fundamentally wrong with the dominant values that ruled America. The movement consumed people and energy—building a collective identity and yet sometimes mercilessly leaving the wreckage of personal pain and damage behind. We were never saints; we could use and abuse people. But the movement also became my home, allowing me to understand that I was not alone in how I thought and acted.

In retrospect, political circumstances that indelibly marked the peculiar time of the Austin antiwar movement created different spheres of life. What I know now, and did not know then, was that vibrant political movements need a distinctive sociocultural milieu with strong roots to sustain and nurture their resilience. The counterculture generated a particular way of life. The emergence of a distinctive set of communitarian values, with their stress on sharing and mutual aid, distinguished our way of life from the competitive ethos of the capitalist marketplace. Various modes of expression—hairstyles, headbands, blue jeans and long dresses, forms of address, music, underground newspapers, poetry, and other written forms of communication—created a sphere of everyday life outside the conventional and mainstream of American popular culture. Alas, it was not deep enough or self-sustaining to remain intact beyond the late 1970s. Over time capitalist commodity culture subsumed almost all of these alternative modes of social life.

How They Saw Us

My goal is to compare my personal recollections with available police records, newspaper accounts, and communications with friends. The aim of this voyage of discovery is not only to connect the personal with the political but also to uncover the visible signs of the quasi–police state this cumbersome bureaucratic security apparatus created. I have a pretty solid understanding of what I believed at the time and what I sought to accomplish. I began with a moral claim grounded in my conscience: The war in Vietnam was wrong, I would not participate in it, and I would actively speak out against it. Over time I came to believe that the war was a visible expression of US imperialism and that racial and gender discrimination were integral features of a system of oppression that pervaded everyday life. I have remained curious to know what the various agencies of the security apparatus—from their extensive observations and investigations of me—thought I was doing.

On a broader front, what can my personal journey through this period of contentious politics reveal about this historical conjuncture, the nature of repression, and the commitment of young people to stand up for what they believed was right? So if the style of this autobiography seems self-indulgent and even a bit pretentious (to follow Timothy Garton Ash), the purpose is not. I engage in a critical exploration of not only archived records and old newspapers but also my "lost self," "the life of the person I was then."[4] In searching for this elusive being who no longer exists, I also seek to uncover a vanished time, buried under layers of mythology, half-truths, and 1960s nostalgia. "The personal is political" was a key rallying cry of the second-wave feminist movement of the late 1960s and early 1970s. By embracing this moral code, we sought to remake the world. In telling my story, I make no pretense to separate my personal views from the political turbulence that surrounded us.

I focus a great deal of my story on the entanglements of my friends and me with law enforcement and security agencies. In every instance I stress how repressive they were. At first glance it may appear that the forces of repression overreacted to what was at best a minor irritant and never a threat to national security at all. This way of seeing has some merit. Yet another way of interpreting the repressive power of security-surveillance agencies is to argue that even under conditions of formal constitutional guarantees of freedom of speech and of assembly, law enforcement agencies saw it as their duty and responsibility to suppress dissent by any means necessary. I favor this second interpretation. I do believe that constitutional freedoms and civil liberties are more or less a thin veneer—a cloak of respectability and feigned tolerance at the edges and margins—covering over a much deeper impulse toward state repression.

Situating the Austin Antiwar Movement in the Terrain of Scholarship

Scholarly and journalistic accounts of the upsurge of popular protest in the 1960s and 1970s are extensive. Orthodox leftist accounts of the sixties—most notably Terry Anderson, Todd Gitlin, and Kirkpatrick Sale—focused an inordinate amount of attention on big cities, elite colleges, and the academically enriched state universities, identifying key figures from these particular places as the most significant actors in contributing to the wellspring of ideas at the root of the New Left and antiwar politics.[5] While much of this effort has used a wide-angle lens to provide a panoramic overview of insurgent politics during the 1960s and 1970s, much less of this scholarship has focused on popular movements rooted in local communities. In countering what he regards as a misplaced elitist interpretation of the New Left, Kenneth Heineman tells the story of the origins and development of the antiwar movement on non-elite, land-grant campuses in upstate New York (SUNY at Buffalo), Pennsylvania (Penn State University), Ohio (Kent State University), and Michigan (Michigan State University). His detailed account helps to reshape our understanding of the antiwar movement as a much more broadly based, and hydra-headed, expression of antiwar politics.[6]

With a little sleuthing, one can uncover a plethora of microhistories of antiwar protest and countercultural dissent in out-of-the-way places.[7] What these studies of local movements that originated outside the national spotlight demonstrate is how the particularities of place—especially those locations infused with a conservative political culture and hostility to countercultural movements—not only shaped the aspirations and overall aims of political activists but also fashioned law enforcement responses to them. Douglas Rossinow, for example, traced the roots of the antiwar movement in Austin in Christian outreach groups.[8] Likewise, John Moretta examined the unique blend of counterculturalism and political activism that distinguished the Austin movement from other places.[9] Sarah Eppler Janda, for example, focused on student activism in several cities in Oklahoma.[10] John Ernst and Yvonne Baldwin examined the historical trajectory of the antiwar movement in Louisville, Kentucky.[11] Robbie Lieberman drew attention to student protest at several Midwestern universities—the University of Missouri, the University of Kansas, and Southern Illinois University—during the 1960s and 1970s.[12] Focusing on the student movement at University of Wisconsin–Madison, Matthew Levin traces the paradox that developed over time: As sites of higher education became increasingly entangled in the Cold War politics of the federal government, university campuses became centers of opposition to the global reach of US foreign policy.[13] Singular events that took place in Madison—most notably the 1966 draft protests, the 1967 sit-in against Dow Chemical, and the 1970 Sterling Hall bombing (housing the Army Mathematics Research Center)—have become part of the political fabric of the sixties, key touchstones at a time of confrontational and sometimes violent protests during the antiwar years.[14]

To be sure, the antiwar movement in Austin did not arise in a vacuum but formed one small piece of a larger, nationwide mosaic of insurgent politics at the time. The contours of popular politics in Austin not only conformed to the rhythms and patterns of national trends but also assumed distinctive characteristics all of its own. In short, the antiwar movement made itself; that is, it fashioned an autonomous course of action determined by the concrete circumstances of its existence. Yet at the same time, it was made by its entanglements within a complex web of repression: an autocratic university administrative apparatus coupled with local law enforcement agencies.

This particular balance gave the Austin antiwar movement a historical specificity that can only be understood in relation to local struggles elsewhere. In terms of the strategies and tactics of marches, rallies, building occupations, and mobile confrontations with law enforcement, the Austin story was intertwined with, and reflected, political currents that played out in the concentrated centers of political protest across the country. Yet what distinguished the Austin antiwar movement was not only the extent to which political activism and countercultural challenge to the existing normative conventions that sought to preserve the "Southern way of life" overlapped, but also the relatively notable tameness of political factionalism that tore political organizations apart elsewhere. In Austin political activists did not gravitate (with few exceptions) to the rigid organizational formats of Marxist–Leninist parties or to adventurist fantasies of the Weather Underground.

On Reading My Surveillance Files: Finding My Ghostly Self, or My Historical Doppelgänger

In order to trigger my own powers of recollection, I came to rely heavily on an unlikely source—law enforcement security files that focused on my activities. It is a strange feeling, really, to realize that I am dependent on my vigilant pursuers—the FBI and other security agencies—to give me some useful clues about myself that help to animate my fading memory of events that happened so long ago. Relying on professional voyeurs is unnerving and uncomfortable.

To paraphrase Timothy Garton Ash (writing about his exploration of secret police files collected by the Stasi in the German Democratic Republic), what a gift to memory is a police file.[15] Reading references to me in these police reports allows me to situate myself in time and place. It is a bitter pill to swallow to learn from these files containing references to me that, as Timothy Garton Ash has put it, "how much I myself have forgotten about my own life."[16] Looking at these police reports, I can only gesture toward an imaginative reconstruction of who I once was—optimistic, determined, committed, idealistic, quite sure of myself and my political beliefs, and perhaps too overconfident and naive.

Reading these security files on myself has brought some relief: For decades I always wanted to find a way to revisit my past and assuage my nagging curiosity about whether the power of my memory to recall events was somewhere close to the truth. Reading the detailed security report from an undercover spy (a fellow PhD student in the Department of Sociology) who reconstructed a casual conversation with me over fifty years ago brings memories rushing back. Yes, everything this undercover informant recalls me saying, I must have said, or at least something like it; what she recounts me saying certainly sounds familiar. Reading these files also brings a deeper understanding of myself as a young man. In retrospect, I wish we—and I—would have pushed more forcefully against the war machine, the churning capitalist engine behind it, and the racial discrimination that accompanied it. I am haunted by the knowledge that an entire security apparatus set its sights on monitoring us, frightened that we would somehow upset the status quo. I am also distressed by the awareness that FBI agents, local police, and undercover informants had few if any qualms about breaking existing laws to suppress us, and even to lure us into illegal acts.

The reliability of sources matters a great deal. I depend on a combination of police surveillance reports, contemporaneous newspaper accounts, occasional recollections of friends who were there with me, and my own memories (albeit selective). These sources provide different versions of events in the past. In the "cold, outward eye" of undercover police informants, I appear as just one of many possibly subversive individuals who happened to attract their attention and to merit inclusion in their periodic reports.[17] Under the surveillance gaze of security agencies, I am not an actual person but a personification of a minor evil that required monitoring. This caricatured construction of who I was motivated them to report on my activities, observe my organizational affiliations, and take surreptitious photographs of me.

In contrast, in my own self-recollection, I appear as a complex person, a bit unsure of what I was feeling, thinking, and doing. Spectral and elusive, personal memory leaves out much more than it recalls. The weakness of hindsight is that it strips away indecision, errors of judgement, and poor decision-making. My own faulty memory notwithstanding, the gaps, elisions, and silences in the official police reports limit my capacity to make sense of what the forces of repression knew about us, what we thought, and what we planned. Police surveillance reports capture on a minuscule portion of what we were thinking and doing. Yet there is a double strangeness here: As I reviewed these FBI files that I obtained through the FOIA requests, I know—and here I do trust my memory—the FBI did not get their facts straight either. Leaving aside their unreliability, getting the "facts" from FBI files is one thing; trying to interpret what they mean is another. In reading these FBI files, I have come to understand that the lens through which they filtered their reports is alien to me. They saw malcontents, troublemakers, and subversives everywhere. The FBI interpreted our planning disruptive demonstrations as worrisome and worthy of the attention of law enforcement. In contrast, I come away from my reading of these security reports with the realization that the security agents actually understood very little about us.

As I read over the security files that I collected, I discovered references to me. I appear in fragments scattered here and there across multiple information depots. I discovered a number of police surveillance photographs taken of me. I appear in grainy footage of a police surveillance video for about three seconds before the camera moves down the line of protesters.

As I explored these security files, I immediately became aware that there seemed to be no coherent rules governing how they were collected, classified, and stored. It was as if the security agents handling these documents seemingly put them in a box or file folder without much thought. There seemed to be no systematic approach to the gathering of information and its storage. While the list of contents suggested that the files were distinguished by different subjects and by particular events, the actual contents revealed a much different story. There is no rational order of things. As I worked through the documents, I found that the arrangement of documents only occasionally followed a coherent chronological order. For the most part, sorting in terms of sequential dates was largely nonexistent. Sometimes the dates on documents went backward in time, only to reverse course halfway through the file. Whole clusters of documents were bundled together, yet without any respect to their actual occurrence in time.

It is evident that the security agents in charge of the collection and organization of these documents approached their task in a rather haphazard manner. I have found written documents correctly attributed to me. I also found other materials in the files that I know that I wrote, yet without attribution to me.

In surveying the operations of the security agencies aligned against the antiwar movement, I have come up against the challenge of compensating for the incompleteness of the available documents that I was able to obtain through FOIA requests and archival searches. By themselves, the available documents do not yield a complete or coherent picture of what we were doing and why we did what we did. The paucity of documentation has left plenty of room for conjecture or reading between the lines.

Getting Outside Assistance in Unlikely Places

I needed help. I turned to two semiautobiographical accounts in which the authors encountered similar paradoxes with trying to make sense of their security files: Katherine Verdery, *My Life as a Spy: Investigations in a Secret Police File*, and Timothy Garton Ash, *The File: A Personal History*.[18] Verdery recounted her experiences as a long-term academic researcher in Romania during which time the secret police—the Securitate—compiled a massive surveillance file on her. Ash wrote a memoir about what the Stasi, the secret police in the German Democratic Republic, collected about him when he was living in Berlin in 1978. The insights that I obtained from these two autobiographical accounts provided me with a great deal of assistance in putting my experience in the antiwar movement in Austin into some perspective. Verdery begins her journey with several observations that were quite useful for me. As she remarked, "There's nothing like reading your secret police file to make you wonder who you really are."[19] It is fair to say that I expected that there would be some coherence and consistency in the records collected about me. Perhaps, in a moment of vanity, I expected to find something more than just passing references. After all, as Verdery put it, having a police security file "confirms our [vain] sense of our own importance."[20] What I found was less than satisfying and rewarding, yet it was still exciting.

As she pored more closely over the security files kept on her, Verdery realized these reports and documents were not written to be read by her, and hence were "under no requirement to be intelligible."[21] My experience with reading security files about myself was similar. My expectation that I would discover some consistency and coherence proved exasperating. Reading my security file amounted to something akin to an archeological excavation. Digging, and more digging, only produced fragments and shards of information. I was unable to make sense of the jumble of times, places, and events. The chaotic organization of the documents even made them unusable to the security agencies that might have wanted to make sense of them.

Verdery's observations made my task easier in some ways and more challenging in others. Because I am not bound by any rules of engagement that the security agencies utilized in collecting and storing information about me, I am free to organize these random anecdotes in whatever way I see fit. Yet the challenge arises from the fact that these shards, remnants, and scattered references do not allow me to construct a composite picture of myself as they saw me.

From reading reports collected about me, I came to realize that the security agencies regarded me as a dangerous radical that posed a potential threat to what they regarded as national security. They spied on me to figure out what I was saying and doing. To paraphrase Timothy Garton Ash, if that was *their plan of action*, then my plan of action in telling my story "is to investigate their investigation of me."[22]

Who Was I? The Value of Self-Exploration Through the Eyes of Someone Else

Reading through these various security documents, I am left with an uncanny feeling as a kind of out-of-body experience. As Verdery put it, "Reading my file is like spying on myself."[23] So true. Scrutinizing page after page of documents on the computer is akin to archival research with the caveat that I am trying to find mention of myself in the text. As I pored over these documents, I found myself looking attentively for the appearance of my name. Think about it: I am looking for the appearance of the name of a person who existed fifty years ago and has disappeared into the shadows of vanishing time. That person no longer exists, but it was once me. My story is a fragmented tale, pieced together from disconnected pieces of evidence—my own recollections, newspaper accounts, hearsay, and the biased judgements of security agents.

Surveying these documents triggered a panoply of emotions, ranging from apprehension (what did these undercover informants say about me?), surprise (seeing a photograph of myself taken surreptitiously), regret (numbers of participants at demonstrations could have been higher), remorse (sadness with coming across the names of friends no longer alive), satisfaction (some demonstrations turned into spectacular events), and jolted (the extent to which undercover informants successfully infiltrated our movement, pretending to be our friends and comrades). Over time I have moved from harboring resentment with what security officers did to a kind of curiosity and fascination with how they approached their surveillance tasks.

I faced two daunting challenges: First, how am I to make sense of what I was discovering? And second, how am I able to come to grips, emotionally and otherwise, with the fact that I am studying myself, or at least that person whom I vaguely remember who existed fifty years ago? To speak openly, I am not exactly sure what I am trying to do here. Because my primary intention in undertaking this research- and-writing project is to uncover the person (the younger "Martin Murray") that the security police constructed (and fictionalized) in their surveillance, I have constructed a kind of memoir, but one that is built around the results of research—some of which is aimed at uncovering "me myself" as I apply the tools of the archival researcher "to my own experience."[24] Since a great deal of evidence that I make use of in this story is about the events in which I engaged as an active participant and with other people with whom I interacted, it is not simply an autobiography. Because my goal is to try to bring together two strains of thought usually handled separately—piecing together a fragmented story of myself as the target of that surveillance and unearthing the activities of the security regime that grew out of control in Austin—I have produced a hybrid sort of work.[25]

While my primary concern is to reconstruct my historical doppelgänger from five decades ago, this story is at the same time an account of the security apparatuses, as Verdery put it, charged "with policing the line between inside and outside, between 'friend' and 'enemy.'" In imagining the "'true motives' of 'subversives' whom they were surveilling," these law enforcement agencies were prone to blur the distinction between fact and fantasy. In the process of watching us and documenting our activities, security agents created fictionalized characters who conformed to their imagined Others. What I learned from this investigation is that the various security agencies did not work from the same playbook, with the same goals, or with the same levels of expertise. The agencies that formed the security apparatus were themselves fragmented and suffered from a great deal of compartmentalization, rivalry, and poor communication.[26]

At the end of the day, reading my security files has proven to be both exhilarating and frustrating. It is gratifying, in a perverse sort of way, to learn that security agencies took what I did in the antiwar movement seriously enough to identify me as a "troublemaker" and "subversive," and sometimes even a "ringleader." As Verdery argued, "This is what is happening to me as I read my file: my familiar is made strange."[27] Because security police believed I was worthy of monitoring, I must have been doing something to clog up the war machine. Yet at the same time, reading these security files is also frustrating. I come away with so many unanswered questions: Why me? How did I draw the attention of the security apparatus? How did the recruitment of undercover informants take place? How many were there in our midst? How many undercover informants were there in total?

Reading these security files has enabled me to uncover some of the secrets of the security apparatus. But what have I not uncovered? What remains forever unknown and unknowable? To what extent were my phones wiretapped? Did I have close friends whom I trusted who were undercover agents? If the security files represent a kind of production of knowledge, from what I have seen, I would say they did a rather clumsy, poor job.

The Paradox

In trying to make sense of the security apparatus aligned against the antiwar movement, I begin with a paradox: On the one hand, the various security and law enforcement agencies aligned against the antiwar movement were able to put together (at best) a comprehensive and ubiquitous system of monitoring and surveillance. This security apparatus focused on information gathering coupled with an almost obsessive fixation with record keeping. On the other hand, these security agencies displayed a surprising inability to really understand what was happening and why. They seemed truly incapable of grasping that antiwar activism was motivated by real efforts to end the immoral, illegal, and unwinnable war in Southeast Asia, to challenge enduring racism, and to counteract the sexism and misogyny that pervaded popular culture. Political activism in Austin was certainly part of a wider national movement for change but was never directed to act at the behest of some shadowy, central command rooted in Communist subversion. The security agencies could not break from their underlying premise that the Austin movement was a creature not of its own making but an entity put into motion by some secret puppet master orchestrating our every move. Schooled in the anti-Communist propaganda of the 1950s, the security agencies from the FBI to the local criminal intelligence division of the APD were fixated on how the specter of Communists—whether CPUSA, SWP, or the PL Party—were able to manipulate naive youngsters into doing their bidding.

Despite gathering literally mountains of information, unleashing countless number of undercover informants, and conducting all sorts of electronic eavesdropping, the security agencies did not really know what to do with the vast assemblage of data that they had collected. Their interpretive skills were weak and ineffectual. The security agencies were simply unable to overcome their "fundamental legitimacy deficit"—to borrow a phrase from Mike Dennis in his analysis of the Stasi in the German Democratic Republic.[28] In short, despite our inadequacies and our flaws, the antiwar movement in Austin was motivated by legitimate goals that over time were shared by more and more people and gained widespread acceptance.

What is relatively well-known is how the FBI at a national level employed a full toolbox of methods—legalized repression, disinformation, extralegal dirty tricks, and even outright assassinations assembled under the Counter Intelligence Program (COINTELPRO) efforts—to stem the tide of rising political dissent during the 1960s and 1970s. The rise of the antiwar movement and political protest was matched by national, state, and local efforts to monitor political activists and undermine their efforts. A number of scholars and journalists have uncovered the hidden story of the FBI and its orchestrated work of clandestine surveillance and political repression of alleged subversive activities. Early accounts, including those of Pat Watters and Stephen Cillers, Frank Donner, and Nelson Blackstock, marked the opening wedge of an outpouring of exposés uncovering FBI monitoring and harassment of suspected subversives.[29] Subsequent research by others, including Richard Betts, David Garrow, Kenneth O'Reilly, James Kirkpatrick Davis, David Cunningham, Seth Rosenfield, and Ward Churchill and Jim Vander Wall, extended and expanded the secret operations of the FBI's carefully crafted counterintelligence efforts, known collectively as COINTELPRO, directed against key figures in the antiwar movement and against African American, Chicano, and American Indian civil rights activists. In the end, law enforcement agencies that constructed the vast security apparatus drew any and all individuals and their political organizations into their nets, targeting alleged subversives deemed threats to national security.[30] This research and writing on the FBI's campaign directed against political activists has contributed significantly to drawing attention to the extent of coordinated surveillance that often spilled into the clouded terrain of illegal methods designed to prevent the exercise of civil liberties.[31]

Systematic surveillance and political repression at the local level has received far less attention in scholarly research and writing than the broad, sweeping accounts. While much is known about the broad scope of political repression at the national level in in the 1960s and 1970s, much less is understood about how policing agencies operated at the local level against political activities. In addition to the federal efforts of the FBI, military intelligence, and other national security agencies, local (city and state) agencies also added their own efforts to monitor and harass movement activists.

In filling in these gaps in the literature, some scholars have used a more finely grained approach to explore the efforts of local policing agencies to monitor and suppress political dissent in local settings. In a meticulous examination of undercover police work in Chicago, Los Angeles, New York, and Philadelphia (as well as Washington, DC, Detroit, New Haven, Baltimore, and Birmingham), Frank Donner exposed the seamy underside of law enforcement. He focused his attention on so-called Red Squads, domestic surveillance units attached to police departments across the country that engaged in widespread police misconduct and violations of protected freedoms.[32] Similarly, other scholars have revealed how local, state, and federal authorities investigated, monitored, harassed, and intimidated political activists engaged in antiwar, civil rights, and other progressive causes in such local settings as New York City and Los Angeles.[33] Johanna Fernández, for example, deconstructed a treasure trove of police surveillance files to uncover the efforts of law enforcement agencies to suppress the Young Lords, from their origins as a Chicago street gang to their emergence and decline as a political organization in New York City.[34]

In *Spying on Students*, Gregg Michel focuses on the concerted law enforcement campaigns directed against New Left and progressive student activists in the South during the 1960s. In this pathbreaking account, Michel has revealed how law enforcement agencies made use of extensive surveillance and illegal tactics in their efforts to crush dissent. Frequently overlooked and ignored in the scholarly literature, white Southern activists worked alongside their African American counterparts in civil rights struggles, organized political opposition to the Vietnam War, and embraced the alternative lifestyles rooted in the countercultural rejection of conventional norms. While African American activists bore the brunt of police surveillance and repression, federal law enforcement agencies such as the FBI and local police intelligence units known as Red Squads subjected white Southern activists to extensive, intrusive, and illegal means of repression.[35]

More specifically, the extralegal roles of undercover informants and agents provocateurs have remained largely unexplored.[36] There is, of course, the well-documented case of Thomas (Tommy the Traveler) Tongyai—a young man who moved around college campuses in upstate New York from

1968 to 1972, seeking out radical students and pontificating about "the revolution." Tommy the Traveler was the quintessential agent provocateur, urging students to "kill the pigs," offering to obtain guns and bombs, and urging them to burn buildings. In carefully unpacking FBI files and local law enforcement records that he was able to obtain through FOIA, Gregg Michel exposed the role of undercover police informants in Memphis and Nashville.[37] In a similar vein, Michel has uncovered how local Red Squads maintained a close watch on political activists affiliated with the Southern Student Organizing Committee (SSOC), an organization with chapters spread across dozens of college campuses in the South.[38] Law enforcement agencies monitored the activities of the SSOC through the deployment of undercover informants and, most notably in Mississippi, infiltrated the local chapters, actively seeking to discredit key figures and sow internal discord through various illegal tactics. At least at the start, the FBI's interest in SSOC, "like so many of its investigations of this era, focused on whether the group was controlled by communists or was sympathetic to communist causes." Michel has exposed how local FBI agents (with the approval of J. Edgar Hoover) relied upon "covert and often illegal tactics, including wiretapping, intercepting mail, planting false stories in the media, and working with the Internal Revenue Service (IRS) to audit and challenge tax returns" to undermine and disrupt legitimate and legally protected protest activities. He concludes that law enforcement efforts that aimed at undermining the SSOC were "not qualitatively different" from similar methods targeting such better-known organizations as Student Nonviolent Coordinating Committee (SNCC) and SDS. This parallelism "thus further helps to reincorporate white southern progressive activists into the narrative of the movements of the 1960s."[39]

The Surveillance Machine in Austin

The layered security apparatuses became, in effect, a secretive "state within a state," whose clandestine operations were able to escape scrutiny and to avoid public oversight for quite some time. These security agencies proved quite capable of acting relatively autonomously from the conventional checks and balances to protect the civil liberties of citizens. Nevertheless, they were unable to stop the hemorrhaging of support for the war in Vietnam, to channel the struggle for civil rights and Black liberation into a nonconfrontational direction, and to hold back the countercultural upsurge that challenged bedrock American values arrayed around a strident faith in capitalism, an unquestioning belief in conventional gender roles, and a willingness to turn a blind eye to racism in its institutional and outright overt forms of discrimination. Once unleashed, rising antiwar sentiment and the questioning of authority took on lives of their own. Rather than suppressing dissent, the security apparatuses—in all their guises and masquerades—actually fostered oppositional politics.

On a broad front, the strange mélange of forces aligned against us often tried to coordinate their efforts at repressing free speech, cleansing the campus of nonstudent agitators, and tackling anything they considered too radical or potentially disruptive of the status quo. To the extent that the UT administration and the local law enforcement and security agencies communicated with each other in order to arrive at a common plan of action, they conspired against us. The heart of any conspiracy is shared intent and agreement to act together with a common purpose. As chair of the Board of Regents, Frank Erwin had a particular vision for what the university should be and how it should operate. He shared this vision with the highest authorities in the university administration and with local security agencies. In carrying out the plan to rid the campus community of "student radicals" and "outside agitators" alike, the Board of Regents and the university administration enlisted the support of campus security (Allen Hamilton) and UT System security (George Carlson) as enforcers to ensure the kind of peace and tranquility that their superiors desired. On a broader front, the Criminal Intelligence Division of the APD (under the leadership of Lt. Burt Gerding) was drawn into this cabal because of its assigned role of monitoring political activities that spilled over the boundaries of what they considered legitimate dissent. In the minds of the defenders of the status quo, every and all criticism of the established order of things was tantamount to embryonic subversive behavior. The line between legitimate dissent and illegitimate subversion was arbitrary and capricious.

The thread running through seemingly disconnected events—perhaps starting with the March 1969 SDS National Council meeting in Austin, followed by the 1969 Chuck Wagon uprising, the anti-ROTC demonstration (spring 1970), the May 1970 mass mobilization after the invasion of Cambodia and the Kent State killings, the Armadillo May Day Tribe and the May Days demonstrations in Washington, DC, (May 1971), the protests at the LBJ Library dedication, and the mass student strike in spring of 1972—was increasingly heightened security presence. The security forces sought to coordinate their efforts and to shift from monitoring and surveillance of political activities toward a more proactive stance of infiltration and disruption. Not only did they seek to use existing laws to entangle antiwar activists in legal defense cases, but they also mobilized more formidable regional policing units (not run-of-the-mill local cops) outfitted with tear gas, Mace, clubs, and better training to stop our marches and disrupt our demonstrations. Rather than relying on agile cops to arrest us on the spot at marches and demonstrations, they came to depend increasingly upon photographs to identify protesters and then arrest them at their convenience. Despite the overall ineptitude of the security agencies, the level of surveillance and suppression of basic civil liberties were completely disproportionate (and out of touch) to any actual threats. This disconnect highlights how even the most banal challenges to authority and the repressive use of the law seemed to those security agencies determined to restore their version of political stability.

The FBI and local security agencies were not content to simply monitor events and activities, but instead sought to actively influence and shape any and all efforts to challenge the system. Besides their assortment of dirty tricks, the security agencies used the repressive power of the law to discipline political activists. Despite their desire for security omnipotence, the security policing agencies that operated in Austin suffered from bureaucratic ineptitude, information overload, poor coordination of effort, miscommunication, and a lack of a genuine understanding of the motives and goals of the individuals and political organizations they targeted for surveillance and monitoring. In the end, they floundered and failed.

PART 1

Formative Years

Chapter 1

Formative Years

Learning to Take Chances and Make Unpopular Choices, 1965–1967

Where I Was From

It is difficult if not impossible to pinpoint a single event, or even a cluster of events, that marked my personal transition from a somewhat naive working-class kid growing up in the 1950s and 1960s in the San Francisco Bay Area to an antiwar activist at the University of Texas. I was born in Oakland. In 1947 my father and mother decided to move east of the Berkeley Hills away from Oakland to a small but growing town called Walnut Creek, located about twenty miles inland. My four brothers and I experienced our version of *Wonder Years* in a modest home in a suburban neighborhood in what at the time amounted to an out-of-the-way "bedroom community" servicing the Greater San Francisco / Oakland Bay Area.

We were raised Roman Catholic, but religious commitment never permanently stuck with any of us. My father, who graduated from the same high school that four of the five Murray boys attended, never went to college. He served in the US Navy during World War II and was posted at Alameda Naval Air Station. He started his working life as a truck driver and eventually settled into a six-day a week job at a nursery in Walnut Creek. My father worked there continuously for over forty years before the business closed down. My mother graduated from high school in Oakland and never worked outside the home. Our parents were politically moderate, yet they were curious and open-minded. They never pushed back against my growing radicalism, and over time they adopted antiwar views inspired in part by the pacifist tradition in the Catholic Church.

Coming of age in the San Francisco Bay Area (rather than a less progressive or "radical" environment) strongly influenced the way I understood the growing political ferment and dissatisfaction in the United States during the 1960s. The fact that I commuted twenty miles away from home to attend a Catholic high school in Berkeley (St. Mary's College High School) certainly made a difference in my outlook on life. The San Francisco Bay Area was a key focal point in the emergence of the (northern) Civil Rights Movement, the growing anti–Vietnam War sentiment, and the broader political-cultural explosion that is now loosely called "the sixties." My political awareness came in graduated stages, in a series of plateaus and building blocks, which shaped my antiestablishment political consciousness. I remember the House Un-American Activities Committee (HUAC) hearings in San Francisco in May 1960. I recall civil rights demonstrations in 1964 protesting discriminatory hiring practices at car dealerships on Van Ness Avenue (Auto Row) in San Francisco. These events made an impression on me, but it was something I did not realize until years later. These breaks with the illusion of political conformity eventually led me away from the safety-first, sheltered environment of the working class suburban outpost of Walnut Creek.

Actually, the sixties is a rather ill-fitting and imprecise label that carries a great deal of nostalgia and misrepresentation in autobiographical writing and scholarship alike. The experience of breaking away from the strait-jacket conformity of the Cold War 1950s was not shared equally. Plenty of my high school and college friends supported the war in Vietnam, enlisted in the military services, and served tours of duty in Southeast Asia. Some died there, their names etched on marble and preserved forever in Washington, DC, at the Vietnam Memorial. Some returned home, forever scarred by the experience.

During my high school years, my class aspirations were not particularly ambitious. Even though both my twin brother and I graduated at the top of our high school class and could easily have been admitted to prestigious schools, it was more or less a foregone conclusion that we would attend a local Catholic college. My twin and I were the first persons in our large family to attend college. It seemed so foreboding and somewhat terrifying. When I entered University of San Francisco (USF) in fall 1963, I decided to major in mathematics. I excelled in mathematics in high school and thought, at least in the back of my mind, I might have a career as a high school mathematics teacher. I was astonished when my twin brother announced that he planned to enter a premed track when he entered St. Mary's College (Moraga). Becoming a doctor, lawyer, or even a PhD seemed so far beyond my grasp that I never considered any profession like medicine or the law or higher education as a career option.

USF was a conventional university with an autocratic Jesuit administration. Besides taking a required undergraduate course in anti-Communism, I registered for courses in the Reserve Officer Training Corps (ROTC) program. Participation in the ROTC program for at least two years was mandatory for all male students at USF. As I understood it, USF (along with other Catholic colleges) had suffered with declining enrollments during the Great Depression. Many of these colleges made a devil's bargain with the US government after the end of World War II. In exchange for obtaining financial assistance from the GI Bill, these Catholic colleges agreed to host ROTC programs and require male students to enroll, at least for the first two years.

During my four years at USF, I looked elsewhere in the Bay Area for inspiration and excitement. I went exploring politically. During October 1964 I ventured to the University of California at Berkeley campus at the start of the Free Speech Movement. I started attending antiwar rallies and demonstrations in Berkeley and Golden Gate Park in San Francisco. I began to pay attention to antiwar sentiment that originated in Catholic pacifist circles. My views began to crystalize around the idea that—no matter what—I was never going to serve in the military. Once I became comfortable with that decision, the rest just fell into place. My prowar college friends at USF began to refer to me facetiously as a "pasty-faced white peace creep," a term attributed to George Lincoln Rockwell, an avowed neo-Nazi who founded the American Nazi Party. It was all in jest.

Around April 1965 I received a formal letter from the officer in charge of ROTC at USF, Colonel So-and-So, congratulating me on my "outstanding performance" in ROTC classes and inviting me to "go upper-division" (junior and senior years) on the regal road to joining the US Army as a commissioned officer. With two more years in ROTC, I was guaranteed a military rank of second lieutenant and the choice of branch of service. While many of my fellow students went for the deal in order to avoid the draft and a lowly rank in the military service, I refused the bait. Over the course of the two years that I was enrolled in the program, I had become very disillusioned with the war in Vietnam and the concerted propaganda efforts that promoted it.

This whole process involved a face-to-face meeting with the colonel in his office in the ROTC building. Sometime in April I marched into his office dressed in my military uniform. As was standard protocol, I stood at attention and smartly exchanged salutes. The colonel said to me in an authoritative voice, "Congratulations, son, you have been invited to go upper-division." On hearing this verbal invitation, I screwed up a bit of courage and blurted out in words I still remember: "Sir, I wish to decline the offer since I have moral reservations about the war in Vietnam."

One would have thought a grenade had exploded in the office. He jumped up from behind his desk, pointing a finger at me, and yelled red-faced, "I will make sure you get drafted when you finish college." I was dumbfounded. I was surprised that a small gesture from me provoked such an angry response from a person of his stature. Initially, and for years afterward, I interpreted his reaction as something personal, something about me and my disrespectful attitude and immaturity and that I had somehow personally rejected his wisdom and his dedication to God and country. He seemed completely oblivious to Catholic teachings about following one's own conscience, a dictum introduced in my moral philosophy courses at USF. For the longest time, I did not tell anyone what happened in that room.

Years later it dawned on me that what Colonel So-and-So had blurted out to me in the anonymity of his office was not at all something just between him and me. What I assumed at the time was a deeply personal experience—a confrontation with state authority—was actually a collective one. He viscerally understood that if all young men shared my views, the military would not have a compliant army to fight the war. This is where my individual biography intersected with history. I came to the realization that he was a petty enforcer trying to preserve the institutional support that was necessary to fuel the war effort. His vow to get me drafted was not personal but institutional. The colonel was only trying to hold the line against anyone questioning the authority of the US military to decide what was best for the USA in terms of fighting foreign wars. While he himself might not have been fully conscious of his place in the system, he was trying to conceal fissures in the war machine, and I happened to be inconveniently in the way. The ROTC program at USF was only a small cog in a conveyer belt channeling enthusiastic, "patriotic" young men into assigned roles in carrying out US foreign policy in far-off lands.

The response of the university senior administration to the growing student opposition to the war in Vietnam and mandatory ROTC was shocking. For the university administration, taking a pacifist stand was verboten. This callous reaction to our pleas brought me to the abrupt realization that questioning the wisdom of the Vietnam adventure was more than an issue involving one's conscience and a moral choice. To grapple even at a personal level with the moral dilemma of Vietnam was tantamount to challenging the entire institutional apparatus that supported and sustained the war machine. The senior university administration fell in lockstep behind the doctrine of a "just war," appealing to the totally unconvincing "If we don't stop Them there, we'll have to fight Them on the Mexican border" pseudo-argument. Failing to win the war of words with their rhetorical bravado, the dean of students moved to expel all students who failed to register for ROTC and fired the faculty advisor to the student anti-ROTC group.

The Draft Board and Me: My Experience with the Selective Service System

Selective Service regulations required (by law) all male US citizens and immigrant noncitizens between the ages of 18 and 25 to have registered within thirty days of their 18th birthday. I complied with this regulation. Enrollment as a full-time student in college kicked the can down the road.

In the early 1960s to 1973, Selective Service regulations allowed full-time students to obtain a 2-S status indicating their "good standing" in making progress through college with at least a 3.0 (B) grade point average. This 2-S status allowed college students to avoid the draft. After completion of four years of college, this 2-S status automatically changed to a 1-A classification. This 1-A status alerted the local draft board (located, in my case, in Martinez, the county seat of Contra Costa County) that the person holding this dubious status was eligible for the Selective Service draft. As the date of my college graduation loomed on the horizon, I began to seriously contemplate how I was going to respond to the draft and military service. What was difficult was how to execute a plan to avoid military service.

As I saw it, I had three options. The first option meant that I would wait to be classified as 1-A, submit to the required physical examination at the Oakland Army Induction Center, and hope that I would be granted a 4-F classification (physically or mentally unfit for military service) or 1-Y classification (physically or mentally unfit except in the eventuality of full-scale outbreak of global war). This option was the preferred outcome, but it was far from guaranteed. If the results of the physical examination declared that I was fit for service, then within a month or so the draft board would have issued an order for me to report for induction into the US military. To refuse induction was a serious crime.

To get to this point meant that I had reached a crossroads—my little Rubicon, so to speak. I could submit to induction, or refuse. I was adamant about my decision to refuse induction. If I refused induction, I would be tried before a military court and sentenced to at least two years in prison for draft refusal.

The second option required leaving the country. Unlike many of my contemporaries, I never seriously considered emigrating to Canada, following in the footsteps of countless numbers of draft-age young men who fled across the border. Estimates of the total number of draft dodgers and military deserters who slipped over the Canadian border due to their opposition to the Vietnam War range from 50,000 to 125,000. An untold number of other resisters simply disappeared in countries all over the world.[1] I always told myself that Canada was too cold, but that was not the real reason. I was simply not prepared to abandon family and friends. So I knew I was going to stick it out, whatever happened. I was not going to jump ship and go over the border to the north. In the end this "Canada option" did not constitute a lifelong banishment. While many draft dodgers returned home under a blanket amnesty issued by President Jimmy Carter, about half actually decided to stay where they were.

There was a third option. Rather than take my chances with the Selective Service process, I decided to apply for conscientious objector (CO) status as my student deferment was about to expire when I graduated from USF in June 1967. The process itself was not straightforward or easy. This option was tricky; I had to convince the draft board that I was sincere in my claim that I was opposed to all wars under all conditions, including self-defense. This position was "turn the other cheek" in the extreme. If the draft board refused my request for CO status, I would remain in the 1-A category, waiting to go through the physical examination and possible induction ("call up") to active duty in the US military.

Applying for Conscientious Objector Status

Conscription was one of the single most hotly contested issues throughout the Vietnam War. As the antiwar and antidraft movements gained momentum, they intersected with other social movements of the 1960s, especially the Civil Rights and emergent Black Power Movements. While those who refused induction or applied for conscientious objector status were few in number in the mid-1960s, the upsurge in opposition to the Vietnam War coincided with concerted efforts by church groups and antidraft counseling services to stand in opposition to conscription. Popular opinion that initially regarded these draft dodgers as antipatriotic and anti-American gradually shifted to a more nuanced understanding of the moral dilemmas posed by military service.[2]

The Selective Service System was a rather large and cumbersome bureaucratic agency designed to ensure a steady stream of foot soldiers for the war in Vietnam. In the early 1960s, volunteers for military service provided sufficient numbers, but before long the draft became a necessary instrument to fill the military ranks. Upon reaching the age of 18, all young men were issued a draft card by the Selective Service System, which all of us were required by law (and under penalty of arrest) to have in our possession at all times. My draft card number was 4-31-45-25. I still have the small card, now frayed and wrinkled, as a token of a strange time.

I decided to apply for CO, or 1-0, status. I framed my application on religious grounds in the idiom of the Catholic pacifist tradition. I had thought about applying for CO status for a long time. The criteria for classification for 1-0 status were explicit about which persons were excluded from consideration. These criteria are worth quoting in full:

> Exclusions from Classes 1-0 and 1-A-0
>
> Persons who beliefs are "essentially political, sociological, or philosophical views, or merely personal moral code" are ineligible to be classified as a conscientious objector. Such persons consist of two groups:
>
> (a) those with beliefs of religious, moral, or ethical nature, but whose beliefs are not deeply held; and
>
> (b) those who objection to war does not rest at all upon moral, ethical, or religious principles, but instead rest solely upon considerations of policy, pragmatism or expediency.[3]

In short, local draft boards maintained a great deal of discretion to determine whether a person met the standards of 1-0 status or not. They had autocratic power to determine one's fate.

What I had forgotten was how long and drawn-out this application process proved to be. Sometimes a happenstance discovery can come to the rescue of failing memories of particular events. Several years ago, as I was going through old boxes in my basement with the intention of downsizing and throwing away unwanted papers, I discovered a nondescript large envelope that contained a variety of materials that I had collected at the time I applied in June 1968 for CO status with my local Martinez (California) draft board. On the outside of the sealed envelope there was a penciled notation, "CO info," written in my mother's distinctive handwriting. In the same box, I discovered a second envelope upon which my mother had written "C.O. letters, Martin Murray." My mother saved these documents for me and kept them stored away for perhaps forty years. Otherwise, they surely would have been discarded, lost, or inadvertently left behind in some hasty move from one living place to another. These documents proved to be invaluable memory aids, triggering recollections of my experience with the Selective Service System. With the passage of time, my memory of much of my interaction with the Selective Service System had faded into oblivion. The whole process was a painful experience, and I just wanted to forget it.

I initiated the CO process when I sent a letter dated 15 June 1967 to local Board No. 31, Martinez (California). In the letter I stressed my commitment to nonviolence in the pacifist tradition of Roman Catholicism. I did not at this time submit a formal application for CO status. In response I received a form letter on 7 September 1967 with the box checked stating "your file does not contain an SSS Form No. 103 indicating that you have or will re-enter college or are or will be pursuing a full-time course of instruction. Request your school to file form No. 103 within 30 days after the beginning of the school year." I complied with this request and asked the registrar at the University of Texas at Austin to inform the Selective Service Board that I was enrolled in the PhD program in philosophy.

On 6 June 1968, I wrote again to Local Board No. 31: "Approximately one year ago I expressed my sentiments to you in a letter (June 15, 1967) with regard to my conscientious objections to military service. I expressed my moral repulsion toward the use of weapons of violence and the institutionalized killing that accompanied them." I continued, "Within this last year, I have had time to think about what I had related to you previously and had formulated a stricter, and clearer, position in my mind. The conclusion I have reached is simply a stronger and more dedicated commitment to my previous Christian beliefs and responsibilities. Therefore, I should like to request that you send me as soon as possible SSS Form 150 for COs so that I might outline more completely the foundations and consequences of my positions and beliefs." The following day, 7 June 1968, Margaret Greeley, executive secretary, Local Board No. 31, sent me SSS 150 as requested, informing me that I "may come into the Board at any time to read the various types of work which have been approved for civilian work in lieu of induction."

I formally submitted my SSS Form 150 in a sixteen-page, single-spaced application on 17 June 1968, and I asked eleven people—mainly Catholic priests and nuns—to write letters to the draft board on my behalf, attesting to the sincerity of my beliefs in my request for 1-0 (CO) status. Virtually all of those I asked to write letters on my behalf were friends of my parents. In framing my instructions to these letter writers, I followed a template provided by the Central Committee for Conscientious Objectors from their offices in San Francisco. On 2 July 1968, the draft board rejected my application for CO status and reclassified me as 1-A, eligible for the draft and subject to induction following a physical examination. On 26 July 1968, I wrote to Local Board No. 31 to appeal my 1-A classification, and I requested a personal appearance before the board to express my views.

Along with Reverend Michael Donahoe, pastor at St. Peter Martyr Church (Pittsburg, California), I appeared before my draft board at 9:00 p.m. on Monday evening, 5 August 1968, to appeal my 1-A classification. Members of the draft board consisted of local business owners, civic leaders, school teachers, and other "notable" men in Contra Costa County. Many were veterans who served in the armed forces in World War II or Korea. They were utterly perplexed why such a "good Catholic boy" would even contemplate "avoiding the draft." I was the first one to apply at my draft board for 1-0 (CO) status—and the first one to obtain it. I must have made a persuasive case. The catchment area for the Martinez draft board were draft-age young men who largely came from working class families and who often did not attend college. The pool of young men facing induction into the armed services was large.

With the growing antiwar sentiment swirling in the Bay Area air, I was clear about two things: I would not serve in the US armed forces and certainly would never go to Southeast Asia as part of the US military mission. Making this decision was actually easy. If I obtained 1-0 status, I was prepared to accept alternative service for two years in lieu of induction into the military. If I did not obtain 1-0 status, I was willing to go to jail.

While I was in no position to realize it at the time, I played a small part as a CO in a much larger groundswell of draft resistance.[4] The number of civilian COs grew from 17,900 in 1964 to 61,000 by 1971.[5] It is important to bear in mind that it is not possible to identify a single coherent and unified ideology behind draft resistance. Young draft-age men refused induction for a variety of reasons, including but not limited to objection to the constitutionality and legality of the Vietnam War, refusal to bear arms, objection to inequities in the Selective Service System and conscription, and many other reasons. At the end of the day, over half a million draft-eligible young men refused the draft by outright resistance or evasion, but only eight thousand went to trial, and the courts only managed to convict four thousand because the criminal justice system was overwhelmed with the sheer numbers of cases.[6]

In looking at the origins of Vietnam-era draft resistance, Amy Rutenberg exposed the deep racial and class inequities of the Selective Service System and conscription during the Vietnam War. Starting from the observation that young men avoided military service as often as they volunteered to serve in the military, she reveals how, in the main, it was draft-age white men from positions of class privilege who were able to evade military service by taking advantage of deferments, exemptions, and other loopholes, while racialized working-class men from disadvantaged backgrounds became primary targets for conscription.[7] Between 1965 and 1968, the Selective Service System oversaw the induction of approximately nine hundred thousand men into the armed forces, tripling the previous induction rate of one hundred thousand per year. In 1967 approximately 48 percent of the army and 16 percent of the entire armed forces consisted of draftees. Of the 6 million Americans who served in Vietnam, 25 percent of them were draftees.[8] In 1969 the Selective Service System introduced the draft lottery with the aim of both increasing the numbers of military personnel available for service in the Vietnam War and addressing inequities in the previous conscription system.[9]

Waiting for the Axe to Fall

As my application for CO status was under consideration, I was required to submit to first one and then a second mandatory preinduction physical examination conducted by military physicians at military bases. My first physical examination took place at the Oakland Army Induction Center. It was indeed a harrowing experience. I do not recall how I arrived at the sprawling complex in the summer of 1968. Hundreds of nervous young men anxiously milled around the doors for the scheduled physical examination process. As the doors opened precisely at 8:00 a.m., uniformed soldiers began bellowing out orders to the crowd. The shouting and harassment never stopped. Uniformed soldiers herded us anxious young men into a large, cavernous room with rows of desks at one end. We were instructed to stand in a line and present our papers when called forward. To begin the process, we were ordered to strip down to our underwear and stand virtually naked in long rows with other young men.

In retrospect, I now understand that this enforced disrobing was a deliberate exercise to humiliate and embarrass all of us potential recruits. Then it was off to one station after another: military physicians and orderlies administered hearing tests, eye examinations, anal checks, and more. Army personnel demanded that recruits present physicians' reports indicating bad feet, missing limbs, or other physical or mental ailments that indicated that the young man was "unfit" for military service. I distinctly remember a medical officer yelling at a portly young man wearing women's undergarments, "What do you mean you are homosexual, you lying piece of shit?" As I moved past, onto the next station, I could still hear military personnel piling abuse onto this young man. The chances of this cross-dressing tactic resulting in a 4-F classification ("homosexuality" was regarded as a mental illness that made a young man unfit for service) were minimal at best. In virtually all cases, the US Army drafted these young men anyway.

After weeks of waiting, I received a letter from my draft board informing me that I had failed the eyesight test. This physical impairment resulted in a change of my draft status from 1-A to 1-Y. The last thing the US Army wanted was for some infantryman losing his glasses on the battlefield. Today, branches of the US military service do not disqualify recruits on the basis of poor eyesight. There are plenty of other tasks to do that wearing glasses is not a hindrance.

Yet the Army Testing Center was not convinced of the accuracy of the eye test. Induction officials demanded that I submit to a second physical examination, this time at Fort Sam Houston in San Antonio, since I was enrolled in graduate school at the University of Texas in Austin. On the appointed day in September or October 1968, I took a military-organized bus from an appointed staging area in downtown Austin to Fort Sam Houston. This second humiliating experience cemented my understanding of the social processes at work. The US military understood that it had first to deprive its young recruits of their individuality before molding them into a cohesive fighting force.

After spending most of a day in both places, I came to realize that the overwhelming numbers of young men sent as cannon fodder to Vietnam battlefields were Black, Hispanic, and poor white youth. US Army physicians behaved like bored cattle inspectors. Army doctors were to medicine what military music is to music. They were as disengaged as we, the assembled recruits, were frightened. Some middle-class white men were able to obtain attestations about alleged physical disabilities from their personal family physicians back home. This "cheating" amounted to a cottage industry. Trick knees, flat feet, and old broken bones were common excuses. The poor Black and Hispanic kids—and poor white working-class kids, for that matter—did not have that option.

For what seemed like the longest time, I remained entangled with the Selective Service System, trying to sort out my draft status. In retrospect, I now realize how anxiety-provoking this waiting proved to be. On 2 November 1968, I received notification from L. L. Gornall, lieutenant, US Marine Corps (the "Joint Examining and Induction Station Commander, Ft. Sam Houston") that I was "found not acceptable for induction under current circumstances." In other words, my poor eyesight had landed me a 1-Y classification. During the summer of 1969, I finally received official notification of my CO draft status. I remember the day distinctly because my father hand delivered the registered letter from the draft board to me at the place where I was working at a summer job in my hometown of Walnut Creek.

Thinking about this in retrospect, I am really grateful for the moral support of my parents for what at the time were certainly rather unpopular political views. My parents were moving toward embracing a kind of liberation theology approach to Catholic doctrine. They began to take up friendships with antiwar priests, nuns, and fellow Catholics. We became one big antiwar happy family.

I suspect that my local draft board in Martinez had so many draft-age young men to fill their quotas for induction that my twin brother (who also applied for CO status) slipped through the cracks. I also suspect that my twin brother and I were the first and only draft-age young men to apply for CO status at the Contra County (Martinez) draft board. We were anomalies. Strange little Catholic "peace creeps." The members of the draft board probably wished that we would just disappear into thin air.

Despite the capacity of the Selective Service System (with the assistance of local draft boards) to churn out the numbers for induction into military service, the entire process was gradually breaking down. For example, 14,303 young men were ordered to report for military duty at the Oakland Army Induction Center in 1970. Close to half failed to report, and 712 refused induction.[10] This kind of collective refusal was a largely invisible and unacknowledged feature of undermining the war effort.

In retrospect, I can see that my proactive decision to defy the Selective Service System marked a watershed moment for me. I was on the slippery slope to radical politics, never to return to conventional ideas. If I had gone to graduate school somewhere other than the University of Texas, I would have remained in the radical camp of politics, but I would not have taken the historically specific direction I did. I never regret going to UT Austin and the Lone Star State. It was not long before I arrived in Austin that I found a welcome home in the antiwar movement.

Chapter 2

Gaining Traction in the Lone Star State, 1967–1969

In September 1967 I entered the PhD program in philosophy at University of Texas at Austin. My choice of University of Texas was not, in the least, grounded in serious rational calculation about future career prospects. Unlike those students who attended elite undergraduate universities and made their choice of graduate programs on the basis of future opportunities for professional or academic careers, I more or less blindly made a choice. I was very interested in going to the South. Besides other options for attending graduate school, I was admitted to Tulane University in New Orleans and UT Austin. I decided to go to UT for virtually no other reason than I had never been to Texas or to the South.

I traveled by Greyhound bus from Oakland to Austin in late August to begin my first semester at UT Austin. The journey seemed interminable. I never considered traveling by plane since it was more expensive than the bus. I settled into university-supplied housing and diligently directed my attention to graduate studies. It was an exciting time of new discoveries. From the start I found graduate courses in philosophy to be uninteresting and leaden, and not connected to real world events or concerns. At lunchtime I began going to the Chuck Wagon cafeteria, where I began to make a few friends. I remember meeting this woman who was ten years older than I. She had several children and was enrolled in undergraduate courses. She was very sad. I later discovered that Charles Whitman, the sniper perched at the top of the university tower on 1 August 1966, had shot and killed her husband as he stood on Guadalupe Street a considerable distance away from the lone shooter.

Settling into a routine at the University of Texas proved to be a somewhat strange and lonely time. I came knowing no one, and I was cast adrift on a campus that by that time numbered close to thirty to thirty-five thousand students. By and large the student body was very socially and politically conservative. Fraternities and sororities seemed to be everywhere. They were the most popular student organizations on campus. I found my fellow PhD students in the Philosophy Department to be very uptight, rather nervous, and exceedingly boring. With a few exceptions, the faculty in the Philosophy Department were conventional in their outlooks, focusing on their own particular (narrow) areas of research and teaching.

SDS as the Focal Point: 1967–June 1969

In Austin there were glimmers of an alternative social and political culture visible at the edges. When I arrived in August 1967, SDS already had a presence in university politics and protests.[1] Students had joined with the Campus Interracial Committee to protest against racial segregation in university dormitories and participated in sit-ins at segregated restaurants. The fledging SDS chapter was actively involved in civil rights struggles and in resistance to the Selective Service System and the draft. In April 1965 SDS members staged a protest at the LBJ ranch outside Austin. Photographs depicting the protest received national attention. In October 1966 ten women staged a sit-in at the Austin Selective Service Office. On 23 April 1967, SDS called a rally on the campus to announce protest action against the visit of Vice President Hubert Humphrey. Six speakers at that rally—Alice Embree, Gary Thirer, Tom Smith, Dick Reavis, Dave Mahler (all from SDS), and John Lefeber (Young Democrats)—were summoned before a disciplinary hearing, charged with violating university policy on unauthorized meetings and rallies, and faced with expulsion from the university. The furor surrounding this event became known as the University Freedom Movement.[2]

Many of the early activists had roots in youth organizations affiliated with Christian churches, and they discovered their political awakening in this moral milieu. These early building blocks contributed a solid foundation for the Austin SDS chapter as a formidable political organization. This background was also true for me. My experience with the Catholic-sponsored Amigos Anonymous group that engaged in community development work in central Mexico shaped my views about social justice. I lived in the small town of Apaseo el Grande for the summers of 1965 and 1967.

Unbeknownst to me at the time, police monitoring and surveillance of SDS was in full swing by the mid-1960s. According to published COINTELPRO documents, the FBI San Antonio field office dispatched at least two undercover agents to begin monitoring the small Austin SDS chapter sometime in 1965. These FBI agents linked their surveillance efforts with their local FBI contact, Lt. Burt Gerding, the head of Criminal Intelligence Division of the APD.

Documents in the Allen Hamilton Papers deposited at the Dolph Briscoe Center for American History at the University of Texas at Austin paint a rather sinister picture of the extent to which the security forces were willing to go from the start.[3] Allen Hamilton, affectionately known as Chief of the Forty Acres, served as UT Austin campus security chief from the late 1950s until 1970. The records—covering a period roughly from 1963 to 1970—amount to a treasure trove of information that reveals a great deal about law enforcement agents and their surveillance techniques.

It seems that Hamilton had secretly stored his police files, hidden away for decades in a large box under his bed at home. His son only discovered them after his father's death in 2005. After unearthing this cache, Hamilton's son set out to sell them to Half Price Books, a bookstore in Dallas that specializes in buying and reselling used books and other printed materials. Recognizing the importance of the materials, the owners of Half Price Books arranged to donate the files to the Briscoe Center. But before turning over the full collection of materials, they allowed Thorne Dreyer, Alice Embree, and a few others to photocopy the political files, including police surveillance papers.

In a thoughtful exposé that reveals the role of Allen Hamilton in mounting a surveillance campaign against UT campus radicals, Thorne Dreyer provides a partial glimpse into the comings and goings of official policing agencies.[4] The files in the Hamilton Papers indicate beyond the shadow of a doubt the extensive efforts that the campus police department made to identify, monitor, and follow students and faculty members whom they found suspicious. The assembled files include more than five hundred pages of police department memos, some produced by undercover informants. The files also contain lists of names of campus "drug users" and political activists, along with photocopies of newspaper articles and political leaflets. The Hamilton files also contain over 250 surveillance photographs capturing protest events and those who participated. While some of these photographs are close-ups of individuals, others are panoramic views with individuals identified by hand-scribbled notations of names.[5]

As Thorne Dreyer put it, "And there are names, lots of names, probably close to a thousand. Some typed, some scribbled, some photocopied from petitions and sign-in sheets collected at meetings and rallies." These materials provide a window into a historically specific time, or as Dryer put it, "a formative period of creativity, iconoclasm, and growing political consciousness" that eventually evolved into a mass antiwar movement. As disorganized and sometimes unfocused as we were, we managed to expose and undermine the US war machine in Vietnam, and to challenge the principles of capitalism and the practice of imperialism. As flawed as it was, the antiwar movement offered an alternative vision of a life-affirming culture that stood against racism, misogyny, homophobia, and class oppression. The documents in the Hamilton Papers show how the security forces "reacted—often overreacted" to the perceived threats to law and order. These papers also reveal how little the campus police and the university top administration "really understood about what was happening in the streets" and in the growing countercultural communities that blossomed in Austin.[6]

Much of the material contained in the Hamilton Papers focuses on the UT SDS chapter. Until the fateful dissolution of the organization in June 1968, SDS carried the weight of antiwar and other political activities at UT Austin. The files on UT campus radicals include an extensive list (covering thirty-two pages) of over 250 names of suspicious persons "associated with SDS"—with street addresses, phone numbers, hometowns, high schools attended, and other background information such as fathers' names and occupations. Sometimes these files contained physical descriptions: Vicky Kirk is a "colored female" and Gary Chason is "growing a beard." There is similar information on the University of Texas Committee to End the War in Vietnam (UTCEWV), the Texas Student League for Responsible Sexual Freedom, and other groups.[7]

Files in the Hamilton Papers reveal the names of two undercover informants who spied on SDS: one, named Jeff Garner, played a minor role as SDS treasurer for a time in the mid-1960s but was never a significant leader in the group. What is unclear is whether Jeff Gardiner was a real name or a pseudonym for this undercover informant. The other, John Economidy, was editor of the *Daily Texan*, the UT student newspaper, in 1966–1967. The Hamilton files contain signed memos to Chief Hamilton concerning SDS activities that originated from both of these undercover informants. Gardiner specialized in providing detailed accounts of SDS meetings and functions, planned activities, factional splits, national SDS policies, and "the comings and goings of members." For his part, Economidy played a more proactive role, providing both Chief Hamilton and Lieutenant Gerding with lists of names of political activists and photographs of individuals and events.[8]

Hamilton and his coterie of campus cops worked closely with the APD and other security agencies, like the FBI and military intelligence. In his citywide role, Gerding coordinated his criminal intelligence activities with Chief Hamilton. Yet, in the rigid hierarchy of policing agencies, Gerding was top dog. Hamilton remained Austin police chief until 1970, when he went to work as a security consultant for the UT System in the office of his friend George Carlson.

The spying on Austin political activists revealed in the Hamilton Papers constituted only a minor tributary in a surging river of repression. One cannot underestimate the magnitude of surveillance efforts by local, state, and federal agencies directed against those involved in the antiwar activism and countercultural lifestyles of the 1960s and 1970s. The FBI, with its secret COINTELPRO, formed the centerpiece of an extensive "surveillance state" directed at disrupting and undermining the movement by using any means necessary.[9]

As we began to tentatively (with some grace, a little flair, and a great deal of naiveté) "rage against the machine," we attracted the attention of a vast security apparatus that committed itself to literally destroying us. We did not realize at the time how far and to what extent the various security agencies were aligned against us. From the start undercover informants attended SDS meetings and spied on political gatherings. The Criminal Intelligence Division of the APD monitored activities and tapped phones. Police photographers began to compile to vast trove of photographic images of people and events.

In March 1966 an FBI COINTELPRO memo declared that SDS leaders in Austin were "overzealous idealists with personality problems."[10] Despite the astronomical growth of the New Left in Austin and elsewhere, the FBI was never able to move away from looking at supposed "individual deviance," "personality disorders," and "character flaws." They were never able to offer more than psychological explanations for our nonconformist behavior. This inability to look to structural causes for dissenting politics kept them in the dark for quite some time.

Sit-In Against Marine Recruiters, Mid-November 1967

I did not arrive in Austin as a completely naive newcomer to insurgent politics. From my experience in the San Francisco Bay Area attending antiwar rallies and free speech rallies at the University of California–Berkeley campus, I was acutely aware of the signs of protest. I had already begun the journey seeking CO status with the Selective Service System.

It was not long before I found what I was looking for in Austin. On 14 October 1967, I attended an antiwar demonstration in downtown Austin at the State Capitol building. It was on this occasion that a new faculty member, Larry Caroline, delivered the speech to several thousand onlookers that set in motion his dismissal from his position at UT Austin. In retrospect, I can now see that I was being drawn into the circle of left-wing antiwar politics, first as an attentive observer and eventually as an active participant.

On 14 November 1967, after finishing lunch with some new friends at the Chuck Wagon in the University Union, I walked down the long hallway to exit the building. As I walked past a large alcove room about thirty feet long and twenty feet wide, I noticed a bit of a commotion. I stopped to observe. At the far end of the alcove, three or four Marines were either standing or seated at a folding table filled with pamphlets and surrounded by signboards that proclaimed "Serve your Country. Join the Marines." Around ten to fifteen young people were sitting on the floor, blocking access to the Marines. Those demonstrating had effectively disrupted the Marine recruiting efforts. A lot of shouting and yelling was taking place. I witnessed some angry people who opposed the sit-in who pushed and kicked their way past and over the protesters.[11] I was captivated. I was against the war in Vietnam, so I sat down, joining the sit-in.

Organized by the UTCEWV, an SDS affiliate, this sit-in was the first in a number of high-profile demonstrations as part of a "fall offensive" designed to confront the university's complicity in the war effort. For the next several days as the sit-in wore on, I became an everyday active participant in the protest. By the end of the week, the small room was overcrowded with those sitting in and with supporters of the Marine recruiters. These counterprotesters jeered at us, pushed their way through the bodies on the floor, stomping and kicking, elbowing their way to the front. I noticed several middle-aged men watching the protest from the far edge of the crowd. Some of my fellow protesters blocking access to the Marines told me that the tall, thin one with a sly grin on his face was Lt. Burt Gerding, the well-known head of the APD criminal intelligence division, euphemistically known as the Red Squad. At the time I did not think much of Gerding's presence. Over time I came to experience the central role he played in spying on the antiwar movement. In FBI documents that I discovered later, I learned that plainclothes special agents from the FBI San Antonio office coordinated with Gerding to observe this sit-in against Marine recruiters in the University Union.[12]

I was inspired by the dedication and sophistication of the protestors and the capacity of the leaders to remain totally unfazed in the face of intimidation and shouts like "Commie bastards" and "pinko beatniks." During this

Lt. Burt Gerding, head of Criminal Intelligence Division, Austin Police Department, striking a pose. Courtesy of Alan Pogue, photographer.

sit-in demanding the expulsion of Marine recruiters from campus, a person in the crowd who was against the protest shouted at one of the apparent leaders, Dick Reavis, "Go back to Russia." Dick, who was holding his Coke bottle by the top of the long neck (as he always did), slowly spilled out his words in a distinctive southern drawl: "No, I don't think so. I'm kind of partial to China myself." This quick retort was an early glimpse at Maoist ideology—the roots of the Progressive Labor (PL) Party—a faction that broke SDS apart in 1969. Dick became a PL stalwart.

Participation in this sit-in drew me into SDS. I started going to weekly meetings held on campus. I was surprised that only about ten to fifteen people attended. The group included Gary Thiher, Larry Caroline, Scott Pittman, Harvey Stone, Robert Heilbrunner, Bobby Minkoff, Mariann Vizard, Alice Embree, and a few more. What impressed me the most was the clarity of vision, the dedication, and the lack of hesitancy. I was committed.

After I had attended only about two campus SDS meetings, I became aware of police surveillance. As I was casually walking along a hallway in the University Union late one morning, a middle-aged man in a cheap suit greeted me cheerily by name with a with a hearty, "Hey, Martin, so I see that you've joined SDS." It was Burt Gerding. I knew at that moment my presence had been noticed. Suddenly, I realized that I was not a random, anonymous participant in a demonstration, using my rights of free speech to offer my opinion. In the mind of Gerding, I had passed from the shadows of anonymity into the glare of light: a subversive to be watched and monitored. Biography blended imperceptibly with history. Chance inadvertently deposited me at that demonstration, and commitment made me stay. It was not that I had chosen to become "political" but that I was compelled to make political choices in turbulent times. Starting around 1963 and perhaps into late 1970, both Gerding and his sidekick, Allen Hamilton, head of UT campus security, were permanent fixtures around political events on the university campus. Despite serving different security organizations, they teamed together to monitor protest events, to spy on political organizations, to record our names, and to identify our "leaders."

I remember this early period in my growing attachment to left-wing antiwar politics in Austin as exhilarating. For the first time in my life, I discovered like-minded people who were not afraid to confront the assembled powers that be. What distinguished the Austin SDS chapter (and the growing political movement in the region) was a visceral rejection of top-down national politics. The Austin SDS chapter was one of the first in the country. Students constituted a sizeable contingent of SDS members, but the majority of participants were nonstudents, dropouts, and alienated youth looking for a home to express their antiwar and antiestablishment politics. From the beginning Austin SDS was not an exclusively student movement.

The early years of political activism in Austin were particularly lean. It was difficult for students and young people to step outside the political mainstream. The university had what the administration called the free speech area—a small patio the size of a middle-size classroom accommodating about one hundred students and surrounded by buildings. The chair of the Board of Regents for the University of Texas was Frank Erwin, who had strong ties to the conservative wing of the Democratic Party in Texas and connections with the elite oil business class in the state. Around 99 percent of the enrolled student body was white. The first Afro-American scholarship football player, Julius Whittier, made his debut in 1970, only a few seasons after the Texas Longhorns fielded the last all-white national championship team in the history of college football in 1963. The Ku Klux Klan was quite active locally, with a presence in the police department. Public facilities like movie theaters and restaurants in Austin had only been formally racially integrated since 1966, the year before I arrived. Business owners of public facilities were openly hostile to so-called nonwhite people.

Yet in the midst of these rapidly changing circumstances, new forms of cultural and political expression took root and grew. SDS veterans from the formative years pointed with pride to a 1965 sit-in at the LBJ ranch outside of Austin, a demonstration that received national media attention. The 1966 SDS national secretary, Bob Pardun, and the 1967 national secretary, Greg Calvert, both moved to Austin. Both had developed a healthy disregard for internecine power struggles in the Chicago National Office. Each in his own particular way preached a populist gospel that elevated themes like prairie power to the level of a political principle. Almost overnight Austin became the hub of a regional-cultural movement spreading east to Houston, south to San

Antonio, and north to Dallas and Denton, also including Norman (Oklahoma) and Little Rock (Arkansas). Started in 1968, the Oleo Strut coffeehouse near Fort Hood military base in Killeen became a key gathering place for active-duty soldiers. Political activists at the Oleo Strut published an underground antiwar newspaper (the *Fatigue Press*), organized boycotts, created a legal office, and organized antiwar rallies and marches. The prairie fire message resonated through the region, blending decentralized organizational structures with a plainly anarchist disrespect for authority of all types.[13]

Texas populism has a long history, and the peculiar brand of 1960s anarcho-syndicalist thought that took hold in Austin was both a blessing and a curse. The Austin SDS chapter operated on a model of persuasion and consensus, tapping into the deep roots of Texas irreverent populist traditions. Meetings were often long and drawn-out events, with heated discussion and occasionally rancorous debate extending long into the night. Austin SDS never succumbed to the Marxist–Leninist party formations or the Weather Underground madness that originated out of the 1969 SDS collapse. Around early 1968 the local leadership of PL introduced into meetings a mode of politics that demanded adherence to a single perspective framed around building a so-called worker-student alliance. Despite lining up behind their democratic-centralist organizational format, PL supporters never amounted to much more than a shrill, vocal minority singing their class purity chorus with a unanimous voice. The countercultural "hippie" faction remained a strong yet politically unorganized current. Anti-imperialist and Marxist study groups and action caucuses of various sorts formed and re-formed without the dominating presence of disciplined sect groups that seemed to plague SDS and other progressive student groups elsewhere.

However, there was a negative side to the deep-seated anarchism and populism that reigned supreme in the local Austin SDS chapter. Anti-intellectualism was rampant. Reading and learning about various political traditions was never high on the agenda. Most hardcore activists failed to understand the relevance of theorizing about strategies and tactics of political protest. They tended to worship action for its own sake and had little patience for thinking about how to build our base beyond alienated youth and cater our message to previously untapped constituencies. Formed at the inspiration of

Greg Calvert, an Austin-based Movement for a Democratic Society (MDS) took the movement off the campus, focusing on bringing a New Left political analysis to nonstudent constituencies like social workers, young lawyers, teachers, and low-level government employees.

Austin was also home to a deeply rooted populist-liberal tradition. A journal, called the *Texas Observer* under the editorship of Ronnie Dugger, published muckraking pieces that exposed corporate greed, the hypocrisy of political elites, and government corruption. The *Texas Observer* attracted such well-known writers as Molly Ivins, Willie Morris, Jim Hightower, and Kaye Northcott. Radical lawyers, disgruntled writers and journalists, and assorted other cranky freethinkers all swam in this sea of iconoclastic disregard for Texas conventions.

Demonstration Against General Harold K. Johnson

After the success of the sit-in against Marine recruiters, we decided to target every official display of support for the war effort by directly confronting the "war makers." The university administration invited General Harold K. Johnson, chief of staff of the US Army, to give a formal address at the University of Texas on 30 November 1967. Official invitations like this one were designed to show university support for the war effort in Vietnam. This planned speech offered a wonderful opportunity to both test our resolve and measure our capacity to mobilize our own forces. For days we members of SDS distributed leaflets in anticipation of his visit. The leaflets named corporate capitalism and the military-industrial complex as those who profited from the war.[14] About four thousand people attended the speech.

We organized into two separate groups: One entered the auditorium, making lots of noise, heckling, and disrupting the proceedings. Those who entered the hall dressed in black and whitened their faces with grease paint "to remind [those in attendance] that people are dying [in Vietnam]." Before General Johnson arrived, this group performed a rousing guerilla theater skit uncovering the relationship between corporate enterprise and the military-industrial complex profiting handsomely from the war in Vietnam. The *Dallas Morning News* estimated that 250 protesters walked out of the speech chanting and shouting antiwar slogans as they departed. The number was surely more than this estimate. A second group of about the same number remained outside, passing out leaflets and engaging in heated conversations about the war. I was part of this contingent.[15]

General Johnson put forward the standard litany of excuses and erroneous justifications for the US presence in Vietnam: "[We] are there to preserve freedom [and] to preserve their [meaning the protesters'] right to dissent"; "We are in Vietnam, I repeat, by invitation," to resist Communist tyranny; and "also because we now know that a threat to freedom and peace anywhere in the world is a threat to free men."[16] One cliché after another. Following the walkout, and as people were filing out at the conclusion of the speech, we converged on the exit to the Union Building where the speech took place, holding aloft signs with antiwar slogans and chanting, "Hell no, we won't go."

We made a calculated choice to use confrontation and disruption as deliberate tactics to spread our message. We were not going to be silent, standing stiffly like speechless sentinels holding placards and signs. Disorderliness and direct action were the way we got attention for our ideas and how we attracted new members. With all tactics something is lost and something is gained. We certainly alienated some people permanently with our boisterous protest, but we also triggered an interest in others.[17]

Around this time General Paul "Ramrod" Harkins, the former chief of Military Assistance Command, Vietnam (MACV), gave an invited address to a Catholic social fraternity at UT. I wrote an opinion piece for the *Daily Texan* in which I chronicled the long string of lies used to justify US military intervention in Vietnam. I was quite proud of this short piece (fully excerpted in appendix 2). I had gone to the university library to do research, reading everything about how the United States became involved in Vietnam. I signed the piece, "Martin Murray, SDS member." Collectively speaking, we were beginning to identify the underlying cause for the war: capitalist imperialism.

The Larry Caroline Affair, 1967–1969

The events surrounding the firing of philosophy professor Larry Caroline are often referred to as the Caroline Affair. This rather bland designation for the controversy carried none of the true seriousness and trauma that

Larry Caroline, dismissed professor, at rally. Courtesy of Prints and Photographs Collection, camh-dob-017294, Dolph Briscoe Center for American History, University of Texas at Austin.

accompanied these events. Larry Caroline joined the Philosophy Department as an assistant professor without tenure starting September 1967. From the start he joined the local SDS chapter. On 14 October 1967, several days after the CIA assassinated "Che" Guevara (9 October 1967) in Bolivia, Caroline delivered a well-crafted speech at an antiwar rally at the State Capitol. I participated in the rally with perhaps several thousand others. I remember distinctly what Larry said. After listing a litany of flaws and contradictions in the capitalist system and identifying the organized efforts of liberal politicians to change these injustices, he went on to conclude, "You can't change things one at a time. The whole bloody mess has to go. What we need is a new American revolution." I was impressed with this systematic dismantling of the liberal fantasy of working diligently inside the system to bring incremental change.

These words ignited a firestorm of controversy. Not tied to the truth, newspapers reported that Caroline had called for a "bloody revolution." The negative publicity enraged the chair of the UT Board of Regents, Frank

Erwin, a bigger-than-life figure who oversaw the University of Texas system like his personal fiefdom. Like a Shakespearian tragedy, the ending was already inscribed in the beginning. The die was cast, so to speak. Erwin set out to terminate Caroline's contract by any means necessary. On 3 June 1968, he announced that the Board of Regents were terminating Caroline's contract as of May 1969. We in SDS held a rally—staged as a funeral for academic freedom—and over 1,500 onlookers joined the protest. This abrupt dismissal set in motion a yearlong sequence of protest rallies and public meetings.

Erwin found in the person of John Silber, the dean of the College of Arts and Sciences, his willing and able executioner. Silber had already built a reputation as a take-no-prisoners hatchet man. Originally hired to shake up a sleepy university, he replaced twenty-two of twenty-eight department chairs in his first four years as dean. A short man with an aggressive approach to just about everything, Silber had a way of disarming those whom he first met by sticking out his left hand to greet people. He openly waved around his withered right arm (the result of a birth defect), and he treated it not like an impediment but a weapon. Silber saw himself as a neo-Kantian scholar. He looked upon rationality and logical argument as the means to promote what he considered his own liberal values of fairness and tolerance. He was on the side of the angels. Yet at his core he was an arrogant, intolerant bully who struggled to win every argument. He refused to succumb to anyone. John Silber saw himself as a crusader for the moral high ground of traditional liberalism. Instead, he exposed the wicked underbelly of illiberal intolerance and deceit.[10]

After these early clumsy efforts to orchestrate Caroline's dismissal by fiat, Erwin and the top university administration were forced to follow their own bureaucratic procedures that had been established to protect faculty and employees from arbitrary firing. Shifting gears, the top administration turned to their attention to finding a way to manipulate their own rules to dismiss Caroline. The furor gathered new momentum after the university administration reopened the case in fall 1968, raising issues both about academic freedom and about which administrative bodies were ultimately responsible for hiring-and-firing decisions in university departments.

In Spring 1968 the eleven-member Budget Council of the Philosophy Department (the governing body of the department) had voted to terminate

Caroline's contract when it came to an end in May 1969.[19] In October 1968 the Budget Council reversed its previous decision, voting 6–5 to extend Carline's contract. In so many ways, the Budget Council change of heart (by the narrowest of margins) was a charade. The Board of Regents had voted unanimously four months earlier in June 1968 not to renew Caroline's appointment, and this elite body had the final word on the matter.[20]

While the council deliberated in a closed-door session, SDS sponsored a protest rally in support of Caroline and the right to free speech. Silber's hand-picked chair of the Philosophy Department, Irwin Chester Lieb, tried to resign in protest over the vote that did not go in his favor. Not to be undone, when the decision reached the dean's office, Silber rejected this departmental recommendation and upheld the decision of the regents to terminate Carline's contract. President Norman Hackerman, an Erwin supporter, backed his decision. It was over.

Larry Caroline taught his final semester in Spring 1969. I worked as a teaching assistant for one of his last classes. While Silber had proclaimed publicly that Caroline misled his students with sophistry and specious reasoning, the opposite was the case. In my view Larry Caroline was a careful thinker who exposed students to all points of view. He used reason to persuade students to think critically. He let me read one of his dissertation chapters entitled "Why be moral?" In essence, he argued that moral beings exist in communities, and for communities to function fairly, all members ought to treat others in the ways they themselves would wish to be treated.

After the initial uproar over the speech subsided, Caroline spoke at all sorts of protest events where he defended his right to freedom of speech and clarified what he meant by "revolution." As the deliberations of dismissal entered into the bureaucratic maze that is a signature feature of university governance everywhere, Caroline slowly withdrew from the spotlight. He turned to alternative education and was a founding member of Greenbriar School, an experimental educational project designed to redefine how youngsters are taught and how they learn. For me, it was sad to see such a brilliant person with enormous potential to become a great scholar and teacher pushed aside. Larry never really recovered while he stayed in Austin, just waiting for an opportunity to leave. He was a victim of political repression. Larry eventually moved with his wife Dina Caroline (who became a well-known medical doctor) to Philadelphia, where he returned to his Orthodox Jewish roots, working as a fundraiser for Jewish schools.

Ten Days of Protest and Resistance, 21–30 April 1968

One striking feature of how we organized opposition to the Vietnam War was how inventive we were in orchestrating multiple types of protest over many days. The Ten Days of Protest and Resistance, 21–30 April 1968 is an illustration of our confidence to sustain momentum over ten days. An FBI undercover informant reported that fifty or sixty SDS members attended a meeting on 4 April 1968 to plan upcoming protest activities. This undercover informant identified Mariann Vizard as the key figure in taking the lead in proposing a connected series of events. On 21 April we started with a mass leafleting of the campus and surrounding streets, announcing our plans. On 22–23 April we organized a mock state fair event laid out in front of the University Tower, featuring a large monopoly game wherein the names of large corporations holding military contracts were substituted for properties. The aim was to use an air of humor and satire in a carnival-like atmosphere to identify the absurdities of imperialism by making fun of the corporate beneficiaries of the military-industrial complex. On Wednesday, 25 April, we scheduled a rally and demonstration at the defense research laboratory on the UT campus. On Thursday, 26 April, we resuscitated the tradition of Gentle Thursday, an event involving music, singing, and dancing—an impromptu "gathering of the tribes" that the university administration had tried to ban in previous years. On Friday we planned a rally in solidarity with student strikes taking place around the world. On 28 April (Saturday), we in SDS joined with the antiwar group called the University of Texas Committee to End the War (UTCEWV) in a march from the UT campus and down Congress Avenue to the State Capitol. While affiliated with SDS, the UTCEWV was an independent, broad-based mass organization that opposed the Vietnam War, and called for immediate withdrawal of US troops. Rooted in the progressive elements of churches and religious groups, the UTCEWV advocated nonviolent direct action. At root it remained a liberal organization committed to bringing about reforms in the political system. We looked upon the joint march as a way of winning them over to a more radical interpretation of US imperialism. On 29 April (Sunday), we sponsored a picnic in one of the many Austin city parks. On 30 April (Monday), we organized a teach-in on the UT campus focusing on the war and racism.[21]

We certainly did not know it at the time, but the San Antonio FBI field office coordinated their monitoring of the events with Criminal Intelligence Division of the APD and statewide Texas Department of Public Safety (DPS). Several undercover informants—deemed "reliable" and with "continuing value"—provided the raw data for a cascade of FBI memos monitoring our actions. These undercover informants identified Mariann Vizard as their primary "person of interest."[22] A careful thinker and brilliant strategist, she was a self-acknowledged member of the CPUSA.

Don Weedon Gas Station Protests, 3 May 1968

Don Weedon epitomized the Texas good ole boy persona. He was the full package, all stuffed and rounded into one. Weedon was firmly rooted in local Longhorns football culture, and he was a walking, talking platform for all the recidivist ideas that this sociocultural world of Texas football exuded. He was a well-known racist and general bigot. He developed a well-deserved reputation for not serving African Americans and long-haired hippies at his Conoco gas station. Weedon had played football at Austin High School, became a defensive star for the University of Texas Longhorns, and went on to play in the National Football League for one year with the Philadelphia Eagles in 1947 (after his service in the Army during WWII). As his football career was ending, Weedon opened a Conoco gas station on the northwestern corner of Thirty-Fourth and Guadalupe. Like many other small business owners with ties to the UT football program, Weedon was alleged to have regularly hired football players on "no-work, full pay" sweetheart deals that supplemented their scholarships. For campus work, it was rumored that one summer job for a football player consisted of watching the University Tower and reporting if it fell over. Football was the focal point of local culture, and trading in football stories was the verbal currency that tied all sorts of otherwise very different people together in a shared camaraderie.

On 3 May 1968, Austin police arrested around forty-two people at an antiracism demonstration that took place at Weedon's Conoco station. The cause of this protest lay in the events of a week before. On the night of Saturday, 27 April, Weedon physically attacked an African American UT student named Leo Northington. As a member of a local rock band, Northington was playing music that night at the Lemon Tree Club. Weedon was at the club watching the heavyweight title fight between Jimmy Ellis, an African American boxer, and Jerry Quarry, a white contender. This boxing match was to crown a new heavyweight champion after Muhammad Ali was stripped of his title after his conviction of draft evasion. Weedon began to question other patrons at the club as to whether they would like to place a bet on the "n——," as he himself was willing to put money on the white fighter. Weedon then began to verbally assault Northington and eventually punched him several times without any provocation. Northington filed charges. Rather than arresting Weedon, the APD called him on the phone to advise him of a summons for his arrest. Weedon was charged with simple assault, a charge that carried a maximum fine of $200. Eventually, Weedon plead guilty and the court issued him a paltry fine of $20.

Larry Jackson, a leader of Austin SNCC and the primary organizer for the Community United Front (CUF), a Black Panther type of neighborhood organization, called for picketing and protest action at Weedon's Conoco gas station on 3 May. By early afternoon around 135 protesters arrived to begin parading on the sidewalk in a circle around the station. As a swelling crowd of demonstrators tried to block automobile access to the station, APD officers rushed in, arresting CUF activists Larry Jackson and Grace Cleaver, along with several others. Groups of protesters, plus a contingent of Weedon supporters from the Hook' M bar across the street, joined the fray. The demonstration spilled into Guadalupe Street, with demonstrators sitting down and blocking traffic. APD officers arrested thirty-three persons for refusing to move off the street, charging them with unlawful assembly, and several others on the more serious charges of resisting arrest. None of the counterprotesters were arrested.

The Gerding Papers contain a whole file on the Don Weedon gas station protests. These police reports focus primarily on the efforts to block cars from entering the gas station and other acts of civil disobedience. As head of the Austin Red Squad, Gerding seemed most interested in the role of Larry

Jackson, the key person in a small Black Power movement in Austin. What the Gerding Papers completely ignore is the presence of the Ku Klux Klan (KKK) as a counterdemonstration force at the protests. KKK members drove around the edges of the mass demonstration, occasionally brandishing shotguns that they pointed out the windows of their pickup trucks, aimed in our direction. On two occasions some yahoo KKK guy pointed a shotgun directly at me out the window of a pickup truck from no more than six feet away as the driver drove slowly around the outer boundaries of our picket line. At the time I did not think too much about the danger. In retrospect, I should have been much more concerned.

This demonstration cemented an alliance between SDS and the conjoined Austin chapter of SNNC and the CUF. Out of its small office in East Austin, the CUF organized tutoring programs and sponsored a free breakfast program for children (modeled on the Black Panthers). Larry Jackson was a charismatic figure and an eloquent spokesperson for Afro-American liberation. He was involved in protests to build a Black Studies program at UT. CUF members (and Anthony Spears and Velma Roberts in particular) were permanent fixtures along Guadalupe Street across from the UT campus, selling Black Panther newspapers and collecting funds for their free breakfast program.

Entanglements of Local and National Radical Politics

What is interesting to note is that the APD Criminal Intelligence Division was beginning to take an interest in the relationship between the local Austin movement and SDS national politics. Gerding describes in detail what happened at an 11 July 1968 meeting of Austin SDS following the June 1968 National Council meeting in East Lansing. He reported with alarm that PL (a Maoist party) had "taken over" national SDS. This claim was wrong. He then observed that "the current [Austin] SDS chapter openly admits that they are Communists and spends a good deal of time discussing the <u>coming Revolution</u>, and the great psychological boost that a US withdrawal in Viet Nam will have since they feel this will prove to workers all over the world how US imperialism can be beaten."[23] Not a particularly deep thinker and not to be confused by complexity, Gerding turned to the principle of parsimony as a problem-solving device (otherwise known as Ockham's razor), adopting the spurious view that the simplest explanation was usually the best one. For Gerding, SDS was a Communist organization committed to ending the war in Vietnam in order to hasten the coming revolution. Armed with such deductive reasoning that enabled them to ignore countervailing evidence, the security agencies could always find what they were looking for.

In the fall of 1968, the APD Criminal Intelligence Division, working "with information from two reliable sources," became alarmed that the New Left was planning "very significant actions in the near future." These sources indicated that while in the past local SDS chapters decided on their own programs of action, this condition "was no longer the case." Released on the eve of the SDS National Council Meeting in Boulder in October 1968 (organized under the slogan "Boulder and Bolder"), Burt Gerding reported that the "[Tom] Hayden–[Rennie] Davis faction of SDS was probably going to make a move to expel Progressive Labor from SDS."[24] This expulsion did not happen. Besides getting the forecast of an upcoming expulsion wrong, Gerding failed to comprehend that both Tom Hayden and Rennie Davis were both inactive in national SDS at that time. Once again, misinformation that the local security agencies relied upon contributed to a failure to truly understand what was happening on the ground in Austin.

Talk of this national friction reverberated to the local Austin SDS chapter. Tensions rose between the PL faction and the rest of SDS. Because it was an organized faction that always voted as a singular block, PL was able to assert its positions unequivocally. Yet PL never consisted of more than a handful of hardcore members. It never managed to shape the direction of SDS. The Criminal Intelligence Division issued a warning to Chief Miles of the APD and to local FBI agents to be on alert for possible unrest around upcoming elections. This proactive move suggested that the Criminal Intelligence Division was shifting from a largely monitoring and surveillance role to one of anticipating future events and actively trying to disrupt or prevent them from taking place.[25] During this period criminal intelligence reports submitted to the APD consisted of a lot of naming of names, the identification of alleged leaders, and information about planned demonstrations.

Our own local success in building SDS into an organized presence on the UT campus and beyond underscored our thinking about creating a regional alliance of local SDS chapters in other cities and college towns in Texas, Arkansas, and Oklahoma. On 18–20 October 1968, we in Austin sponsored a regional get-together with SDS chapters in Houston, Dallas, Denton, San Antonio, Norman, Stillwater, and more to coordinate our efforts regarding antiwar protests, combating racism, opposing the elections, supporting draft resistance, and dealing with repression. The leaflet announcing the meeting declared (in capital letters), with a bit of bravado: "SDS IN TEXAS AND OKLAHOMA IS GROWING AT A FANTASTIC RATE! THERE ARE NOW MORE THAN TWENTY GROUPS AND CHAPTERS, AND SDS IN THESE TWO STATES IS COMING CLOSER EVERY DAY TO A TRULY FUNCTIONAL REGION. BUT OUR GREATEST OBSTACLE—ISOLATION—MUST STILL BE OVERCOME." The leaflet also noted, in an ominous gesture to the future, "Repression is coming down hard on radicals and activists all over the country, and Texas and Oklahoma are no exception. We must struggle together."[26]

The SDS Texas-Oklahoma Regional Office (located in Dallas) released a statement—included in FBI files—that claimed that 130 SDS members from all over Texas and Oklahoma attended the regional conference. The principal focus was to expose the national elections scheduled for 5 November as "a hoax and a fraud." This leaflet announced five sites for anti-election demonstrations—Austin, Dallas, Houston, Norman, and Stillwater—involving thirty SDS chapters in the region. The slogan for the planned student strike (to coincide with rallies and marches) on 4 and 5 November was "No Class Today! No Ruling Class Tomorrow! SDS." The underground newspaper *Dallas Notes* promised to print seventy-five to a hundred thousand copies of their anti-election issue. SDS promoted the idea that the election consisted of a choice among the Three Stooges (Nixon, Humphrey, and Wallace). We distributed posters that caricatured the images of these three politicians. This SDS attack on electoral politics represented a clear break with the reformist, gradualist (work-within-the-system) agenda of liberalism.[27]

FBI undercover informants at the 18–20 October regional meeting reported a growing split between the PL faction and everyone else. One informant reported that "newer SDS chapters did not want anything to do with PL." Those SDS members who participated in this regional conference voted not to hold one massive rally in Austin to oppose the November national elections (the PL proposal), but instead to endorse dispersed demonstrations at multiple sites as a more effective way to build the antiwar movement across the region.[28]

In January 1969 the FBI issued a lengthy (sixty-three-page) report evaluating the activities of various SDS chapters in the Texas-Oklahoma region. Profiles on the SDS organized presence included the Texas-Oklahoma Regional Office collective and local chapters at Southern Methodist University, University of Texas at Arlington, West Texas State (Canyon), East Texas State (Commerce), North Texas State (Denton), Texas Technical College (Lubbock), and Midwestern University (Wichita Falls). By 1968 we had built quite a presence in out-of-the-way locations in Texas and Oklahoma. What was missing from this report were evaluations on SDS chapters at University of Oklahoma (Norman) and Oklahoma State University (Stillwater), both places where SDS was active.[29]

While we did not know it at the time, all SDS local chapters were subjected to COINTELPRO disruptive tactics and infiltration by undercover police informants.[30] It seems that every SDS chapter in Texas and Oklahoma had at least one undercover informant spy in their midst, reporting up the chain of command to FBI national headquarters. The FBI operated with the unspoken assumption that young people exercising their rights to speech and assembly was the slippery slope to subversive and seditious behavior. The San Antonio FBI field office mailed anonymous, and untraceable, letters to key University of Texas officials. The letters contained "more than a mere criticism of the university's administrators for allowing the [regional] SDS meeting" to be held on the campus in October 1968. Various FBI field officers reached agreement that the anonymous letters should come from "an irate taxpayer who objects strongly to allowing a revolutionary group like SDS to hold a meeting on the campus of University of Texas." Taking their dirty tricks even further, FBI field offices agreed that the letter should include observations—obtained from undercover informants who attended—about what transpired at the event to show the true nature of SDS. Under this directive, the faux persona—an irate letter-writer code named Dillon O'Rourke—was born.[31] For a long period of time, Dillon O'Rourke—an FBI invention—routinely mailed letters to university officials and local newspapers complaining about subversives. His irate letters appeared in various newspapers over a number of years.

Confrontational Politics and Disruptive Tactics

While SDS was the focal point of the student movement, other organizational nodes began to emerge. On 12–14 December 1968, a conference on Legal Defense for Political Dissidents took place in Wimberley, Texas. Martin Wiginton, Greg Calvert, Jim Simons, Cam Cunningham, and others played a large role in organizing this get-together. This seemingly small event triggered a massive upsurge in building and coordinating legal defense efforts for political activists throughout the region. This conference was attended by over one hundred Texas lawyers, representatives from SNCC, SDS members, twenty to twenty-five law students, and about ten law professors.

Until its untimely demise at the June 1969 national convention in Chicago, SDS functioned as the main focal point of antiwar activities in Austin. Thursday night organizational meetings ranged in numbers from fifteen or twenty of us during lull periods to three hundred or more participants during periods of heightened, frenzied activities. We organized around what we called Armed Farces Days and disrupted ROTC events. We demonstrated against corporate recruiters for companies like Dow Chemical, against the CIA and military recruiters, and against prowar speakers. SDS spearheaded the drive to push our message out from the narrow confines of the campus, spawning MDS with connections with social workers and high school teachers and a radical law office that handled the growing number of political court cases. We mimicked each and every national trend or spectacular event. We had our own Stop the Draft Week, our own People's Park, our own anti–Selective Service demonstrations, and our own marches that coincided with mass rallies in Washington, DC.

Little protest actions not directly connected to SDS erupted here and there. In February 1969 the university administration closed down the play *Now the Revolution*, performed by the university-based Curtain Theatre, on the grounds that the performance contained an indecent display of nudity. Five UT students were charged with using abusive language directed at DPS intelligence officers during a campus meeting to organize protest against the closure of the play. They pleaded no contest in court and were fined for their "offense."[32]

Following in the footsteps of main protests at other universities, like the Third World Student strike at San Francisco State University that turned into a major confrontation, an organization in Austin called African Americans for Black Liberation (AABL) issued a list of eleven demands to the UT administration. These demands included a call for the creation of a Black Studies program, a change in admission policies in the university to allow for the enrollment of more Afro-American students, and increased financial aid for minority students. The announcement of these demands triggered a campus-wide protest movement that came out in support. SDS took the lead in initiating a campaign to support the AABL demands. Larry Jackson, spokesperson for the AABL, led a group of Afro-American students to briefly occupy the administration building in support of the AABL demands. We discussed what to do in a series of hastily called SDS meetings. Some wanted us to seize a building in solidarity. I always remember Mariann Vizard, a cogent thinker who always saw the bigger picture, arguing that to support the cause for the formation of a Black Studies Department did not mean we had to engage in the same tactics. We needed to carve out our own path for support and solidarity. While we could have easily occupied a university building, we fanned out over the campus, distributing leaflets, sponsoring discussions in dormitories, and maintaining a picket of the university administration building.

The arrest of Jackson stemming from his conviction on charges of assault on a police officer during the Don Weedon protests the previous spring only added fuel to the fire. In conjunction with four consecutive days of protests, SDS supporters of the AABL demands went to classrooms to talk with students and explain the issues. Almost without notice we had entered into a period that seemed like continuous protests and demonstrations.[33]

New Left Education Project

A number of us—me, Doyle Niemann, Ann Locklear, Alan Locklear, Barbara Wuench, Paul Turner, Steve Krinsky, and several others—decided to proactively advocate for an educational mission, rather than simply an agitational role, for SDS. While our rallies, marches, and demonstrations were always accompanied by the distribution of leaflets and flyers, we felt that we needed to provide more in-depth analysis of the issues of the day. The New Left Education Project (NLEP) came into existence; it epitomized our efforts to put our ideas into print rather than simply rely on verbal rhetoric. Like activists who set up tables on the University of California at Berkeley campus (which led to the Free Speech Movement), we decided in the early fall of 1968 to create a mobile literature table that we moved from location to location around the campus. We saw the literature table as a convenient mode for dissemination of educational materials and as a vehicle for provoking discussion and debate with people who happened by.

Two or three of us volunteered to staff the table virtually every day of the week during the midday hours around lunchtime. We reprinted short papers on the history of SDS, the war in Vietnam, racism, and other topics. We obtained printed materials from national organizations. We sold buttons and bumper stickers. We had announcements for upcoming events. We even printed a list of the items we had available and the cost of each.

We in NLEP were able to stir a great deal of interest. Curious passersby stopped at the table to talk, sometimes timidly at first, and see what we were offering. We got into some great arguments, and even shouting matches, with those who opposed our political views. We were successful in starting and engaging in critical dialogue. We developed our debating skills, memorized arguments for getting out of Vietnam, and learned how to articulate the nature of US imperialism.

We also began to write and print our own analyses of issues around the UT campus. A memo prepared by an undercover informant in January 1969 identified "Martin Murray, a graduate student, assisted by Professor Clifton Grubbs, Professor of Economics," as the persons responsible for the preparation of "a rather lengthy article on Walt Rostow which is supposed to be to be distributed on campus tomorrow."[34] Mention of Walt Rostow on the UT campus was an acutely sensitive issue. Rostow served in the LBJ administration as national security advisor until 20 January 1969, when he vacated the post after the election of Richard Nixon as president. Unwelcome at elite prestigious universities where he had worked previously, he accepted a tenured position in the Economics Department at UT Austin. Rostow achieved a great deal of notoriety for the oversized role he played in shaping US foreign policy in Southeast Asia during the 1960s. He was a fervent anti-Communist, well-known for his belief in the virtues of capitalism and free enterprise. Rostow was one of the most ardent and vociferous hawks in the Johnson administration, calling for escalation of the war, expanded bombing campaigns, and even a ground invasion of North Vietnam. For us he was a symbol of US imperialism, and we were determined to expose his presence on the UT campus. We believed that we needed to supplement our slogans, chants, and one-page leaflets with a deeper analysis. I wrote the long critique of Rostow to provide some analytic foundation for our denunciation of the war in Vietnam.

I found this pamphlet denouncing Walt W. Rostow in the Gerding Papers in a box containing assembled leaflets from the New Left that Gerding had collected in the 1966 to 1968 period. Weirdly, the fifteen disconnected pages of this document were scattered randomly, mixed in with other documents in the files. Needless to say, Rostow was a target of our ire. Whenever he spoke at a public forum, we were there in force to protest. Several SDS members (including David MacBryde) enrolled in one of his large lecture courses and did their best to disrupt whenever they could.

Looking through the Burt Gerding Papers, it is clear that the university administration at the highest levels were quite annoyed with the efforts of NLEP to proselytize, and they were merely biding their time and waiting to pounce on us for violating rather malleable university rules regarding "solicitation." If one were to believe that the matter of SDS selling literature on campus was merely an internal bureaucratic procedural issue about university governance and compliance with rules, one would be gravely mistaken. Shutting down the NLEP-SDS literature table was part of a broader repressive strategy that brought together both on-campus and off-campus security

Cover page of "Defender of the Faith" Walt Rostow pamphlet. Author's collection. Reconstructed design courtesy of Patrick Young, Michigan Imaging.

forces with the tacit approval and participation of the university administration. Even a cursory review of the Gerding Papers reveals deeper and more sinister motives for shutting down the literature table. The matter of selling literature represented a microcosm of the broader mobilization of the security apparatuses: While the university administrators and campus security officers ostensibly took the lead, they coordinated and colluded with the Criminal Intelligence Division of the APD and the FBI with the goal of disrupting and curtailing the outreach work of NLEP and SDS.

In addition, these various security agencies linked their strategy of repression to what they regarded as SDS and NLEP political endorsement of labor rights on campus. Beginning in late 1968, undercover informants focused their reports (labeled "Memorandum for Understanding") on SDS support for a boycott of food services, particularly the cafeteria known as the Chuck Wagon, in support of workers who were demanding decent wages and better working conditions. The undercover informants reported on active picketing and the placement of the NLEP literature table outside the Union Building near where the Chuck Wagon was located. Of course, the literature table and the small crowds that gathered to argue and debate attracted the attention of university officials, UT campus security, and the Austin police. An APD memo (dated 29 January 1969) identified NLEP as an SDS subcommittee responsible for selling literature. Subsequent police correspondence reveals their calculated decision to try to shut down the literature table under university regulations forbidding solicitation of funds on campus property.[35] What I did not know at the time, and did not fully comprehend until I read the Gerding police files, was that shutting down the literature table was an orchestrated effort involving the participation of the university administration, campus police, and the APD Red Squad under the direction of Lieutenant Gerding.

Unbeknownst to us at the time, I later learned that Lawrence Franks, UT dean of men, spent weeks spying on those of us who were staffing the NLEP literature table with binoculars from his third-floor window in the administration building. University administrators concluded that "if any action is contemplated, suggest at about 11:00 am is the best time."[36] Sure enough, one fine day (30 January 1969) during spring 1969 registration, Lawrence Franks and Edwin Price, assistant dean of students (flanked by several uniformed campus security officers), approached the literature table all decked out in the bravado that comes with authority. They announced to those sitting at the literature table that NLEP was in violation of university rules prohibiting "commercial solicitation" (Regents' Rule 6.11) because SDS did not have prior approval to sell our materials on campus. Besides that, the two deans declared that they considered accepting donations while passing out literature to be a violation of the "commercial solicitation" rule. According to APD police reports, the NLEP members staffing the table greeted these administrators quite rudely. I was not there when this verbal scuffle took place. I am sorry to have missed such a hilarious event.

> New Left Education Project
> [Mimeographed statement for distribution, no date]
>
> The New Left Education project grew out of a real need within the New Left to both create a systematic radical analysis of this country and the world, and to disseminate that analysis to the public at large through literature and discussion. Although greatly hampered by lack of funds and oppressive restrictions, we are pressing ahead toward our goal of creating and demonstrating a coherent radical analysis that can be understood by a troubled and confused public. Our aim is not just to develop a critique of our society and the role it plays in the world, but also to explore alternatives which could lead to a humane society built upon socialist values.
>
> Martin Murray, principal author[37]

February 1969 Disciplinary Hearing

Along with another SDS member (Alan Locklear), I was charged with violating university rules regarding commercial sales on campus property. Alan and I were each issued summons to appear before separate disciplinary hearings to determine our fate. University authorities considered nonattendance as tantamount to an admission of guilt. So in this sense, I was required to attend this disciplinary hearing. If we were found in violation of university regulations, we faced possible permanent expulsion from the university, and hence termination of our degree programs. University officials separated Alan Locklear and me, scheduling my disciplinary hearing to take place a week before his.

Faced with such a dire outcome, we immediately enlisted the pro bono services of Mark Levbarg, an attorney affiliated with the Austin chapter of the American Civil Liberties Union (ACLU), to represent us in these hearings. Collectively, we fashioned a two-pronged defense. On the broad front, we prepared arguments claiming that the university did not have the power to "enjoin sales on campus" because we were protected by the First Amendment guaranteeing freedom of speech, including the dissemination of religious and political materials. Attorney Levbarg prepared a legal brief in which he referred to two cases based on the same amendment that were already adjudicated in courts of law. One case involved Cornell University and six students who were selling poetry on campus in violation of a university rule. The court ruled that the students could sell their poetry on campus because to limit them would be in violation of their rights of freedom of the press and freedom of speech. The other case that Levbarg highlighted involved a company town that stopped Jehovah's Witnesses from selling religious materials. In the final decision, Supreme Justice Hugo Black ruled that when the town was founded it became public, and therefore it could not prevent religious literature from being sold.

In a narrower vein, we argued that we were not actually "selling" literature but passing it out free of charge to interested persons, and if they wanted to make a contribution to help defray the costs of printing the material, we would gladly accept donations. In counteracting the university administration's case, we sought to undermine the blanket condemnation of our action by pointing out the inconsistent enforcement of these antisolicitation regulations: fraternities and sororities sold tickets for raffles and events all the time.

I was, quite frankly, surprised and thankful for their sloppy detective work. Campus security could have enlisted the support of undercover agents to actually purchase literature from us, or they could have walked away with our price list, which was in plain sight on the table. In rummaging through boxes in my basement, I came across a full-page leaflet that listed materials available for sale at the NLEP literature table and their prices. If campus security and the university administration had recovered this incriminating piece of evidence, our defense might have been compromised.

Documents in the Gerding files make clear that the university administration was biding its time, preparing for a longer legal battle. An APD internal memo, prepared by an undercover informant and released on 20 February 1969, reported that "ACLU attorneys advised some SDS members that the solicitation of funds is a violation of the constitutional rights of students to collect money for friends in trouble."[38] The university administration seemed sufficiently worried that they might not win their case against Alan and me. On 28 February 1969, on the same day my disciplinary hearing was scheduled, APD memos reported that President Norman Hackerman had decided to delay action on the "solicitation of funds" rule in order to get further legal clarification. Lawyers for the university put in motion a rewriting of the rules that included the acceptance of cash donations as tantamount to solicitation. Campus police responded that they regarded this new tactic as a "beautiful technique" to stop us from carrying out our nefarious actions.[39]

In the meantime, the wheels of motion on my disciplinary hearing were already in motion. From records in the police security files, it was quite clear that Burt Gerding and the Criminal Intelligence Division were carefully monitoring from afar what was happening. In a handwritten memo labeled "SDS meeting," an undercover informant reported that university officials had summoned Martin Murray and Alan Locklear to appear before a disciplinary hearing, and that SDS "will try to get [the hearing] open, by force if necessary."[40] I remember that the hearing remained closed. But I also remember that security personnel prevented a rather unruly crowd of SDS members from entering the room; they remained outside for the duration of the proceedings.

The closed disciplinary hearing took place in the administration building on late Friday afternoon, 28 February 1969, and lasted well into the evening hours. During the marathon proceedings, it was quite clear that Dean Franks, who headed the university disciplinary team, was quite serious about making an example of me. He was all business, dressed in a suit and tie, and refused to make eye contact. Franks and his administrative assistants produced documentary evidence noting the days and times the literature table was in operation. They provided numerous photographs taken by campus security of SDS members at the table. The overconfident university administrators seemed pretty assured that they had nailed us.

On our side, Mark Levbarg was brilliant. His argument was that we were not technically selling literature but only accepting donations from a grateful public. Our main defense focused on whether university officials had proof that we were actually engaged in commercial solicitation. It may be that campus security and undercover APD informants did have information that we were indeed selling literature, but the university and APD officials were unwilling to have the undercover informants offer testimony against us because this would have exposed their identities and compromised their further usefulness to them. Dean Franks frantically pleaded that he personally observed us taking money with binoculars from the third floor of the administration building. That was not sufficient evidence. I claimed ignorance, declaring that I did not know about the rule because I was not at the literature table when Dean Frank and Dean Price had come by to warn us.

In his closing remarks, Levbarg presented a motion requesting that the five-person faculty-student disciplinary panel decide the constitutionality of the university-imposed antisolicitation rule. After both sides presented their final arguments, the joint faculty-student disciplinary committee went into closed session. In their verdict, based on a 4–1 vote, they reached the conclusion that I was not guilty because of the vague wording and definition of "commercial solicitation." In their written report, the disciplinary panel declared that I was not in violation of the rule because "the acceptance of donations of funds does not mean commercial solicitation or selling." They also sidestepped the larger legal issue, voting that they could not decide on the constitutionality of the antisolicitation rule.

I was acquitted of all charges of wrongdoing. We were, of course, elated and relieved. An ad hoc group of our supporters had gathered in the hallway outside the hearing room, anxiously awaiting the outcome. When the disciplinary board announced their verdict, cheers and yelling filled the cavernous corridors. We went to Scholz Beer Garden to celebrate our victory. Six days after the hearing, Margaret Pack, interim dean of students, wrote a letter addressed to Alan Locklear and Mark Levbarg, stating that "upon recommendation of Mr. Edwin B. Price, Assistant Dean of Students, the complaint against you [Locklear] for alleged violation of the Regents' Rule 6.11 has been dropped." University administrators did all they could to save face. "This is not to be understood as establishing a precedent for future fund solicitation on campus," the letter concluded. Deans Frank, Price, and Pack held firm that commercial solicitation was prohibited on campus unless prior approval has been obtained.[41]

Levbarg presented the case to a regular board meeting of the Austin chapter of the ACLU. The board agreed to revisit the case in the eventuality that SDS was cited in violation of the commercial solicitation rule. For NLEP the issue of selling literature never surfaced again. We in NLEP continued with the literature table for the next several weeks, until enthusiasm from among our ranks dwindled. We were always sure to announce that we were not selling literature but were only accepting donations. That ploy worked.

All in all, the university administration and the campus police miscalculated, unable to convince a disciplinary panel that we had overstepped their rules. In subsequent months the Gerding Papers contain only passing reference to the NLEP and our literature table activities. An (undated and unsigned) leaflet that I wrote appears in the police files. It was entitled "You Cannot Buy Our Literature." In this leaflet that we distributed to students on campus, I outlined our constitutional rights to free speech and exposed the university administration for trying to suppress our literature table. The leaflet focuses most attention on the decision of the Board of Regents forbidding not only the sale of literature on campus but also the collection of funds to defray the costs of producing this literature. This leaflet appears in the police files without comment and out of context. Files in the Burt Gerding Papers even contain an internal memo prepared by Alan Locklear, pleading with fellow SDS members to support the efforts of the NLEP and bemoaning the fact that besides himself, Martin Murray, and Doyle Niemann, volunteers were not stepping up in sufficient numbers to keep the project going.[42]

In late April 1969 an undercover police informant reported that the NLEP continued to hold regular meetings on Friday nights.[43] This spy wrote that the NLEP agreed to test the university sales policy and set up a table on 21 April 1969. Consensus in the meeting was that if and when a university administrator contacted whoever was at the table and announced the rules and regulations prohibiting selling literature, that whoever was staffing the stable should immediately terminate sales. In a follow-up "Memorandum for Information" (dated 5 June 1969), the undercover agent reported that NLEP decided to set up two tables: one inside University Union where literature would be sold (this selling was authorized) and one outside for advertising only. Consensus at the SDS meeting was that NLEP was not looking for a confrontation at this time.

That is the last mention of the NLEP and the literature table in the Gerding Papers. Certainly, the refusal of the university to move from its stated policy that taking donations was tantamount of commercial solicitation did not disappear. But enforcement was obviously lax and actually nonexistent. Yet the threat of further harassment targeting commercial solicitation had a chilling effect. We in NLEP did not openly and blatantly challenge university regulations but continued to surreptitiously accept donations—or whatever one would want to call taking money for literature.

I certainly did not realize at the time, but upon reading my FBI files I learned that the San Antonio FBI Field Office took an inordinate interest in the NLEP and the disciplinary hearing that dismissed the charges against me for unauthorized sales of literature on campus. I am really perplexed as to why they cared so much about what amounted to a university matter. These FBI files contain two newspaper articles on the NLEP solicitation case.[44] The interest of local FBI agents in NLEP indicates how far they were willing to go to look into what they considered subversive activities. In distributing literature we were only exercising our Constitutional rights, yet that seemed to trigger a response from the security apparatuses.

All in all, this imbroglio bears the decided imprint of the 1964 Free Speech Movement at University of California–Berkeley. But we were never able to turn the suffocation of our literature table into a free speech controversy. Too bad. We were soon overtaken by larger events involving the Chuck Wagon.

Yet NLEP and solicitation of funds has to be placed in a wider context of UT campus life in the late 1960s. Fraternities and sororities—the dominant groups on campus—maintained a high social profile. They routinely solicited funds on campus, selling tickets to such events as Round-Up (when frat "boys" chased sorority "girls" and dragged them into big cattle pens) and Old South Day (an afternoon barbeque followed by a dance, the tradition of which was for yahoo frat boys on horses to hire young African American kids from East Austin to carry written invitations to the doors of sororities to request dates for the evening festivities). Even if they had violated some obscure rule, no frat boy or sorority sister would have been dragged before a disciplinary hearing. All sorts of religious groups and social clubs routinely sold literature and tickets for events on campus. Despite its claims to neutrality and equal protection, the law operates in mysterious ways.

In the wake of the dismissal of the disciplinary charges against Alan Locklear and me, university authorities did not rescind their rules and regulations regarding solicitation of funds on campus grounds. In fact, they expanded their restrictions to incorporate "accepting donations" as a subcategory of "solicitation," thereby effectively tightening the noose around free speech. The university administration was bound and determined to prevent *The Rag* underground newspaper from being sold on campus.

On 8 July 1969, the Board of Regents went to the 167th District Court of Texas (Judge Tom Blackwell) to seek an injunction against the NLEP, which they improperly identified as the sponsor for *The Rag*, the Radical Media Project, and some eighteen individuals. In their suit filed in district court, the regents asked for a permanent injunction against the sale and distribution of newspapers such as *The Rag*, *Challenge* (the PL newspaper), and publications associated with the NLEP, except those allowed inside the Student Union Building. For years this case wound its way through the courts, pitting the Board of Regents against the ACLU. After a great deal of wrangling, the case eventually reached the Supreme Court, which returned it to a lower court. On 19 January 1973, Judge Bell of the Fifth Circuit Court upheld the earlier rulings that the restrictions on sales on literature on campuses were unconstitutional. At last, a victory for free speech.

From Political Awareness to Political Consciousness

In those early heady days in SDS, we learned from doing. SDS was less an organization with a formal membership and clear program of action and more a collection of disgruntled individuals and alienated youth who gravitated to different clusters of like-minded friends. We acted impulsively, sometimes motivated more by theater and performance than by rational calculation.

"The virtues of SDS also became its vices," Dick Reavis wrote in a 1992 essay. "Our open-ended meetings were conducted in what might be called Free Association English."[45] We employed a lot of rhetorical catchphrases that were often imprecise and emotive. We never took the time to define imperialism, capitalism, socialism, and communism. We literally jumped from one issue to another, without prioritizing the expenditure of time and energy and without carefully weighing the consequences of our actions. Acting impulsively often resulted in miscalculation, but spur-of-the-moment actions also signaled a great deal of experimentation and creativity.

The Austin SDS chapter was particularly anarchic, historically linked with a deep Texas populist tradition and thoroughly entangled with countercultural hippie currents. We had not yet mastered the conventional adage, "Political awareness is knowing which side of the barricades you are on; but political consciousness is knowing who is there with you." We attracted new adherents less by political persuasion than by the audacity of action. We measured our successes more by numbers of participants in demonstrations and rallies than by deeper understanding of political issues.

In those early days, SDS activists gravitated to inchoate political positions often associated with key individuals. Greg Calvert was one such polarizing figure. When he came to Austin, perhaps in the fall of 1967, he immediately became involved in the local SDS chapter. Greg had taught at Iowa State University in 1963, where he had formed an SDS chapter. He was elected national secretary for SDS in 1966 as part of the prairie power move away from the East Coast. Greg had an unparalleled, commanding presence unmatched by any other. In his quiet manner and careful thought, he was indeed charismatic. I first met Greg at an off-campus meeting called to plan the defense for Larry Caroline after he was fired. At first Larry was the centerpiece of the meeting. But as Larry increasingly deferred to Greg, it was clear who was the dominant figure in the group. Greg introduced a degree of theoretical clarity and sophistication into debate and discussion. In graduate school he had studied the French Revolution and its aftermath. I remember a comparison he made between Dean John Silber and Charles Maurice de Talleyrand-Périgord: "shit in a silk stocking." That image has stuck with me for fifty years.

In *A Disrupted History: The New Left and the New Capitalism*, Greg Calvert and Carol Neiman laid out a theory of the "new working class"—the new strata of teachers, social workers, health care workers, and low-level professionals (like engineers, architects, and lawyers in huge firms) that originated out the transformation of capitalism away from a total reliance upon the labor of the industrial proletariat.[46] This analysis called for organizing off campus and building what was called the Movement for a Democratic Society (MDS). Greg was some years older than most of the political activists who formed the core membership of SDS. He felt more comfortable building alliances with off-campus progressives than with sitting through long SDS meetings with endless debates that involved as much posturing as clear thinking.

Under FOIA requests I was able to obtain an estimated four hundred pages of files that the FBI had accumulated on Greg Calvert. These records were collected by the Internal Security Division of the FBI and classified as secret and confidential. FBI agents noted that in 1967 he was "constantly traveling throughout the county on behalf of SDS." Whether he spoke at large or small gatherings, FBI agents were always in attendance. Greg was arrested at the antiracist Don Weedon gas station protests in May 1968. He was involved in legal challenges to the university's decision to bar the SDS National Council meeting from the UT campus in March 1969. He was one of the organizers of the "Movement Legal Services" conference in Wimberley. He took the lead in building a legal defense team for Chuck Wagon 21 in November and December 1969. He rarely if ever attended SDS meetings. He was primarily involved in draft counseling and building the antiwar GI movement.

Calvert referred to himself as a "post-Communist revolutionary." He took the position that Black Power was "absolutely necessary" and argued that the draft was "racist and class prejudiced" and should be abolished.[47] Calvert also argued that the "anti-Draft movement must become part of the anti-imperialist movement. He stressed that the antiwar movement should "support not only drafter resisters but also deserters and to encourage desertion from the Armed Forces."[48] In reviewing the FBI files collected on Calvert, I was surprised to learn the extent to which the security agencies—the FBI through various field offices, Secret Service, Military Intelligence, and the Criminal Intelligence Division of the APD—covered Calvert in a virtual "security blanket," reporting on his attendance at meetings, recording his speaking engagements around the country, and collecting large quantities of his essays. I counted no fewer than ten FBI undercover informants who reported regularly on his goings-on. Local FBI agents regularly consulted with Burt Gerding about Calvert, opening lines of communication between local law enforcement and the national security agencies.[49]

There was a group of old-time SDS-ers from 1964–1967 who clustered around *The Rag* underground newspaper. This group was strongly influenced by the growing hippie counterculture, and their politics gravitated to performance and theater more than careful analysis. *The Rag* mixed political commentary with a strong dose of countercultural antipolitics. One key organizational expressions of this kind of loosely knit group was the formation of Mother's Grits Anarcho-Terrorist New Left Beatnik Evangelical Travelling Troupe, a band of merry pranksters who traveled around Texas and Oklahoma in the summer of 1968, stopping at small college towns to promote a unique blend of direct-action politics and antiestablishment counterculture. While they represented quite different political orientations, Jay McGee (of notorious Motherfucker fame) and Martin Wiginton were both comfortable with dissimilar political styles and were the driving forces behind Mother's Grits. This strange collection of pot-smoking and beer-drinking free spirits used a combination of guerrilla theater, rock-and-roll music, and political speeches to bring their message to places in Texas and Oklahoma off the beaten track of radical politics. Through its undercover informants dispersed around the region, the San Antonio field office took note of Mother's Grits, associating their activities with a kind of gospel of anti-Americanism.

Certainly by 1968, if not before, a small but dedicated group of activists associated with PL had built a presence in the local SDS chapter. According to PL, the only true and genuine revolutionary force was the industrial proletariat. For PL the narrowly focused strategy of building the worker-student alliance was the way forward for SDS. In this view the role of SDS was to act as a funnel to enlist students, not to fight for their own interests and causes but to become a subservient partner in the great proletarian revolution.

There were at least two leading figures in Austin SDS who were also linked to the CPUSA. Mariann Vizard and Larry Waterhouse played important and significant roles in building SDS. I never once heard them try to propagandize, and I never once saw Communist Party literature. The main Trotskyist groups—the SWP and its twin affiliates, the Young Socialist Alliance (YSA) and the Student Mobilization Committee (SMC)—had their own organizational presence separate from SDS. On many occasions we worked together, particularly on building large rallies and demonstrations. Under the tutelage of the SWP, the YSA and the SMC maintained a rigid adherence to single-issue politics and shied away from unauthorized marches and rallies. We disagreed strongly with both these positions. We found their slogan, "Bring the troops home now," too constraining if one wanted to raise issues about US imperialism. The faction of the antiwar movement to which I was attracted—the strongest current—paid considerably less attention to the niceties of legalism. Just because law enforcement officials said we could not march did not mean that we would obey.

The tiny Spartacist League (Sparts, as we called them) remained in SDS. Their membership never reached more than perhaps half a dozen at most. They held to the view that the Vietnamese revolution had gone astray due to too much Soviet influence. They always carried banners at large marches that proclaimed in bold lettering, "All Southeast Asia must go Communist." Their purity of political line meant that they were totally irrelevant. They were only an occasional annoyance. I found the Sparts to be a collection of largely lonely people, not particularly socially adept, who found comfort in abstract slogans.

For the most part local Austin SDS consisted of an evolving mélange of tendencies—anarchists, anarcho-syndicalists, socialists, unaffiliated Marxist–Leninists, countercultural hippies, second wave feminists, and more. All struggled to get their positions heard and sought through votes in SDS general meetings to get sponsorship for their proposed actions. What distinguished the local PL-affiliated activists from the rest was simple: PL was a national organization with headquarters in Boston. As a democratic-centralist organization with the requirement of following the party line, PL leadership told the local PL group what positions to adopt, and their members followed along in lock-step.

Clampdown at the SDS National Council Meeting in Austin, March 1969

As a national organization with chapters spread across the country, SDS held a national convention once a year and three National Council meetings that were convened every three months and held in various cities. In preparing for the SDS National Council meeting in Ann Arbor on 26–27 December 1968, we in the Austin chapter authorized Dick Reavis, Myron Bloom, Rene Ochoa, and Larry Waterhouse to attend and act as our representatives. One of these persons was in all likelihood an undercover informant.[50]

In late 1968 the FBI San Antonio field office was alarmed to learn that SDS planned to hold its next National Council meeting in either Austin, San Antonio, or Houston. San Antonio FBI operatives expressed grave concern that if the meeting were held in Austin, it could possibly cause embarrassment to President Lyndon Johnson, since his presidential library was planned to be located on the UT campus. "It is strongly suggested from the Bureau," the memo stated, "that this matter be brought to the attention of the White House so that the strongest possible pressure can be asserted by the White House on UT officials to prevent SDS from having any type of conference at the UT."[51] The machinery of state repression seems to have moved at a snail's pace. If the White House learned from FBI national headquarters of the proposed SDS meeting planned for March 1969, nothing seems to have materialized. The FBI San Antonio field office did not seem to have communicated and coordinated very effectively with UT campus officials.

In early 1969 FBI officials at their Washington, DC, headquarters began to scramble, looking for ways to keep the meeting off campuses in Texas and even out of the state. Once the SDS National Office decided that the Austin chapter would host the National Council meeting in Austin on 28–29 March 1969, high-ranking FBI agents put the wheels of repression in motion. In an internal memo dated 5 February 1969, the FBI headquarters issued a directive to their field offices: "Louisville, Detroit, and Denver will immediately contact logical sources at their respective universities to secure any derogatory information which could be utilized to block SDS from having their meeting at the University of Texas."[52]

The weeks leading up to the scheduled National Council meeting in Austin were indeed a busy time. I joined the organizing committee in charge of making local arrangements: securing venues for plenary sessions and meeting space for subcommittees, finding accommodation for the expected eight or nine hundred visitors from around the country, creating a central communications "hotline," and planning for meals and entertainment. In February we secured permission from the University Union Board in charge of campus facilities to make use of various lecture halls and classrooms to hold meetings. We asked for volunteers to host out-of-town visitors with sleeping space on floors, spare bedrooms, and backyards. We set up a clearing house to handle logistics and deal with last-minute snafus.

It is evident from reviewing files in the Gerding Papers that the Intelligence Division of APD acted in concert with the FBI to mount a concerted campaign to pressure UT administration to refuse to allow SDS to hold the National Council meeting on the UT campus. The security forces mobilized a letter-writing campaign from administrative officials at the University of Colorado at Boulder (where the SDS held a previous National Council meeting) to flood the UT administration with accounts of the "problems" with SDS. In concert with the FBI San Antonio field office, the APD alerted managers of all hotels, motels, and warehouses, in addition to city-owned buildings, to deny SDS the right to use the facilities.[53]

The University Union Board had originally granted permission to hold the meeting at the University Union Building on the UT campus. Yet at the eleventh hour, the Board of Regents and President Norman Hackerman stepped in to reverse this decision. The Board of Regents issued a public statement: "We are not about to let the university be used by subversives and revolutionaries." President Hackerman cited the SDS "intention of destroying the American educational system" and "the lack of educational implications of the meeting" as justification for the refusal to allow SDS to use campus facilities as was originally agreed upon. The FBI faux concerned parent Dillon J. O'Rourke again joined the fray with a letter to *The Daily Texan*, proclaiming that the UT administration should "take the next logical step to expel SDS from the campus entirely."[54]

The FBI took charge of organizing a series of high-level meetings, bringing together top university officials and local security agencies ranging from the Criminal Intelligence Division of APD to the Texas DPS and UT campus security.[55] When they decided they would not make university facilities available for the SDS National Council meeting, the UT Board of Regents and President Norman Hackerman provided the kind of salvation the FBI was seeking. Of course we in SDS believed that the university administration had engaged in a breach of contract when they pulled out of the deal. We enlisted the support of ACLU attorney Mark Levbarg to represent us and to file a suit in federal court charging the UT administration with violating our First Amendment rights to free speech. Our legal efforts were rebuffed. The local federal court denied SDS an injunction against the university. SDS then appealed to the Fifth Circuit Court of Appeals in New Orleans. We lost this legal fight to overturn the barring of the National Council meeting on the UT campus.[56]

We staged rallies condemning the university's decision, but our protests fell on deaf ears. The Faculty Council rejected a proposal put forward by progressive faculty to request that President Hackerman and the Board of Regents reconsider the decision to ban SDS from the use of campus facilities. In a vote of 23–14, the Faculty Council took an additional step to pass a resolution extending a vote of confidence in President Hackerman. It was clear that moderate and conservative faculty were against us. Our fate was sealed.[57]

The Gerding Papers contain various reports on the SDS National Council meeting.[58] Documents prepared by various security agencies exclaimed with great glee that the local FBI San Antonio office was able to convince university authorities to bar SDS from the use of campus facilities. They were indeed proud to say that this prohibition against SDS marked the first time a university administration had undertaken such effective counterintelligence measures.[59] In assessing the success of their COINTELPRO efforts, the San Antonio FBI field station proclaimed that "the bold and sophisticated operation launched under this [COINTELPRO] program" was successful in blocking SDS from the use of university facilities. They bragged that their effort "shows that this program is an effective weapon in counteracting the New Left." In defending their machinations, the FBI National Office applauded the Texas state legislature on passing a resolution in support of the university administration for standing up against SDS. Not to be ignored, the San Antonio field office took credit for bringing the UT Board of Regents together with the university administration to agree to prohibit SDS from using campus facilities.[60]

This last-minute refusal to allow us to use any campus facilities was part of an orchestrated security plan designed to throw us off balance and disrupt our meeting plans. It worked, sort of. For us this exclusion was an annoyance but not a deterrent. At the end of the day, this counterintelligence campaign amounted to not much more than a Pyrrhic victory for the repressive political forces aligned against us. The decision of the UT administration to reverse an earlier agreement simply confirmed the belief of political activists that in suppressing the right to free assembly, the security forces were deeply committed to political repression rather than respecting our rights to free assembly. Denying us the right to use university facilities strengthened the resolve of SDS participants to come to Austin from far and wide.

The security agencies were confident that they had successfully prevented the SDS National Council meeting from taking place in Austin. They were wrong. We scrambled to secure alternative venues: the local YMCA, the Catholic Student Center, the Methodist Student Center, All Saints Episcopal Church, Presbyterian Student Center, University Christian Church, and Hillel. Along with Rene Ochoa, I worked with the managing director of the Catholic Student Center to open their doors to us. We rented an auditorium at the YMCA. We firmly believed that we had outmaneuvered them. We actually did.

On the eve of the National Council meeting, we engaged in a flurry of activities. Reports submitted to the APD Criminal Intelligence Division consisted of a lot of naming of names and identifying organizations.[61] Yet, as was often the case, undercover informants inaccurately identified organizations, leaders, and activities. For example, a January 1969 FBI memo refers to an organization called the ALF and incorrectly identifies this group as the American Liberation Front. In mimicking an organization in Washington State that called itself the Seattle Liberation Front, a few of us (maybe five in all) started calling ourselves the Austin Liberation Front (ALF), and we wore buttons with the name attached. In their haste to submit reports, undercover informants often produced wildly exaggerated and inaccurate information.

On the eve of the SDS National Council meeting, we busied ourselves with other protest activities. While we remained organizationally distinct, the Austin SDS chapter always worked in concert to support the local SNCC chapter (headed by Larry Jackson) and protests around Black Liberation. At a 20 March meeting with 250 SDS supporters in attendance, we laid out plans for what we considered our spring offensive. A few days later at a 24 March meeting of SDS (chaired by me), the 150 SDS members in attendance organized a two-day strike starting 27 March in support of the Afro-Americans for Black Liberation boycott of university facilities. Along with three others, undercover police informant Barbara Roseman took charge of the strike coordinating committee. I coordinated the production and distribution of literature and leaflets. I authored a leaflet calling for the creation of a "Critical University." I found this leaflet tucked away in one of the files in the Gerding Papers.[62]

National Council Meeting

The SDS Nation Council opened on 28 March with large meeting at Catholic Student Center starting at 11:30 a.m.[63] As the proceedings got underway, it was immediately obvious from the nature of the debate that the seeds of organizational self-destruction had already been sown. In retrospect, it is not difficult to see how the posturing and the backdoor maneuvering were a dress rehearsal for the sectarian infighting that marked the demise of SDS three months later. The public discussions were quite rowdy and rancorous. The National Office collective (grouped around Bernadine Dohrn, John Jacobs, Bill Ayers, Mark Rudd, and Mike Klonsky) orchestrated the gathering but were clearly not in firm control. The election of Tim McCarthy (a National Office loyalist) as chair seemed to indicate that PL remained in the minority of participants. Yet what was clear is that no consensus on any political issue was even vaguely possible.

The PL faction was organized and quite vociferous in their demands to turn SDS into a platform for the so-called worker-student alliance. National Office speakers made fun of this slogan by reversing the order to a student-worker alliance. Reports submitted by undercover informants characterized the outcome as a kind of (in their words) "Mexican stand-off" where nothing was gained by either of the rival factions. What the Austin National Council accomplished was to greatly solidify positions, setting in motion an inevitable confrontation in June.[64]

In a summary assessment of the National Council meeting presented to his boss, Chief Miles (head of APD), Burt Gerding issued a woolly-headed statement: "It is too early to completely evaluate what the effect of the National Council meeting in Austin will have on the local SDS chapter. The meeting did not unify the existing factions (Friends of Progressive Labor, Marxists, and anarchists) and may have widened the split." For good measure Gerding added a false accusation: "The National Officers of SDS are reported to be under the Southern California wing of the Communist Party, USA [CPUSA] and when the local SDS group learned of this, it was a surprise to them."[65] He was exactly right to say that those of us in the local SDS chapter would have been surprised to learn that the CPUSA managed to control the SDS National Office. This claim was simply not true.

At the Austin National Council meeting, the National Office faction and the PL cadre scrambled to line up votes for their side. Discussion and debate focused not on what SDS could do to expand its presence on college and high school campuses and to build an off-campus base in local alternative lifestyle communities as a way of spreading the antiwar and anti-imperialist message. Instead, proceedings boiled down to efforts by each of the major factions to gain control of the organization and to force compliance with a political line. Most political activists who participated in the Austin meeting did not identify with either faction.

Some of us—undercover police informants identified Paul Turner, Nancy Sweeney, and me as the Austin leaders—sponsored a Workshop on Decentralization. We endorsed a much looser SDS structure in which chapters would remain affiliated with the national organization but were not subject to ideological dictates from above. We attracted close to two hundred participants, but we failed to gain any traction in the plenary debates. In SDS the winds had already shifted in the direction of top-down leadership. As the meetings wore on, debate focused on the nature of Marxist–Leninist organizational structures, the identification of which oppressed agency would lead the coming revolution, and how to recruit a loyal cadre. In a display of a quasi-religious fervor and hysteria, each successive speaker ritualistically denounced the internal enemy (either PL or the National Office) before turning to the anointing of the industrial proletariat, the oppressed African American masses, or antiestablishment alienated youth as the vanguard of the coming revolution. I can only wonder to what extent the FBI and other law enforcement agencies successfully infiltrated leadership positions in SDS and fomented internal dissension.

The National Office functionaries and PL sympathizers were a bit of a sorry lot. The one image that has remained indelibly fixed in my mind is the sight of Bernadine Dohrn sauntering into the foyer of the Catholic Student Union the day before the National Council meetings were to start. Followed by an entourage of hangers-on, she was decked out in an expensive blouse, long earrings, a miniskirt, and high black leather boots. I was surprised: This brash, cocky woman dressed like she was going to an upper-class party at a yacht club was blathering on about being a Communist revolutionary. I thought to myself, "Is this the designer revolution?" I was dressed in my usual Austin uniform: light-blue work shirt, faded denim jeans, and dirty old work boots.[66] If she would have asked, I would not have followed her out the door to get coffee or, for that matter, joined the Weather Underground. Less than six months later, Bernadine Dohrn emerged as the self-proclaimed leader of the adventurist Weather Underground, promising to "smash the state by any means necessary." Posturing and posing—the stylized attributes of inexperienced youth. Revolutions should not be left to youngsters. In retrospect, what was a tragedy is that she actually seemed to believe what she said.

The SDS-ers who came from the Bay Area, Chicago, Boston, and New York acted as if they had landed in the backwoods prairie at the frontier edge of the real revolutionary politics that only they understood. What happened at the Austin National Council meeting was a great example of what NOT to do to build a broad-based movement in opposition to the war in Vietnam and in favor of social justice. The ones that talked the most acted as if Marx, Lenin, Mao, and Stalin knew all the answers to what was to be done. Worse still, they believed that they could translate the words of the masters to the untutored SDS participants from everywhere but the two coasts (and, of course, the Chicago National Office). These "outsiders"—my Texas friends called them Yankees—imported a fervent righteousness unwarranted under the circumstances. Shouts of "Right on!," "Smash the state," and "Up the revolution," and waving Mao's *Little Red Book*, were out of touch with the millions of alienated youth (white and African American alike), angry workers, and women tired of second-class citizenship.

In retrospect, SDS was imploding before our very eyes. The starry-eyed talk of revolution and calls for confrontational tactics were harbingers of the turn to cultlike organizational forms. Marxist–Leninist parties and preparty formations sprung up like dandelions on a wet spring day. This turn toward Marxist–Leninist vanguardism was tantamount to jumping off a cliff, hoping others would follow. What we called "vanguard-itis" was a serious mental disease, in which those caught in its grip suffered from delusional fantasies of the coming revolution.

Ironically, what kept us going was the constant appearance of pressing issues like the endless war in Vietnam, racial injustice, and the bungling of the university administration—which always seemed to us hand us an issue. Ironically, the incipient anti-intellectualism of the Austin antiwar movement paid off. Most political activists in Austin were not interested in hewing to the correct Line of March preached to us from the self-proclaimed leaders of SDS.

Draconian Surveillance: The Embryonic Security State

The severe police clampdown that targeted the Austin National Council meeting illustrates the extent to which law enforcement agencies, and the security machinery more broadly, were willing to go to disrupt political dissent. In my view, what might appear at first glance as routine information gathering is the first step in the direction of a declaration of a state of emergency. The Austin National Council meeting was, in many ways, a dress rehearsal for the accelerated surveillance and repression to come. From the national to the local level, the security apparatus mobilized its formidable resources to harass and intimidate us. In retrospect, I now realize that we did not fully comprehend how far the security agencies were willing to go.

Sometimes just a handful of police security documents can reveal in microcosm a general pattern of repression not at all obvious or visible to those who were the actual targets of monitoring and surveillance. In my view, the strategy that the assembled security agencies adopted around the Austin National Council meeting was not the exception but the rule. Even before the National Council convened, FBI agents managed to obtain a list of delegates (hundreds of names in all) from all over the country who were planning to attend the National Council in Austin.[67] The FBI San Antonio field office distributed all the information they collected about the National Council meeting to the Secret Service (Austin and San Antonio), Office of Special Investigations (OSI), 112th Military Intelligence Group, and the National Intelligence Security Organization (NISO).[68]

Once the meeting was underway, the security apparatuses stepped up their efforts to coordinate the monitoring of the discussions that occurred at the Austin gathering and the surveillance of participants. Security agencies created a special task team with a centralized command post. Along with the FBI, the APD Criminal Intelligence Division spearheaded the planning to blanket bus stations, meeting places, and housing venues with security agents. The Gerding files refer to military intelligence agencies, along with Criminal Intelligence Divisions from the Dallas–Fort Worth, Houston, and San Antonio police departments. The FBI and APD Criminal Intelligence infiltrated our meetings with undercover agents.

Law enforcement agencies established a security grid that extended both horizontally and laterally across space. The Gerding Papers contain one document that chronicles at least sixty separate telephonic reports to the central command headquarters on a single day. This central command station was in contact with police departments and security agents spread across all the major transportation routes into Austin. On the day before the start of the National Council meeting, the security forces covered Austin with surveillance teams, spotters, and undercover informants who tracked virtually every move of the more than one thousand persons who attended the National Council meeting. The security agencies enlisted the support of employees at the Greyhound bus depot, university maintenance crews, and hotel/motel managers to report on the comings and going of SDS members.[69]

As the meetings got underway, the security police spread false rumors that the Texas DPS (the feared Highway Patrol) and elite units of the National Guard were standing by in Austin and San Antonio, waiting for orders to bust up the gathering. In seeking to encourage participants to leave Austin early before the end of the meetings, security agents spread rumors that a DPS helicopter had set up a roadblock near Waco, and police were detaining suspected SDS members who inadvertently drove into this trap, holding them without charge for several hours. Security agents bragged about their success in planting rumors, since this disinformation was able to keep "some of the more militant people off balance." They expressed considerable delight that these false rumors generated a great deal of unease and paranoia.[70]

Specialized security teams conducted visual surveillance on perhaps as many as a dozen houses in which out-of-town SDS visitors, but particularly well-known national officers, were staying. They used undercover operatives who infiltrated meetings and informal gatherings to collect mountains of largely useless information.[71] Like bird watchers looking for some elusive species, agents took great pride in identifying key figures at specific locations and precise times: "Larry Caroline was observed standing on the front steps of the 'Y' with about 20–30 hippies gathered around him"; "Bernadine Dohrn [was] spotted going into the Catholic Student Center"; and Mark Rudd was observed walking nonchalantly on Guadalupe Street. Security agents offered such explicit reports like "the big people [i.e., National Office leadership] are staying at 503 West 14th Street," "anarchists from New York are sleeping in Lamar Park," and Jay McGee ("wearing a sarape and Indian headband") "is writing ZAPATA on the walls of the Y."[72]

Agent Nelson observed that "about twenty hippies are taking a bath in the Littlefield fountain and several are exposing themselves." Military intelligence agents reported that at least twenty GIs from Fort Hood had registered using aliases for the National Council meeting. Houston Police Department Intelligence Division alerted central command about persons (listing them by name) from Houston coming to the Austin meeting. Surveillance teams watched apartment complexes and motels and kept a lookout for chartered buses. Security agents reported the license plate numbers and car descriptions of over about two dozen automobiles. Texas DPS arrested and detained five persons on their way to the National Council meeting at Junction, in the Hill Country.

Security agents paid particular attention to persons loading packages into cars. Agent Hacker and Agent Smith alleged that Steve Fox got into a car (identified by make and license plate number) with a container filled with gasoline. They conducted surveillance but lost track of the vehicle. Agent Peterson identified four people from Colorado who had outstanding warrants for their arrest. Trivial as these reports may sound, they indicated an attention to detail unprecedented in the sinister world of Austin surveillance.

In the Gerding Papers, there is a copy of the full registration list—ironically headed with the caption "Never, ever leave this Log Unguarded"—of all those who signed in to participate in the National Council meeting. In his interview stored in the Gerding Papers, Gerding claimed that "I [in all likelihood, an undercover operative] got the registration book, where everybody signed in and—swiped it for long enough for D.P.S. to make a copy of it."[73] The theft of this list suggests either that SDS internal security was terribly lax or that police undercover agents were able to effectively penetrate and infiltrate what SDS security measures were in place. From this list of names, security police concluded that 1,019 persons (another report estimated 1,050 delegates) attended the meetings, with 226 participants from Austin. Since we know that some participants (especially active-duty GIs) who wished to keep their identities a secret did not sign the registration book, the number of those in attendance was even higher.[74] Eventually this list of delegates reached the San Antonio FBI field office.

Was this extensive "security blanket" an example of overreaction—a security operation that was conducted by overzealous law enforcement agencies competing with one another to gather the most information? Or was it something else? I believe that the extent and depth of this security fixation exemplified the turn to political repression through the suppression of civil liberties like the right to assemble, the right to free speech, and the right to expression. What happened at the Austin SDS National Council meeting was integrally connected with the disruptive strategy that COINTELPRO orchestrated from the headquarters of the FBI in Washington, DC.

Over time investigative journalists exposed the COINTELPRO policies, chronicling the choreographed efforts of the FBI to undertake a series of covert and illegal projects aimed at surveilling, infiltrating, discrediting, and disrupting political organizations.[75] I believe that these unlawful methods of gathering information, actively sowing discord, and using undercover agents to entice unsuspecting activists into illegal actions were not an aberration of overzealous security operatives but a hidden, deliberate, and authorized method of political repression. While constitutional rights have always formed the legitimate bedrock for political dissent, security agencies did everything they could to undermine what civil libertarians have always held dear. In his essay "Repressive Tolerance," Herbert Marcuse laid bare the hypocrisy of a capitalist democracy where alleged "threats to national security" justified a virtual state of emergency, despite the façade of constitutional rights.[76]

A passage from an undated confidential memo in the Gerding Papers is worth quoting in full: "We officers had spread a few rumors that [the] National Guard was standing by and a company of Texas Rangers was in Austin. The delegates were so paranoid they would not walk alone. I believe the action on the part of the UT administration [to bar SDS from the use of campus facilities] had a great deal to do with splitting the SDS organization that fall."[77] In reading these FBI files, I was surprised by how often agents affiliated with one field office or another bragged about all the good work they were doing. The bravado expressed in this undated confidential memo is like the FBI taking credit for the sun coming up every morning.

PART 2

Finding Our Place in the Post-SDS World

Chapter 3

Cut Loose from Our Original Birthplace

The coup de grâce that ended the short reign of SDS as a vibrant student-and-youth movement took place at the SDS National Convention in June 1969 in Chicago. My twin brother and I, along with several other Austin SDS members (Connie Lanham, Doyle Niemann, and Gavin Duffy) drove together to Chicago to participate in the gathering. We witnessed a debacle. Probably eight to ten Austin SDS members in all (Jeff Jones and Rene Ochoa for sure) attended the meeting, including a number of whom were representing PL. I cannot recall the names of the official delegates from the Austin SDS chapter. Two separate reports ("Memorandums for Information") in the Gerding Papers give two different accounts and contradictory lists of elected delegate names. The situation was indeed fluid. In the end it did not matter. Official delegates and nondelegates all voted on formal motions. It was indeed chaos.

The June 1969 SDS National Convention turned out to be a showdown between two irrepressible forces. On the one side, the National Office collective clustered around newly minted revolutionaries who looked to the Black Liberation Movement at home (particularly the Black Panthers) and third world liberation struggles abroad as their sources of inspiration. On the other side, PL, which had painstakingly established new local SDS chapters with the aim of increasing the numbers of their loyal delegates coming to Chicago, came as an organized force. In retrospect, the fiasco was virtually unavoidable. The fool's errand was underway.

SDS National Convention, Chicago, June 1969

The atmosphere around the Chicago Coliseum was tense. Members of the Black Panther Party acted as door monitors, frisking all those lined up to enter. SDS National Office leadership barred cameras and recording devices. They also made a point of excluding the bourgeois press, but that was sort of bravado and posturing rather than anything else. Practically anyone who wanted to get inside was able to do so.

Todd Gitlin provides a brief summary of the Chicago fiasco.[1] Curiously, he provides no explanation of why the National Office collective, which for all intents and purposes represented a temporary (and ill-fitting) alliance between the Revolutionary Youth Movement I (RYM I) and Revolutionary Youth Movement II (RYM II), worked together to carry out the eventual decision to expel PL. My personal recollection of the sequence of events differs from all the accounts that I have read. As the proceedings got underway in a cavernous auditorium, the litmus test for which faction was the most powerful was the first vote to select the official chair overseeing the proceedings. The National Office leaders supported one of their own—Tim McCarthy, the perennial chair of national SDS gatherings. When he lost in a close vote to Jeff Gordon, the PL choice, the final outcome at the National Conference was a foregone conclusion. This decision on selecting a chair indicated that PL forces would be able to muster sufficient votes on all key issues, or at least block resolutions that were not favorable to the worker-student alliance position. PL had clearly stacked the meeting with their supporters. In retrospect, this mobilization of support should not be surprising. The selection of delegates from local chapters was haphazard at best. It was relatively easy for PL to form local chapters, pay membership dues, and send elected delegates to Chicago. PL was playing by the rules, but not in the way that they were intended.

As discussion and debate got underway, rhetoric reached a fever pitch. Realizing that PL had outflanked them, the National Office collective stole the march on their PL opponents by orchestrating a staged walkout of the proceedings. After moving to an adjoining hall to deliberate their next move, the self-appointed leadership of the anti-PL faction returned to the main convention center, seized the microphone, and denounced PL, announcing their expulsion for a variety of original sins. With the exception of the PL representatives, the rest of us from Austin remained more or less neutral during the coup and ensuing bloodletting.

On the third day of the meeting, most of us from Austin gathered in an adjoining hall to listen to Murray Bookchin elaborate on an anarchist alternative to the rampant Marxist–Leninist ideology that seemed to mesmerize the majority of those in attendance. For us the anarchist message was overladen with too much theory and romantic history and consisted of few concrete remedies about how to move forward. We went to Chicago under the umbrella of SDS. The organization had provided an organized focal point for building a broad-based movement for channeling the multiple dissatisfactions of alienated youth. We left without an organizational anchor point.

The SDS National Convention was a total disaster. The non-PL people from Austin were shocked by the high-intensity rhetoric that bore little connection with our own experience. Talk of vanguard parties, Marxist–Leninism, and who would lead the revolution was so out of touch from the overwhelming majority of SDS chapters that were just struggling to maintain a presence and get out their antiwar, antiracist message in their small, out-of-the-way college towns and countercultural enclaves.

When we left the final general meeting on the last day, we went to the supposedly secure parking lot to discover that perhaps as many as two hundred cars had their tires slashed. Symbolically, at least, the forces of repression had seized the day. The message was clear: "We are watching you, and you better be careful." Looking back I think it would be impossible to guess how many undercover police agents participated in the SDS collapse. I am sure that the top leadership of the FBI and other security agencies were overjoyed and simply beside themselves with self-congratulation.

I departed from the SDS National Convention somewhat despondent. Those of us who were aligned with neither faction were left to ponder, What do we do now? What was clear was that SDS had collapsed amid rancorous faction fighting, and there was no way to put it back together again. With the centrifugal forces in command, SDS splintered into countless kaleidoscopic pieces that eventually crystalized into rival organizational fronts going their own way to forge the revolution. The PL group was elated with their hollow electoral accomplishment in Chicago: Claiming to be the "real SDS," they moved the National Office from Chicago to Boston and declared triumphantly that they would carry on as usual. Armed with the slogan "Worker-student alliance," PL groups around the country set out to reconstitute SDS under their control. Feigning openness and tolerance for dissenting views, these reconstituted SDS chapters kept their PL leadership in the shadows and called meeting after meeting to lure in the unsuspecting. It was not long before this false edifice of SDS collapsed under the sheer weight of irrelevance. Young antiwar radicals wanted to put a halt to the war in Vietnam, and they did not believe they had to join a rigid Marxist–Leninist party to do so. At the end of the day, it was just a tale told by an idiot, full of sound and fury and signifying nothing.

The National Office faction took on the mantle of forging what the leadership called a revolutionary youth movement. Over the next several months, the collapse of SDS produced two strategic choices for the non-PL factions: On the one hand, RYM I eventually became the Weather Underground. Its hopelessly adventurist bombing campaign was completely removed from the experience of the broad antiwar movement. On the other hand, RYM II, with its base on the West Coast, eventually split into the October League (and later the Communist Party, Marxist–Leninist) and the Revolutionary Communist Party. SDS as a national organization and a centralizing force for the movement was dead. Linking up with various Marxist–Leninist party formations, each identifying some oppressed group that constituted the "vanguard of the revolution," stifled debate, leaving political direction in the hands of various self-styled leadership elites.

In Austin both these options were off the table. The anarchist and countercultural currents were just too strong to be moved by abstract, arcane rhetoric.

There was a lot of thunder and heavy wind, but the storm quickly passed. Nothing from these two alternative options ever really materialized.

The downward spiral of increasingly sectarian sloganeering and debilitating factionalism largely bypassed the Austin movement. Flush with their victory in Chicago, returning PL members reconstituted the local Austin SDS chapter in late June 1969. The hardcore PL cadre called meetings under the banner of SDS. Some of my friends attended these meetings en masse. They were ever hopeful that an entrance strategy of packing the meetings would be able to oust PL from leadership and reclaim SDS. They were mistaken. Sensing that the tide had turned, we gradually abandoned the idea of keeping the name *SDS* alive.

Perhaps ironically, within several months the PL faction—with its strident rhetoric and narrow focus on building a worker-student alliance—simply dwindled and died. Frankly, who would want to work with a Marxist–Leninist cultlike group that paid more attention to Maoist China than to the war in Vietnam, let alone racism and sexism at home? For some the purity of a political line—even though it could change at a moment's notice—provided a sense of belonging.

As usual, I went to Berkeley for the summer, living in a big house with friends. I participated in rallies and demonstrations in the Bay Area. In one memorable event, I participated in a nighttime "riot" on Telegraph Avenue close to the University of California–Berkeley campus. At one point I scurried past a team of three people—one lookout and two guys kneeling down over a pipe bomb ready to light the fuse—in front of a Bank of America branch. I do not know if the bomb went off or not. Running down the street to avoid tear gas, I was confronted by a line of police about thirty yards in front of me. As a stopped to figure out how to get out of this situation, someone not ten feet behind me pulled out a pistol and shot one of the cops in the leg. Time to run.

Post-SDS: The Kaleidoscopic Movement

Ironically, the collapse of SDS recharged an increasingly hydra-headed political movement that was simply too large and too diverse to be confined within a single organizational format. Crippled by factionalism and beset by political sectarianism, SDS around the country had in the months leading to the 1969 National Convention increasingly lost touch with its mass base of alienated and countercultural youth, and thereby relinquished its leading role as the main coordinating body for national mass protests. SDS had certainly outlived its usefulness as a reliable political-cum-countercultural focal point for a groundswell of pressure from below to bring about change. The antiwar (and antiracist) movement was growing by leaps and bounds. In time the accumulated pressure occasioned by the SDS fiasco gave popular protest a much-needed facelift. Contrary to the mainstream view popularized by the liberal media, the implosion of SDS did not mark the end of the student movement. In actuality college students were increasingly becoming a minority in the antiwar movement. Freed from the strident rhetoric that characterized SDS in its last year of existence, we were able to explore and experiment with all sorts of political strategies and tactics that far exceeded the issues that had defined the student movement.

Certainly by late 1969, there was no longer a single movement but many branches and self-directed iterations of alternative lifestyles and protest politics. These movements grew rhizomatically, no longer tethered to a single organizing core. These currents were overlapping, intersecting, and sometimes conflicting. In Austin the separation between the political Movement and the hippie counterculture was never straightforward. Events like Gentle Thursday, skinny-dipping at Hippie Hollow on Lake Travis, smoking pot, listening to country music at the Lake Austin Inn and the Split Rail epitomized the mixing and matching of political protest and hippie lifestyles. Unlike many other wellsprings of social unrest, the so-called hippie counterculture in Austin blended fairly easily with the political movement.[2]

In trying to publicize our antiwar message and expand our base into the growing youth culture, we made deliberate efforts to connect with the largely nonpolitical countercultural currents that flourished in Austin. I remember how we organized a block party sometime in 1969 on the west side of campus in the student/youth housing area. Some crazy idiot drove his car about forty miles an hour through the crowd, scattering people left and right. I saw one guy who was tossed at least ten feet into the air, only to break his leg.

We suspected that the driver had driven through purposefully to attack the youth culture, but I am not certain anyone ever found out.

I remember how Martin Wiginton organized the 60th birthday party for Kenneth Threadgill, a local legend in the down-home country music scene, at a place called the Party Barn outside of town. Martin's gift from all of us to Kenneth was a gold-plated stirring straw to mix drinks. Needless to say, the huge crowds broke down the fences and turned the event into a free concert. Thousands showed up to hear Janis Joplin sing "Me and Bobby McGee"—the first time she performed the song in public. I was appointed Janis's handler, and remember sharing swigs from a bottle of Southern Comfort with her. When she first came to Austin from Port Arthur, Janis played regularly at Threadgills, the music venue on North Lamar. Janis died several weeks later on 4 October 1969 after the Threadgill birthday party. She was only 27 years old. This event, and other similar signature events, contributed to cementing an alliance in Austin between political militants, alienated youth, and the counterculture. We were swimming in the same sea—all outlaws in Amerika.

Curiously, something else was happening other than sectarian factionalism. Gradually at first but soon with greater ferocity, all sorts of smaller groups aimed at specific goals came into existence. By this time the center of gravity of the Austin movement had slipped away from its original moorings as a narrowly based student organization. New organizational forms, both on and off the UT campus, were popping up everywhere like so many champagne corks. The Women's Liberation Movement was born in this turmoil of movement ferment and recognized male chauvinism as a major impediment that stood in the way of even talking about revolutionary change. The Women's Liberation Movement argued correctly that fast-talking, angry men tended to dominate movements oriented toward demonstrations and public events. Who could speak the loudest and the most forcefully were often rewarded with leadership positions. Women's caucuses began to form in virtually every mass organization. The emergence of the Gay Liberation Movement also became a visible presence in political protests.

Beginning around 1970 New Left organizations and the counterculture movement pivoted away from focusing almost exclusively on antiwar activities and toward institutions that would create a local support network and community alternatives to conventional business practices. All sorts of enterprising small groups started co-ops related to food, housing, gasoline, auto repair, daycare, buying-in-bulk groups, free universities, free newspapers, and free music venues. The Armadillo Press, and later the Red River Women's Press, offered inexpensive printing services. Countercultural communities—organized around shared living arrangements, music, food, and the arts—became too numerous to count. The People's Community Clinic started as the Free Clinic, which opened in 1970 in the basement of a downtown church. The Free Clinic started out offering free consultations once a week at the Congregational Church on Guadalupe Street just across from the University of Texas campus. Volunteers—including doctors, interns, and nurses—staffed the clinic, and the line of patients wrapped around the building. There was definitely a need for medical services in the local community, and the Free Clinic expanded its services to cover more days. The clinic was always short of money. Staff members staged various fundraising events, including music concerts, and applied for grant monies. The People's Free Clinic (now called the People's Community Clinic) somehow kept afloat, and it has continued offering services to this day. In whatever form, these alternative institutions swamped whatever hopes the PL-SDS faction had of dominating and directing all of us to march in lockstep to their rhythmic drumbeat.

Some political activists worked with the Economy Furniture strikers (largely Mexican American workers). Campus organizers turned their attention to creating a teaching assistants union, raising issues regarding pay, working conditions, and availability of childcare facilities. The APD Criminal Intelligence Division reported with alarm that Black militants spoke of "organizing black people into military type units for the defense of the black community."[3]

For the next several years, numerous organizations emerged, grew, reached a high point (usually around a major demonstration or protest march in the fall or spring), withered after the planned event or series of events, and eventually disappeared. These ad hoc and impromptu efforts carried us along like a wave in the ocean. While those of us who generally shared similar political perspectives thought differently at the time, it was clear than no single organization could have been capable of leading, or even channeling, the

Community United Front storefront offices, East Austin.
Courtesy of Alan Pogue, photographer.

huge outpouring of hostility directed against the vast machinery of war, institutionalized racism, and entrenched authoritarianism in the schools, workplaces, and elsewhere. What was also beginning to take place was a concerted critique of our own internal flaws dealing with sexism and homophobia in our own ranks. Certainly by late 1969, if not before, we were engaged in a great deal of coalition building, reaching out to CUF, which was centered around the African American community in East Austin, and working with the a fledging Chicano organization through support for the Economy Furniture workers strike.

Over time we built a fairly strong relationship with the CUF under the leadership of Larry Jackson. In fall 1969 the CUF sought to expand its breakfast for children program—modeled on the Black Panthers—at the old University Y. The CUF received permission to move their breakfast program (involving 250 children at the start) to the Chuck Wagon in October 1970.[4] Besides their free breakfast program for underprivileged children, the CUF also provided draft counseling services, daycare, sewing classes, and a liberation school out of their offices in East Austin.[5]

Those of us who worked closely together politically did our best to exploit available cracks in the system that opposed us. At the university we formed campus-approved student groups that allowed us to schedule the use of campus facilities. We accumulated huge bills for posters, paper, mimeographing, and other services, and then we abandoned the organization without paying. On the legal front, we aggressively countered the increasingly sophisticated efforts of the police and security forces to use the courts to keep us off balance. We filed class-action suits, we organized group-defense strategies for common offenses like disturbing the peace or marching without a permit, and we used nonviolent resistance tactics to fill the jails on several occasions.

While they could never keep pace with our changing tactics, local law enforcement agencies and the security apparatuses were busy as well. We knew that policing agencies watched, followed, wiretapped, and photographed us. We suspected that undercover informants from the Criminal Intelligence Division of the APD and the FBI had infiltrated our movement, but we did not know for certain who they were. In this murky world of espionage, there was only a thin line separating those undercover informants who attended meetings and gatherings with the aim of reporting their findings to their superiors, and those surreptitious police agents who actively engaged in trying the steer the antiwar movement in particular directions. We also knew that agents provocateurs sought out the vulnerable, the careless, and the unsuspecting, trying to entice them into illegal acts, often involving guns and explosives, that could be prosecuted via conspiracy trials. Across the United States, the Chicago Eight conspiracy trial was perhaps the most recognized in the 1970s. But others, like the Seattle Seven conspiracy trial, were also noteworthy.[6]

Picking up the Shattered Pieces: Building Alternative Institutions

A radical student activist in Germany, Rudi Dutschke, coined the slogan "The long march through the institutions" to describe a strategy for bringing about fundamental transformation within the established order. The "long march" entailed working against the established institutions while working within them—not simply "boring from within" but rather replacing them and building a better a more humane alternative. The concerted effort to build counterinstitutions offered an embryonic vision of the new, more equitable social order that we hoped to create. For me this strategic focus offered a much greater potential for change than the Marxist–Leninist sectarian parties. The emergence of a wide range of alternative institutions and countercultural initiatives grew in tandem with the antiwar movement, contributing to the success of both. The proliferation of food co-ops, the CUF breakfast program, alternative schools and alternative university classes at the YMCA, tutorial services for the poor, a Free Clinic offering health services for those who could not afford to pay, expanded legal services, a Gay Liberation group, support services for women, and involvement in organizations to assist striking workers symbolized the growing awareness that building alternative institutions offered a playbook for undermining the system. *The Rag*, our underground newspaper, the Radical Education Project, Latin American Policy Alternative Group (LAPAG), and more functioned as alternative sources of political information not available in the mainstream press. Alex Calvert, David MacBryde, and others worked tirelessly to build the Armadillo Press, printing leaflets by the thousands and countless numbers of political pamphlets. Along with Vietnam veteran Terry Dubose, Greg Calvert and others devoted their energies to draft counseling. The law office of Simons, Cunningham, Coleman, Nelson, and Howard handled politically oriented legal matters. I know that this list is much longer. Although tentative and fledgling, these steps offered a glimpse of an alternative to the world of exchange grounded solely in the competitive capitalist marketplace.

A number of dedicated political activists turned their attention to local labor struggles. The strike at the Economy Furniture assembly facility provided a focal point that blended struggles for workers' rights with Mexican American politics. The work stoppage began in November 1968 after company officials refused to recognize the vote of workers to form a local branch of the Upholsterers International Union. Mexican Americans comprised 90 percent of the four hundred workers, almost a quarter of whom were women, employed at the facility. At the time Economy Furniture was the largest company in the furniture-making business in the tristate area of Texas, Arizona, and New Mexico. UT students and political activists joined with local Catholic churches to support the strike. The movement came to be known as the Austin Chicano Huelga. City officials denied protesters the right to march. They called in the Texas Rangers, who loaded picketers onto buses and drove them ten miles outside of Austin and left them to walk home. The strikers organized boycotts of Economy Furniture products, pickets of stores selling Economy Furniture, and leafleting all around Austin.

In October 1969 the Students for Strikers demonstrated in solidarity with the Economy Furniture strikers after an unprovoked incident in which the police used chemical mace to assault the picketing workers. Supporters of the striking workers went to the protest "armed with equipment resembling Mace preparations: hair-drier hoses, scuba masks, handkerchiefs over the face and signs saying, 'All power to the workers, No more Mace in the face.'"[7]

In January 1971 the federal court of appeals upheld the decision of the National Labor Relations Board to recognize Local 456 as the legitimate representative of the workers and ordering Economy Furniture to enter into collective bargaining. In the ensuing agreement, Local 456 won major concessions from the company, including back pay of up to $13,500 per worker. Support for the union organizing effort came from outside. On 7 February 1971, United Farm Workers' Cesar Chavez led a march and rally of more than five thousand people at the Texas State Capitol. The strike last three years before it ended in a negotiated settlement.[8]

The Fall 1969 Marching Season

The year 1969 was a turning point for escalating antiwar protests that spilled beyond University campuses and into the mainstream. By the fall of 1969, a pattern for organized rallies and marches had emerged; Austin antiwar activists synchronized our own fall and spring marching season to coincide with national mobilizations. In the fall of that year, organizers in the DC-based National Vietnam Moratorium Committee sponsored propeace and antiwar rallies and marches that spread around the world. The date of the first moratorium was 15 October 1969 in Washington, DC. In its coverage of the first marches, an article in *Time* remarked that the moratorium had brought "new respectability and popularity" to the antiwar movement.[9] In various locations all over the United States, over 15 million people took part in marches against the war on 15 October.[10] In response to the great success of the 15 October moratorium, Richard Nixon appeared on national television on 3 November asking for the political support of the "great silent majority" of Americans for his Vietnam War policy.[11]

In solidarity with the national moratorium in Washington, DC, we in Austin organized a day of protest activities, including a march from campus to a rally at the State Capitol. On the morning of the march, we began with picketing and leafleting of all the main entrances to the campus announcing the event, followed by teach-in discussion groups on the Main Mall. By noon a large crowd had assembled in front of the Tower. A *Daily Texan* reporter remarked that "many classrooms were emptied while students attended moratorium-sponsored activities." We attracted more than twelve thousand people to take part in the procession down Congress Avenue and to the rally at the State Capitol. At the time this event marked the largest march in Austin history. The march attracted sorority and fraternity members as well as student-athletes, professors, young mothers with children, working people, "members of various clubs, and people of all races." "Greeks and SDS members sat side by side and neither seemed to find it uncomfortable," the same *Daily Texan* reporter observed. This kind of "Give Peace a Chance" rally was designed to attract a large crowd around the single issue of withdrawal from Vietnam.[12]

The SMC (affiliated with the YSA and the SWP) played a large role in organizing the event but did not control its political message. It was a partnership effort. The broad-based stance adopted by the march-and-rally organizers gave a tameness to opposing the war. It attracted liberals and those who were curious and just wanted to learn more. At the end of the day, this nonconfrontational approach complemented the core militant factions who were always spoiling for a fight.

During this Moratorium Day protest, students boycotted classes and guerilla theater skits entertained participants and curious bystanders alike. Speakers at the State Capitol included a mix of Vietnam veterans and spouses of soldiers serving in Vietnam, in addition to others who focused on the history of US involvement in Vietnam, atrocities in the war, US imperialism and the capitalist economic roots of the war, and the support of University of Texas for the war machine. Larry Jackson of SNCC and the CUF stirred the crowd when he urged people to get off the campus and into the community to organize ordinary people around their real needs.[13]

The 15 October moratorium rally and march in Austin was a huge success in bringing out huge numbers of people to oppose the war, and it buoyed our spirits. It marked a good start for our fall offensive against the war, which included sponsoring demonstrations against CIA recruitment on campus and building support and organizing buses for a second moratorium in Washington, DC, scheduled for a month later on 15 November 1969. An estimated half a million people attended the mostly peaceful November march and rally, an event that organizers proclaimed was the largest antiwar protest in US history. This moratorium rally followed the March Against Death demonstration held the day before, when an estimated forty thousand people paraded down Pennsylvania Avenue carrying signs with the names of dead US soldiers and names of destroyed Vietnamese towns and villages. A security force of forty thousand US Army troops and police were deployed to guard government buildings and facilities.[14] Antiwar activists sponsored parallel demonstrations in dozens and dozens of cities and towns across the country. In Austin we did our part, organizing a huge protest rally and (once again, unauthorized) march to the State Capitol building.

Looking for a Movement Home in all the Wrong Places

In the fall of 1969, after the reality set in that SDS was finished as a movement center, we set about reconstructing organizations to carry forward the antiwar and antiracist message. We created numerous organizations with various names, usually selected to plan for the next "big action." Not to be deterred, some of my movement comrades turned to the SMC as an alternative organizational framework for mounting antiwar protests. We all knew that the YSA, the student wing of the SWP, controlled the SMC. But some political activists thought it was possible to steer the SMC away from its SWP roots. They were wrong. In a confidential "Memorandum for Information" on 20 October 1969, an undercover informant reported that Jeff Jones caused a "hassle" in an SMC meeting when he requested that all YSA members stand up and reveal their political identities. All in all, of the forty persons in attendance, about half were YSA members. This confrontational tactic brought about a performative walkout of non-YSA members. Despite its affiliation with YSA, the SMC was a somewhat fluid organization. In late October SMC held an event featuring two non-YSA speakers in order to mobilize protests against CIA recruiters on campus. In light of an anticipated mass rally and confrontation, the CIA recruiting team called off their visit.[15]

Yet in the end the SMC never wavered from its singular focus on staging peaceful antiwar rallies and marches. Under the outside guidance of the YSA, the SMC never addressed racism and sexism head-on and always hewed to the line of legal protest. Eventually this single-minded focus failed to attract much of a mass following.

The success of these two moratorium antiwar marches, combined with what was clearly increased political militancy during the fall of 1969, led to much greater repression. Law enforcement agencies experimented with new ways to keep the movement off balance. Interspersed between the October and November moratorium marches were two events of local provenance that profoundly reshaped the Austin movement. The Waller Creek incident and the Chuck Wagon Riot did not originate out of opposition to the war in Vietnam. Each in their own way, these two events reflected the widening and enlarging of the base of operations for insurgent politics that grew in opposition to the arbitrariness and autocratic approach of the university administration.

The Waller Creek Incident, 21–23 October 1969

At the University of Texas, football was king. After all, the Longhorns won the NCAA national championship in the 1963 football season—the last all-white football program to do so. The Longhorns consistently came out on top of the Southwest Conference and were frequent participants in the annual Cotton Bowl staged every New Year's Day in Dallas. Loyalty to the university, the steady flow of alumni donations and gifts, and just plain old Texas pride were deeply rooted in football culture and "Hook 'em Horns." After discussion and debate, the Board of Regents decided that the football stadium was just too small to accommodate the loyal fan base. Calls for expansion spilled over into reality. The footprint for the expansion meant leveling Waller Creek, a small stream that meandered past the west side of the stadium. Frank Erwin, chair of the Board of Regents, took the lead in promoting the planned enlargement of the stadium.

In May 1969 the Board of Regents approved final plans for the expansion of Memorial Stadium by placing a new building (known today as Bellmont Hall) along the west side of the stadium. Designed to house the administrative offices of intercollegiate athletics, its roof supported an upper deck to the stadium with new seating capacity for fourteen thousand more football fans. The total cost was just over $12 million, though because of its mixed use, about 70 percent of the financing came from Permanent University Fund bond proceeds, the rest from the sale of seating options in the stadium. Ironically, the Board of Regents announced their plans on Earth Day, a day of awareness of the need to preserve the environment. To make room for the new building, expansion plans called for the removal of the giant live oak and cypress trees that had shaded the western gates of the stadium for decades. All in all, campus planners proposed the elimination of thirty-nine mature trees and the paving of the bed and banks of the creek in order to support erosion control.

Taking their cue from the emergent ecology movement, a group of environmentalists, especially those aligned with the UT School of Architecture (SOA), raised objections to the destruction of a place of natural beauty and opposed plans to transform the creek into a paved drainage ditch. Faculty and students affiliated with the SOA created substitute proposals to save Waller Creek.[16] A common thread running through the various points of opposition was the desire to have more public input on future building development of the campus. SOA faculty and students met with President Hackerman, proposing a week's delay in the start of the project in order to encourage more discussion. In the meantime, two botany professors and some UT law students partnered with the local Sierra Club and filed for a temporary restraining order to halt construction, though any court order would not be issued until midmorning on Wednesday, 22 October.

Protests began on Monday, 20 October, after the temporary restraining order was lifted and contractors with bulldozers arrived at the stadium to begin removing the trees along the west side of San Jacinto Boulevard. But when the construction company turned its attention to Waller Creek on the next day, more than fifty sign-carrying protesters took direct action, blocking the path of the bulldozers. An undercover police informant working for Security Chief George Carlson warned the campus security about the planned sit-in in front of the bulldozers. Protesters had planted saplings and shrubs the Saturday before, with the aim of drawing attention to the aesthetic features of the meandering creek. The university administration ordered the protesters to remove these before Monday morning.[17] Of course, that did not happen.

Protesters distributed leaflets announcing, "Slow growing, straight stretching, TREE POWER." Starting at 7:00 a.m. university maintenance workers removed these newly planted trees as protesters fanned out in front of the bulldozers.[18] All along the disputed section of Waller Creek, dozens of people had climbed up the trees and refused to come down. These were cedar, live oak, pecan, and maple trees—many of them well over a century old. A few protesters took part in an all-night vigil at the site, warming themselves with a huge campfire. These "tree lovers," as newspaper reporters repeatedly referred to them, were concerned that construction crews might return in the dark to finish their dirty work.[19] Other protesters arrived at sunrise and climbed the branches with the hope that they could delay any action before the expected restraining order was issued. This organized tree-in, where protesters tied themselves to branches with ropes, forced a daylong halt to construction efforts along Waller Creek.[20] A number of us, less than a week after organizing a huge march and rally in Austin to coincide with the national Moratorium in Washington, DC, mobilized our friends to join the tree protests.

Rather than provoke a more serious situation, Dr. Bryce Jordan, vice president for Student Affairs, instructed the crews not to resume clearing the

Waller Creek Protests, November 1968. Protester dragged from tree. John Yates, UT Texas Student Publications, photographer. Courtesy of Prints and Photographs Collection, camh-dob-017295, Dolph Briscoe Center for American History, University of Texas at Austin.

site until they received instructions from the president's office. This delay infuriated Frank Erwin. He arrived in person at Waller Creek early in the morning, surveyed the scene, and, ignoring the pending outcome of the legal case, personally directed the work crews to begin clearing the trees. Without even bothering to contact President Hackerman, Erwin personally took charge of calling in campus, city, and state law enforcement agencies, along with a fire truck with an extended ladder, to remove student protesters from the trees as quickly as possible.

This event marked the first time the university administration had used noncampus security on such a large scale. As hundreds of chanting protesters gathered to watch, police used ladders and safety nets to bodily remove tenacious protesters who had climbed higher and higher into the upper branches of the trees. Erwin was in a hurry to beat the restraining order. Hovering around the scene of destruction, he demanded that the bulldozers get to work and ordered police to use force to get the protesters out of the trees. Erwin ordered the contractor to "head for the biggest trees first." "Get these big trees down as soon as possible," he allegedly said. "After they're down, the students won't give a shit."[21]

As recounted by a reporter for the *Daily Texan,* Erwin ordered the police to "arrest all the people you have to." "After school administrators and campus police asked for cooperation and instructed the protesters to clear the area," one reporter wrote in the *Austin American*, "police began moving in to pluck the demonstrators from their perches on the branches of the two largest trees on the southwest corner of San Jacinto and 21st street."[22] Police used fire truck ladders and nets to pull protesters from the trees. In removing one of the last remaining holdouts, police even sawed off a huge tree limb with a person still clinging desperately to it.[23]

With the protesters scattered, police formed lines to secure the construction zone as bulldozers and crews set to work to remove the trees. As the trees came down, a photographer captured an image of Erwin applauding wildly. The courts issued a temporary restraining order a little before noon, but it was too late.[24]

The sight of police officers and firefighters yanking and dragging protesters out of the trees was a public relations disaster. Newspapers in

Frank Erwin, chair of University of Texas Board of Regents, overseeing the removal of trees at the Waller Creek Protests, October 1968. Courtesy of Prints and Photographs Collection, di_01352, Dolph Briscoe Center for American History, University of Texas at Austin.

"Trees and People Belong Together" protest sign affixed to chopped down tree at the Waller Creek Protests, October 1968. Johnny B. Jenkins, photographer. Courtesy of Prints and Photographs Collection, di_06084, Dolph Briscoe Center for American History, University of Texas at Austin.

Austin and across the state published these somewhat comical images. By Thursday the "Battle of Waller Creek" had become a major news item across Texas, and newspapers from Los Angeles to New York even covered the story. The local *Austin-American* newspaper provided extensive coverage, even including an entire photographic montage.[25] Images of the forcible removal of protesting students from trees appeared in newspapers as far away as Paris. The Battle for Waller Creek proved to be a real embarrassment for the UT administration.[26]

The three-day protests over the clearing of trees ended when the bulldozers pulled away after their destructive work was finished. All in all, twenty-seven protesters were arrested and charged for violations ranging from disorderly conduct to use of abusive language and interfering with the right to work.[27] The sheer number of arrests, the police use of excessive force to remove protesters from trees, and Frank Erwin's complete disdain for the protesters substantially increased the awareness of the need to preserve the environment.

On 22 October, as construction crews stopped for their lunch break, a group of between eight hundred and a thousand people grabbed branches large and small, towed them out of the creek bed, and carried them in a long procession from the Waller Creek site to University Tower. Protesters piled branches and limbs to block the entrance doors to the university administration offices. Undercover police informants identified the leaders of the group carting tree branches to the main building as Doyle Niemann, Ann Locklear, and a number of well-known anarchists (the self-styled Motherfuckers) like John Lane.[28] Fearing for their own safety, the senior administration locked the doors to the building. When a fire broke out in a trash bin in a bathroom, their suspicions were realized. They called in campus police for protection.[29]

Forced to retreat under this mounting pressure, President Hackerman agreed to negotiate with a small group, drawn almost exclusively from the SOA. In the discussions he agreed that the university would not pave over Waller Creek and instead would create a cement flue as part of the stadium extension plans. Over the next week or so, students and faculty mounted protests. Cutting down the trees proved to be such an egregious affront to environmental preservation that even moderate and apolitical groups like the

Tree limbs blocking entrance to the Administration Building during the Waller Creek Protests, October 1968. Anarchist John Lane is in the center. Courtesy of *The Cactus* Yearbook, Prints and Photographs Collection, di_06085, Dolph Briscoe Center for American History, University of Texas at Austin.

Campus Young Democrats and the Campus Young Republicans were drawn into supporting an "Axe Erwin" rally.[30]

The anger and resentment over the failure of negotiations to produce positive results did not subside. The following Saturday afternoon (25 October), after the big trees were removed, a large crowd replanted fifty saplings along the creek bed in an organized "plant-in." Demonstrators distributed thousands of leaflets to the crowd attending the UT and Rice football game at Memorial Stadium.[31] While protests at the Waller Creek site died down, the legal cases dragged on for months. Twelve of the twenty-seven people arrested pleaded nolo contendere to disturbing the peace charges. But nine protesters held out, demanding trials so that they could plead their cases in court.[32]

Now, fifty years later, the SOA has been given the green light to take charge of the much-needed cleanup of the riverbed and the beautification of the water course. What was once an unruly stream—parallel to Shoal

Creek—coursing through the university campus is now a tourist-entertainment venue when it empties into the Colorado River downstream.

The events at Waller Creek brought together two strands of protest. In the first instance, protesters directed their ire at the senior university administration and Board of Regents (led by Frank Erwin), challenging the arbitrary use of power to shape the physical environment of the campus. The core of this sentiment was the slogan, "The days of the university being accurately referred to as Frank Erwin University must come to an end." In the second instance, these protests signaled a growing awareness of the contradictions between the destruction of the natural environment and the unrestrained building practices of university administrators and real estate developers. The Waller Creek incident was a signature moment, a catalyst that triggered a radical ecology-environmental movement that was relatively autonomous from antiwar activities.

The antiwar movement was no longer the only focal point or single fountainhead of political dissent. The wanton destruction of trees triggered a mass, militant confrontation with the police and the university administration. Many of my activist friends and I participated in the Battle for Waller Creek. We in the antiwar movement came to realize that the organizations with which we were affiliated were no longer the single driving force behind political protest. The willingness to rise up had spread, tapping into new constituencies and triggering the birth of new causes.

Curiously, the security forces not only failed to grasp the significance of the protests but they also misunderstood the sheer spontaneity of the protest action. Criminal Intelligence Head Burt Gerding and Security Chief George Carlson focused on organized groups and their leaders, thereby completely misreading the fluidity of the protests. In a handwritten note, an undercover police informant said that Eddie Arnold (a police officer attached to APD) could identify key people, including Judy Smith, Doyle Niemann, Barbara Wuench, and well-known hippie-anarchists (Jay McGee and Dick LeClair). So what? At the Waller Creek events, "leaders" did not orchestrate the protests. "Leaders" actually followed the animated crowd.[33]

Over the course of the week before the outbreak of demonstrations at Waller Creek, the composition of the group opposing the removal of trees changed significantly. At the start there was a large cross-section of the campus, especially those associated with the SOA and the emergent environmental movement, involved in early demonstrations and discussion. But "radical elements" gradually took over leadership (whatever that actually meant) and filled the ranks of those who participated.[34] Yet the security forces completely misjudged what was happening. Undercover police informants issued a number of reports to their superiors. One reported that "present feeling among 'radical activists' on UT campus is that the tree incident is absurd, but it something for the 'straight people' to become involved in." This same undercover informant offered the opinion that some of the radical activists compared the tree incident with Gentle Thursday—that is, a frivolous event that was about having lighthearted fun rather than engaging in real politics. Another parroted this same point of view: "Most of the 'leftists' indicated that they did not want to become involved."[35] These reports from undercover informants greatly underestimated the involvement of "radical elements." These police spies misread the situation.

Yet another undercover informant reported—correctly—that the Spartacists, YSA, Communist Party, and the SWP were not taking leadership roles in the protest movement. "At present, SDS [actually, already a moribund organization] is the only 'radical activist' group taking part, and their purpose is to turn it into a student power issue that can be exploited."[36] While it is true that the organized Marxist–Leninist political parties scoffed at the Waller Creek protests, these groups were actually irrelevant. It was not SDS, which had disappeared, but former SDS-ers and a wide variety of new young political militants who participated in the Waller Creek events, sharing the spotlight with the new radical ecologists, mainly affiliated with the SOA. We were a leaderless anarchist mass.

Chuck Wagon Police Riot, 10 November 1969

The Chuck Wagon police riot marked a watershed. The furies descended upon us, and we fought back with a tenacity not seen in earlier confrontations with law enforcement agencies. The combination of APD officers, the Texas DPS, and campus security pushed us out of the Chuck Wagon cafeteria by

Clockwise, from far left: Roy Breaux, David MacBryde (with a cigarette), Alex Calvert, Martin Murray, unidentified woman, Paul Spencer, and Paul Turner, sitting at a table in Chuck Wagon. Courtesy of Alan Pogue, photographer.

the use of excessive force. Not deterred or defeated, we outmaneuvered them, scattering in the face of tear gas, dividing their forces and gathering ours when needed, pelting them with bottles and rocks, and engaging in literally hand-to-hand skirmishes. We attacked, breaking prisoners free from police vans, puncturing tires, and transforming the entire area into a fluid battleground. In so many ways, the veil of propriety was lifted. They knew what we knew: If the chance arose, we would fight back—even with rocks and bottles and wrestling matches. There is nothing like a police riot to quickly alter consciousness. Respect for the public face of law enforcement—police out of control—reached a low point.[37]

Let me tell you the whole story. I have relied upon my personal memories, assorted newspaper accounts, and particular internet sources to reconstruct these events as best I can. What is certain is that the Chuck Wagon Riot marked a turn from passively waiting for the security forces to attack us at peaceful protests and marches to actively defending our turf and taking the fight to them.

The Chuck Wagon was the main campus cafeteria in the Student Union Building, located close to Guadalupe Street (better known as the Drag). It served a standard menu of uninteresting college food, including inexpensive coffee and sandwiches. There were booths along the edges and moveable tables and chairs in the middle. It could accommodate perhaps 250 people without feeling too crowded. The Chuck Wagon was a popular hangout for student radicals, countercultural hippies, and nonstudents alike. I could never go to the Chuck Wagon without running into someone I knew.

The Chuck Wagon Riot originated out of a rebellion against the arbitrary power of the UT Board of Regents and their surrogate functionaries rather than arising specifically out of the pressing issues of the war and racism. An expanding number of "street kids" with nowhere else to go gravitated to the Drag that ran along the west side of the UT campus. Some of these wayward youngsters found a kind of soulful refuge in the Chuck Wagon. In time, the presence of these underage nonstudents drew the attention of the press. The conservative-leaning *Austin American-Statesman* published an over-the-top, exaggerated editorial in which the authors feigned outrage against what they considered behavior beyond propriety, labeling those who frequented the Chuck Wagon as "pot smokers," "street people," and "non-student scum," and called for the university administration to "clean up" the mess. In retrospect, I wonder if law enforcement agencies teamed up to convince the *Austin American-Statesman* to publish this editorial.[38]

One of the main excuses the university administration gave for restricting the use of the Chuck Wagon to university, faculty, students and staff was the "problems" created by street kids, drug-dealers, and other untidy riffraff. I really cannot recall large numbers of youngsters frequenting the Chuck Wagon, but I might not have noticed because I did not care. Shortly after the inflammatory editorial appeared in the *American-Statesman*, two plainclothes police officers stormed unannounced into the Chuck Wagon with the aim of apprehending a young female runaway popularly known as Sunshine. She tried to run but was unable to avoid the grasp of the arresting officers. Hostilities escalated dramatically when some of Sunshine's street friends reacted angrily, shoving and cursing the police, denouncing them as "pigs." Several protesters blocked the doors to the Chuck Wagon, temporarily preventing the plainclothes officers from leaving with their captive. In order to prevent the crowd from rescuing Sunshine, an undercover officer named Brownlow handcuffed himself to her. An official police report filed in the George Carlson Papers confirmed that when asked to identify themselves, one of the arresting plainclothes officers pulled out a pistol, stuck it in the stomach of one those who confronted them, and declared, "This is the only ID I need." If that display of bravado were not enough, he threatened to shoot anyone who obstructed their path to the police vehicle.[39] This dramatic show of force was unprecedented. The assembled protesters quickly moved aside. There seems to be circumstantial evidence to suggest that the plainclothes officers of the APD entered the Chuck Wagon without even notifying campus authorities.[40]

A mingling crowd of about 150 outraged protesters encircled the police car, slashing tires and kicking at the doors. As the departing police cars carted poor Sunshine away to juvenile detention, angry protesters followed, throwing rocks and bottles. Later that afternoon protesters went to the police station to file a complaint about the police officer brandishing a pistol during the capture of Sunshine. The police arrested four of those whom they recognized as coming to Sunshine's defense, charging them with disorderly conduct.[41] The raid on the Chuck Wagon to seize a child was clearly a provocative act. The plainclothes police could have waited outside and confronted Sunshine when she was alone. The APD wanted a visible display of force that would provoke a response.

"Please Don't Take Our Sunshine Away"

The story of Sunshine is part of a wider narrative about the emergence of a great cultural chasm—the severe breakdown of the conventional nuclear family structure. In this moment of cultural crisis, the center could no longer hold. In a revealing account published in the *Austin American-Statesman*, reporter John Bryant described Sunshine as an "innocent looking, freckle-faced sixth grader [who] looks like any other 12-year-old girl." "She taps her feet, keeping time to an inner core of youthful energy," Bryant wrote. "She wiggles her nose when she is upset. And she doesn't like wearing a dress." Yet Sunshine—whose given name was Sharon Faye

Marsden—was no ordinary sixth-grader. By her own admission, she began smoking marijuana and dropping LSD when she was 10 years old. She ran away from home and began living with so-called street people who hung around the Drag (Guadalupe Street) across from the UT campus. Sunshine claimed she had landed a job as a clerk at a local head shop. On 6 November, one day before her 12th birthday, Sunshine was nabbed in the Chuck Wagon. Her story was similar to an escalating number of similar stories of children running away from dysfunctional homes. By November 1969 the number of runaway juveniles handled through Austin juvenile courts had reached four hundred persons. It was like a mini-epidemic.[42]

Sunshine was not a typical runaway. Declaring that she was "just out of control," the Travis County chief probation officer signed authorization papers transferring custody of Sunshine from her mother's care to Marshall Cooper, head of a minimum-security juvenile facility called Girlstown located about fifty miles outside of Lubbock. Girlstown was literally in the middle of nowhere, on the flatlands of West Texas, a barren landscape littered with oil rigs and meandering cattle. Sharon Marsden appeared at her court-appointed hearing wearing a new dress and black shoes that her mother purchased for her in anticipation of her going away. Before she left for the airport, Sunshine discarded her new clothes and put on blue jeans and a boy's shirt. She refused to communicate with her mother. She adamantly rejected her mother's efforts to show affection. As Sunshine boarded the single-engine Comanche light plane for her two-and-a-half hour ride to her new prison-home, there were no tears, no kisses, and no hugs.[43] One can only guess that Sunshine bided her time in detention before making an escape and finding her way to San Francisco or New York to disappear into the burgeoning youth culture that defined the times. I only hope that Sunshine found some peace and tranquility in her new life.

The spontaneous, angry response to the police invasion of the Chuck Wagon to apprehend Sunshine gave the university administration the excuse they wanted. Although the Student Union was in theory governed by an autonomous board with a student majority, the senior administration pounced on the opportunity, looking for a way to rid the Chuck Wagon of "the imaginary non-student menace."[44] At an emergency meeting held on Friday evening 7 November, the day after the confrontation over the seizure of Sunshine, the Student Union Board capitulated to administration pressure and swung their support for the a new ruling that only faculty, students, and university staff who presented their valid identification cards were permitted to enter the cafeteria. This controversial decision came on the heels of District Attorney Bob Smith's call for an immediate Travis County Grand Jury investigation of seemingly nefarious goings-on at the Chuck Wagon.[45] This investigation led the district attorney to declare that the Chuck Wagon was a "public nuisance." Campus police claimed that the Chuck Wagon had become a den of iniquity, harboring youthful runaways, providing cover for drug dealing and alleged prostitution, and allowing for the destruction of property and disorderly conduct.[46] What was clear was that the district attorney's office, the APD, and campus security had been carrying on a lengthy investigation of alleged drug abuse and how the Chuck Wagon had become a "sanctuary for juvenile runaways."[47] These flimsy excuses were merely a pretext for closing this popular dining facility to Non-University people. The real reasons were more sinister: The senior administration looked upon the Chuck Wagon as a kind of liberated outlaw space that had embedded itself in what university officials considered their sovereign territory. Along with the campus security, the senior administration wanted a show of force.

This new ruling barring nonstudents from the Chuck Wagon clearly signaled the intentions of the university administration to demonstrate their control by reclaiming lost terrain. Those of us who frequented the Chuck Wagon on a regular basis regarded it as a free zone, or liberated territory, that belonged to us. A considerable number of antiwar activists who frequented the Chuck Wagon moved in and out of formal enrollment at the university. This fluid pattern of maintaining student status and dropping out was common. Despite hyperbolic allegations to the contrary, there were no real outside agitators on campus.

On Saturday morning (8 November) student employees standing by the entrance began to check university IDs. The fact that the president (ad interim) of the university, Bryce Jordan, was in the Chuck Wagon when it opened to oversee enforcement of the new rule provides sufficient evidence to support the view that the senior administration was complicit in the decision and had simply pushed the supposedly autonomous Student Union Board out of the way. Around 8:30 a.m., Paul Spencer and David Pratt walked into the Chuck Wagon. Both refused to show IDs. Almost immediately they were confronted by President Jordan (decked out in a business suit) and flanked by two UT police officers. Jordon blurted out, "Paul, you know you're not supposed to be in here." The fact that Jordan could identify Paul, knew of his nonstudent status, and had prior knowledge that he planned to come to the Chuck Wagon that morning meant that he had information supplied by someone inside the movement. (Paul had been a student, but that semester he was a nonstudent studying to pass several advanced placement exams.) As Paul started to respond, Jordan ordered the cops to "take him." It is important to note that David Pratt also did not show an ID when he entered the Chuck Wagon, but he was a registered student and participated in student government. In the ensuing melee, Paul was arrested and charged with disorderly conduct and aggravated assault on a police officer. As a result of this confrontation, the university administration simply shut down the Chuck Wagon to everyone for the day.[48]

In many ways the Chuck Wagon Riot marked a decisive moment in which movement activists were willing to engage in direct confrontations with armed security forces. Around midmorning on Monday, 10 November, I joined a huge impromptu protest rally and demonstration on the West Mall just outside the Student Union Building. The discussion centered on how to reclaim the Chuck Wagon. As the day wore on, the size of the crowd expanded exponentially as more and more students, nonstudents, and activists heard the news of the Chuck Wagon shutdown and came to the protest. What was clear from the start was that this unruly crowd was not going to acquiesce to the cafeteria closure without some sort of direct confrontation. There were plenty of angry people in the crowd who wanted to take action. One particular agitator stood out from the rest. A tall, muscular man, slightly older than the typical student and bearing a distinctive black tee shirt, urged the crowd to storm the building. He called himself Duke, and he seemed to appear as if out of the blue, never seen before or after the events of the day. In retrospect, many of my friends strongly suspected that he was an agent provocateur. A couple of photographs stored in a university collection of images are all that remain to indicate his presence.

Suspected agent provocateur known as Duke photographed in courtyard before the Chuck Wagon Police Riot, November 1968. Courtesy of George Carlson Papers, camh-dob-017274, Dolph Briscoe Center for American History, University of Texas at Austin.

Actually, it did not matter. People were going into the Chuck Wagon no matter what. After about an hour of angry speeches, a sizeable number of the crowd grew weary of talking and decided to march en masse into the popular dining hall. In his transcribed oral history interview, Burt Gerding declared that the protesters "forced their way into" the Chuck Wagon. This claim is simply not true.[49] The Chuck Wagon doors were open as always, and perhaps a hundred or more angry protestors simply walked single file into the Chuck Wagon without showing IDs and right past startled student monitors who were haphazardly checking identification at the door.

The occupation began. As the hours passed, the crowd swelled to over six hundred persons, some sitting on the floor, others standing on chairs and tables, and still others pressed against all four walls of the cafeteria. Those who were occupying the cafeteria debated what to do. Protesters in the room were in an angry mood, unwilling to accept vague promises of the Union Board to hold a student referendum in two weeks' time. Some protesters burned their orange ID cards, prompting cheers of support from the crowd.

Martin Murray speaking to a crowd inside the cafeteria during the Chuck Wagon Police Riot, November 1968. Undercover police surveillance photograph. Circled numbers represent police identification with names of Martin Murray (1) and Steve Russell (2) listed on the back of the photograph. Courtesy of George Carlson Papers, camh-dob-017273, Dolph Briscoe Center for American History, University of Texas at Austin.

The senior university administration responded to this affront to their authority by calling in the campus police and the Texas DPS, who gathered out of sight. The assembled law enforcement agencies were dressed for battle. Uniformed cops backed with police vehicles standing at the ready surrounded the University Union Building. They announced a 4:00 p.m. deadline to vacate the premises.

We were not a disciplined group, and the threat of arrest triggered a range of responses. Perhaps a dozen or so volunteers decided to stage a civil disobedience protest by staying inside the Chuck Wagon and going limp when the police came to arrest them. While this kind of civil disobedience was standard fare for protest demonstrations, I thought that sitting down in front of angry cops was not a particularly good idea. I thought that the going limp tactic was an invitation to the police to start beating us. As was typically the case with large, leaderless crowds seeking to find consensus, discussion and debate lingered on, right up to the 4:00 p.m. ultimatum. As the deadline approached, hundreds of people filed out of the Chuck Wagon and into the University Union corridor, seeking an escape. Uniformed police blocked their exit. All in all, perhaps a thousand people were positioned in ways that were intended to prevent the police from entering the Chuck Wagon.

In the confusion demonstrators received mixed signals. In pleading with demonstrators to leave the Chuck Wagon, the head of the Union Board of Directors told the crowd that he had assurances from the UT administration that the police were not going to make arrests. Shortly thereafter, W. L. Purse, assistant chief of campus police, announced to the crowd, contrary to earlier assurances, that at 4:15 p.m., the police would close and lock the doors and arrest anyone—both student and nonstudent—who remained. As some began exiting the doors, about seventy to one hundred helmeted DPS riot-trained officers and the special riot squad of the APD joined the campus security force, and they marched double file into the Union building, making their way down the hall to the entrance of the Chuck Wagon. Some members of the National Guard stood nearby, supposedly to observe and learn.[50]

As they entered the Student Union, this phalanx of security police, all decked out in riot gear, scattered protesters far and wide. As if responding to some prearranged time management protocols, the assembled police units reached the doors to the Chuck Wagon almost exactly at the original 4:00 p.m. deadline. Rather than choosing to enter the Chuck Wagon through the kitchen doors, they decided that they would engage in a frontal assault. As the riot police began to push through the glass doors at the entrance to the Chuck Wagon, those protesters inside who had decided to leave and were trying to exit came face to face with their worst nightmare. It was like an unstoppable force bumping into an immoveable object.

As they forced their way into the Chuck Wagon, the police broke through the double glass doors at the east entrance, shattering glass everywhere. An equal number of police filed in the north entrance. Chaos ensued as the cops tried to push their way inside and protesters tried to evade the tear gas and the nightsticks and slip through the police lines. Dozens were trapped inside with no obvious way to escape. Using clubs and their large bodies, the

Hand-to-hand skirmishes between police and protesters during the Chuck Wagon Police Riot, November 1968. Courtesy of Prints and Photographs Collection, di_06989, Dolph Briscoe Center for American History, University of Texas at Austin.

cops pushed people away from the front doors and back into the cafeteria. Amid the chaos of broken glass, overturned chairs, objects flung into the air, and a great deal of yelling, a full-blown riot had begun.[51]

I was one of the groups that remained inside the Chuck Wagon when the police burst in. There was literally no place to go. Tear gas filled the crowded space. State police indiscriminately sprayed chemical Mace into the faces of protesters in the crowd. The surging mass of panic-stricken protesters forced me to the back of the room where I was caught, unable to move, against the wall near the back kitchen door. Even if I wanted to leave the Chuck Wagon, it would have been impossible. Dozens of people blocked my pathway to the doors. Besides, if I had left by the available exits, I would have walked right into an angry horde of law enforcement officers looking to hit people. As the advancing cops grabbed people next to me, I thought all was lost. Then, just as a burly cop reached for me, I felt a hand on my back as someone yanked me by the shirt, forcing me to tumble backward through the rear door and to relative safety. I looked up. It was Judy Smith, a fellow radical who saved me from arrest. If she had not rescued me from the mayhem, I would have had suture-covered head wounds and would have been one more defendant in the court case.

This police assault triggered an hour-long spree of violence and mayhem that spilled from the University Union building into surrounding streets. As I ran around to the front of the Union building, a pitched battle was taking place. Riot-equipped state police outfitted with steel helmets and face visors, nightsticks, and chemical Mace tried in vain to disperse the angry crowds. They were indeed vicious, beating protesters whom they could catch and arresting everyone who did not run. They fired tear gas indiscriminately, completely unconcerned about where it might land. General mayhem ensued. Protesters chanted, "Sieg Heil, Sieg Heil," "Oink, Oink," and "Pigs off campus."[52]

Scuffles broke out in numerous locations. There were no police lines, only angry cops flailing at protesters. Those of who had escaped ahead of the police assault teamed up with the hundreds milling around the edge of the Union building, converging on the police from the rear. In numerous incidents when police officers tried to detain demonstrators, protesters prevented their arrest by pulling them out of the grasp of law enforcement officers. Some protesters had come prepared, dressed in heavy boots and sturdy helmets. It was clear that the police had not expected or prepared for protesters to actually fight back, using roving street tactics to taunt the police and throwing rocks and bottles. "The crowd of both students and non-students swelled outside the Student Union Building," the *Houston Post* reported the next day, "as the arrested persons were loaded into the van and both onlookers and angry participants in the confrontation poured into the street."[53]

In order to deal with mass arrests, the police had brought in two large panel trucks to haul away those whom they had nabbed. They lowered the hydraulic tailgates of the vans to make it easy for them to collect prisoners. The police succeeded in apprehending some of the protesters and putting them inside the vans, awaiting transport to jail. One clever protester reached over and cut a line to the hydraulic lift on the back of one of the trucks, spraying hydraulic fluid everywhere. Another had disabled one of the truck tires, rendering the police exit a sloppy affair. In the confusion of flying objects, the Mace-filled air, and plenty of verbal abuse, the police left the rear door of the prison truck momentarily unguarded. What a propitious opportunity. One fearless protester seized the time, rushing forward to swing open the rear door, enabling our captured comrades to escape into the crowd. This audacious action caught the cops completely off guard. It was totally gratifying to witness prisoners able to scamper to freedom.

We followed the police contingent as they retreated, their prisoners locked away in the vans. Crowds surged after one lumbering truck. A cordon of police formed behind it, walking backward as a handful of officers ran out in front, until the truck "out-distanced the mob."[54] From eyewitness accounts it is clear that police officers had targeted specific people for arrest—Paul Spencer and Bill Meacham, for example. The cops moved through crowds of screaming protesters, avoiding the surging mayhem, in order to grab those they wanted.[55]

As the crowd eventually melted away, the police were surely disappointed. They had turned their attempt to enforce a rather stupid rule into a wider confrontation that brought attention to the autocratic behavior of university administration officials and their willingness to use excessive force. They may have cleared the Chuck Wagon, but we won the battle for hearts and minds. It was an cxhilarating victory.

We learned later that the Student Union governing board had voted to call off the police and was still deliberating what to do as the 4:00 p.m. deadline approached. President Jordan intervened, overruled the board decision, and gave a green light for the assembled police units to invade the Chuck Wagon.[56] We were disorganized and unprepared for the mayhem that ensued. The police were even more disorganized and unprepared. By charging through the only two exits, thereby leaving no route for escape, their heavy-handed police tactics made what might have been a straightforward civil disobedience sit-in, with protesters going limp and submitting to arrest without confrontation, into a mini-uprising.

The Chuck Wagon Riot marked a turning point. We were no longer passive participants at marches and peaceful rallies, waiting in dread for the inevitable police attacks. We fought back, grappling with police, throwing rocks, sticks, and bottles, and tossing tear gas canisters back into police ranks. I learned that one should not pick up tear gas canisters with bare hands and toss them like a baseball in front of one's eyes. The right way to return tear gas canisters to their owners was with gloves and a sidearm toss, away from the body.

Not long ago I discovered some newspaper clippings on the Chuck Wagon Riot that I had stored away in an impromptu archive of sorts. These accounts are filled with hyperbolic posturing that is humorous in retrospect. One account referred to police moving "through a screaming, chanting crowd of several hundred persons, many of them *dressed as hippies*."[57] Another reporter added, "For a short time Monday afternoon, the University of Texas was a battleground of the most violent, ugly sense of the word." "Preparing for the 'sad drama' to come, police officers for the most part were jocular. Many were laughing. None seemed to anticipate what was to come." "If that's what they want, then we will give it to them," District Attorney Bob Smith bragged. "The police moved against the mob in the hall, igniting brief but violent scuffles." Law enforcement officers referred to those arrested as "prisoners." "The mob roared with glee as when a loud hiss told them that one of the tires on the truck had been punctured or the air released from it." "Throughout the intermittent skirmishes," Lynn Taylor reported, "officers were kicked, hit with fists, and spat upon. Instances of the police losing their temper appeared rare."[58]

It seems to me that Lynn Taylor was not in attendance at the same police riot in which I participated. The police were out of control. They had come spoiling for a fight, and they got much more than they bargained for. A close-up photograph of a young woman trying in vain to cut into a tire was accompanied by a humorous caption: "A UNIVERSITY tire gets the knife."[59] I witnessed this young woman (Pam Stubblefield) trying desperately to puncture the tire of a police van by sawing it with a pocketknife. There was nothing humorous about this. Her photograph appeared in the *Austin American-Statesman*. Other puncture artists were more successful. Thinking about that

Police mug shot of Pam Stubblefield, charged with felonious destruction of property for allegedly trying to disable a truck tire with a pocketknife during the Chuck Wagon Police Riot, November 1968. Courtesy of George Carlson Papers, camh-dob-017271, Dolph Briscoe Center for American History, University of Texas at Austin.

incident later, I realized that a pocketknife was no match for a vehicle tire. Wire cutters to rip off the air-intake value or a sharpened ice pick to stab the tire were much better weapons for disabling vehicles.[60]

The Messy Aftermath

Security documents showed without a shadow of a doubt that law enforcement agencies regarded the clearing out of the Chuck Wagon not as a university matter alone but as part of a larger effort to deny antiwar activists a safe place to gather on campus. We learned later that DPS had deployed special riot-trained patrol personnel from a six-town area centering on Waco to converge on Austin if more disturbances erupted in the coming days. Once again, the various policing agencies exaggerated the so-called threat to security in order to clamp down hard on dissenting voices.[61] There were reports that the FBI told the Austin police to hold four protesters—Jay McGee, Bill Meacham, Paul Spencer, and Albert Cambio—overnight. The Austin police reported that the FBI wanted to question the four suspects on possible violations of a federal warrant that prohibited crossing state lines to incite a riot.[62] This was a ludicrous accusation since all four lived in Austin.

What was clear was that Burt Gerding played an oversized role in the Chuck Wagon events. In his interview in the Gerding Papers, he brags about recruiting a local radio/television reporter named Mike Simpson to spy on us. Apparently Simpson played a role in identifying a suspected arsonist on the UT campus sometime in the fall of 1969 and reported this person to the police department. From this initial contact, Gerding began using Mike as an undercover source. At Gerding's behest Simpson pretended to be an objective observer reporting on the Chuck Wagon events, recording speeches and interviewing a number of protesters outside the Student Union before the police invaded the cafeteria. Simpson supplied Gerding with copies of his recordings and tape-recorded interviews. The police plan was to use these tape-recorded interviews in the court case against the Chuck Wagon defendants. Gerding donated these materials to the Briscoe Center as part of his papers collection.

In several photographs taken inside the Chuck Wagon after protesters were forced out, Alan Pogue captured the presence of Gerding standing with police. Why did Gerding seem to attach undue attention to what university officials claimed was a matter of misuse of campus facilities? It is evident that Gerding and the Criminal Intelligence Division of the APD treated the Chuck Wagon events as something to do with radical "subversion." One can only imagine that the decision to clear out the Chuck Wagon was an orchestrated effort undertaken by security agencies—APD, campus security, and Texas DPS—to undermine insurgent politics. No matter. The police caused a riot, and we fought back. The events contributed to building the movement, not disrupting it.

The George Carlson Papers contain a number of internal police reports detailing their response to the Chuck Wagon incident. The aim of these reports was to seek to give the security forces the justification for their heavy-handed response. These efforts were as ludicrous as they were self-delusional. Their response amounted to a cover-up. The security agencies clustered around the reigning mythology that students and nonstudents alike forcibly entered the Chuck Wagon, thereby triggering the police response. In fact, the security agencies had prepared for this eventuality. Those outside on the mall attending the rally simply walked into the Chuck Wagon unimpeded around 11:15 a.m. In a "General Offense Report" (10 November 1969), Chief of Campus Security Allen Hamilton declared that campus security had twenty officers onsite and the DPS had twenty more en route. At this time Hamilton called all motorcycle and warrant officers to order in the assembly hall of the APD headquarters. He reported that seventy-five to a hundred unauthorized persons were inside the Chuck Wagon and that they had been given until 4:15 p.m. to leave the premises or face arrest and be charged with disorderly conduct. This report severely underestimated the number of protesters inside the Chuck Wagon and ignored the thousands of protesters outside.

Hamilton admitted that APD officers and campus police had already agreed upon arrest procedures for the transfer of prisoners in two large UT vans. It was also planned beforehand that the UT campus police would lock the Chuck Wagon doors at 4:15 p.m. and "all inside (illegally) would be arrested." As an indication of considerable preplanning, Hamilton reported that the APD would "handle the perimeter guard, including the west side of the building and the protection of the trucks used for prisoner transportation." A police photographer was onsite to take photographs of prisoners as they were loaded into the awaiting vans. In short, despite their public proclamations that they were unprepared for the severity of the riot, the security forces were considerably more prepared for battle than what they acknowledged.[63]

In the confusion, however, law enforcement officers attacked earlier than the 4:15 p.m. deadline. As the officers entered the building and reached the foyer to the entrance to the Chuck Wagon, one police report attested that "a large number of those inside ran outside breaking the aluminum and glass doors. Several officers were kicked, cursed, and spat on as they entered." Well, I was there. The law enforcement officers at the door were responsible for breaking the glass doors to gain entry. This police report conveniently ignores how police officers beat, kicked, and assaulted those inside the Chuck Wagon with chemical Mace, seemingly less interested in making orderly arrests than in displaying their wanton power of repression. Captain J. C. Fann, APD, noted that District Attorney Robert Smith was present during the entire incident, giving advice and undoubtedly offering encouragement.[64]

The Story Continued

A massive rally held the following day demanded clemency for those arrested and an end to the use of outside law enforcement agencies on the campus. A number of us were convinced that agents provocateurs had instigated the occupation of the Chuck Wagon. Even if there were agents provocateurs in the crowd urging us to commit illegal acts, the street fighting (which many called a police riot) would have happened anyway.

We also triggered a backlash. In a letter to the *Daily Texan*, Thomas Johnson, a (supposed) graduate student in the English Department, complained about "filthy, smelly adolescent bums that come to the Chuck Wagon every day, occupy large sections of it and make themselves totally obnoxious." "It was necessary to clear these deadbeats [and troublemakers] out of the university," he concluded.[65] Perhaps this irate letter originated with the COINTELPRO faux letter-writing campaign. Who knows? In the referendum sponsored by the Union Board and conducted about a week later, students voted to close the Chuck Wagon to nonstudents. This vote represented a setback for us. The Chuck Wagon remained closed to nonstudents for more than a year. The Board of Regents overturned a Union Board decision on 10 November 1970 that would have reopened the Chuck Wagon to anyone, including nonstudents. The regents justified their decision by claiming that "street people" who were known drug users would once again establish their nefarious headquarters in the Chuck Wagon should it be opened to the general public.[66]

Yet every cloud has a silver lining. It was our good luck that a number of those arrested were actually innocent bystanders and passersby. At least four of the people arrested on the spot were people who were not involved in the protest at all. Overenthusiastic police arrested a Navy ROTC cadet in uniform for simply not moving fast enough to get away. They also arrested two unsuspecting women students walking by, minding their own business, on the way to class. Sometimes necessity is the mother of invention. We posted bail for all those arrested and promised to provide legal assistance free of charge. Forming a legal defense committee for all those caught in the dragnet was a stroke of genius. We included everyone who participated in the riot with those who were simply bystanders or passersby. We were smart. Those innocent onlookers were a great cover for us malcontents.

A few weeks later, the Travis County Grand Jury handed down indictments on twenty-one Chuck Wagon protesters. Not all of those arrested onsite were included in the indictment. The grand jury dropped charges against those innocent bystanders whom the police had arrested. This list of those indicted included eight people arrested during the incident and a large number of others identified through police photographs as troublemakers.[67] The police use of photographs to identify people and arrest them later marked a shift in their tactics. The security forces expanded the use of surreptitious photographs for arrests at a later date in subsequent protest events.

The twenty-one people were charged with inciting to riot and malicious destruction of public property (the three slashed tires). These felonies carried a penalty of two to twenty years in prison. The prosecution relied upon a legal theory of conspiracy—individuals unknown to one another yet acting in concert. Under the application of this conspiracy charge, it was unnecessary to show that an individual committed felonious acts, only that this person was part of a crowd that did so. According to existing Texas law at the time, all persons who participated in and around the Chuck Wagon in an "unlawful assembly" were implicated in the felony charges. The university issued a reported that listed the damage to tires at less than $160.[68] In order to add substance their case, campus security provided a photograph of knives that were confiscated from nonstudents. This photographic evidence was a way of alleging that "outsiders" who came onto the UT campus were sometimes "armed and dangerous."[69] Another photograph contained in the George Carlson Papers shows a display of "weapons" collected at the Chuck Wagon protests: a long knife capable of easily puncturing tires and three smaller pocketknives.[70]

In the aftermath of the Chuck Wagon Riot, UT campus officials assessed the damage to equipment. In a confidential "Interview Report—University of Texas at Austin, November 12, 1969," maintenance personnel reported on the destruction of property. One truck suffered from three flat tires, a disabled hydraulic cable for lifting the tailgate, and a broken windshield due to rock damage. Investigators identified twelve separate punctures from an ice pick on one tire and pocketknife stab wounds on two others. A second truck had a punctured tire due to a pocketknife. All in all, it was a good day for the protesters.[71]

Sheriff's deputies served warrants on as many of those who were listed in the indictment as they could locate, and bond was set at $2,500 each. APD jailers did nothing to prevent inmates from beating our people while in jail. For example, defendant Bill Meacham filed a malpractice suit against university health services personnel who treated him for a broken rib, a punctured lung, and assorted bruises while an inmate at Travis County Jail. He remained hospitalized for eight days after his release from lockup.[72] Years later, Bill Meacham recalled these events:

> At some point we all went outside [from the Chuck Wagon] to make a lot of noise, and the police either attacked us or threatened to attack. There was a police vehicle there, and I knelt down and tried to saw off the valve stem of one of its tires. My knife was small and dull, and I failed. In the jostle of the crowd, I gave up and moved aside.
>
> A day or so later I learned that the cops were looking for me. I got a haircut to try to hide. I was in a sandwich shop or coffee shop or something and Bert Gerding came in and looked around. I said loudly, "Hey, Bert, who are you looking for?" He looked at me without recognition and said he had some people in mind.
>
> I left and went home, intending to sneak in the back door, but it was locked, so I went in the front way. Shortly thereafter the cops pounded on the door, forced their way in and arrested me. I, along with 20 others, had been charged with destruction of public property. We were the "Chuckwagon 21."
>
> In jail I was put in a cell with several other guys, none of whom I knew. They were of a whole different social class from mine. I was a white, middle-class student, and they were Black, working class,

> or criminal class guys. I was, in comparison, much weaker and more naive; they were street fighters. I had no idea of the appropriate social rules to follow. We were given some uninspired food, and several of the guys put their bread (white "bunny" bread) aside, so I put mine with theirs. Later I went to get mine and eat it, and found out that I had broken a social rule. One of the guys got mad and told me I didn't have permission to get the bread. My infraction was an excuse for him and some others to beat me up and kick me in the ribs. I was very freaked out. I think the cops put me in there on purpose, hoping I would get beaten up to teach me a lesson. Somehow I got bailed out the next day. Went to the campus health center and found out that I had a broken rib. I guess I was put in a hospital bed overnight because I remember someone bringing me pot brownies while I was in there. I think I was still pretty stoned when I got released and made my way home in a bit of daze.[73]

A number of those who were indicted were not initially arrested. When he surrendered to the APD in early December, John Lane became the sixteenth person to be arrested on felony charges.[74] Robert Arnold became the seventeenth person arrested on felony charges after he turned himself in to police on 2 December 1969. When Pam Stubblefield, the young woman who tried unsuccessfully to slash the tire of the police van, turned herself into APD on 4 December, there were still three fugitives (including Sonny Litchmna) still at large, and two others (Dick Le Clair and Peter Quant) hid from the police in the old University Y auditorium and left town immediately after the DA issued warrants for their arrest.[75]

The coconspirators became known as the Chuck Wagon 21. Those indicted consisted of a wide range of hardcore activists and a few who just spontaneously jumped into the fray. Building a defense strategy for the Chuck Wagon 21 became a significant part of political work over the next several months. Greg Calvert and Martin Wiginton took the lead in pulling together a prominent legal team and, along with Jim Simons and Cam Cunningham, in drafting a legal strategy. We formed an ad hoc legal defense committee for the twenty-one persons arrested on various charges, mostly misdemeanor violations (like disorderly conduct) but a number of felonies, including aggravated assault on a police officer, destruction of property, and conspiracy to carry out the destruction of property. Several prominent local activists affiliated with the self-styled Motherfuckers (actually called Up Against the Wall Motherfuckers)—Jay McGee, Dick LeClair, and Randy Carley—were indicted as coconspirators. While the Motherfuckers seemed more interested in defying authority than in political analysis and action, they were full of energy and verve. The Motherfuckers offered a great deal of theatrical and comic relief, but their off-the-cuff provocative style complicated the public image of "innocent victims" of police brutality when the Chuck Wagon 21 faced an assortment of charges, some of which presented the possibility of long jail terms.

A movement law office (called the Austin Law Commune) opened its doors in early October 1969. Initially with only two lawyers, Cam Cunningham and Jim Simons, the law office had its hands full. They alone could not carry the heavy lifting of political defense for the Chuck Wagon 21. We quickly realized that we could not expect our other lawyer friends to drop their own private practices to devote the kind of energy and time required for the defense. We wanted to draw a lot of attention to the case, so we decided to bring in some high-profile hired guns to give us visibility.

With deep entanglements in local Texas liberal culture, Martin Wiginton had built strong personal friendships with a wide range of progressive (but not-so-radical people) from his days working on the failed campaign Ralph Yarborough for the Texas governorship in 1966. Known as Smilin' Ralph, and having popularized the slogan "Let's put the jam on the lower shelf so the little people can reach it" in his campaigns, Yarborough was a permanent fixture for many years in the progressive wing of the Democratic Party. Returning to his roots, Martin was able to enlist the services of such prominent liberal lawyers as Warren Burnett, the well-known criminal defense attorney from Odessa; the famous San Antonio lawyer and political icon Maury Maverick; Sam Houston Clinton; and David Richards, constitutional law professor at UT and husband of future governor of Texas Ann Richards.

In seeking to cobble together an ad hoc defense for the Chuck Wagon 21, Greg Calvert suggested getting in touch with the National Lawyers Guild and the Center for Constitutional Rights in New York City, particularly the attorneys Bill Kunstler, Leonard Weinglass, and Arthur Kinoy. Greg wanted them to give us advice about how to construct a proactive legal defense that was not just about getting charges against the defendants dropped but also about using the case to promote our politics. After some discussion the center agreed to dispatch Bill Kunstler to come to Austin to assist us. He brought along a young lawyer named Beth Livezey, who was a partner in a legal collective called Bar Sinister located in Los Angeles. The Bar Sinister collective owned an old school building, which they transformed into offices, a kitchen, and living quarters for about thirty people who lived there. Beth was fantastic. She worked tirelessly to prepare us.

I really liked working with Martin Wiginton and Greg Calvert, so I devoted my energies to the defense work. I remember a time at a meeting in the kitchen at the home of David Richards when Ann Richards—with her distinctive white hair piled high on her head—drifted into the room. At the time she was the dedicated spouse of her well-known husband, before she became the electrifying and fiery Ann Richards, governor of the state of Texas.

Despite our high-profile legal connections, Jim Simons and Cam Cunningham in fact assumed the lion's share of carrying out the bulk of the actual legal work, drafting petitions to the court, collecting evidence, and constructing a strategy for courtroom proceedings. We formed a broad-based defense committee that brought together most of the twenty-one defendants and their supporters. We were able to use this platform both to introduce constitutional issues regarding free speech and matters of procedure and to raise all sorts of questions about police brutality, indiscriminate arrests, and proper and legitimate use of public buildings on the university campus. We called protest rallies and distributed leaflets in the name of the Chuck Wagon Legal Defense Committee. One main substantive feature of the arguments for the defense was to inquire just how was it possible for twenty-one defendants to all be held equally responsible for damage done by one person to one truck tire. The prosecution countered that all twenty-one defendants had conspired to commit this crime due to joint participation in the events. In terms of legal liability, the conspiracy statute was particularly vague and broad in its possible interpretation.

District Attorney Bob Smith went for the big win but in the end failed to even get the case to court. Think about it. Declaring a crowd to be an "illegal assembly" and then arresting some at a time when an alleged felony (destruction of property) was taking place, and then adding more to the list from photographs and police eyewitness accounts, is a rather lengthy legal stretch. Legally speaking, the police and district attorney could have charged anyone who participated in the "illegal assembly" with a felony. When thousands could have been indicted, charging only twenty-one persons was obviously a bit arbitrary. While the prosecution would never admit it, the police targeted specific people for arrest.

Defense for the Chuck Wagon 21 defendants came from all quarters. The UT Student Assembly voted to collect funds and channel these donations to students charged with indirect property destruction on 10 November. The Student Assembly stopped short of providing funds for those charged with assault or direct property damage.[76] On 6 January 1970, a group of nine university students and faculty members, joined by the Campus Young Democrats, filed a lawsuit in federal district court challenging the constitutionality and the application of statues under which twenty-one sealed grand jury indictments were issued. Along with Judy Smith, David Pratt, and Paul Turner, I was one of the four UT students who joined the suit. We held a press conference to explain our legal action.[77]

Chuck Wagon Legal Defense Fund Leaflet
"Citizens of Austin Your Freedoms Are at Stake"

You could go to prison for attending a peaceful meeting to express your views. Texas law defines an assembly of 3 people or more to be a riot. If a crime is committed or if there is a threat of violence. 400 people in and around the Chuck Wagon on November 10th 1969 may be liable to minimum prison term of two years because a few others damaged tires worth $160.00 altogether. Under Texas law all persons participating in the assembly are implicated in this felony. We feel that this interpretation of the law is unconstitutional because it destroys the basic rights of the 1st amendment of all Texans.

Signed by John Henry Faulk, Larry Goodwin, etc.[78]

MERRY CHRISTMAS

From Chuckwagon Defendants:

Bob Rankin, Randy Carley, Jay McGee, David Pratt, Bill Meacham, Paul Spencer

Copy of Christmas postcard depicting some of the Chuck Wagon 21 charged with crimes after the Chuck Wagon incident. Courtesy of David Hamilton (Pratt).

In early February the Chuck Wagon Legal Defense Fund issued a plea to anyone who witnessed the events of 6 and 10 November to come forward to offer testimony at the scheduled trial. The purpose of the testimony was to help prove that the district attorney had used selective enforcement procedures in deciding whom they were going to indict and prosecute. On the other side, the district attorney's office said that tape recordings (conducted by undercover informant Mike Simpson) and photographs taken by the DPS formed the basis for arrests of some of the Chuck Wagon 21 and constituted a strong foundation for a successful prosecution.[79]

After extensive conferencing on 6 March 1970 between District Attorney Bob Smith and our lawyers (Jim Simons, Cam Cunningham, Sam Houston Clinton, Maury Maverick, and Warren Burnett) representing the remaining nineteen defendants (two were severed from the case), a decision was reached to postpone the preliminary hearing. While the date of the jury trial on 6 April remained open, the felony conspiracy case against the Chuck Wagon defendants had begun to unravel.[80] It seems that the prospect of facing the eloquent verbal gymnastics of Maury Maverick in the courtroom sufficiently intimated the District Attorney Bob Smith, who subsequently agreed to drop most of the legal charges against virtually everyone. The DA singled out Paul Spencer for special attention, charging him with numerous counts of lawbreaking. In order to claim a small victory, the DA wanted Paul Spencer to accept a plea bargain for thirty days in jail and probation. Knowing that he had been the one assaulted in the Chuck Wagon, Paul refused the deal and eventually just left town.

There were other victims among us of the Chuck Wagon uprising. The felony charges had lasting impacts on many lives. Randy Carley went underground, changed his name to Travis, and retreated to an Oregon farm for a time. Dick LeClair also changed his name. Peter Kwant disappeared. Paul Spencer never returned to Austin except for a couple of brief visits.[81] Some of my good political comrades dropped out of movement politics for several years because they got freaked out by the street fighting.

The Outcome

First and foremost, thousands of students who either participated in the imbroglio or simply looked on learned that the police would indiscriminately beat and attack anyone in their line of fire. In this sense the police relinquished their ideological masquerade that they were there to serve law-abiding citizens and only arrest lawbreakers. The trust was gone.

The police also lost their aura of invincibility; they were chased off the campus grounds by an angry and determined mass of protestors. I cannot remember the outcome of when and how the Chuck Wagon returned to normalcy. I seem to recall that the cafeteria remained closed for some time. When it reopened, if there were monitors at the door checking for proper identification, that system of surveillance must have lasted no more than twenty minutes. The administration could not round up a reliable crew of pseudo-police to keep nonstudents out.

The closing of the Chuck Wagon was the opening round in an escalating show of force by the senior university administration (acting at the behest of the University Board of Regents) to assert their unbridled authority over campus grounds and to reclaim lost turf. While they often bungled through issues in ways that only made things worse for them, I believe that the university administration reasoned that they could get away with restricting entry to the Chuck Wagon because eventually the nonstudent targets of their opprobrium would move somewhere else. I do believe that their real goal was to break up networks of student and nonstudent radicals by denying them shared space on campus. The Chuck Wagon Riot was only a small piece of a much larger transition toward more militant tactics. While it proved to be sheer bravado, many political activists came to believe that a revolutionary situation was just around the corner.

The security forces resorted to new forms of repression, including using photographs to arrest people after the conclusion of demonstrations, to tap phones, and to expand the work of undercover informants. An increasing number of political activists began to call themselves guerillas and revolutionaries. We began to learn about protection against tear gas, how to engage in various acts of sabotage, and how protect each other from arrests. After the Chuck Wagon Riot, activists published and distributed such information in pamphlets and underground newspapers. We had come to believe that we needed to be prepared to protect ourselves and fight back in street actions.

These events sparked a war of words between liberal faculty and a group of Chuck Wagon 21 defendants. At root many liberal faculty members were upset that outside police forces violated the sanctity of university space. These liberals regarded the university campus facilities as sacred ground set aside for reasoned debate and rational discourse in which the intended outcome was never a violent confrontation but a mutual consensus under the principle of "we respectfully agree to disagree." What a liberal platitude! Steeped in the early twentieth-century mythology of academic life as a metaphorical place—an atmospheric Ivory Tower where those pursuing knowledge for its own sake were happily cut off from the rest of the world in favor of their own endeavors—these truly naive liberal faculty members could not break free from the ideal that the university constituted a state of privileged seclusion. Fantasies die hard.

The disciplinary action taken against six students in April 1967, which sparked the University Freedom Movement, and efforts to prevent *The Rag* and the New Left Education Project from distributing literature on campus should have disabused head-in-the-sand liberal faculty who held to the mistaken belief that the university was a hermetically sealed enclave separate from the nastiness of real-world politics. Released in March (more than three months after the riot), a detailed, eleven-page faculty senate committee report (called the *Grubbs Report*, after its chair, Professor Clifton Grubbs) pontificated about the unacceptable behavior of nonstudents in the Chuck Wagon yet put "part of the blame" on the university administration for "the incident which brought DPS officers and violence to the campus for the first time." The *Grubbs Report* concluded that the university administration lacked a coordinated response and reacted with confusion to the events. In short, the *Grubbs Report* blamed the unfortunate turn of events on a failure to communicate a top-down plan of action. The faculty senate recommended that the district attorney "should consider whether, in view of the confusion during the events of Nov. 10, so serious a charge as that of a felony is justified with regard to those persons who are not accused of direct destruction of property and who are liable, if at all, on felony charge, only indirectly and vicariously."[82] In their findings the *Grubbs Report* focused an inordinate amount of attention of juvenile "street people" who frequented the Chuck Wagon, engaging in mischief, panhandling, and sleeping.[83] To focus so much on nonstudent youth who came to the Chuck Wagon enabled the *Grubbs Committee* to appear as evenhanded and fair. But arriving at a way to deal with alleged misbehavior in the Chuck Wagon was to complicate a problem that was related in its entirety to police overreaction. Because we were convinced that the *Grubbs Report* contained information that would assist our legal defense, we demanded that the fact-finding committee release its findings. They did not comply.[84]

Everyone at the Chuck Wagon that day witnessed firsthand police violence and wanton brutality. In a blatant effort to combat negative publicity and to control the narrative, supporters of the police action flooded various media outlets with vain attempts to justify the law enforcement invasion. A report in the *Daily Texan* sought to disparage the Chuck Wagon protests, claiming that campus police were victims of abuse, and that they "don't make policy" and "only enforce the law as it stands." Chief Allen Hamilton defended his officers, whom he claimed did not overreact to hysteria and "handled themselves well." He also referred to an incident in which a juvenile nonstudent arrested on campus claimed that she made twenty-five dollars a day (a hearty sum in terms of the value of money at the time) by panhandling.[85] Entering into the fray, President Norman Hackerman defended university administrators against the charge that they did not actually know what was going on, claiming that Campus Police Chief Hamilton was authorized to act without consultation to bring in outside law enforcement.[86]

In response, the Chuck Wagon defendants issued a critique (prepared by Martin Wiginton) claiming that Campus Police Chief Allen Hamilton had indeed coordinated his security efforts by consulting the higher authority of Regents Chair Frank Erwin. The Chuck Wagon defendants blamed the entire incident on police overkill, demanding that all charges be dropped. While Steve Van (Union Board president) and Joe Krier (Students' Association president) said that they had evidence of dope dealing and prostitution coming out of the Chuck Wagon, the actual proof for this accusation never materialized.[87]

What did we learn from the Chuck Wagon police riot? What we gained from our experience was that the UT campus grounds offered no security against the heavy hand of outside law enforcement agencies. The Chuck Wagon imbroglio reinforced the fault lines between "us" and "them" and helped to render even minor compromise beyond reach. It also put to rest the illusion that the campus was open to outsiders who were free to make use of university facilities. Law enforcement overreaction and police use of clubs and tear gas produced a groundswell of support for our brand of countercultural politics. For those who were appalled by the police action, we came to understand the misrule of law. Even today, as of March 2024, there are posted signs outside the Student Union Building warning that "these facilities are available to faculty, students, and staff who can produce a valid ID." The Chuck Wagon is gone, a victim of remodeling of the University Union. It seems that the university administration is unwilling to forget.

The Chuck Wagon confrontation came on the heels of the Waller Creek protests. It is important to examine the chronology closely. Timing is everything. Both these incidents did not emerge directly out of the antiwar movement. They arose out of an interwoven, complex sequence of confrontations with law enforcement located both on campus and in Austin. The early period of protest, characterized by efforts to proselytizing against the Vietnam War, had evolved into a hydra-headed upsurge against what was deemed illegitimate authority.

The Law Commune Is Born and Grows

What evolved out of Chuck Wagon 21 legal effort was the consolidation of an organized legal arm for our movement. Quickly, the primary work of the Austin Law Commune was directed at political cases (both high-profile and rather mundane), including work with Vietnam veterans, drafter resisters, protesters arrested at demonstrations, and the like. Police regularly used the tactic of arresting people at rallies and demonstrations and charging them with such crimes as disorderly conduct, refusal to obey a lawful order, failure to disperse, and even resisting arrest and assault on a police officer. As the frequency, size, and militancy of demonstrations increased, the numbers of those arrested (and charged with felonies) escalated dramatically. The lawyers and legal aids in the Austin radical law collective worked tirelessly for us, and they worked for free. Despite the myriad felony charges leveled against us over the years, very few people were actually convicted.

The seeds of what eventually blossomed into the Austin Law Commune were sown at the 12–14 December 1968 Movement Legal Services held at a dude ranch in Wimberley, Texas.[88] This gathering called for the creation of a statewide legal defense structure. Martin Wiginton—whom an FBI special agent referred to as an "obnoxious 'old man's hippie"—took the lead in organizing this event.[89] Over the years Austin lawyers like Cam Cunningham and Jim Simons had come to the defense of active-duty GIs at Fort Hood for refusing to obey orders. The work of these lawyers, including Bobby Nelson and Brady Coleman, who also joined Law Commune, was invaluable to us. Within time the FBI wrongly identified these law offices as a "weatherman contact point" to justify wiretapping.[90]

Jail time in Austin was to be avoided at all costs. The Austin City Police stepped up their brutal treatment of antiwar activists jailed for various offences. Local police frequently placed our people in overcrowded cells with redneck thugs. Inmates beat and sodomized a self-styled Motherfucker and Vietnam Veterans Against the War (VVAW) member named Peter Kwant while he was in the Travis County Jail after his arrest on charges of first-time possession of marijuana. Movement lawyer Cam Cunningham filed a suit against the police. It was common knowledge that lockup police encouraged inmates to assault antiwar activists.[91]

Finally, our antiwar movement had sunk some deep roots in the fertile terrain of growing dissatisfaction with the US government, its failed war effort in Vietnam, and its inability to respond adequately to the legitimate demands of the civil rights struggle and the emergent Black Power movement. We were no longer a fringe element that could be easily dismissed as anti-American troublemakers. We were part of a groundswell of popular dissent. The battle lines were drawn more crisply than ever before.

Chapter 4

Direct Action and Disruption

Establishing a Public Presence for Popular Protest, 1970–1971

A coalition of political groups that originated outside the organizational framework of the antiwar movement planned a rally and march for 11 January 1970. Leaders of the coalition had applied for a parade permit, which the Austin City Council, as usual, denied. The debate that preceded the planned march focused on whether to march without legal authorization or postpone the event. We decided to proceed under any circumstances. Our ability to coordinate with so many different groups (ten to fifteen in all) was impressive: LUCHA ("the Struggle," a Mexican American group), UT Mexican American Student Organization, La Raza Unida, staff members of the *Rag*, SMC (who opposed marching without a valid permit), the Waller Creek Group of radical ecologists, Austin Welfare Mothers organization, representatives from the *Fatigue Press* (Fort Hood GI underground newspaper), Young Democrats from UT Austin, the Chuck Wagon Defendants, the ACLU, the SNCC, and the CUF breakfast program. Two features of the march and rally (organized under the banner "United We Speak") stood out: First, we were able to bring together racially diverse constituencies with a wide focus on protesting repression in local communities. Second, the antiwar message was not front and center. In order to avoid confrontations, the 250–300 marchers stuck to the sidewalks, proceeding from First and Congress Streets to Woolridge Park.[1]

Over the next several months, it became clear that we in the antiwar movement had grown weary of organizing one mass rally and march after another. Our antiwar protest meetings were filled with young people looking for political direction. In a confidential intelligence report submitted 4 May 1970, Burt Gerding actually got the story right: "Much of the ex-SDSers on campus have been drifting from one organization to another and not always supporting any one organization such as the Student Mobilization Committee (SMC)." In spring 1970 some non-PL and non-SWP/YSA antiwar activists formed what they called the Radical Alliance (RA) as a way of catalyzing antiwar sentiment. The RA (with police undercover agent Barbara Roseman as part of the leadership team) targeted University of Texas complicity in the war machine, particularly defense contracting and ROTC. In his confidential report, Burt Gerding claimed, "As usually happens when any action is initiated, MARTIN WIGINTON, and his two close associates LARRY CAROLINE and GREG CALVERT, usually step in and try to assume a prominent role in any action." This claim was only partially accurate. By this time both Greg Calvert and Larry Caroline were almost totally absent from campus organizing. Calvert was involved in building MDS (recruiting young professionals to the antiwar cause) and GI draft counseling, and Larry Caroline was connected with Greenbriar, an alternative school located outside Austin. In contrast, Martin Wiginton emerged as the key organizer of protest events. He was masterful in his attention to details: planning strategy, building coalitions, and constantly pushing for "street action."[2]

Stop the Draft Week, March 1970

The first Stop the Draft Week protests took place in October 1967 on college campuses and often spilled over into marches and rallies at local military facilities. The Oakland/Berkeley demonstrations that focused on the Oakland Army Induction Center in October 1967 turned into a massive riot in the streets of Oakland. In March 1970, responding to the national call for another round of Stop the Draft Week protests, we in Austin decided to participate in a local way.[3] We pulled together a group that included a contingent of Vietnam veterans from the local chapter of VVAW, lawyers, former SDS members, and some local high school students who were active in building antiwar sentiment in their schools. Altogether, we numbered around twenty to thirty people. I remember Martin Wiginton, Cam Cunningham, Billy Pope, David MacBryde, Steve Krinsky, Gretchen MacBryde, Steve Russell, Terry Dubose, Peter Megaw, and I in the group. We identified four high schools as targets for our actions during the week starting March 16: William B. Travis on Monday, A. N. McCallum on Tuesday, Stephen F. Austin on Wednesday, and John H. Reagan (now renamed Northeast Early College High School because John Reagan served in the Confederate government) on Thursday. We determined that it was legal for us to remain in the parking lots and on public sidewalks, but if we went on school grounds we would be asked to leave in no uncertain terms.[4]

In preparation we printed plenty of literature, including information leaflets on draft counseling services that were available in Austin and pamphlets on the war in Vietnam and US imperialism. In alliance with the New Mobilization Committee, the newly minted Gerard Winstanley Memorial Caucus (GWMC, consisting of radical sociology PhD students) took the lead in creating publicity for the event, passing out leaflets and writing a letter announcing the days of protests and high school locations that appeared in the *Daily Texan*. Perhaps it was this event that attracted the attention of George Carlson, head of security for the University of Texas System. He opened a file on the Winstanley Caucus and initiated a channel of communication with an undercover informant (a female PhD student in the Sociology Department) who reported to him about us.

A couple of Austin High School students, Peter Megaw and Alma Sollinger, created a comic book–like flyer for distribution at the various high schools to announce our arrival. The Armadillo Press, with which Peter Megaw was involved, printed the comic book. We agreed to avoid confrontation at all costs and to try to engage in serious conversations. We decided that the noon lunchtime hour offered the best opportunity to engage in meaningful discussions with curious students.

We went to Travis High School at lunchtime on Monday. Of course, prowar students did everything they could to intimidate us and drive us away.

The students that crowded around us were loud and boisterous and tried to prevent curious onlookers from talking with us. Yet we nonetheless managed to distribute a great deal of literature to eager students. We later learned that the high school football coach encouraged students to confront us.[5] On Tuesday we went to the McCallum High School. The dozen of us who gathered at the parking lot at noon were met with a combination of curiosity and hostility. As a newspaper reporter observed, "'short-haired' students who assembled across the street" pelted us with a few rocks and several eggs. One minor fistfight broke out. On the third day, we visited Austin High School, where the students who helped organize the effort and created the comic book leaflet had formed an ad hoc group to sponsor a rally in support of our visit. It was clear that tensions were escalating: The *Austin American-Statesman* carried news stories about how UT college students were spreading antiwar, pro-Communist propaganda at local high schools. Austin High School was considered to be more liberal than the other schools, but I learned later that the shop teacher mobilized a group of prowar high school students to physically oppose us. At noon we lined up across the road separating us from the school. The prowar students yelled at us and stormed across the street just as a group of Austin High School students, including a number of African American youngsters, came across the road and joined us. A little bit of rock throwing ensued, but Steve Russell and some of the other VVAW members stepped forward and stopped the assault in its tracks. They spoke the same language as the prowar students and quickly succeeded in engaging them in real conversations on the realities of Vietnam. When the antiwar students recognized that the hoped-for outcome of conversation had begun, they melted away to let talking unfold, unaffected by the presence of their prowar fellow students.[6]

The fourth day, at Reagan High School, was a wild roller-coaster ride. When the lunchtime school doors opened precisely at noon, a group of around a dozen students literally ran the seventy-five yards to the parking lot where we were standing in a cluster. Led by well-known members of the Reagan High School football team, this unruly crowd made a beeline for us. The first one to get to us was a short, wiry youngster who proceeded to leap headfirst, like a heat-seeking missile, into our group, which had bunched together for protection. The furies were unleashed. In the ensuing melee, the prowar students yelled obscenities, threw punches, and ripped at our literature. Counterdemonstrators chased and beat an antiwar student. Without the possibility of dialogue, we retreated—unsuccessful but unbowed.[7]

It turns out that the principal at Reagan High School had come on the loudspeaker system early in the morning, announcing to the student body that the Communists were coming to the school and told them in no uncertain terms that they were not to go to the parking lot at noontime. He then played the national anthem and asked the students to stand and recite the lines of the Pledge of Allegiance in respect for American democracy. Rather than a deterrent, this announcement had amounted to a call to arms.

Later on Thursday afternoon we held a demonstration at the Selective Service System offices, declaring their work to be a "public health hazard."[8] All in all, we were pleased with what we accomplished over the course of the week. Our Vietnam veterans were really successful in engaging in conversations with the high school students. What began as hostility mostly turned into really good discussions. The vets were believable. In effect, we had taken our message away from the confines of the university campus and established a presence where we were not welcome. As time went on, the movement became less tied to it college student roots, branching out into the wider community.

It so happens that the *Austin Statesman* newspaper assigned a young reporter, Barbara Worley, to cover the antiwar rallies at the four high schools. We won her over to our cause. In time she changed her name to Vernell Pratt, and became a leading figure in the Soeur Queens, a self-described all-girl honky-barroom band that produced a songbook called *Songs of Sisterhood.* The songbook was dedicated to spreading the message that "women in prison are prisoners of war."[9]

We were aware that high school students in Austin were becoming increasingly politicized and confrontational with administrative authorities in their schools. The route into politics came via the attraction of the countercultural movement. Until I read the Burt Gerding Papers, I did not know the extent to which the APD Criminal Intelligence had begun to take seriously the rising tide of political agitation and unrest among Austin high school students. A single APD intelligence report, dated 11 October 1968, under the subheading,

"'*The Roach*' Subversive Publication for Travis-Crockett High Schools," provides a window into dissension emerging in Austin high schools. In his report Burt Gerding recounts a conversation with the parents of Linda Adair, a former student at Travis High School and a first-year student at UT Austin. Mr. Adair reported that his daughter "had turned hippie, uses Marijuana and L.S.D. and has lived at various hippie pads with her ex-boyfriend."[10] The principal object of concern was the production and distribution of an underground newspaper called *The Roach*, essentially an information flyer that promoted the drug culture and contained an antiwar message. The Criminal Intelligence Division contacted the principals at both Travis and Crockett High Schools, who reported that unknown individuals had clandestinely distributed copies of this paper on their campuses. High school authorities were bound and determined to identify the culprits and root out dissent.

The Gerding Papers contain a copy of the first issue of *The Roach*. Of course, the term *roach* (like joint) was countercultural slang for a marijuana cigarette. In their opening statement, the editors of *The Roach* wrote that the purpose of the newspaper was "to test the reaction of the school [administration] to a trial in free speech and the press; to provide a means of student protest in writing; to do something which will bug the school establishment, and hopefully blow the fuse in some old robot teachers; to write uncensored material which will probably get us expelled, but will, of a certainty, give us great SATISFACTION." One contributor wrote that "the student is but a robot, a learning machine." Using capital letters, editors at *The Roach* also ridiculed "THE OLD BELLOWING BULL," an old-time football coach at Travis High School who memorized these words: "IF YOU DON'T GET CHILL BUMPS WHEN THEY PLAY 'DIXIE,' THEN WE DON'T WANT YOU HERE AT TRAVIS."[11]

The War Machine and ROTC

It's always the old to lead us to the wars
It's always the young to fall
Now look at all we've won with the saber and the gun
Tell me, is it worth it all?
. . .
But I ain't marching anymore
—Phil Ochs, "I Ain't Marching Anymore"

The practice of statecraft consisted of more than the repressive security apparatus. The war machine functioned as the vanguard of US imperial ventures at the time of the Vietnam War. Without the draft and the training of an officer corps, without university research facilities and large-scale corporate enterprises devoted to armaments production, the war machine would not operate at full capacity. We targeted all of these visible symbols of US imperialism.

Both in SDS and in other organizations in which I participated, one of our favorite targets was ROTC. In alliance with other organizations, we in the GWMC played a major role in organizing an anti-ROTC demonstration on 23 April 1970. In a discussion with Lt. Burt Gerding, Special FBI Agent Howard Riley came to believe that the GWMC "dreamed up" the 23 April 1970 ROTC demonstration at a "pot party" on the night of 22 April 1970.[12] We in the GWMC distributed leaflets under the rubric of the Anti-Creeping Meatball Coalition to announce the anti-ROTC demonstration. Under the heading, "Red Carpet Welcome for the Top Brass!!!!!!!!" we declared "Rise up and abandon the Creeping Meatball." I have absolutely no clue what the "creeping meatball" referred to.[13]

An estimated seventy-five protesters invaded the ROTC annual inspection for over an hour, marching around and trying to disrupt their solemn ceremonies, harassing the cadets and squirting them with water pistols. The *Daily Texan* printed a picture of me (without attribution) under the caption "Protesters Disrupt ROTC Inspection."[14] A staff reporter for the *Austin Statesman* described the protest in this way: "Hoots, jokes, taunts and a barrage of squirt gun spray greeted officers of the 4th Army Headquarters of San Antonio and the University Army ROTC cadets as they had come to inspect."[15] The well-known "yippie" John Lane kissed one of the Cordettes, the women's ROTC auxiliary. For this action law enforcement officers later charged him with aggravated assault, and he was given a bail bond of $1,000 (a huge sum at the time).[16]

This interruption of the annual ROTC ritual was sufficiently noticeable that it drew the attention of George Carlson, security chief for the whole UT System.[17] We were successfully able to hoist the NLF flag from the flagpole at the military parade. The military officer corps demanded

Anti-ROTC disruption, 23 April 1970. We inspect the "troops." Sponsored by the Anti-Creeping Meatball Coalition and Gerard Winstanley Memorial Caucus. Unidentified military officers on far left. Bill Meacham (*left side*) is in a white jacket and holding a clipboard, inspecting our troops. John Lane (*center*) is bearded and wearing a blue shirt. Doyle Niemann (*far right*) has his head down and is wearing shorts. David Dye (*second row*) is bearded and wearing a checkered shirt and smiling. He was subsequently fired from his teaching assistant position in the Department of Sociology. Courtesy of George Carlson Papers, camh-dob-017277, Dolph Briscoe Center for American History, University of Texas at Austin.

that the campus police arrest us, but they hesitated and then backed off. Watching us from the heights of their dormitory rooms that overlooked the parade grounds, students cheered us on and started playing the Phil Ochs song "I Ain't Marchin' Anymore" at full blast, serenading everyone with a strong antiwar message.[18]

Thinking about this response of dormitory residents in the months that followed, I realized that the goals at the start of the antiwar movement were to bring awareness and trigger action in opposition to the war. Now I realized that we had moved to the next stage. Rather than building political consciousness, our actions at the ROTC parade simply reflected general sentiments that were already there.

Anti-ROTC disruption, 23 April 1970. Steve Krinsky (*left*) and Doyle Niemann (*right*). Courtesy of George Carlson Papers, camh-dob-017276, Dolph Briscoe Center for American History, University of Texas at Austin.

Undercover police informants working with the Criminal Intelligence Division of APD observed the presence of the following members (and friends) of the GWMC—Steve Krinsky, David Dye, Molly Minus, Richard Minus, James Gundlach, Jan Marsten, Billy Pope, and Nancy Folbre. What was notable is that no arrests were made at the scene. Using photographic evidence of alleged wrongdoing, APD officers arrested ten people (including Steve Krinsky, Jan Marston, David Dye, Richard Minus, Doyle Niemann, and John Lane) on disorderly conduct charges not at the demonstration itself but over the next several weeks. In an ominous shift in law enforcement tactics, delayed arrests became a favored police tactic for the next several years.[19]

The damage to us was not finished.[20] Undercover police photographs provided the evidence that university officials needed to begin dismissal proceedings against vulnerable university employees with temporary contracts. In July 1970 the university administration announced that five teaching assistants—Steve Krinsky, Doyle Niemann, Jan Marston, David Dye, and Richard Minus—who pleaded guilty to disorderly conduct stemming from the anti-ROTC demonstration on 23 April were fired (or dismissed from voluntary work) from their paid positions.[21] Despite spirited protests mounted by the newly formed Teaching Assistants Association, the terminations remained permanent. Several of those dismissed ended up dropping out of their graduate programs.[22]

Nixon Invades Cambodia and the National Guard Shoots Students at Kent State: The World Is Turned Upside Down

Spring 1970 proved to be a landmark moment for the Austin antiwar movement. When President Nixon ordered US ground troops to invade Cambodia on 28 April 1970, he waited two days to announce on national television that the cross-border incursion had already begun. With resentment already building around the country over the seemingly endless war in Southeast Asia, this military escalation felt like the final straw. The invasion of Cambodia lit a powder keg, and it exploded.

We of course were already planning yet another rally and march for early May to coincide with national protests. Veterans of the antiwar movement met off campus at the YMCA to make plans. We decided not to bother to request a parade permit from the city council because of the consistent pattern of refusal to allow us to march in the streets. We planned a march route around the campus to end at the West Mall for a protest rally. As we publicized the event, we made no public acknowledgment or any mention of the plan to march in the streets because that would have alerted the police. As a prelude to the coming protests for the following week, we gathered on the patio in front of the Student Union Building on Sunday, 3 May, to burn an effigy of Richard Nixon.

The Kent State Massacre on Monday, 4 May, changed everything. The Ohio National Guard opened fire on a largely peaceful rally protesting the invasion of Cambodia and the presence of the National Guard presence on campus, killing four (including one innocent bystander) and seriously injuring nine other unarmed protesters. The Kent State incident marked the first time that any student had been killed in an antiwar gathering in United States history.

"Four Dead in Ohio" (Jeffrey Miller, Allison Krause, William Schroeder, and Sandra Scheuer). The Crosby, Stills, Nash, and Young song became an anthem: "Tin soldiers and Nixon's comin! We're finally on our own." Yes, we learned in a split second that we were on our own, without support except ourselves. Liberals believed that the system of laws, institutions, and electoral politics offered legal protection for law-abiding citizens. How wrong they were.

After Kent State and then the Jackson State police shootings on 15 May, when city and state police opened fire, killing two students, we came to viscerally understand our situation. In so many ways, the killings at Kent State and Jackson State marked a watershed in antiwar and antiracist politics in the United States. After Kent State many of us came to the realization that in order to step up our opposition to the Vietnam War, we could no longer depend upon the hollow shield of liberal platitudes about the neutrality of the law to protect us from repression. We found ourselves in a swirling vortex in which political stances were rapidly polarizing into two opposing camps, where differences (in ideology, lifestyles, and future goals) appeared across multiple fault lines. Living under circumstances in which we believed choice was exhausted, we felt we could not find a way to express our outrage other than direct confrontation. We began to see ourselves as fugitive outlaws in the shadows of legality. We were renegades occupying the frontier of a new dawn.

The fatal shootings at Kent State triggered an immediate and massive outrage on campuses and alternative lifestyle communities around the country. More than 4 million students participated in organized walkouts at hundreds of universities, colleges, and high schools, the largest student strike in the history of the United States at that time. These events undermined public support for Nixon's Vietnam policies and set in motion a national dialogue over ending the Vietnam War.

Suddenly, the political sentiments were unsettled and the world seemed turned upside down. Over the course of the events following the invasion of

Cambodia and the Kent State killings, a groundswell of popular anger spilled over into action. The willingness to use the Austin police and the Texas DPS officers as a visible force of repression, coupled with the callous disregard for human life displayed at Kent State, galvanized the Austin movement. Previously apathetic, disinterested, or even hostile students and community people joined the seemingly endless round of rallies, marches, and demonstrations. On Monday evening (4 May) a broad coalition of antiwar organizations and community activists gathered to call for a student strike and construct a list of four demands. The demands included (1) calling for an end to university complicity in the war machine; (2) expressing outrage over the invasion of Cambodia and issuing a demand for an immediate withdrawal of US troops; (3) condemning the attempted murder of Bobby Seale and seven other members of the Black Panther Party; and (4) endorsing the CUF and its breakfast program, including a demand to overturn the denial of a solicitation permit for this organization to collect funds on campus.

For four straight days, we filled the streets with angry and suddenly mobilized marchers. The huge outpouring of support for antiwar politics was unprecedented in terms of sheer numbers. Those of us who assumed leadership of the mass expression of protest were both jubilant with our success and horribly saddened by the senseless murders at Kent State. Day after day, increasingly larger crowds ignored the steadfast refusal of the Austin city officials to grant our formal requests for parade permits. We engaged in a series of unauthorized marches from the UT campus stronghold to the State Capitol building, located at the edge of downtown several miles away. These extralegal marches invariably resulted in daily clashes with law enforcement officers blocking our route.

Now, of course, the hardcore militants among us were spoiling for confrontations with the police. The local VVAW contingent insisted that they lead the marches, and sure enough, rather than doing an end-run around the police blockade at the corner of Guadalupe and Nineteenth Streets as we always did, they charged directly into police lines. Chaos ensued. The first three days of demonstrations and marches—Tuesday through Thursday, 5, 6, and 7 May, involved breaking around police lines, running down the streets, and converging on the State Capitol grounds.

"We Will Never Forget Kent State," 5 May 1970.
Courtesy of Alan Pogue, photographer.

As the news of what happened at Kent State reached us, a veteran leader, Martin Wiginton, filed an application with the City of Austin on 4 May for a parade permit for the following day. This application is preserved in the George Carlson Papers. "This parade permit request is submitted on short notice," Wiginton wrote, "because Richard Nixon did not give advance notice before ordering US troops into Cambodia." He estimated that two to eight thousand marchers would participate, marching from what he referred to as "Frank Irwin's University" to the State Capitol building. The application was ignored.[23]

On Tuesday, 5 May, we swung into action, engaging in picketing and mass leafleting that called for a student strike. We quickly set up plans to leaflet at high schools, shopping centers, downtown street corners, and university dorms. After an impromptu rally (including speakers from CUF, Chicano groups, and Women's Liberation) attended by over eight thousand people that began around noon, we staged an unruly march around campus, passing classroom buildings and dormitories to gather support. In a hand-written report, a political informant remarked about a march around campus

"Pigs 5, Students 0" sign at rally, 6 May 1970. The sign indicates the injuries to police versus injuries to protesters on an unauthorized march to the Stte Capitol the day before. Courtesy of George Carlson Papers, camh-dob-017270, Dolph Briscoe Center for American History, University of Texas at Austin.

on 5 May: "[I] do not believe we can control [the march around campus]." "Lot of straight kids and are teed off," the report continued. "A lot of liberals have become radical."[24]

On the north side of campus, the march veered off its predetermined course. The front line of the marchers moved onto the Drag. This unauthorized march elicited a hasty police response, and various skirmishes between police and protesters took place along the route, culminating with a confrontation at the State Capitol building. More than six thousand marchers had taken over the streets. At Nineteenth Street an unprepared contingent of police officers blocked the path of the march. The VVAW contingent at the front line of the demonstrators headed straight toward the police, while the rest successfully carried out an end run, bypassing the police by moving to the left. We used this tactic again when we reached

Fifteenth Street, totally confusing the police cordon. We broke away and headed for the Capitol. A large assembly of armed police in riot gear with bayonets and a supply of tear gas canisters proved no match for mobile protesters. All in all, we evaded police roadblocks three times, outflanking them and outsmarting them. Fistfights broke out between police officers and protesters, who threw rocks and bottles and set a few cars on fire. Police deliberately fired tear gas canisters over the heads of chanting crowds gathered at Eleventh Street and Congress, cutting off lines of retreat before they charged the protesters. Police arrested at least five protesters on the spot. Dozens of protestors invaded the Capitol building, and law enforcement agencies fired tear gas inside the Capitol Rotunda to dislodge the unwanted visitors. As a result of the melee, seventeen people were treated at local hospitals. Eleven were protesters and five were police. After retreating to the relative safety of the campus grounds, remaining protesters lowered the flag at the ROTC building to half-mast before police drove them away and stood guard.[25]

My twin brother and I made a home movie of these events, and I still have the video. There is plenty of marching, tear gas, and several burning cars. Innocent onlookers and bystanders were harassed and arrested. The police spared no one in their rampage. That evening a huge gathering of over ten thousand people gathered on the West Mall in front of the University Tower to discuss the day's events and plan for the next day.

Perhaps what disturbed the APD most was that the Texas DPS apprehended five militants traveling from Houston to Austin. Law enforcement agents reported that this group was in possession of a .45-caliber automatic pistol, a shotgun, and numerous clubs and fighting sticks. Intelligence reports also indicated that two other carloads of militants from Houston were en route to Austin with weapons and ammunition.[26]

In a news conference after the 5 May riot had subsided, Chief Robert Miles of the APD promised, "We will be much better prepared tomorrow, a much better supply of tear gas for one thing. Tomorrow we will have more manpower and more equipment." Governor Preston Smith chimed in, promising that he would resort to "whatever alternatives are at hand" to enforce compliance with the law.[27]

Police at demonstration, ready for action, 6 May 1970. Courtesy of Alan Pogue, photographer.

The next day, Wednesday, 6 May, various political organizations came together to sponsor an all-day rally and teach-in that brought more than ten thousand people to demand that the university be shut down Thursday and Friday. Speakers included representatives from a range of groups and tendencies, including CUF leaders speaking against the war and in support of their breakfast program. As police helicopters circled overhead, there were speeches on US imperialism, race consciousness, and women's liberation. After a rally at the ROTC building, we orchestrated a 4:00 p.m. march to the J. J. Pickle Federal Building. Some leaders discussed storming the building, but in the end the crowd decided against it. Protesters had come prepared for violent confrontations with the police and more tear gas: Many wore heavy boots and long pants in the May heat, carrying wet rags or gas masks and rubbing Vaseline under their eyes to protect against tear gas.[28]

An undercover informant—who may have been Joe Lawley, from Naval Intelligence—suggested that the crowd could reach five thousand marchers ready to fan out after the noon rally and disrupt classes. This same informant worried that "Black [participants] are pushing for a march whether permit or not." Doyle Niemann, Paul Turner, David Pratt, Larry Jackson, Paul Spencer, and Gavan Duffy were preparing an injunction to permit marches off campus. Because they could not identify a leading organization capable of orchestrating the protest actions, undercover informants suggested that the crowd was restive and unruly, and that protesters were "sitting around, waiting for action. They do not know what to do—could go either way. No leadership." The undercover informant claimed there was "no leader—which is bad." For the security forces, this lack of leadership meant they did not know what to expect.[29]

This false impression that leadership was missing failed to take into account that key figures from various organizations—veterans of the antiwar movement—were engaged in deep discussions about how to coordinate our actions and how to mobilize the thousands who rallied to our cause. One core aim was to inform and educate those who were drawn to protest out of anger but came without a firm understanding of the politics behind protest. We knew that we needed to provide an understanding of the goals of the antiwar movement. Following a noon rally, we sponsored dozens of teach-ins spread across multiple venues on campus grounds. These teach-ins included the GWMC on "Sociology and Tear Gas" held in Garrison Hall, the Venceremos Brigade and Cuba Outreach, Free Bobby Seale, racism in Austin, the Chicano Struggle, Gay Liberation, the GI movement, and why the war expanded to Cambodia. All of these activities were a prelude to a raucous march the next day to the J .J. Pickle Federal Building and the State Capitol.

As day turned into night on Wednesday, 6 May, a festival-like atmosphere unfolded. As a component of the student strike, we sponsored a camp-out on the university mall involving thousands of students and community people. Hundreds of people brought sleeping bags and spent the night under the stars on the mall, local musicians played, and even fraternity and sorority members came by, unable to contain their curiosity. One undercover informant went so far as to suggest that hungry protesters might attempt to steal food at the nearby student dormitory, Jester Commons.[30]

Police Officer holding tear gas dispenser, prepared for battle, 6 May 1970. Courtesy of Prints and Photographs Collection, e_ppc_00052, Dolph Briscoe Center for American History, University of Texas at Austin.

Contingent of police officers firing tear gas canisters on protest march, 6 May 1970. Courtesy of Prints and Photographs Collection, e_ppc_0028, Dolph Briscoe Center for American History, University of Texas at Austin.

In an APD intelligence report labeled "Further Activities of General Strike on UT Campus" and dated Wednesday, 6 May 1970, Lieutenant Gerding reported with alarm that demonstrators at a nighttime rally held up a sign that read "Pigs–5, Students–0." The sign indicated that at the march the day before, five police officers had sustained injuries during clashes the previous day, while no students were badly injured. Gerding observed, "It became apparent that a great number of otherwise uninvolved students were becoming radicalized and would participate in the action, such as occurred on May 5, and is planned for May 6." It is gratifying to hear this admission. We had done the long, hard work of proselytizing. When the crisis erupted, we were ready to bear the fruit of our endeavors.[31]

Gerding reported that campus radicals were making two "impossible demands" on President Norman Hackerman—close the university for a week and open up space for a legitimate occupation of university facilities.[32] Of course, Hackerman did not accede to these demands. On behalf of the university administration, he issued a predictably constructed response: "The university will remain open to all who wish to attend classes." The chair of the Board of Regents, Frank Irwin, announced on 7 May the unanimous decision of the regents that "during the remainder of the current semester the institutions comprising the UT System shall remain open and

Unauthorized protest march, 7 May 1970. Martin Murray (*front, far left*), Doyle Niemann (*center*), and Johnny Gevissa and Steve Krinsky (hoisting National Liberation Front flag, *right*). Johnny B. Jenkins, photographer. Courtesy of Prints and Photographs Collection, e_ppc_0049, Dolph Briscoe Center for American History, University of Texas at Austin.

available to those students who wish to attend regularly scheduled classes and examinations." In the interim, the Faculty Senate (in a rebuke to the regents) voted to suspend classes.[33]

We closed down the university anyway. During these tumultuous days, we stopped all normal university business, occupying buildings and holding impromptu teach-ins. Actually, the university shut itself down, straining under the sheer weight of its inertia and irrelevance as a space of higher learning. The university as a machinelike entity that carried out its bureaucratic business as usual on a daily basis just imploded. University staff just did not show up for work. We occupied university buildings without any opposition.

On Thursday morning, 7 May, demonstrators set up picket lines to support the strike. Teach-ins and mini-rallies erupted everywhere.[34] Handwritten police undercover reports announced with alarm, "Groups of striking students barged into classrooms unannounced, calling for a boycott of classes." We sponsored teach-ins on numerous topics. The boycott effectively brought everyday activities to a standstill. The usually timid faculty

In the streets, 7 May 1970. Doyle Niemann is carrying the National Liberation Front Flag on the left, and Johnny Gevissa is center right. Johnny B. Jenkins, photographer. Courtesy of Prints and Photographs Collection, e_ppc_0027, Dolph Briscoe Center for American History, University of Texas at Austin.

called an emergency meeting, voting by a wide margin to cancel classes and requesting the city council to grant a parade permit. Efforts to get a parade permit from the city council for Friday ended in failure. Protesters gathered and decided to march in the streets with or without official authorization. In a panic Governor Preston Smith called out the National Guard, and they arrived in full riot gear. Carloads of counterprotesters and Texas rednecks cruised the Drag with their shotguns at the ready. It was indeed a tense and ominous atmosphere.[35]

Confidential reports found in the Gerding Papers provide some insight into what the APD and other policing agencies were thinking. The FBI placed sharpshooters on top of the Tower and snipers on top of buildings between the campus and downtown. About two hundred riot-equipped police lined up along Twenty-First Street. Shouting "Pigs off Campus," protesters managed to push the police back to Nineteenth Street. One authoritative report claimed that police units were under orders to shoot and kill anybody who came off campus. The police were determined not to allow anyone to get onto the Austin streets.[36]

The university was shut down and ceased to function with any semblance of normalcy from Tuesday through Friday. The GWMC (including me, Steve Krinsky, John Houghton, Gary Fitzgerald, Richard Minus, Carlo Ginoletti, Jim and Carol Gundlach, Sarah Rosenbaum, and Jan Hullum) virtually seized the sociology department offices located in Garrison Hall. We hung a huge National Liberation Front (NLF) flag out the second-floor window overlooking the main quad underneath the tower; it flew for about a week before we took it down. (I still have NLF and Pathet Lao flags that we made for demonstrations.) Caucuses emerged in the School of Architecture, the Law School, and departments like political science, English, and history. We linked these caucuses to build a shut-it-down movement on the campus. Almost overnight the scope and depth of the protest movement exploded, the ideological commitment to constructing an alternative vision of education suddenly became relevant, and the extent to which core radicals were able to reach out to new constituencies who had never been active or involved in protest politics in the past appeared as if by magic.

Liberals who up until this time refused to sponsor or participate in rallies and demonstrations suddenly found their nerve. Seeing an opportunity to reclaim a bit of relevance, they wanted to seize the high ground of leadership. Jeff Friedman, a third-year law student at UT School of Law, jumped into the fray, bypassing us and, along with several fellow law students and professors, filed a legal petition with the federal court to request permission for a march on city streets on 8 May. He and his liberal Law School colleagues were granted a parade permit to march from the university to the State Capitol for a rally. This march was the first that city officials ever allowed to take place. The radicals were forced to share the spotlight with "Give Peace a Chance" liberals, who hijacked the legal negotiations with the City of Austin. Perhaps not surprisingly, the city council remained adamant, refusing to grant a parade permit. A groundswell of popular protest arose against this decision. At the end of the day, a federal court order overturned the council decision, allowing a march on Friday, 8 May. In his judgement US District Court Judge Roberts viewed the Austin parade permit ordinance, which was used time and time again to outlaw marches, to be unconstitutional.[37]

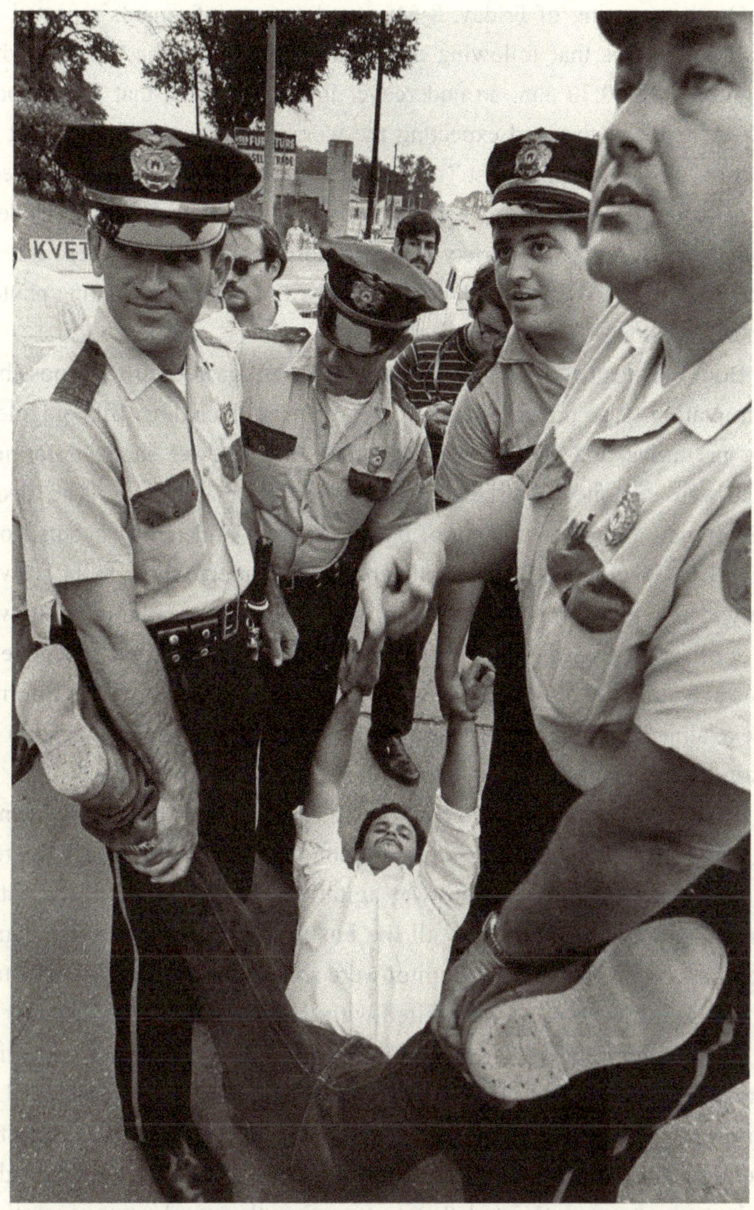

Police contingent arresting a protester, 7 May 1970. Courtesy of UT Texas Student Publications, Prints and Photographs Collection, e_ppc_0043, Dolph Briscoe Center for American History, University of Texas at Austin.

On the morning of Friday, 8 May, undercover informants reported in handwritten notes that following the federal court order the "Law is with the group." At 10:30 a.m. an undercover informant noted that "everybody freaked, apprehensive and expecting the worst." "[I] do not know what is going on. Will have rally first." The same undercover informant observed: "lot of straight kids, moderates, but do not know what [to expect]." Undercover informants from a variety of law enforcement agencies were out in force. They mingled freely with the large crowds of protesters, taking photographs at random.[38]

Both the security forces and protest marchers geared up for a possible confrontation. The police issued riot equipment, including fifty goggles, forty gas masks, and twenty-four respirators. At least three dozen uniformed police were stationed at strategic points along the march route. The Texas DPS brought a huge contingent of police officers. Undercover agents from APD, Texas DPS, and military intelligence were scattered through the crowd. One undercover informant noted that marchers were assembling wet-towel kits to offset tear gas, and were "expecting trouble, size of crowd will govern [how much trouble]." Adding a sense of comic relief, this undercover informant exclaimed, "Those present on the main mall gave a standing ovation to Austin Police. Fantastic, great, super."[39]

The 8 May march was the crowning achievement of the spring events of 1970. This peaceful parade was a monumental success and represented the culmination of years of antiwar agitation. The entire City of Austin was brought to a standstill, as all the businesses along the march route from the campus to the State Capitol were shut down, traffic was diverted for hours, and the streets were filled with thousands of protesters. All in all, the march stretched for miles, filling the streets and sidewalks with protesters. It took a full thirty-five minutes for the marchers from the UT campus to pass beyond Congress Avenue. Marchers arrived at the Capitol grounds before the last contingents left the campus departure point. Independent observers estimated that twenty-five thousand persons participated—the third or fourth largest street demonstration anywhere in the country at this time.[40]

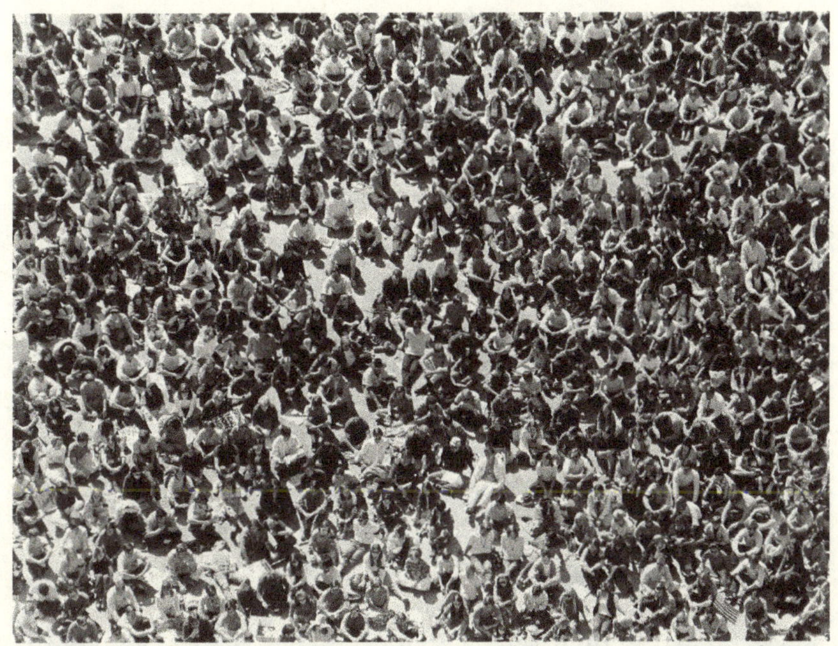

Rally in preparation for mass march and demonstration, 8 May 1970. Courtesy of Prints and Photographs Collection, camh-dob-017293, Dolph Briscoe Center for American History, University of Texas at Austin.

On Friday, 8 May—the last day of an exhaustive wave of building take-overs, marches, and rallies—Jeff Friedman, a person who was never active in the antiwar movement before or after, seized the reins of control over the liberal opposition to the war in Vietnam. With the determined look of a leader, Friedman rode in an open car at the head of the march, waving and cheering, feeling quite self-important about his newly discovered notoriety. He was proud of his instant interest in antiwar politics and his conversion to a new brand of political expression that was completely unfamiliar to him and his colleagues. Behind Friedman and the car, the first line of marchers at the head of the parade solemnly carried a casket that was painted red, white, and blue. The second line of marchers carried seven American flags, some of which were altered with peace signs replacing the stars. Included in this medley was a yellow flag inscribed with "Conscription without Representation is Tyranny: Don't Tread on Me."

Mass march, 8 May 1970. An estimated twenty-five thousand on protest march, the third largest demonstration in the country. Johnny B. Jenkins, photographer. Courtesy of Prints and Photographs Collection, camh-dob-017292, Dolph Briscoe Center for American History, University of Texas at Austin.

This protest march and rally at the Capitol consisted of a whole range of political organizations and constituencies. Dozens of newly formed groups march behind their own self-made banners: "Austin High School Students—Stop the War," "Travis County Medical Doctors for Peace," and so on, seemingly ad infinitum. The tiny Spartacist League group carried their broad banner "All

Mass March, 8 May 1970. Courtesy of Alan Pogue, photographer.

Southeast Asia MUST go Communist," next to a hastily formed "High School Teachers for Peace" contingent participating in their first public antiwar protest. Marchers for "Gay Liberation" mingled with the angry VVAW collective. For one brief moment, the world was indeed turned upside down. Only one person was arrested—a youngster from Houston charged with abusive language.[41]

Active-duty GIs, Fort Sill (Oklahoma). Courtesy of Alan Pogue, photographer.

Over the course of the May 1970 demonstrations, large numbers of protesters were arrested on charges ranging from resisting arrest and failure to comply with a lawful order to disorderly conduct and assault on a police officer. There were a few arrests on charges of destruction of property. For example, Joe Crawford (an undercover informant) witnessed Laredo Cole trying to set fire to a building. In September the courts convicted Cole of attempted arson.[42]

In May 1970 Friedman pretended to be a leader. In time he was able to parlay his proverbial fifteen minutes of fame as a campus activist into a politically acceptable effort to propel himself into elected political office. In 1971 he became the youngest person ever elected to the Austin City Council. In 1975, at age 30, he was elected mayor of Austin, campaigning on a liberal reformist agenda. Widely known as the "hippie mayor," Friedman had cobbled together a loose alliance of young liberal-leaning voters, including African Americans and Chicanos, to build his electoral coalition. His time in office was short-lived. Within a few years, he was gone.

In a real sense, we had achieved the impossible. The counterculture served as a bridge linking various disparate subgroups in a common,

Gay Liberation contingent at mass march and demonstration, 8 May 1970. Courtesy of Alan Pogue, photographer.

albeit temporary, bond. Longhairs and rednecks mixed freely and cordially in Austin's country-and-western bars. After 1970 Texas "torpedoes" (foot-long, rolled joints) were everywhere, and the feared drug bust for users and small-time dealers became almost extinct. This free-wheeling spirit came in the wake of severe repression for possession of marijuana in earlier years. Also seemingly overnight, the majority of young Austin residents—students and nonstudents alike—had turned against the war in Vietnam. Alternative lifestyles flourished, communal living arrangements were the norm: being mellow and doing your own thing were honored values to be emulated, praised, and aspired to.

The events of April–May 1970 triggered widespread outrage that penetrated into the thick layers of the liberal mantra of working within the system. In the run-up to this large march, all sorts of players clamored for a piece of the action. The invasion of Cambodia and killings at Kent State turned the tide, suddenly giving legitimacy to opposing the war in Southeast Asia. Appalled by Nixon's Cambodia invasion and killings of students, ad hoc liberal groups were spurred to action, suddenly declaring their opposition to the war in Vietnam. While certainly not unique to Austin, liberal groups sought to assert themselves into leadership roles in political opposition to the Nixon administration's widening of the war. In the long run, this blending of liberal and radical participation transformed antiwar sentiment from what began as a fringe position into a mainstream political issue. While they had remained bystanders and docile up until this point, all sorts of groups and individuals now turned up. Timid and unable to take a stand before, the Faculty Senate voted to support the 8 May march and volunteered to send dozens of "march monitors" with the goal of creating a cordon sanitaire between the massive police contingents and the protest marchers. Paternalistic liberal do-gooders to the end!

On 15 May 1970, police opened fire on an antiwar demonstration at Jackson State College, killing two protesters. While this horrible event cried out for general outrage and protests, it received very little attention at the time. The radical faction of the antiwar movement staged a protest rally, but we did not achieve the same support as we did for the shootings at Kent State.

Assessment

> The entire University swarms with hippie types. Unbathed, unshaven, barefoot, bearded, etc. hunkered around in little groups all over the campus and surrounding areas, like bewildered animals. . . . The lethargic characters barely look as though they may be in the human race. . . . For far too long now colleges and universities, under the false guise of "academic freedom," have been spawning grounds for treason and degradation.
>
> Henry Fessi, disgruntled parent[43]

The dividing lines between the antiwar movement and the establishment were clearly drawn. Outside observers—like Henry Fessi, perhaps an FBI COINTELPRO invention—were unable to comprehend that something was happening that they did not understand. The movement had merged with an alternative lifestyle and offered a different way of seeing the world.

The May 1970 strike was the most forceful display of student power in the New Left antiwar movement. It marked the highpoint of popular antiwar protests following years of student activism and community mobilization throughout the 1960s. Campus administrators and law enforcement agencies learned some valuable lessons on how to control or undermine popular dissent. The UT administration and the Texas legislature adopted a series of regulations restricting the rights to peaceful assembly and free expression, including creating obstacles standing in the way of parade permits and permission for rallies. Building and grounds officials introduced antiriot landscaping and physical engineering, breaking up the large, open space both on the West Mall and inside the Student Union. The university administration authorized the construction of a new wall along Guadalupe, and new buildings were designed with many doors and lots of glass to make student occupations more difficult. In clear violation of the US Constitution, campus officials restricted free speech areas and established limited hours for assembly. UT police were armed, acquired full law enforcement powers, and were given original jurisdiction in the campus area. At the same time, the student movement opened spaces for the recognition of new rights for ethnic minorities and women. New regulations eased in loco parentis restrictions, inaugurated places for student participation in faculty committees, and challenged admissions policies that restricted access for minority groups.[44]

Until the May 1970 events, we were primarily a disparate bunch of agitators, trying to build a movement and broaden consciousness against the war, racism, and misogyny. After the massive marches and occupation of the university during the first week of May 1970, the widespread consciousness against the war and against the established political order had swung to our side. After this time we were like free-floating agitators swimming in a vast sea of political opposition.

Expanding Repertoire

We expanded our repertoire of tactics and addressed new audiences that would have been impossible to reach just a few months earlier. Student Body President Jeff Jones (with deep and longstanding roots in the antiwar movement) and his student government group began to speak at fraternities about opposition to a proposed tuition increase and against the war. Those of us not affiliated with the electoral coalition holding power in student government worked with local non-university antiwar groups linked with local churches. In June a coalition of yippies and a newly formed liberal-radical group called Outreach (that worked in support of the George McGovern campaign) targeted the annual convention, sponsored by the Texas State American Legion, for high school students called Boys State held on the UT campus. Former Texas State Attorney General Waggoner Carr was the keynote speaker at the earlier 1969 Boys State convention. He urged the assembled crowd of youngsters to "take the offensive against the longhaired mad dogs and dirty rattlesnakes" of their generation. Carr singled out SDS (no longer an active political organization) as "Hitler-type revolutionaries" who have "kidnapped college presidents, closed colleges, barricaded buildings, ransacked official records, forced college deans to walk before them like prisoners in a chain gang, howled curses and foul words at respected public officials, demanded huge sums of money from our nation's churches with the threat to seize all churches and hold them if the money is not paid." Undeterred in his unhinged diatribe, he claimed that SDS "is spreading its poisonous tentacles" into high schools. "In my youth it was the Nazi movement that threatened to destroy America. In your day, it is the SDS," he shouted. "I, for one, are tired of being on the defensive. I am American and proud of it. Our land is not perfect but while you and I are working together for a better day, I am not going to sit idly by and watch these radical subversives destroy us." He ended his speech on an us-versus-them rhetorical note: "The militant minorities [meaning African Americans] are doing all the demanding. It is you and I who should be making the 'non-negotiable demands' of them. Well, let's get started. Are you ready? From this moment on, let's take the offensive."[45]

Wow. Fiery words indeed. While his strongly worded plea may have deterred many, at least some were curious enough to engage. A group of about fifty antiwar activists marched to Jester Hall, where the high school students were staying. The march on the first night led to a near confrontation over the distribution of leaflets calling for a high school bill of rights and antiwar literature. The second night antiwar activists were able to engage in sometimes heated but also serious discussions.[46]

The antiwar movement spawned small cells that planned and executed clandestine arson and bombing attacks on symbols of power. In October 1970 campus police responded to an attempted arson attack on the Law School.[47] On several occasions the ROTC Building was firebombed. Law enforcement agencies in Austin began to ready themselves for a wave of arson and bombings. Unlike other hotbeds of antiwar activity, Austin did not experience a great deal of destruction of property due to deliberate acts of sabotage.[48]

A local Austin Women's Liberation group staged a protest over an Alpha Tau Omega fraternity poster announcing an upcoming football game. The poster displayed a woman with big breasts under the sign "Bust UCLA." This protest ignited angry arguments and a huge crowd of onlookers. In September over two hundred people attended a Women's Liberation conference in Austin, advocating abortion rights and the end to sexist treatment.[49] In a parallel fashion, political activists began to engage in campaigns to support workers, sponsoring unionizing efforts among teaching assistants and campus workers. In September 1970 political activists were able to gain the endorsement of the AFL-CIO in support of the formation of a union for university co-op workers.[50]

Electoral Politics as Deviation

Some political activists were more willing to work closely with liberals. For example, during the 1970 campus shutdown, Doyle Niemann and Jeff Jones invited John Kenneth Galbraith to speak at a major antiwar rally. Many of us opposed this invitation, thinking that Galbraith was a well-known liberal and would offer what we thought was the wrong (work-within-the-system) message. The radical/liberal division was closely linked with the fundamental schism—as a matter of principle—between engagement in electoral politics and abstentionism. The electoral campaign of Jeff Jones for University of Texas student body president (1970) caused a great deal of rancor in movement circles, dividing friends from one another. For most political activists, participation in local Democratic Party politics was beyond the pale of respectability, even though some of our most trusted comrades flirted with participation in mainstream politics.

Put into broader perspective, the division between electoralism and abstentionism (or rejection of electoral politics) was real but not particularly significant. For sure, Mariann Vizard, Gavan Duffy, and others became involved in the Frances "Sissy" Farenthold campaign in the Texas Democratic Party gubernatorial primary in 1972. Victoria Foe, Judy Smith, and Pat Cuney engaged in local Democratic Party politics. According to Doug Rossinow, they "engineered a virtual takeover of their local Democratic Party precinct in Austin," and "without necessarily meaning to, [Cuney and Foe] rode the McGovernite 'new politics' wave to influence partisan politics."[51] I know for a fact that Cuney and Foe were never supporters of George McGovern. Yet some antiwar activists believed that through working in liberal Democratic Party causes, they might be able to steer them in a more radical direction. In the end, this entrist strategy produced few positive results.

There were those abstentionists—and Martin Wiginton, who himself had a long history of working in Democratic Party politics, was the key person here—who strongly objected to what he regarded as meaningless charade that merely reinforced faith in the American two-party system. The abstentionists also believed that the essence of the early SDS ideal of participatory democracy ran directly counter to conventional two-party electoral politics, and, furthermore, there were other, more effective methods of grassroots political organizing that inspired ordinary people to "take control over their own lives."[52] The abstentionists adamantly opposed any and all participation in electoral politics not only because it played into the liberal illusion that gradual reform with the established system was possible, but also because it was a waste of valuable energy that could be devoted to other more fruitful endeavors.

We kept up our protests, moving seamlessly into community activism that took us off campus. On Halloween 1970 (31 October), we organized yet another march (coinciding with marches around the country sponsored by the National Peace Action Coalition [NPAC]) to the State Capitol to not only protest the Vietnam War but also raise all sorts of other issues. This ecumenical march included the SMC, Gay Liberation, Women's Liberation, and many other groups. This march attracted the attention of the head of security for the UT System, George Carlson, because of a large contingent of antiwar activists coming from Houston and elsewhere.[53] That evening we sponsored street parties in the student residential neighborhoods near the UT campus. Upset by the affront to their authority to control the streets, APD officers arrived and tear-gassed the predominantly student and hippie crowd.

Antiwar sentiment spawned new organizations and new targets for protest. A group called Direct Action, with roots in church-based pacifist traditions, took the lead in organizing antiwar actions with inventive tactics. While I was not part of this organization, it was effective. In December 1970 Direct Action sponsored an anti–war tax march and rally at IRS building and at the nearby downtown headquarters office for Southwestern Bell Telephone. Campus police arrested two Direct Action members, a Catholic priest, and a member of American Friends Service Committee when they slipped onto the playing field during the Texas-Arkansas football game, carrying a huge banner that read "Don't Pay Telephone War Tax."[54]

Confrontation, Direct Action, Militancy, 1971–1972

After the large-scale marches and rallies following the Cambodia invasion and the killings at Kent State and Jackson State, the movement in Austin began to drift inexorably toward two distinct poles: one more countercultural and the other calling for direct action and political engagement. At the countercultural end of the spectrum, there were those who tired of marches and rallies without any seeming progress on ending the war. These people believed that continuous marches and confrontational politics were a dead end, and they retreated into self-built communities and alternative institutions as their personal way to opt out of the system. At the political end of the spectrum, there were those of us who advocated continued engagement with politics, identifying capitalist imperialism as the source of oppression and exploitation, and calling for direct action and more confrontational politics.

Those of us who saw ourselves primarily as political activists were confronted with a novel and contradictory situation. We were no longer preoccupied with finding creative ways to convince ever greater numbers to accept our antiwar message. Within the broader community and youth movement, we faced what in the end turned out to be a losing battle. While we were able to mobilize consistently large numbers for rallies and demonstrations for particular events, we were unable to engage the counterculturalists in the kind of sustained day-to-day preparation required to reach out, and win over, new constituencies, particularly working-class communities. Large numbers of alienated youth simply chose to withdraw ("drop out") of the political struggle to change structures and institutions.

Within the political left, we also came face-to-face with or own ideological differences, stylistic preferences, and accumulated contradictions. These had remained a bit frozen while we took on antiwar and antiracism work. In Austin many veteran stalwarts of the early antiwar movement had either left town for extended periods or were somewhat inactive.

Yet from around late 1969 to 1973, the leadership core of the antiwar movement remained relatively stable. Anywhere from thirty to sixty people more or less took turns serving as leaders of myriad organizations, caucuses, and groups that emerged, developed, and collapsed. Ideologically, there were at least three separate currents. One tendency argued for building a broad anti-imperialist, prosocialist front that would both reach out to nonstudent, nonyouth working-class constituencies and maintain a high level of visible militancy. I gravitated to this position. For a time we turned toward strategic thinking, attempting to evaluate how other movements had confronted similar dilemmas and pushed forward. The visceral anti-intellectualism of the New Left in Austin was too strong, and this current that called for building nonsectarian political organizations—and certainly not Marxist–Leninist parties—never gained sufficient traction to reach a place of hegemony or dominance. I was always a bit uncomfortable with this current because many of the radicals who found a home here seemed a bit mesmerized with detached theoretical reflection and were too critical of direct action and street politics.

Another tendency promoted a kind of self-conscious populism grounded in a kind of free-floating radicalism, measuring its success in the ability to work with liberals who flocked to the movement after spring 1970. While many of us preached against electoral politics and against making alliances with liberals and the Democratic Party, these self-conscious populists gravitated to the view (often unstated) that we should downplay the politics of anti-imperialism and socialism and instead embrace a sort of reformist populism as the most effective way to bring the Vietnam War to an end.

The third major current demanded action, and sometimes (unfortunately) action for its own sake. This "action faction" embodied the anti-intellectualist currents that were always strong in the Austin movement, and those who adhered to this position strongly believed that only confrontational politics would be able to force the powers that be to abandon their commitment to the war in Vietnam. The goal of this movement faction was to mobilize large demonstrations, take to the streets, and clash with the police. This ideological current emerged as the most powerful tendency during 1971–1972, but it was unable to sustain momentum after the Paris Peace Accords of January 1973. While I certainly had my intellectual reservations, I worked most closely with this faction.

Despite the gravity of the issues that bound it together, the Austin movement was also internally divided along a number of fault lines. The contradictions of racism and sexism divided the movement from the beginning. In Austin very few African American, Chicano, or other minority groups participated fully and actively in the student, youth, and community movements. The one exception was the GI movement clustered around VVAW. The Austin movement failed miserably here to build a multiracial organization. Yet by way of an explanation, Black and Chicano activists wanted, and insisted on, their own separate organizations. By 1968 some SDS women formed consciousness-raising groups as separatist organizations. By the 1970s the fully fledged Women's Liberation Movement had ballooned to enormous proportions. In so many ways, radical women were much better at transcending differences to get their message of misogyny and sexism into the wider mainstream. By 1971 small and dedicated affinity groups like the Women's International Terrorist Conspiracy from Hell (WITCH) were engineering their own independent actions, like impromptu guerrilla theater operations and painting graffiti such as "Free Food Today" on supermarket walls. Gay and lesbian groups formed their own autonomous organizations.

In retrospect, I can locate the lack of political unity in the Austin movement in a historical perspective that at the time I was not able to fully comprehend. We developed a sufficiently sophisticated critique of US imperialism and offered a naive yet workable understanding of socialism as an alternative to corporate capitalism. We tended to look at socialism through rose-tinted glasses, and did not grasp the multiple variants of the collective ownership of the means of production and did not fully understand how political authority operated. As products of our social upbringing in the post–World War II period, we were totally unprepared for how to confront the issues of racism, sexism, and homophobia.

Early Spring Flowers, 1971

Between 8 February and 25 March 1971, the Army of the Republic of South Vietnam launched a failed military campaign called Operation Lam Son 719 that involved a cross-border incursion into Laos. This operation depended upon massive US air support.[55] On 10 February 1971, a coalition of antiwar groups and leaders—including Jeff Jones (People's Peace Treaty), Bobby Gonzales (GI movement), Melissa Singler (YSA and SMC), and in all likelihood a representative from CUF—shared the stage for the rally on the Main Mall in front of the tower. This rally against the invasion of Laos attracted only a small crowd of a little more than a couple of hundred people. We were very disappointed.

We kept up the pressure on selected targets, particularly military recruitment efforts on campus. On 19–20 February 1971, we organized a two-day protest against Navy recruiters.[56] Under the slogan designed to be provocative, "Join the Navy and Kill Slope Heads" (in retrospect, a terribly racist slogan, and something we should be ashamed of), we organized marches, rallies, and guerilla theater against Navy recruiters. For our Thursday and Friday rallies, we were able to attract about 150 people for each event. VVAW played a significant part of our messaging.[57]

Broadly speaking, the success of our antiwar rallies and marches triggered a backlash. A group of religious fundamentalists and self-avowed conservatives sponsored a rally attended by three to four hundred people on the grounds of Texas State Capitol. Using slogans like "Victory over sin," "Victory over Communism," and "Victory in Christ," rally organizers called for complete victory in Vietnam.[58] We watched at a distance. Their efforts were amusing, and somewhat pathetic.

Chapter 5

Expanding the Terrain of Confrontational Politics, 1971–1972

The antiwar movement did not evolve and mature in isolation. While we did not fully understand it at the time, our collective efforts by late 1970 had moved from strictly protesting the war through rallies, demonstrations, and marches to embracing strategic resistance directed at the war machine that sustained military intervention in Southeast Asia. Looking beyond the routine protest cycle of rallies and marches led invariably to engagement in more provocative confrontational politics.

Simultaneously, the antiwar movement became entangled in a wide-ranging critique of power and privilege. In practice the sentiment in opposition to the war in Vietnam developed in concert with a multitude of other struggles directed against oppression: the Civil Rights Movement and the turn to Black Power, efforts to combat poverty in America, the Women's and Gay Liberation Movements, environmentalism, and opposition to corporate control over food systems.

The antiwar movement worked to establish linkages with both active-duty GIs and returning veterans. Law enforcement agencies ranging from the FBI and military intelligence to the criminal intelligence division of the APD took a keen interest in expanding surveillance of these activities. The VVAW in Texas had created sixteen different chapters spread all over the State. In early 1971 the VVAW organized a conference in Austin. Police undercover informants stole the list of the two hundred registered participants. This list of names can be found in the George Carlson Papers.[1] In April local Women's Liberation groups sponsored an International Women's Day that consisted of workshops, consciousness-raising groups, and rallies. On 4 April political activists worked with CUF to sponsor a large demonstration in memory of the legacy of Martin Luther King.

Austin Spring Offensive, April–May 1971

At a national level, the People's Coalition for Peace and Justice (PCPJ) emerged as the organizational focal point for the shift from protest rallies and demonstrations to direct action. The PCPJ seized the time, calling for a mass, nonviolent, civil disobedience campaign scheduled for late April and early May 1971 in Washington, DC. The direct action contingent of the Austin antiwar movement took up the challenge. We formed a group called the Armadillo May Day Tribe (AMDT) to coordinate our activities under the broad umbrella of the PCPJ. As we wrote, "the planned strategy for the Mayday actions is to concretely pressure the US government to bring an immediate, total cessation of hostilities with the people of Indochina through massive civil disobedience."[2]

Working in tandem with the PCPJ, we organized a series of local activities to coincide with the series of events designed to culminate in the planned May Days demonstration in Washington, DC. The local calendar of events for the week of 12–18 April included an organized telephone call-in to Bergstrom Air Force base and picketing at the main gate to invite active-duty GIs to participate in the planned GI solidarity march, and a tax refusal demonstration at Southwestern Bell Telephone Company to call for nonpayment of taxes. Austin Veterans for Peace (under the leadership of Terry Dubose) sponsored the picketing at Bergstrom Air Force Base on 15 April. Besides creating committees to leaflet at local high schools, and to reach out to church groups and civic organizations, we began publishing a weekly newsletter providing information on our protest activities.

On 17 April the AMDT sponsored a regional conference at Greenbriar School, outside Austin, to make final preparations for the May Day demonstrations. The gathering consisted of antiwar activists from Texas, Oklahoma, and Arkansas. Out-of-town contingents included groups from the campuses of Southern Methodist University (Dallas), North Texas State University (Denton), and UT at Arlington, in addition to activists from Fort Worth, Houston, Norman, Stillwater, Little Rock, and Fayetteville. Our aim was to consolidate our forces and coordinate our efforts. Over several weeks we sponsored workshops on how to engage in disruptive tactics and offered medical advice about how to avoid serious injuries (wearing long-sleeved shirts, long pants, and heavy boots) and how to treat injuries like abrasions, broken bones, and concussions.[3] Participants at the meeting claimed that stretching metal chains across streets were an effective way to disrupt traffic. Others suggested pouring blood and oil in front of the Texas Petroleum Institute in Washington, DC.[4]

As a prelude for what was to come, we sponsored a GI-civilian solidarity march on 18 April. Over 1,500 protesters, including more than 200 active-duty GIs, participated in a march that started at the campus and proceeded to the State Capitol. As usual, the local VVAW contingent deliberately charged into police lines, engaging in street fighting with the police.[5]

May Days Demonstrations, Washington DC, 3–5 May 1971

The Armadillo Tribe has come
To shut Scott Circle down
When we get there the first they'll hear all through this fucking town
Fuck you, in the nose
In the nose
In the nose
[Repeat][6]

Some events refuse to shrivel and disappear in our collective memories. The 1971 May Days demonstrations in Washington, DC, is one of them. At the time I regarded these protest events as just one more in a string of national mobilizations. Yet over time I realized that the series of events in Washington, DC, in April–May 1971 were significantly more inventive and more audacious than any other challenges to state authority that we tried.

In my judgment the highpoint of antiwar protests in the US was the April–May 1971 demonstrations in Washington, DC. As a matter of fact, these activities were not a single event but multiple protest activities that converged at the same place at more or less the same time. What national organizers from a vast coalition of organizations and groups called our Spring Offensive, a whole series of protests that began on 18 April in Washington, DC, were designed to be seventeen straight days of nearly nonstop political action. The audacious plan of action began with VVAW protests, culminating with a mass march on 24 April at the Capitol and followed by the mobile civil disobedience tactics designed to bring the city to a standstill beginning on 3 May and lasting three days.[7]

Let's take a step backward in time. In January–February 1971, VVAW had organized its three-day Winter Soldier investigation in Detroit. Former soldiers exposed and publicized the atrocities and war crimes of the war machine in Vietnam.[8] The event was the launching pad for VVAW-sponsored demonstrations in Washington, DC, in the spring. The anger, frustration, and guilt of returning veterans culminated in what VVAW called Operation Dewey Canyon III (named after a real-life series of small-scale incursions into Laos and Cambodia in 1970), a self-styled "limited incursion in the country of Congress." These protests lasted from 19 to 23 April, and included camping on federal grounds, a trip to Arlington National Cemetery to honor fallen soldiers, lobbying efforts with members of Congress, and a sit-in on the steps of the Supreme Court Building. The high point of this series of events was the well-publicized two-hour march past the Capitol, in which disheveled, shaggy-haired Vietnam veterans dressed in military fatigues tossed their medals and accommodations over an eight-foot-high police barricade to demonstrate their opposition to the Vietnam War.[9]

Washington, DC, swirled with protest activities. There was literally room for all sorts of political groups with many different perspectives. The VVAW protests were followed on 24 April by a huge antiwar march of over half a million people—the largest-ever demonstration opposing a

US war. The observations of a student reporter from the University of New Hampshire is worth quoting in full:

> People perched on traffic lights. People hanging like lichen from trees in the front yard of the Capitol building. People crawling on statues. People as far as the eye could see down Pennsylvania Avenue, stretching twenty, thirty, forty or fifty abreast; endless people to the right and left, some old, some middle aged, but mostly young. Saturday afternoon, April 24, Washington, DC, The "final" police estimate of the crowd was 175,000 but it is rumored that it was finalized by one in the afternoon, when the march had just begun and people were still filling the yard of the Capitol. They had not even begun to pack the surrounding streets and parks. People in the march say between twice and three times the police estimate would be closer to the truth. Student organizers claimed the size of the crowd was over a half million.[10]

The 24 April march, sponsored by the NPAC, appealed to the broadest possible range of antiwar sentiment and at the same time opposed any and all tactics (including civil disobedience and sit-ins) that went beyond legally permitted protest.[11] This "Give Peace a Chance" moratorium that consisted in the main of a liberal-radical coalition orchestrated yet another of its high-profile "babies and balloons" marches and rallies. Yet for the first time, other constituencies challenged the single-issue focus of the NPAC moratorium. For example, a United Women's Contingent joined the march to express solidarity with sisterhood. This largely festive protest march took place in tandem with large-scale sit-ins outside the Selective Service Agency, the Justice Department, and other government agencies.

This annual spring peace march in Washington, DC, sponsored by NPAC was followed by what were the most significant and bold street protests of the entire antiwar period—the 1971 May Days demonstrations. The increasingly militant wing of the antiwar movement had come to the conclusion that mass mobilizations, including marches and rallies, around legally sanctioned protest had reached their limits of effectiveness. The PCPJ emerged as the organizational focal point of the militant faction. Unlike the NPAC, with its singular focus on "get out of Vietnam now," the PCPJ favored a multi-issue approach to antiwar organizing and sought to build alliances with national organizations as a way of drawing connections between foreign and domestic policies of the US government. A key element of the PCPJ strategy centered on the advocacy of a separate peace between the people of the United States and the people of Southeast Asia (the Joint Treaty of Peace, more commonly referred to as the People's Peace Treaty). The People's Peace Treaty began with the words, "Let it be known that the American and Vietnamese people are not enemies."[12]

Organized around the provocative, ambitious, and utterly utopian slogan, "If the government won't stop the war, we'll stop the government," a leadership coalition consisting of the PCPJ and the pacifist War Resisters League called for three days of civil disobedience to literally shut down the US government through disruptive tactics beginning on 3 May. The self-styled "direct action" protest brought together the most militant activists in the antiwar movement, with the aim of using small "affinity groups" to block major intersections and bridges in Washington, DC, to bring normal government functions to a complete standstill. As the widely distributed *Tactical Manual* put it, "The aim of the Mayday actions is to raise the social cost of the war to a level unacceptable to America's rulers. To do this we seek to create the specter of social chaos while maintaining the support or at least toleration of the broad masses of American people."[13]

The motley crew of action-oriented militants in Austin—me included—were captivated by this proposed national action, and we feverishly began making plans to participate under the aegis of the new organization—the AMDT—that we created just for this purpose. The undertones of anarchism, adventurism, and anti-intellectualism that accompanied the long process of building toward the Washington, DC, protests once again split the Austin movement. The militant rhetoric frightened away not only the timid but also those who believed that disrupting the lives of ordinary commuters would only backfire against us. Some objected to the putatively anti–working class tactics of disrupting traffic and generally causing havoc in a largely Afro-American city. For some of us, the purism of this position was stultifying. We recognized that the everyday lives of working people would certainly be disrupted, but we reached the conclusion that we needed to proceed anyway. At the same time, the firmly entrenched countercultural hippie wing of the movement declared that the planned protests were just another national demonstration that would not accomplish anything.

I understood the objections to this sort of national extravaganza demonstration calling for a heavy dose of civil disobedience and chaos making. But I decided that the potential gains outweighed the downsides. I participated wholeheartedly in building support for a southwest regional contingent for the May Days demonstrations. We organized groups from about a dozen cities and college towns throughout Texas, Oklahoma, and Arkansas. All in all, we gathered together around 250 people to make the long trek to Washington, DC, in Volkswagen vans, rented buses, and overstuffed automobiles. We gathered in Washington, DC, at private homes of friends and acquaintances, church basements, and university dormitories.

The PCPJ leadership took a hands-off approach, in part to avoid the possibility of becoming enmeshed in a conspiracy trial like the Chicago Eight after the organized disruption of the 1968 Democratic National Convention in Chicago. The PCPJ called on contingents from different regions of the country to team with so-called national constituency groups (Women's Liberation, Gay Liberation, welfare rights organizations) to decide on their own their specific targets, strategies, and tactics within the overall framework of nonviolent civil disobedience. As the pamphlets we distributed made clear, "The execution of specific plans has been left to the discretion and philosophy of regional groups and national constituency organizations."[14] Everyone understood that civil disobedience and disruption were slippery terms, covering a variety of tactics, including minor destruction of property and physical blockading.

The PCPJ leadership made available an elaborate twenty-four-page *May Day Tactical Manual* that was distributed months in advance to local collectives. It identified twenty-one key bridges and traffic circles as targets, with photographs of each, detailed descriptions of the surrounding topography, and their location on a comprehensive map of the entire city. As local collectives announced their plans to participate, the PCPJ leadership assigned these contingents specific locations to disrupt, blocking traffic with barricades, stalled cars, and available trash. The larger objective was to make carrying out business as usual completely impossible.[15]

In addition to the *May Day Tactical Manual*, which identified specific targets for civil disobedience and traffic disruption, the PCPJ national headquarters issued a host of other pamphlets and printed materials for mass distribution. One large pamphlet (which I have in my possession) was entitled "May Flowers. May Day" with the NLF flag emblazoned on the front page. Besides reproducing once again the sites in Washington, DC, targeted for disruption, this twelve-page broadsheet consisted of specific messages from particular constituencies. The Gay May Day Tribe (Washington, DC) mentioned its connections with the Gay Liberation Fronts in Austin and elsewhere. Another short essay called "Trouble over Bridged Waters" stated explicitly, "The unanimous agreement that the target we chose should not involve disruption of the black community, or in any way invite further repression of black people in Washington."

May Days, 1971: Our Tet Offensive in the Nation's Capital

"The largest and most audacious direct action in US history is also among the least remembered," the historian L. A. Kauman argued, "a protest that has slipped into deep historical obscurity."[16] On 3 May, after nearly two weeks of continuous antiwar protests in Washington, DC, many thousands of protesters set out from all over the country to accomplish something extraordinarily brash and brazen: paralyze the functions of government for three days. In retrospect, this call to action was indeed incendiary, if not quasi-insurrectionary. The Jefferson Airplane soundtrack "We Are All Outlaws in the Eyes of America" was a perfectly appropriate setting. Those of us who participated discarded any liberal illusions that law enforcement agencies would respect our civil liberties and protect our rights to assemble peacefully. We knew that the Washington, DC, security forces were determined to stop our actions by any means necessary, short of mass shootings. We understood that our tactical inventiveness would work for a while. "The tactical advantage underlying the May plan was now apparent, the asymmetrical warfare of a guerrilla force against a standing army," Lawrence Roberts correctly observed. "It was nearly impossible [for the security forces] to defend against small decentralized bands, who could shift on a dime . . . choosing spots that weren't even on the original list in the Mayday tactical manual."[17]

Organized from Austin, the AMDT brought together a ragtag combination of countercultural hippies, hard-core radicals, peace activists, and women's and Gay Liberation groups. What distinguished May Days from earlier demonstrations/rallies was the distinct combination of three features: direct action, nonviolent civil disobedience, and a decentralized organizational structure. Direct action stressed proactive engagement and tactical mobility rather than passive marching along a predetermined route. We were nimble. Nonviolent civil disobedience allowed for extralegal tactics. We did not feel bound to obey laws prohibiting blocking traffic, building impromptu barricades, and disabling cars and trucks. Finally, an innovative decentralized organizational structure called for breaking movement action into small units, called affinity groups, in order to function autonomously from a central command. Ranging from three to fifteen people, these affinity groups planned their participation jointly and took part in their actions collectively. The idea of affinity groups drew its inspiration from anarcho-syndicalist notions of shared responsibility and the real need for security, especially to combat undercover police infiltration.

The *May Day Tactical Manual* made no secret of the targets and objectives. The assigned target for the Texas contingent—participants drawn primarily from Austin but also recruited from around the region—was Scott Circle, a strategic point along a major traffic route into the heart of the city. Scott Circle was the traffic congestion point where Massachusetts Avenue, Sixteenth Street, and Rhode Island Avenue converged and crossed. It was located three blocks from Dupont Circle (assigned to the New York May Day contingent). We were delighted. I remember meeting with friends to study the *May Day Tactical Manual*, which described Scott Circle as filled "with much open land," with "open space in front of the Australian Embassy and the infamous National Rifle Association." The copy of the *May Day Tactical Manual* that I kept is marked with notations and instructions.

Beginning in early March, we held weekly meetings to finalize plans and coordinate activities for our participation in the May Days Demonstrations. In our printed leaflets, we declared, "So you people out there in

Longhorn Land be thinkin' and talkin' about this. . . . If you want, you can make your place in the New Action ARMADILLO ARMY and Stop the war in May." Our preparation resembled a ragtag volunteer army planning for battle. In our efforts to maximize efficiency in the field and to minimize the need for centralized coordination, we divided into about fifteen to twenty self-sufficient traveling groups who were responsible, logistically speaking, for getting back and forth to Washington, DC, and for keeping track of any lost or arrested comrades. Our motto was "No comrade left behind."

Antiwar protesters were encouraged to carry FM radios to receive precise instructions from a local radio station broadcasting updates. National May Day Tribe organizers had made contact with sympathetic soldiers in the military police units from Fort Bragg who were ordered to "protect" Washington, DC, but who promised to keep protesters informed as to troop movements.[18] Protest leaders worried that helicopters were to be dispatched to teargas demonstrators. Some suggested that in retaliation protesters fly kites with long wire "to fowl helicopter rotors" as had been done in a demonstration in Berkeley (California).[19]

I traveled to Washington, DC, from Austin in a convoy of two Volkswagen minivans. It was indeed a motley squad, eleven of us in all, split into three affinity groups of three to four enthusiastic disrupters each. We came prepared. Our uniforms consisted of long pants, heavy jackets, and work boots (not too heavy for running but sturdy enough to withstand stomping by police). We carried food and water, cash for bail money, a lone item of personal identification (usually secreted in our boots), Vaseline for dealing with tear gas, and color-coded bandanas to identify ourselves. Some of us brought three-pronged nails for dropping in the streets to flatten tires, canisters of sand (for dumping in the gas tanks of stalled cars), and wire cutters to use in disabling car tires. We also brought gloves for carrying heavy materials. We etched in ink on our covered arms the phone numbers of the ad hoc legal assistance group established in Washington, DC (May Day Legal Aid—833-9480) to handle the anticipated mass arrests. We were ready for battle.[20]

The PCPJ leadership assigned us to a movement center in Washington, DC, where we congregated with fellow protesters from our region. We stored

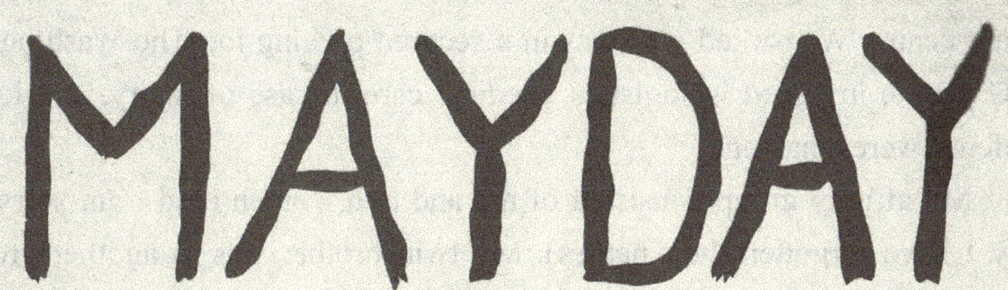

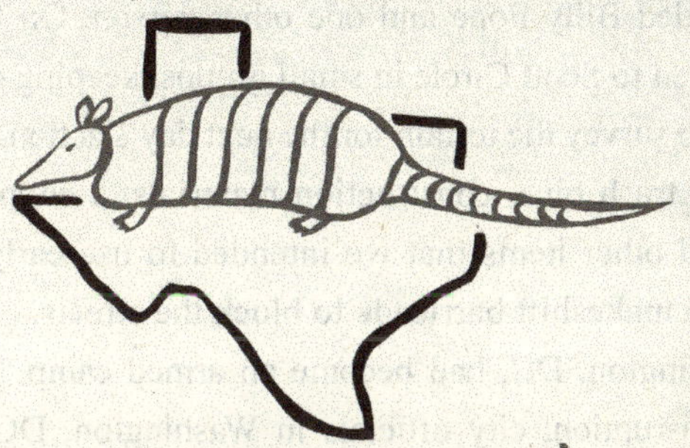

Mayday: No Business as Usual, Armadillo May Day Tribe poster. Gift of Grace Hedemann. Courtesy of Political Posters, Labadie Collection, University of Michigan, Ann Arbor.

wallets, valuables, and other personal items in secure lockers at the movement center. We parked our vans in a secured parking lot. The Washington DC people involved in logistics, medical care in case of injury, and legal defense were amazing.

My affinity group consisted of me and two women (and I am sorry to say I have forgotten their names). My twin brother was in another group that included Billy Pope and one other person. On the evening of 2 May, we ventured to Scott Circle in small groups, keeping out of sight as much as possible to survey the terrain for the next day's action. My three-person team identified trash bins, construction materials, a couple of discarded utility poles, and other items that we intended to use early the next morning in building a makeshift barricade to block the streets.

Washington, DC, had become an armed camp. To maintain order and prevent disruption, city officials in Washington, DC, deployed more than 4,000 paratroopers from the US 82nd Airborne Division (some of whom had just returned from Vietnam) with another 4,000 in reserve, 5,100 officers of the DC Metropolitan Police, 2,000 members of the DC National Guard, and federal agents that were already in place, in addition to park and Capitol police units. Paratroopers and Marines deployed via helicopter to the grounds of the Washington Monument.

Every monument, public park, and traffic circle in Washington, DC, had troops stationed to protect its perimeters. Despite this unprecedented show of militarized force, we managed to disrupt the normal functioning of government for three days.[21]

We arrived at Scott Circle on the morning of 3 May around 6:30 a.m. Automobile traffic was flowing tentatively through the circle. City officials and law enforcement agencies had warned commuters to try to get to work hours earlier than normal, and this advice worked because traffic flows were heavier than usual at this hour. Some affinity groups had arrived before us, and they were busy carrying out as much disruption as they could. Once my team flew into action, we were able to stop traffic in its tracks. We built a makeshift barricade on the lane leading into downtown with everything we could carry, rip up, and throw into the street. In our affinity group, we would take turns, one watching for police on motorcycles and the other two carrying poles, bricks, and other heavy objects into the street. Cops on motorcycles came and parked a short distance away. They were afraid of us.

Altogether at Scott Circle we were more than a couple of hundred strong. The motorcycle police called in reinforcements. Heavily armed police units arrived in a convoy of vans. They piled out, rushing at us with clubs. Confrontations ensured. Then they teargassed us. All in all, we held Scott Circle for more than two hours before we were driven away.

The police charged into groups, arresting anyone they could grab. But the police were no match for our mobile tactics. I saw streets littered with abandoned cars, their tires flattened and distributor caps removed. Tow truck operators were busily pulling cars off the streets. Some roads were blocked with makeshift barricades of burning trash bins and tires, bricks and large stones, and whatever else could be lifted and piled high. Some protesters sat down in the streets, blocking traffic. I myself thought that this tactic was unwise, inviting beating and arrests by frustrated and angry police.

As we moved away from Scott Circle, we saw that tear gas blanketed the city. Brief skirmished broke out everywhere. Small knots of protesters numbering perhaps ten to twenty strong stood their ground, and they fought back with punches, throwing bricks and bottles, and returning tear gas canisters. Roving bands carried the message of protest everywhere throughout the downtown areas. As police cars whisked away the arrested, ambulances carted off the wounded and injured. As we moved toward downtown, there was chaos everywhere.

Outnumbered, police units clustered together in packs. We avoided them. I saw one of our fellow protesters proudly displaying at least twenty distributor caps. He said he just opened the hoods of stopped cars and pulled the distributor caps out, disabling the car. This was a great tactic to block the streets. As we walked and ran to avoid the cops, I remember sprinting to avoid a barrage of tear gas. Someone in our group shouted, "Hey, look, there's the White House." Sure enough. That was the first time I ever saw the White House—running past in a cloud of tear gas. To this day I cannot venture past the White House without the urge to run.

As the day wore on, we stopped for coffee breaks at local cafeterias and watched the action in the streets unfold before our eyes. By early evening we retreated to our secure redoubts, pleased with ourselves. On 3 May, the first day of the protest actions, around eight thousand people were arrested, the largest number for any single day in US history. All in all, close to fourteen thousand protesters were arrested during the three-day battle for the streets of Washington, DC. On the first day, no one I knew had been hurt and only a few arrested. Alice Embree was nabbed and charged with theft of public property. She had grabbed an unattended police gas mask. The figure registering the numbers of injured and arrested changed in the next several days. As the numbers of arrests declined, the numbers of those injured increased. Law enforcement agencies changed tactics, beating rather than arresting. They were determined to get us off the streets, and making arrests wasted their time and effort.

On the second day, we emerged from our hideouts, ready for action. Police and army units were better prepared and were out in force, securing routes into the city. We tried to build some barricades but were not as successful as the first morning. My affinity group sort of free floated, moving around the best we could, linking up with other groups to do as much disruption as possible. Word passed around to converge on the Department of Justice for a massive sit-in. I met up with Martin Wiginton and his affinity group. We talked about sitting down and blocking the entrances to the Justice Department. We decided one of us had to stay out of jail to coordinate legal defense. We flipped a coin. He won (or lost, depending on how one judged the circumstances). He sat down and was eventually arrested and carted off to a makeshift prison at the Washington Coliseum. He led a breakout effort, and the security police rewarded him with a broken arm. I remained a free person, anointed with the task of calling lawyers to set up bail releases.

The combined forces of law and order were clearly surprised by the level of ingenuity, the levels of militancy, and the endurance of the May Day protesters. They were certainly not prepared to handle the sheer number of arrests. When the jails were filled to capacity, the security forces stockpiled the spillover in emergency detention centers, such as a huge practice field near JFK Stadium on the outskirts of the city. On the second day, the police deliberately abandoned their initial plans of making sweeping arrests of anyone they could lay their hands on. I saw many protesters handcuffed to bike racks and street poles. Police vans scoured the streets, loading up these captured comrades and hauling them off to jail. As Roberts observed, "By early Tuesday [4 May], two thousand prisoners were stretched out uncomfortably on the oval floor of the Washington Coliseum, a sea of exhausted refugees hip to hip, right up to the wooden barriers at the edges. Many more sat in the bleachers. . . . Thousands more detainees were scattered in various lockups around the city, but this [Washington Coliseum] was the largest group."[22] The security forces mistakenly believed that the threat of arrest would frighten away most protesters, allowing them to focus on the most militant protestors who decided to stick to the original protest plans. No way. Many of those arrested the first day returned to the streets once they were released.

Shifting gears, the police adopted completely different tactics. Their tactical adaptation was tantamount to a martial law under an authoritarian regime. In order to keep the number of arrests to a minimum, they attacked protesters and beat them, leaving them bruised and bleeding in the streets. I distinctly remember seeing these two undercover police officers—one white and one Black—dressed in military fatigues festooned with political buttons and slogans ("Stop the War," "Free all political prisoners," "VVAW"). They were driving through the streets in a yellow Volkswagen beetle. The white cop tied his ponytail with a hair clip and the African American cop wore a military jacket with a "Free Angela Davis" button attached to the front pocket. On several occasions I witnessed these two undercover agents carry out the same modus operandi: They would drive up to a group of unsuspecting protestors, jump out of the car, and hail their intended victims with the appropriate shouts of "Power to the People!" and clenched fist salutes. Once within striking distance, they pulled out short clubs concealed in their clothing and proceeded to beat people mercilessly before strolling off to their car.

The police had crossed a line of legality and propriety in broad daylight. Once the thin veneer of legality was stripped away, the ugly core of police-state tactics came to the surface with a vengeance. I realized that we had passed over a threshold into a police state, a virtual state of emergency that enabled the security forces to do whatever they wanted to do.

In processing thousands of prisoners, the Justice Department under Richard Kleindienst adopted a bold tactic that was both unethical and illegal: The young Justice Department attorneys processing the arrest reports on 3 May were given instructions from Attorney General John Mitchell to "fuzz up" the time and place of arrest. They were also supplied with a list with names with badge numbers of seven police officers. The lawyers randomly entered the name of one of these in the space for "arresting officer." "In other words," as Roberts argued, "the Justice lawyers were told to falsify the record to establish grounds for an arrest that would otherwise be indefensible in court."[23] On the third day, 5 May, the remaining affinity groups that had not been arrested put up sporadic resistance wherever and whenever we could muster sufficient numbers. In the end we tried to mass our remaining forces in a large-scale demonstration at the US Capitol. Protesters came to present members of Congress with the results of the petition drive to sign the People's Peace Treaty. Another twelve hundred people were arrested on charges of unlawful entry of Capitol grounds or unlawful assembly. Many of those detained "languished in a cellblock below the federal court house." About half of these thousand or more remaining prisoners refused to be fingerprinted, "insisting that their rally had been legal and the arrests not." Cells intended to accommodate two people held twenty to forty detainees each. Police refused to allow public defenders into the dungeon to talk with their clients.[24]

As we withdrew from Washington, DC, on the morning of the 6th, we left a city filled with the signs of battle: ripped up utility poles, trash everywhere, and the lingering smell of tear gas. While we did not successfully shut down Washington, DC, for three days, we wreaked havoc, causing the Nixon administration to call out US Army troops, the National Guard, and the full complement of Washington, DC, police contingents. Every newspaper in the country reported on these events. If we did not successfully shut down the government, we certainly garnered a great deal of attention for trying. The mainstream media was apoplectic, putting out a stream of damning condemnation of unruly lawbreakers trying to stop the government. We really paid no attention to their diatribes.

The AMDT returned home to Austin weary but virtually unscathed. No one was seriously injured. A few of us were charged with felonies (resisting arrest, assault on a police officer, grand theft), but in the hopeless confusion of the overburdened judicial system, these charges were eventually dismissed. The legal defense team in Washington, DC, did a marvelous job in getting cases dismissed and freeing our "political prisoners."[25]

As the story trickled out about the extralegal overreach of the security forces, the District of Columbia Human Relations Commission released a scathing fifty-nine-page report that showed that more than half of the more than 13,400 arrested at the May Days demonstrations did not violate any law. The report said that while the remainder of those arrested may have violated some law, only about one-quarter were actually apprehended by police while committing an illegal act. Moreover, the commission found that the main criterion by which the arrests were made appeared to be "evidence of youthful appearance, such as long hair, casual dress, or the wearing of protest button," rather than "evidence of an unlawful act." An impromptu survey of arrest sheets on the first groups of protesters detained showed that 90 percent were under the age of 25.[26] The commission also noted that the failure of a "substantial number" of police officers "to wear badges or name-tags" seems to "have encouraged officers to act in ways for which they could not later be called to account." The suspension of emergency field arrest procedures by the Metropolitan police department, "on the advice of the Justice Department and without the approval of the city administration," violated minimum due process requirements. The circumstances and legality of the arrests were further muddled by the entering by police "arresting officers" of the generic charge of "disorderly conduct" in nearly every case, contributing to the subsequent inability of the city attorney's office to successfully prosecute many of those arrested for alleged criminal behavior.[27]

Months later the thousands of protesters who were falsely detained were able to receive financial compensation for illegal arrests. Activists learned important lessons from the May Days demonstrations. Traditional pacifists learned that they could translate their commitment to nonviolence into relevant militant action, not avoiding but embracing confrontational politics. Militant activists came to recognize that mass protests could use nonviolent tactics to great advantage. We all learned to minimize our differences and to see the strength in a range of tactics.

Those activists in Austin who did not travel to Washington, DC, for the May Days demonstrations organized a series of local events. During the first week of May, activists leafleted near the UT campus and downtown to inform people about the People's Peace Treaty. They managed to obtain hundreds of signatures on a petition requesting an Austin referendum to endorse the treaty, which called for immediate withdrawal from Indochina, the establishment of $6,500 as a minimum yearly income for all American families, and the immediate release of all political prisoners. Activists also conducted roving guerilla theater actions at shopping centers and public gathering places. On 5 May protesters organized a No Business as Usual day, requesting all businesses and schools to close down, and held a protest rally at the Austin State Capitol. Thousands attended.

May Day Leaflet
List of events in DC

1 May	Celebration of People's Peace
2 May	Poor People's March
3 May	PCPJ focus on the Pentagon
4 May	Focus on Justice Department and demand freedom for all political prisoners
5 May	Surround the Capitol to demand ratification of People's Peace Treaty

Austin Parallel Activities

1 May	Leafleting on campus to support People's Peace Treaty
2 May	Leafleting of churches in the morning and large commercial stores in the afternoon in support of People's Peace Treaty
3 May	Rally in support for minimum family income at Austin State Capitol
	Austin Veterans for Peace, Direct Action, and May Day Tribe sponsored rally at Capitol Rotunda
4 May	March around Travis County Jail in support of demand to free all political prisoners
5 May	No Business as Usual—call for a strike at businesses and schools
	Guerrilla theater downtown at Selective Service and then at J. J. Pickle Federal Building

> A group called High School Direct action endorsed People's Peace Treaty
> An estimated seventy-five high school students gathered at the State Capitol and marched down Congress Avenue passing out leaflets
> Specters of Death—nine people with faces painted and wrapped in grey-blue robes—led the march
> Representatives of the AMDT showed up to tell them about demonstrations at Selective Service and the Pickle Federal Building later in the afternoon[28]

Nicolaus von Hoffman, a reporter for the *Washington Post*, wrote a wonderful article on 6 May 1971 where he refers specifically to the well-disciplined "Texas group." Here "you got," he says, "stamina and the restraint that put the requirements of tactics above the acting out of anger." With "Washington on the ropes," he continued, protesters "exhausted the police force until it has begun to lose its normally good disciple and indulge in indiscriminate and promiscuous busting of most anybody young looking or different." "The people arrested for blocking traffic here have already spent nearly as much time in jail as [Lt. William] Calley has for My Lai."[29]

Certainly at the time neither I nor my antiwar comrades would have imagined that the FBI would take such an oversized interest in our impromptu, somewhat clumsy efforts to disrupt the normal operations of the federal government during the 3–5 May 1971 May Days demonstrations in Washington, DC. We knew that the over-the-top slogan "If the government won't stop the war, we will stop the government" was sheer rhetorical bravado and wishful thinking. We knew that our ragtag army of somewhere between forty-five and fifty-five thousand disruptive protestors were no match for the assembled policing agencies. Our goal was not to stop the government but to draw national attention to the continuing war in Southeast Asia and to offer, by example, an escalation of tactics to include not only civil disobedience but also minor lawbreaking, like blocking traffic, disobeying lawful orders to disperse, disabling vehicles, and fighting back against police attacks. The coordinated efforts of the FBI National Headquarters, the local San Antonio field office, and the Criminal Division of the Justice Department to contemplate bringing felony charges against the leadership of the AMDT under the umbrella of antiriot laws was truly beyond our comprehension.

AMDT and the FBI

Let me start at the beginning. As planning for the 3–5 May 1971 May Day events unfolded, the FBI took an interest in the AMDT following a national planning meeting held in April in Bloomington, Indiana. With the assistance of my lawyer Peter Sorenson, I was able to obtain a vast cache of confidential FBI reports via the FOIA. This stockpile of FBI files consists largely of triangular correspondence between FBI National Headquarters in Washington, DC, the Criminal Division of the Justice Department, and the FBI field office in San Antonio (the jurisdiction for Austin). Responding with a kind of panic, the FBI National Headquarters cast a wider net, drawing in various regional offices in their eleventh-hour efforts to piece together a profile of the Austin AMDT and to figure out what the goals of this organization were with regard to the planning of the May Days demonstrations.

The files span the period April to July 1971 and consist of 106 pages (with 9 pages redacted). These files were not devoted to simply collecting information. The purpose of this correspondence was to explore the possibility of bringing criminal charges against leaders of the AMDT under federal antiriot laws for demonstration activities stemming from the 3–5 May 1971 May Days demonstrations in Washington, DC, under the umbrella of the PCPJ with its headquarters in Washington, DC.[30]

At the end of the day, these FBI efforts to use grand jury hearings in San Antonio to drag leaders of the AMDT into federal court just fizzled out. What hampered their work of exposing the aims of the AMDT was their inability to locate a sufficient number of reliable witnesses willing to testify about the nefarious plans of the AMDT. The FBI realized, to their chagrin, that local law enforcement agencies had devoted too few undercover informants to conduct surveillance and provide actionable intelligence.

The planned Spring Offensive actions for April–May 1971 in Washington, DC, included a vast array of antiwar groups ranging from the NPAC and their all-in peaceful march philosophy, the VVAW and their Operation Dewey

Canyon III, and the PCPJ civil disobedience campaign. In building a broad coalition of individuals and groups from around the Southwest under the umbrella of the PCPJ, we in Austin began holding organizing meetings starting around January 1971. In time we established connections with antiwar groups from places like Fayetteville and Little Rock (Arkansas); Norman and Stillwater (Oklahoma); and Denton, Dallas, and Houston (Texas). Despite our ongoing efforts over many months, the FBI—if their paper trail of documents I received via FOIA can be taken at face value—seems to have overlooked this early preparation. In the documents that I obtained, the FBI head office in Washington, DC, seems to have zeroed in a leadership meeting of the PCPJ held at the Christ United Community Center in Bloomington, Indiana, on 17–18 April 1971. A small number of activists from the AMDT attended the gathering. The FBI noted the Texas license plate of a car owned by Carol Jones. She was not the person who drove the car to the meeting. Interestingly enough, in the initial memo, ill-informed FBI agents identified Bloomington as a city in Illinois, until an FBI operative lower in the chain of command corrected this egregious mistake.

At least four confidential sources advised the FBI headquarters of the meeting, the purpose of which was to finalize plans for the May Days demonstrations. The local FBI office in Indianapolis was able to persuade the Reverend Nevin Danner, pastor of the United Church of Christ, to provide them with some information about the meeting. Danner said that he was "in sympathy with the May Day activity and desired not to identify any of persons involved in the conference." He acknowledged that he observed firsthand some of the proceedings, and he reported that the discussions were "all of a non-violent nature." In the end, he did identify several individuals whom he knew personally from Bloomington, or with whom he spoke at the meeting.[31]

The FBI field office in Indianapolis admitted that they had "no live coverage of the conference." Watching from outside, special agents observed sixteen persons entering the premises on 17 April, and FBI agents were able to identify eight of them. Most of those they identified were representatives of the National May Day Committee (MDC), based in Washington, DC. In a memo from the FBI director to the San Antonio field office dated 26 April 1971, and captioned "Demonstrations sponsored by PCPJ," the FBI head office referred to two meetings—one in Bloomington, Indiana, on 17 April 1971 and another in Austin on 20 April 1971. In issuing instructions to the field offices in Springfield (Illinois) and San Antonio, the FBI National Office advised that your "investigation should consist of the re-contact of the original sources [i.e., undercover informants] and the contact of any additional available logical established sources for the purpose of obtaining the fullest available details regarding the events at those meetings and subsequent meetings held for the same purpose."[32]

While the FBI took a keen interest in the Bloomington meeting sponsored by the national office of the MDC, they failed to identify three political activists from Austin who were in attendance: Pat Cuney, Jeff Jones, and Sam Jones from the VVAW. In personal correspondence Pat Cuney recalled that around twenty-five people attended the meeting in Bloomington, the purpose of which was to coordinate efforts for the mass protest action. Pat remembered a giant map of Washington, DC, placed on a large table. The political activists who attended the meeting purposely divided up targets for each organization to concentrate on. Participants took care not to pair political organizations committed to nonviolent civil disobedience tactics with those that were more open to extralegal activities, like pulling distributor caps out of cars, puncturing tires, piling trash in the streets to block traffic, and fighting back if attacked by the police. Pat also recalled that as they left the meeting, they discovered that their car tires were slashed. She assumed it was the FBI.[33]

Trying at this late hour to leave no stone unturned, the FBI head office mobilized their vast army of undercover informants to find out what was happening on their watch. "Information should include identity of persons in attendance, specific statements made with particular reference to plans for violence, identity of leaders and information as to whether or they were involved with persons from out of state." It is not difficult to fathom that collection of this information had all the makings of building a criminal case along the lines of "conspiracy trials."[34]

A "confidential source who has supplied reliable information in the past" reported to the FBI field office in San Antonio on a meeting on 17 May 1971 of the AMDT held at Greenbriar School outside of Austin.

The meeting was restricted to AMDT members, and particularly local activists who were planning to go the May Day demonstrations in Washington, DC, in May. Approximately thirty-five people attended the daytime meeting. An estimated sixty people attended the meeting that evening, including representatives from Fayetteville, Little Rock, Denton, Dallas, and Houston, as well as activists from the national office of the MDC in Washington, DC. The undercover informant identified Lori Hansel, Martin Wiginton, Sylvia Hughes, Barbara (last name unknown, but it was Barbara Worley, otherwise known as Vernell Pratt), Bobby Connel, Carol Jones, Bradey Coleman, Cam Cunningham, Robert Hibberry (Hibbard), Jay (McGee), Steve (LNU), John Pearcy, and Mike Wallick. At the meeting Martin Wiginton made it clear that all participants (including the Quakers, SMC, and Vets for Peace) should not engage in any violence before 3 May, as "the AMDT was not interested in getting little old ladies arrested who might be demonstrating with other groups at the May Days activities." After that day an undercover informant in attendance quoted Martin Wiginton as saying, "trashing starts"—understood by the undercover informant "to mean violent disruptive type activities"—would be the order of the day. He also purportedly "encouraged participants to do whatever it takes to 'shut the city down' and suggested that actions which are felonies be conducted by small closely knit groups."[35]

After receiving information from the Bloomington May Day meeting, Sylvia Hughes and Barbara Worley reported that the Texas, Arkansas, and Louisiana contingents were given the assignment of shutting down Scott Circle. Dupont Circle was assigned to the estimated two thousand activists expected to arrive from South Florida. This information from FBI informants may have been incorrect. It was my recollection that groups from New York were assigned to Dupont Circle. It was reported that four to five thousand demonstrators from New York were expected to come to Washington, DC. The undercover informant reported with alarm that "there was talk in Bloomington, of bringing guns to Washington, DC, and of doing extremely violent acts."[36]

Actually, this report is an inaccurate account of how we in the AMDT operated. The leadership cadre was always clear to proclaim our endorsement of civil disobedience but never openly advocated lawbreaking that could result in felony arrests. At the Greenbriar meeting, the activists in attendance resolved that the AMDT, as a group of participants, would not engage in violent acts. Whatever individuals or small affinity groups decided to do on their own, they did so on their own accord. Wiginton advised everyone to conduct major type actions (that is, actions considered to be felonious) in small groups and only with people that were known and trusted.[37] We were fully conscious of the broad strokes of the conspiracy laws that ensnared activists who urged antiwar protesters to cross state lines to commit felonies like destruction of property, assault on law enforcement officers, and the like.

Will Wilson, assistant attorney general, Criminal Division, Department of Justice, sent a hastily written memo to the director of the FBI on 23 April 1971 on the subject of a meeting in Bloomington, Indiana, concerning mass demonstrations in Washington, DC. Wilson proclaimed that the group that assembled in Bloomington on 17 April 1971 had decided that the AMDT would be responsible for shutting down Scott Circle in Washington, DC. At the Bloomington meeting, the group declared that an estimated twelve thousand people planned to participate in the activities organized by the PCPJ and the national organizing center called the MDC. Wilson reported that the "Texas demonstrators plan to pour blood and oil in front of the Texas Petroleum in Washington, DC, and conduct some sort of demonstration at the National Aeronautics and Space Administration." Attorney Laurence McWorter, Criminal Division, Department of Justice, repeated these claims in another memo. Wilson concluded that these planned demonstrations indicated possible violations of the "federal antiriot laws." Framed in this light, he requested that the FBI "conduct an immediate investigation to obtain the fullest details possible concerning possible violations of the antiriot laws, including possible pre-planning of violence" by the AMDT in connection with the 1971 May Days demonstrations.[38]

On 7 June 1971, Will Wilson provided FBI National Headquarters with the report of an FBI special agent who attended the 20 April meeting of the AMDT in Austin. This undercover informant identified six individuals—Martin Wiginton, Lori Hansel, Pat Cuney, Jay McGee, Martin Murray, and

Dianne Simmons—as "persons of interest." This undercover informant at this meeting reported that Sam Jones had spoken openly about a group called New Nations (formed by the Weather Underground) who said that they would engage in the "heaviest actions" at the May Days demonstrations. Several AMDT members advocated that the Austin contingent "do something" to those facilities in Washington, DC, that related directly to Texas.[39]

In a 30 April 1971 memo from A. Rosen to Mr. Sullivan, FBI headquarters, regarding May Days demonstrations and antiriot laws, Rosen identified five groups for special mention: the AMDT, Peninsula Concerned Citizens for Peace (Hampton, Virginia), the Michigan contingent of antiwar demonstrators, and antiwar groups from Cleveland and Columbus (Ohio) and Pittsburgh (Pennsylvania). He called for an investigation into their plans and activities at the May Days demonstrations. The instructions are worth quoting in full:

> Previous experience with the Department [of Justice] has clearly established that they will consider prosecution under Antiriot Laws only after some substantial violence has occurred and will then limit their prosecution to key leaders. In connection with the disturbances in Chicago at the time of the Democratic National Convention where there was extensive violence and damage, we investigated over 1200 cases but prosecution was limited to eight leaders of national prominence. We could expend untold manpower in instituting criminal investigations at this time of all persons whose activities conceivably could result in some technical Antiriot Laws violations before the demonstrations are over. However, this would be an entirely wasteful procedure and could never result in prosecution of more than a minimal percentages of the cases investigated as experience has clearly established that most of those who participate in the demonstrations will not engage in conduct which would warrant Federal prosecution.[40]

Rosen acknowledged that "no matter how much prior investigation might have been conducted, it would still be necessary before prosecution could be authorized to identify the persons who engaged in the violent action that would warrant prosecution and to then prove a connection with prior planning to commit that violence." This language is the platform for conspiracy trials. Rosen referred to Justice Department attorney Laurence McWorter in the Criminal Division "to determine what precisely the Department had in mind at this time and the exact nature and extent of investigation which the Department desires." As a result of these discussions, FBI field offices were instructed to "re-contact original sources and contact any additional established informants to get the identities of participants and up-to-date details of travel and action plans."[41]

What is clear in these correspondence files is that the FBI was fixated, almost obsessed, with finding ways to build a criminal case under federal antiriot statutes. This effort was all part of a wider repressive strategy of ensnaring antiwar activities in charge of conspiracy to engage in felonious activities in Washington, DC. In their correspondence FBI agents were convinced that their legal strategy depended upon "turning" participants in the AMDT demonstrations in Washington, DC, to testify before a grand jury investigating charges of disruptive behavior. To turn individuals to testify against the AMDT, they first had to interview these people and get them to agree to cooperate with law enforcement.

In an undated memorandum to the director of the FBI, Will Wilson (Criminal Division, Department of Justice) declared that in his judgement these plans "indicate possible violations of the Federal antiriot laws."[42] After weighing the information collected about the participation of Austin activists in the May Days demonstrations, the director of the FBI informed the San Antonio field office that the Department of Justice intended to institute federal grand jury proceedings targeting the AMDT at San Antonio on 21 June 1971. In preparation for their legal case, the San Antonio Bureau Office put in motion efforts to interview the six individuals (including me) who their undercover informant identified as attending the 20 April AMDT meeting.[43] The wheels were turning.

An undercover informant advised that two Austin individuals—Kenneth Moore and Larry Leichtman—attended meetings of the AMDT during April 1971 and that these individuals might conceivably cooperate with a federal grand jury. At the start the FBI felt confident that they could convince these two to testify on behalf of the government. The FBI was able to solicit an interview with Ken Moore at his residence. FBI agents got

Moore to sing like a noisy songbird. But the story he told was not what the FBI wanted to hear. While Moore was a cooperative witness, he was unreliable. He openly acknowledged in his FBI interview that he attended several meetings in April 1971 of the AMDT. He told the FBI agents that he was a musician, and his interest in attending the AMDT meetings was simply to party and drink beer. He admitted that he was not interested in the political activities of the AMDT "and, in fact, did not know what the organization was all about. He did not take part in any of the discussions at the AMDT meetings but rather drank a lot and played the drums." Moore recalled going to an AMDT planning meeting on 20 April but could not furnish any pertinent information because he was drunk at the time. He claimed not to know any of the names of AMDT members but admitted that he traveled to Washington, DC, to participate in the May Day demonstrations. He traveled in a blue Volkswagen bus with individuals known only to him as Janet and Mike. When he arrived in Washington, DC, he said he was distressed by the disruptive activities of some of the demonstrators. He claimed that he did not participate in any acts of vandalism, and regretted having gone to Washington, DC. Besides being unable to provide any substantive information, Moore also had a record of arrests: for illegal possession of marijuana, 7 March 1969; for vandalism, 30 April 1969; for theft, 11 July 1969; and for loitering, 5 July 1970.[44] Defense attorneys would have easily undermined the credibility of this witness.

The FBI interviewed Larry Leichtman at his residence on 13 July 1971. Larry freely admitted that he attended a number of meetings of the AMDT in April 1971. He told his FBI interviewers that at "no time did the AMDT members advocate the use of violent type activities in order to shut down the operations of the Federal Government." In his recollection Leichtman was firm in his conviction that discussions always centered on the use of nonviolent tactics, with one exception. Leichtman recalled one particular meeting "at which an individual from Florida, whose name he did not recall, advocated the use of violence and the carrying of guns" during the demonstrations. AMDT members challenged this Florida person, proclaiming they were "adamantly opposed to this type of activity." In all likelihood the Florida man was a law enforcement undercover plant whose purpose was to draw the AMDT into advocacy of illegal activities and crossing state lines to conduct violence.[45]

Leichtman did recall a meeting at the end of April 1971 in which discussions pertaining to the instructions contained in the *May Day Tactical Manual*. According to Leichtman someone at the meeting "referred to information in the Manual which indicated helicopters could be brought down by demonstrators using kites and wire to foul the helicopter rotors." According to him, these protesters used this tactic at demonstrations in Berkeley (California), and these efforts were apparently successful. Leichtman said that the AMDT did not endorse this type of activity. He offered the opinion that approximately forty people attended this meeting, but he refused to identify any AMDT members.[46]

Leichtman traveled to Washington, DC, in a Dodge van and stayed there from 30 April to 8 May 1971. He claimed that he did not become involved in disruptive activities or "trashing." He said he did not observe any AMDT member engaging in any types of violence. As a volunteer medic, he did have the opportunity to treat head wounds resulting from confrontations with the police and the effects of tear gas on demonstrators. He reached the conclusion that "future national organized demonstrations are doomed to failure as were the May Day demonstrations which were expected to be much larger." Leichtman described himself as a nonviolent individual who was "thoroughly disillusioned with the prospect of self-government." He explained that "street actions and demonstrations are as futile in achieving results as is legitimate working within the system." He said he was no longer interested in political activities and intended to devote all his time to scholastic pursuits.[47]

After interviewing Leichtman the San Antonio bureau reached the conclusion that "in view of his cooperative attitude," "he definitely should be considered as a prospective witness to appear before the Federal Grand Jury." Yet efforts to "locate additional witnesses who could furnish necessary [i.e., incriminating] evidence to a Federal Grand Jury" as a means to bring legal charges against the AMDT proved fruitless. An undercover informant indicated that three individuals—George Gowens, Rick Reams and Bill Scherer—"might possibly be cooperative witnesses." But efforts to locate the whereabouts of Reams and Scherer turned up empty, and

Gowens refused to be interviewed. After these failures to obtain cooperating witnesses, the FBI concluded that "the possibility of locating additional witnesses is very remote."[48]

In seeking to demonstrate that the AMDT not only advocated violence but also engaged in illegal activities, the FBI released the names of Austin activists arrested at the May Day demonstrations: Steve Byers (unlawful entry, Justice Building); George Gowans (unlawful entry, Justice Building); Lori Hansel (disorderly conduct, 4 May); Robert Hibbard (disorderly conduct, 3 May 1971); Cathy Wilson (arrested for failure to possess valid driver's permit); Susan Lorenz (unlawful entry of US Capitol); Danny Miller (unlawful entry of US Capitol); and Martin Wiginton (unlawful entry of US Capitol). The San Antonio field office requested background information on these individuals to assist in checking prior arrest records. The Department of Justice (Gary Hagman, Crimes Section, Criminal Division) expressed a keen interest in obtaining this information "at the earliest possible date" in order to present a case to a federal grand jury. Interestingly enough, other Austin activists—Alice Embree (charged with a felony for making off with a police gas mask), Sal Shero (underage at the time), Jeff Jones, and others—were arrested in Washington, DC, but seemed to slip through the surveillance cracks.

On 24 June 1971, the FBI National Office wrote to the FBI San Antonio field office proclaiming that the AMDT allegedly violated antiriot laws by planning to participate in violence in connection with May Day demonstrations in Washington, DC. Departmental attorneys went to Austin in connection with grand jury action and wished to develop witnesses. The FBI head office advised that "interviews with AMDT members who were possible witnesses should be handled independently by Bureau agents and neither a representative of the US attorney nor Departmental attorneys be present. By the same token, Bureau agents should not be present at any interviews that the US Attorney and/or Departmental attorneys may conduct."[49]

From the information they acquired from their undercover informants, the FBI was convinced they could start a criminal investigation of the AMDT. Following an interview with one of their undercover agents, Hagman advised that this clandestine source "appeared to be in an excellent position to furnish all necessary information concerning prosecution of AMDT members under ARL [antiriot laws] statutes." FBI agents in San Antonio and Justice Department attorneys acknowledged that the possibility of prosecution rested primarily on the testimony of this undercover agent. This source had supplied them for years with reliable information. Hagman indicated, however, he was "interested in approaching prosecution without exposing" the identity of the source—"as source would be in personal danger if surfaced."[50] As FBI agents attached to the San Antonio field office put it, "[The] informant [is] of continuing value [and] the unauthorized disclosure of which could result in [her/his] identification and adversely affect the National defense."[51] I actually wonder what they suspected we would do if we discovered the identity of this undercover informant. Surely this spy would no longer be useful to security agencies.

The FBI followed the long-term strategy of keeping this undercover informant safely ensconced in our midst rather than opting for the short-term goal of seeking criminal indictments against AMDT members—a move that would have required them to reveal the identity of their spy. They faced a dilemma of arriving at a course of action. Not willing to expose the identity of this trusted source, Agent Tennyson suggested continuing efforts to interview AMDT members to find weak links. They focused on those who attended the 20 April 1971 AMDT meeting. The undercover source indicated that only three might respond favorably and identified them (names were redacted but they were probably Ken Moore, Larry Leichtman, and George Gowens). When asked, the undercover source indicated that he/she expected the AMDT to continue as an organized group and that he/she would continue to function undercover and continue to be an active member as long as possible.[52]

The FBI did cast a wide net, seeking out antiwar activists involved with the AMDT to try to get them to talk. When FBI agents sought to talk with John Muir, he refused to identify himself and refused to answer any questions without consulting his lawyer, whom he named as Cam Cunningham. This pattern repeated itself. Martin Wiginton refused to identify himself or to answer any questions. Sam Jones also refused to identify himself or to answer any questions. John Pearcy similarly refused to identify himself or to answer any questions. Three Austin activists—Lori Hansel, Steve Byers, and George Gowens—all contacted the FBI by phone, saying that it was their understanding that the FBI wanted to interview him. They all refused to be interviewed without the presence of their lawyers. The FBI never interviewed them. The FBI added me to the mix. Let me quote in full: "An individual who identified himself as MARTIN MURRAY was located at 405 West 12th Street. He was informed as to the identity of the interviewing agents and his interview was being sought in connection with his activities as a member of the Armadillo May Day Tribe (AMDT) at Washington, DC, during May, 1971. Mr. MURRAY stated that he had nothing to say to the FBI. He further advised that his lawyer, CAMERON CUNNINGHAM, of Austin, Texas, could be contacted in this matter. MURRAY was not interviewed."[53]

In their correspondence regarding their investigation of the AMDT, San Antonio FBI agents listed the names of antiwar activists they wanted to interview, admitting that they were unable to locate the whereabouts of Jay McGee, Pat Cuney, and Diane Simmons for interviews. In light of the responses from those who refused to be interviewed, the FBI reached the conclusion that it would be unjustified to continue to pursue those whom they could not locate.

Their favored undercover source indicated that AMDT members "will not cooperate in this investigation. They will make no statements to the FBI and are attempting to prevent issuance of subpoenas for their appearance before Federal Grand Jury." In expressing frustration, the FBI requested contact of any additional available logical established sources for the purpose of obtaining fullest available details regarding the events at Austin meetings leading up to the May Day demonstrations. The FBI acknowledged that only one undercover source attended "the pertinent meetings." Another undercover informant who participated in the May Days demonstrations under the auspices of the AMDT was thoroughly debriefed following his/her return to Austin. The FBI admitted that a third undercover informant was "relatively inexperienced in matters of [national] security interests." One of these undercover informants acknowledged that their first assignment was in fact the 20 April 1970 AMDT meeting, and hence was unable to provide no "additional information."[54] The San Antonio field office attempted to obtain suitable photographs of AMDT members who participated in May Days demonstrations. They wished to use these photographs as identification of individuals and evidence of wrongdoing.[55]

The Austin antiwar movement warned political activists to be aware of FBI efforts to lure people into giving interviews in preparation for grand jury hearings. *The Rag*, Austin's underground newspaper, published a key article entitled "Grrrrand Jury," offering helpful suggestions about what to do. "During the past week, local FBI agents have contacted eight people who work with the Armadillo May Day Tribe," the article stated. "The *Armadillos* were asked to answer questions about the May Day action, and upon their refusal to answer they were told either explicitly or implicitly that if they did not cooperate by answering questions they would be subpoenaed to appear before a Federal Grand Jury in Washington in the near future." *The Rag* article went into didactic mode, advising that the purpose of the grand jury was to function (1) as a witch-hunting device, (2) as an information-gathering agency, and (3) as a fast railroad ride to jail on charges of contempt. *The Rag* article continued, "The Armadillo response to current FBI harassment and to any future grand jury machinations is one and the same: we will not be intimidated. We will not give information to be used against our brothers and sisters. We will continue to engage in those forms of political work that will help make a continuing human revolution a reality." The article finished with a challenge: "[FBI] agent John King, the person who contacted the *Armadillos* has a distinct aversion to talking before lawyers. He must be afraid he will fuck up."[56]

At the end of the day, the FBI decided to put off their efforts to seek felony indictments of AMDT members through the use of grand jury testimonies. All their efforts to use the criminal justice system to charge us under conspiracy laws came to nothing.

The events around organizing both before and after the May Days demonstrations really rattled the FBI. The San Antonio field office zeroed in on Martin Wiginton. Special Agent James King reported that undercover agents were instructed to conduct regular spot checks in the vicinity of his place of residence. A confidential source named as William Hamilton, security officer, Southwestern Bell Telephone Company, supplied Wiginton's phone number to start a wiretap. No less than nine undercover informants reported directly on Wiginton, and these spies produced regular reports on the meetings he attended and his activities.[57] The FBI produced a full profile ranging from where he was born and his academic experience to his full military records (including lists of postings and discharge papers). One undercover informant even reported that he was spotted drinking beer at Threadgill's with some friends. Wiginton aroused enough suspicion for alleged "revolutionary activities" he was placed on the Administrative Index (ADEX), Category II.[58] FBI reports alleged that because of his background, he was "potentially dangerous," a "subversive" who engaged in expressions of strong or violent anti-US sentiments.[59]

"Kick the Ass of the Ruling Class": The LBJ Library Dedication, 22 May 1971

In the long arc of antiwar activism in Austin, some events just refuse to fade and disappear in our collective memories. The disruption of the LBJ Library dedication on 21 May 1971 is one such event. This demonstration—oversized in our recollections years later—marked a pivotal point in our commitment to push for more direct confrontations with the security agencies aligned against us. The LBJ Library demonstrations prompted both delight and unease because we recognized at one and the same time that we were able to successfully disrupt the status quo and that we alienated many people who held antiwar views but were unwilling to engage in extra-legal activities.

Once back in our home base in Austin following the May Days demonstrations in Washington, DC, the AMDT set out to coordinate plans for massive protests against the dedication of the LBJ Library on the campus of the University of Texas. New recruits flocked to our cause, inspired in part by learning how much chaos we accomplished in Washington, DC. In the meantime, we participated in VVAW protests on 16 May at local military installations.[60]

For the LBJ Library dedication ceremonies, we planned carefully.[61] We built a large coalition of political groups to sponsor the protest, making it clear that our intention was to breech the barricades and shut down the event.[62] In the first protest incident connected with the dedication of the LBJ Library, a group of seven self-proclaimed radical feminist WITCHes—all in long dresses, with faces covered in multicolored greasepaint—started their action on Friday afternoon at Peace Fountain, a site located as close as they could get to the LBJ Library grounds. They put a hex on the library. Moving toward downtown the WITCHes continued their roaming demonstration at the studios of KTBC television station before marching to the State Capitol, where they sang and chanted in the rotunda. They then proceeded to the Commodore Perry Building and ended their protest journey at St. Mary's Catholic Church, where the cops arrested them at Ninth and Brazos Streets. In the chaos three WITCHes escaped. Seven were charged with disorderly conduct.[63] Weeks later fifty "sisters" dressed in Halloween costumes showed up at the WITCH trial held at Municipal Court at the main Austin Police station. The judge dropped all charges, and our freed sister comrades were greeted by a raucous crowds of onlookers and well-wishers.

The militancy, inventiveness, and sheer determination of the antiwar movement was matched by a qualitative shift in police strategy and tactics. On the eve of this planned disruption of the dedication proceedings, a combined police task force consisting of the Travis County Sheriff's office, the Texas Rangers, and the DPS served temporary restraining orders (TROs) to fourteen political organizations and twenty-seven protest leaders, including me. Travis County District Attorney Bob Smith sought the order on behalf of the University of Texas System Board of Regents. The aim of these TROs was to dampen the enthusiasm for carrying out a protest action that was bound to result in confrontations between police and protesters, street fighting, and numerous arrests. The security apparatus that was mobilized against us was formidable. It consisted of University of Texas System Security (under the leadership of George Carlson), the local APD Criminal Intelligence Division, the Washington, DC–based Secret Service, and the statewide Texas DPS.

Let me provide some detail. All the security agencies were extremely agitated about the proposed disruption of the dedication of the LBJ Library, especially because President Richard Nixon was one of the invited guests. A "confidential source," who had "provided reliable information in the past," seemed to confirm the worst fears of the various security agencies. This undercover informant observed a large gathering of at least 150 political activists at Eastwood Park (a few blocks north of the LBJ Library) on 19 May 1971. By acclamation the assembled activists agreed to "march through police barricades regardless of the consequences." Martin Wiginton, leader of the group, was overheard proclaiming, "Let's don't get hung up on legality, just get it on up there." He also said that "smaller groups [affinity groups] will definitely plan and implement violetn [*sic*] type actions, which will not be discussed publicly."[64]

The assembled group decided to march on the LBJ Library site from two different directions. We wanted the law enforcement agencies to spread their ranks in order for us to more easily breach the security lines. The primary reason for the demonstration was "to get national publicity because three major Television networks were going to cover the event." The undercover informant exclaimed with a degree of alarm that "the protest appears to be gaining momentum as demonstrators will participate from throughout the State, including a representative number of military personnel from Fort Hood, Texas."[65]

The San Antonio FBI office frantically contacted security agents at the US Secret Service, the 112th Military Intelligence Unit, the Intelligence Division of the APD, the Intelligence Division, Texas DPS, Tenth District Office of Special Intelligence, and the US Attorney (Justice Department). The security agencies debated the use of tear gas to immediately disperse the demonstrators but ruled against this approach. The FBI San Antonio field office kept in close contact with the Secret Service members assigned to protect President Nixon.[66]

We sponsored another warm-up rally at Eastwood Park in the early evening on the day before the planned demonstration. It was a rollicking event, with music and speakers and hundreds of attendees. Toward the end of the festivities, I was approached from three sides by three middle-aged, uniformed police officers, one of whom handed me my very own TRO, instructing me and others to refrain from participating in the next day's planned march and demonstration. The law enforcement officer who handed me the TRO was so nervous that his hands were shaking visibly, like leaves in a heavy wind. He must have imagined me as some crazy Communist or something. The three men represented the local APD, the Secret Service (since LBJ was going to be there), and the DPS.

This rather lengthy document took a blanket approach, naming some individuals who were not involved at all and a host of organizations seemingly almost chosen at random, and consisted of a lot of legal jargon listing restrictions on what we were not permitted to do. The order specifically sought to prohibit the named individuals and organizations from participating in or encouraging mass demonstrations, interfering with the dedication ceremony, obstructing entrances and exits, "arresting" certain persons, and "seizing control of the area set aside for the dedication." The document alleged that our planned activities "were designed, calculated, and intended to and will, at such time and under such circumstances, produce a clear and present and immediate threat or danger to the physical well-being or life of those present and attending such ceremony and other activities as well as damages to property of the University of Texas at Austin." Whew. The security agencies were trying to cover all their bases. We were told that we "constituted a public nuisance." We were restrained and enjoined from, among many things, "conducting or participating in, or encouraging, aiding or urging any other person to conduct or participate in a mass demonstration on the 22nd of May 1971." We were also "enjoined from encouraging, aiding, or urging any other individual to do or perform any act that would disrupt or interfere with the conducting of the dedication ceremonies." Furthermore, we were restrained from "going into or encouraging, or aiding and urging any other person to go into the enclosed prohibited area" for seven days. The document included a street map outlining a designated area where the dedication of the LBJ Library was to occur. This area stretched from East Twenty-First Street to East Twenty-Sixth Street on a north-south axis and Swisher Avenue to San Jacinto / Trinity Street on an east-west axis. This restricted territory was a rather large space.[67]

As an individual and alleged ringleader of various organizations, Martin Wiginton was issued with three TROs. After Martin Wiginton I appeared second on the list of individuals. The list of organizations included the AMDT, Veterans for Peace, CUF, Ragstaffers, Peoples Party II

"Restricted TERRITORY" under terms of a temporary restraining order. LBJ Library Dedication Demonstration, 22 May 1971. Map courtesy of Olaia Chivite Amigo.

(Houston), and the John Brown Revolutionary League (Houston). The TRO listed SWP and YSA, but these organizations actively encouraged their supporters *not* to participate in our planned demonstration. SDS was also named, but it did not exist as an organization. The TRO also identified a group called Children of God. I have no idea what this organization was doing on the list.

This cease and desist order trying to prevent us from conducting a demonstration was tantamount to a declaration of a state of emergency. Reading this twenty-one-page document again, I am amazed at the precise wording contained therein. The purpose of the TRO was to use the law to ensure that all of us were safely tucked away in legal limbo. The language of the document suggests that we were actually a threat to "arrest" the president of the United States.

We called a press conference for the next morning, a few hours before the planned demonstration. We built a bonfire of sorts, and one by one those who received the TROs added them as fuel to the fire. I am not sure why, but I kept my TRO, feeling that I might want to remember the event someday. I am glad that I did not burn my TRO. It may be the last remaining copy available. Some of us (including me) publicly declared that were going to violate these orders. Some others who received TROs elected to stay home and watch the event on television.

In midmorning well-known dignitaries who had arrived in Austin the day before made their way to the planned site for the dedication of the LBJ Library. An initial crowd of about three thousand protesters gathered at the staging area around Peace Fountain on the East Mall. The antiwar demonstrators consisted of students and nonstudents alike, including a large turnout by Mexican American Youth Organization, CUF, VVAW, various women's collectives, and Austin Gay Liberation.

As usual, the SMC/SWP had organized a peaceful protest on the UT campus near the Drag, a pathetic event that gathered the support of somewhere between forty and one hundred people. Never seeking to violate the law and never wavering from their narrow focus on stopping the war and bringing the troops home, the SMC proved themselves to be out of touch with wider political sentiments. The vast majority of activists gravitated toward the more confrontational approach.

On the morning of the planned disruption, we gathered at the site, slowly trickling in with banners, placards, and NLF flags. We were dressed in jeans, heavy boots, and long-sleeved shirts or jackets and had Vaseline jelly around our eyes to protect from tear gas and kerchiefs to cover our faces from unwanted photographs. On the other side of the barricades, the VIP dignitaries who gathered for the formal dedication were a veritable who's who of establishment figures, including President Richard Nixon and Vice President Spiro Agnew (and virtually their entire cabinet), high-powered politicians (John Connally, Dean Rusk, Hubert Humphrey, Barry Goldwater, Edmund Muskie, George McGovern, Birch Bayh, Clark Clifford, and McGeorge Bundy), religious leaders (Billy Graham), military brass (General William Westmorland, General Omar Bradley, General Earl Wheeler), Civil Rights icons (Roy Wilkins), educators (Harry Ransom, Chancellor Emeritus, University of Texas; Frank Erwin, former chair of the Board of Regents), and even Hollywood stars (Gregory Peck). This assembled rogue's gallery came to pay tribute to LBJ and participate with close to a thousand official guests to view the ceremonies. "Notables on Parade," an *Austin American-Statesman* headline screamed.[68] This event received maximum exposure because it was televised live to a national audience and attracted international media coverage.

The security forces established a tight cordon sanitaire around the event site. Uniformed police officers were lined along barricades they had erected to keep us out. They were flanked by dozens of undercover plainclothes cops with walkie-talkies. As the invited dignitaries streamed into the site, we banged on trash can lids, putting up quite a racket that was audible in the television coverage. As usual, the Austin VVAW contingent was quite militant at the front of our lines. These ex-GIs vowed to break through police barriers and deposit their ceremonial medals and ribbons on the LBJ Library steps as a statement of their opposition to the war.[69]

Of course, many of us served with the TROs ignored the proscribed restrictions and proceeded to participate in the protest anyway. The security

LBJ Library protest, 22 May 1971. Courtesy of Sue Mithun, photographer.

forces erected barricades, establishing a two-block perimeter around the library. The dedication site was guarded by 500 officers from DPS, 40 Texas Rangers, and 250 Austin police (including the Austin Tactical Squad), most of them in riot gear. As Nixon arrived and the UT Longhorn Band started playing "Hail to the Chief," members of Direct Action released about 800 black balloons. These floated harmlessly in the air before settling near the festivities, much to the chagrin of the worried attendees.[70] Collectively, we made a lot of noise—chanting, blowing on horns, banging on garbage can lids. In a protest event that borrowed from Operation Dewey Canyon III when VVAW threw their medals over barricades at the Capitol in Washington, DC, on 1 May 1971, Vietnam veterans at the LBJ Library demonstration also returned their medals by tossing them over police barricades. The crowd cheered.

In planning for the event, protest organizers encouraged the assembled mass of demonstrators to engage in some sort of nonviolent civil disobedience action when confronted with the police. In the heat of the moment, militant factions were determined to invade the marked-off grounds of the ceremony and disrupt the proceedings. Some protesters began to throw rocks, bottles, and water balloons at the police on the barricades. After a great deal of pushing and shoving, the VVAW eventually opened up a gap in the police lines and proceeded to cross into the forbidden territory—the ten blocks or so surrounding the library complex. Other protestors followed in their footsteps. As the police fell back in disarray, we poured across the lines, scattering everywhere, running toward the actual dedication ceremony. Some were able to get around the police barricades by going north on San Jacinto, climbing the hill behind the Art Building, and eventually "ended up getting bottled in at the Texas Memorial Museum." One militant contingent split away from the main concentration of protesters, moving toward Twenty-Sixth and Red River, where honored guests and dignitaries were enjoying a hearty Texas barbeque. I was with this group. We were able to break through or skirt around three lines of police. I was with my twin brother. As we sprinted up a slight incline and over a small bridge, a photographer took his picture. My brother reacted instinctively, grabbing the startled photographer by the shirt collar and dangling him over a railing on a bridge. The distance to the ground was about six feet. I pulled my brother off the guy, saving the startled photographer from some unknown fate after an awkward tumble into a creek. Off we ran.

The whiff of tear gas filled the entire site. We were able to disrupt the official ceremony as event planners rushed through the list of speakers before herding the dignitaries off to the relative safety inside the new library building. As the outdoor festivities were coming to a close, we made an effort to reach the war makers in their lair. A handful of us were able to get within shouting distance and successfully confront a few of the assembled dignitaries. But the police regrouped their lines of defense closer to the ceremonies, effectively preventing us from overrunning the site. A combination of tear gas and police batons drove us into retreat.

Our assault on the event was multipronged. As the core of protesters sought to disrupt the event by overcoming the police barricades and charging the site, others took a more rearguard action. As the festivities wound down and protesters scattered, a large contingent moved to Hardin House, a guesthouse where most of the invited dignitaries were staying. Faced with only a few police, some protesters—including one VVAW member I recognized and others—slashed car tires, including those transporting Dean Rusk and Billy

Arrest by plainclothes police, LBJ Library protest, 22 May 1971. Notice the exposed and holstered pistol. Courtesy of Sue Mithun, photographer.

Graham. Event security had parked these cars in a supposedly secure location within walking distance of the event. The police charged into the crowds of protesters near Hardin House, swinging clubs and arresting whomever they could grab.

Later that evening, in a planned nighttime rally and march (to avoid police photographing), we paraded around the edges of the campus and onto Guadalupe Street, probing for police weaknesses in their continued defense of the new library complex. As Kaye Northcott and Jay Brakefield of the *Texas Observer* put it, "Austin authorities said that anyone who can be recognized by police as having been at the rally can be charged during the next two years with abusive language. At least two persons were so arrested Saturday night and charged with disorderly conduct as well. The two insist they weren't even at the demonstration." All in all, twenty-nine were arrested during this day of festivities, three on felony charges (destruction of private property) and the rest on misdemeanor charges ranging from abusive language to disorderly conduct. At least half of those arrested were bystanders and passersby unconnected to the demonstration. There were several injuries to protesters and bystanders alike. Several of these people sued for false arrest. Prosecutors eventually dropped most of the charges.[71]

Our demonstration at the LBJ Library dedication attracted close to ten thousand angry protesters. I heard a rumor that someone in our protest contingent had walked mistakenly into a lecture hall on campus on the day before the planned protest event. The lights were dimmed and the police security forces were showing slides of known activists who were being targeted for arrest on the following day. Undercover police agents, posing as legitimate news reporters, took hundreds of photographs that they later used to identify individuals engaged in illegal activities. The police carried out early morning raids on places where wanted protesters were staying. They usually conducted these raids around 4:00 a.m. This tactic certainly achieved one of its goals of spreading maximum fear among antiwar movement. After this time I always stayed away from home for a few days following demonstrations. I carried my toothbrush with me, not sure where I might spend the night.

The seemingly endless round of rallies and marches continued. In the fall of 1971, we organized a demonstration of around four to five thousand protesters to shut down the federal courthouse downtown. The massive display of police force effectively kept us away from the site. The demonstration seemed to attract only the most militant protesters.

Gradually, and I might say inexorably, the motivations behind antiwar activities underwent a sea change. As the antiwar movement sought to find firm footing during the mid-1960s and onward, issues like the draft and military conscription, coupled with questions about the morality of the Vietnam War, took center stage. Certainly, after spring 1971 the thinking shifted away from questions of individual conscience and the irrationality and stupidity of the US war effort to a broader critique of US imperial ambitions and the identification of the war machine as the structural mechanisms driving the system. Our aims shifted from protest rallies providing testimonials against the war toward new goals seeking to disrupt the machinery of war.

Until the mass eruption of large-scale protests in May 1970, we were primarily political agitators, trying to build a movement and broaden consciousness against the war, racism, and misogyny. After the massive marches and occupation of the university during the first week of May 1970, the broad sentiments against the war had swung to our side.

What had become clear by early 1972 was that we had reached a tipping point. A sufficiently large number of people—students and nonstudents alike—were not only against the war but also open to a broader countercultural message of antiestablishment politics. We worked within a large base in which we did not have to concern ourselves about convincing people to oppose the war. The real issue was how best to mobilize these political sentiments into a common commitment to protest in the streets and to build alternative institutions. We continued to pay attention to young people, fresh into the university, who came intellectually unprepared to actually understand the connections between the war in Vietnam and corporate America. In seeking to tackle our own sexist and misogynist views, we followed the lead of the Women's Liberation movement. We conducted workshops, took part in teach-ins, and engaged in classroom presentations. What was now entrenched was holding meetings and protest events away from the UT campus; we were no longer a student movement.

Our combined strategies and tactics underwent a fundamental metamorphosis. Strategically, we targeted a wider range of locations for mass rallies, and we operated in coalitions with multiple organizations. This cooperation allowed us to keep our numbers of participants high. Tactically, we sponsored nighttime marches in order to avoid the police surveillance and photographing. We adopted more mobile tactics, trying to keep the police off balance. We sought less to mass our forces in the concentrated form of large rallies and demonstrations and more to stress the flexibility of smaller affinity groups operating autonomously.

Sometimes seemingly innocuous events can shed some light on shift ing tactics of the popular movement. On 5 April 1972, a group of approximately ten hippies (including four or five females and from five to eight males) boarded a university-sponsored shuttle bus service owned by Transportation Enterprises Inc. (TEI). They shared a goal. Within minutes one brazen hijacker, described as "a white male, 5-7, 140 pounds, with brown hair, brown-rimmed glasses, wearing blue jeans and sandals," grabbed the keys from the startled bus driver, demanding that he "get off the bus, you scab. We're taking over." This hijacking took place in the midst of a month-long strike of shuttle bus drivers affiliated with the local chapter of the Amalgamated Transit Union. Hours later a man fishing near Lake Austin close to Tom Miller Dam observed about twenty people "wearing old raggedy clothes [with] long hair" who had driven a TEI bus across a shallow downstream waterway onto a small, uninhabited island, abandoning the vehicle and scampering off. In the meantime an unidentified anonymous female who claimed membership in the "Local Union of the International Werewolf Conspiracy" read off a list of demands to be met in exchange for the return of the missing bus. These demands included meeting the demands of the striking shuttle bus drivers and an immediate end to the Vietnam War. I know who the hijacker is. The description of this modern-day Robin Hood (not his real name) was wildly inaccurate. No arrests were ever made.

An undercover informant reported that a party was held at the Guild on Wittis Street to celebrate the theft of the TEI bus. This spy overhead a conversation that alleged that Lori Hansel, Steve Krinsky, Gavin Duffey (the correct spelling is Duffy), and Barbara Worley (a.k.a. Vernel Pratt) were responsible for the heist. This inaccurate allegation is like drawing names out of a hat.[72]

Incidents like this surely would have escalated in scope and intensity if the Paris Peace Treaty had not ended US involvement in the war. During this same week, protesters burned down the Mountain View Army Recruiting Station in Palo Alto. The Holy Cross ROTC building was bombed. Close to one thousand people were arrested in San Francisco for seizing and holding an Air Force recruiting office. Tactics were becoming much more militant.

April–May 1972

"[Protesters are] a goddamned bunch of thugs."
Frank Erwin, chair, University of Texas Board of Regents

In spring 1972 the Nixon administration's decision to undertake a sustained program of bombing attacks against North Vietnam became a focal point for nighttime demonstrations. The mass protests that erupted in Austin were not isolated events. Large-scale antiwar activities came to a boiling point elsewhere, including the closing down of Columbia University and students from Antioch College blocking access to nearby Wright-Patterson Air Force Base. Large demonstrations took place in San Francisco, Los Angeles, and New York. Confrontations between police and protesters broke out over ROTC and other war-related targets at Berkeley, Madison, Ann Arbor, and Cambridge. Small affinity group actions at University of Maryland blockaded a major highway for three nights and battled with the National Guard before the governor declared a state of emergency. The mayor of Ann Arbor, members of the University Board of Regents, and a few professors were among a group of sixteen people who volunteered to go to Hanoi in northern Vietnam as "peace hostages to protect Vietnamese citizens and American prisoners of war from American bombing"[73]

Chronicle of 1972 Protest Activities

13 April	Leaflets at Texas Instruments after bombing of Hanoi
17 April	Leafleting at Bergstrom Air Force Base and rally at J. J. Pickle Federal Building following Haiphong mining; gathering with Bergstrom GIs at Pease Park
20 April	March to Pickle Federal Building
21 April	Student strike, march down Guadalupe to the State Capitol
	March on ROTC, LBJ Library (breaking windows), occupation of main building
24 April	Student strike continues
25 April	All-night vigil at ROTC with Direct Action playing a leading role
27 April	Tactical meeting, Pease Park
29 April	SMC-sponsored march to State Capitol and rally
30 April	First Aid Information and Practical Training meeting, Pease Park
1 May	Disruption of traffic on Lamar in front of Texas Instruments; thirty-one arrested for stopping traffic
4 May	Moratorium Day; Picketing at Texas Instruments
8 May	Haiphong ports mined, meetings and rallies
11 May	Woolridge park rally
12 May	Leafletting at Texas Instruments on Route 183
13 May	SMC-sponsored march to State Capitol
14 May	Candlelight vigil with three to four hundred participants drawn from Peace Groups, a march converging from five collection areas
	Give Peace a Chance sentiments and reading of war dead

In Austin protests rallies and marches against the war came in waves in April and May 1972. On Thursday afternoon, 13 April, close to fifty of us showed up outside the Austin branch of the defense contractor Texas Instruments (TI) at their North Lamar office complex, protesting the production of war-related equipment. We distributed leaflets describing TI's defense contracts for the production of guided bombs, air-to-ground missiles, and a "disposable seismic intrusion detector" dropped over the Ho Chi Minh Trail. We held aloft a huge banner that proclaimed "Stop the Air War, TI War Merchants."[74]

These protests at TI included three separate stages: first, civil disobedience, "wade into rush hour traffic, then sit down and wait for police to arrive"; second, distributing leaflets to stalled motorists, explaining the purpose of the demonstration; and third, affinity groups engaging in small acts of disruption and avoiding arrest.[75]

On 20 April a crowd of around 250 protesters marched to the J. J. Pickle Federal Building. By noon a large crowd gathered in the courtyard of the building where the Bertolt Brecht Memorial Theater Troupe performed skits denouncing the war. Carrying NLF (Viet Cong) and North Vietnamese flags, the "band of protesters marched north on Congress to the rotunda of the Capitol building." Protesters moving off the sidewalks to distribute leaflets provoked physical confrontations with the police.[76] As police attempted to make arrests, protesters fought back, kicking in the door of a police vehicle. Police arrested eight protesters on Congress Avenue and charged them with an assortment of infractions, including disorderly conduct, abusive language, failure to comply with a local order, and destruction of property.[77] With shouts of "On strike. Shut it down! End the war now," the crowd moved into Jester Center and the Business Economics Building, where they disrupted classes, and onto the University Union. The ROTC building closed because of bomb threats.[78]

To summarize observations offered by Bill Meacham, "Years of talking, years of marching, years of rallying, years of fatigue. . . . Last Thursday a new breath, new voices and talent. New songs. Art in the service of the revolution. Song, poetry and [guerilla] theater."[79] Rather than allowing ourselves to become vulnerable to police batons and tear gas during mass marches, we decided to engage in more hit-and-run tactics, outmaneuvering them with small groups operating semiautonomously.

On Thursday evening (13 April) the Student Senate held an emergency meeting and endorsed a resolution in support of the student strike the next day to protest escalation of the war. The senate also issued a strongly worded statement that called for "all bombing by American personnel in Vietnam be halted and American troops be withdrawn immediately."[80] The antiwar message had penetrated into the basic institutional structural apparatus of student government at UT Austin.

That same evening an estimated 250 protesters gathered at a hastily called rally to publicize a boycott of classes to begin the next morning and to lay out a plan of action for the next several days.[81] We assembled a broad coalition of groups working in tandem, including the old AMDT (which police informants claimed was defunct), Direct Action, VVAW, Women's Liberation, Gay Liberation, SMC, YSA, and SWP. Some of the known leaders who participated included several members of the YSA, David Ross (Palestine Solidarity Committee), Sam Jones (AMDT, Vietnam veteran, and known anarchist), Lori Hansel (feminist and anarchist), and me (AMDT). An undercover informant reported that one of our feminist comrades was allegedly in possession of Molotov cocktails at Twenty-First and Speedway, but Jeff Jones persuaded her and others not to use them.[82]

After the rally demonstrators marched around the campus and proceeded to the ROTC building, where unknown individuals broke several windows under the cover of darkness, and the outnumbered police did not make any arrests. The crowd then marched to Jester Center to announce the next day's student strike before veering off campus along Guadalupe Street. Avoiding a confrontation with a police contingent armed with Mace and nightsticks, the crowd "snaked its way through the neighborhood west of campus, flanked at one time by 11 police vehicles."[83]

On the morning of 21 April, dozens of picketers appeared at all main entrances to the campus, distributing leaflets announcing the start of the boycott of classes. We issued a list of demands that included total withdrawal from Southeast Asia, expulsion of ROTC and military contractors, all police off campus, and recognition of Gay Liberation. Morning workshops preceded a noon rally followed by teach-ins on corporate involvement in war, US economic interests in Vietnam, the history of US involvement in Southeast Asia, and history of antiwar movement. These events culminated with a protest march around campus to publicize the strike. Around fifty to sixty UT police officers prepared themselves for "trouble," unveiling recently purchased equipment "brought to campus in the event it is needed." This new equipment represented a technological escalation, as they introduced stronger pepper spray, gas masks, and more sophisticated tear gas "fogging machines."[84]

According to *Daily Texan* reporter Marigny Lanier, "What began as a peaceful antiwar rally at noon Friday followed by a march around campus erupted into a confrontation between approximately 600 to 700 protesters and riot-clad Austin police in the streets." Around midday protesters marched along a preplanned on-campus route from the West Mall where the rally had assembled to the ROTC building. Campus police occupied the building behind barricaded doors. Protesters threw mud and rocks at the building and through open windows. After more than an hour, an estimated 1,500 marchers led by the Austin VVAW chapter broke away from the protest at the ROTC building and moved onto Guadalupe. After a short sit-in that blocked traffic in front of the co-op, the large crowd headed for the Capitol. However, a large force of riot police armed with tear gas, clubs, and gas masks positioned themselves in readiness for a confrontation, blocking off Nineteenth and Twentieth Streets. Angry and unafraid, the VVAW contingent led the charge straight into the police lines. Trying to prevent the protesters from breaking through their defensive positions, police fired tear-gas canisters into the crowd and attacked individuals with chemical Mace. In response protesters hurled rocks and bottles at police lines. One protester, John Kniffin, a VVAW leader, was shoved to the pavement by two policemen and struck with a club several times before being arrested. He was charged with assault on a police officer. As the police pushed the protesters into retreat, skirmishes broke out everywhere, as protesters threw rocks and bottles and police retaliated by indiscriminately beating people with nightsticks.[85]

Another breakaway group, led by a militant women's collective called Women's Action, set their sights on seizing the UT radio-television building. A group of an estimated seven hundred women marched on the radio station. Five campus police officers locked doors and blocked entry at the east entrance to the building, pushing the protesters back. After smashing several windows and breaking through the door on the west entrance, the women demanded one hour of uninterrupted airtime to express their views. As Victoria Foe, a leader of the women's caucus, put it, "We came to you because we thought you would be sympathetic." The purpose of the broadcast would be "to get past the news embargo on the Vietnam War." A spokesperson for the university radio station KUT-FM agreed to a compromise,

Rough arrest of John Kniffin, leader of Vietnam Veterans Against the War (VVAW), Austin Chapter, 21 April 1972. I do believe the man in the center of the photograph with a camera was an undercover informant whom we referred to as "Nick the Cop." I do believe I know his name. Courtesy of Alan Pogue, photographer.

agreeing to allow a six-woman delegation forty-five minutes on the air. Foe blamed big business and foreign investments for the war and the news embargo. "Corporate well-being," she continued, "is what dictates what is good for the country."[86]

These decentralized tactics proved to be an effective way of ensuring that law enforcement agencies were unable to mass all their forces in anticipation of one protest event. As these separate protest events ended, demonstrators regrouped on the Main Mall and decided to meet for rally at 7:00 p.m. that evening. National Guard helicopters followed the crowd from the air.[87]

On Friday evening (21 April) approximately one thousand protesters gathered on the Main Mall, ready for direct action. Protesters came prepared with wet cloths, Vaseline jelly under the eyes, gas masks, long pants, and heavy boots. Speakers informed the crowd how to wash off tear gas, and people sang and chanted. After some heated debate, the crowd decided to return to the ROTC building. By the time the crowd reached its destination, the police had barricaded the building. The crowd, whose numbers had swelled to over three thousand angry protesters, marched to Sid Richardson Hall, the location of the LBJ Library. Protesters gathered in small groups, breaking loose to smash close to a dozen windows. One friend of mine picked up a small sewer cover (about ten inches in diameter) and threw it against a window. Failing to break it on the first attempt, he tried again, this time shattering the window into thousands of pieces. Fearing for their own safety, the Austin police on hand did not respond.[88]

The understaffed Austin police called for outside assistance. An additional group of fifty APD officers in full riot gear bolstered their numbers. In addition to calling on the support of the National Guard, the security forces under the direction of the University of Texas System imported an outside contingent of at least a dozen police officers from as far away as Galveston, Arlington, and Dallas to bolster the embattled local police.[89]

Around 10:30 p.m. protesters once again regrouped on the Main Mall. An initial group of around eighty to one hundred protesters broke through the poorly guarded entrance to the main building, pushing aside the too-few campus police officers who scrambled to get out of the way. Despite some sporadic random destruction and a lot of milling around, protest leaders called for civil disobedience and a sit-in. Antiwar protesters managed to occupy the first two floors of the building before police reinforcements arrived, using back entrances to gain access to the second floor. The building occupation and sit-in were short-lived. After forcing the building occupiers outside with chemical Mace, tear gas, and nightsticks, the police locked the doors and barricaded the building. Law enforcement officers threw one protester down a flight of stairs before beating him severely. When demonstrators started pelting the main doors with rocks and breaking windows, a reinforced contingent of campus police chased the people onto the mall and formed a line in front of the building. Approaching from the north and south, riot-equipped Austin city police entered the fray, lobbing tear-gas canisters into the crowd, pursuing demonstrators as they tried to escape. As protesters headed east to Guadalupe, the National Guard sprayed tear gas from helicopters and law enforcement officers on the ground arrested nine people.[90]

The protests were not over. Two hours after the main building had been cleared, police officers used tear gas to break up a boisterous demonstration on Guadalupe Street. Police ordered the crowd to "clear the area in one minute." But within thirty seconds, they began to spray tear gas into the crowd.[91] Law enforcement officers arrested at least eight protesters in these incidents, bringing the total of the day to twenty-five persons detained. Participant observers claimed that protesters were Maced and beaten indiscriminately when police cleared the streets with a barrage of tear gas. For the next several hours, the conjoined forces of law and order continued to spray tear gas to break up small crowds.

When this tactic did not work, the police headed through the residential areas west of campus, scattering groups of protesters who dared challenge their authority and harassing and beating anyone unable to escape. For the first time, the campus and the surrounding residential neighborhoods were literally transformed into a battlefield. The police cordoned off university grounds, locked buildings, guarded entrances with nightsticks and Mace, and pounced on small groups of protesters who scattered when they sensed danger.[92] At 11:00 p.m. police investigators discovered two unexploded Molotov cocktails on the roof of the TI building. Two hours later protesters deliberately set fires along Guadalupe Street. All in all, it was a long and eventful day.[93]

The real threat of continuous turmoil prompted the APD and campus security to request that the National Guard remain in Austin to occupy the campus. In order to announce their presence, National Guard troops marched in formation with rifles, gas masks, and steel helmets. They blanketed the entire area with tear gas—just like dogs marking their territory by peeing on a tree.

The VVAW took the lead to handle bail for the twenty-five persons arrested during various demonstration events during the day and evening of Friday. On Saturday morning there was a chaotic scene at Austin police headquarters as protesters gathered to welcome the release of their comrades. News reporters observed what they considered the "mass confusion" of city police, UT campus police, and the Texas DPS.[94]

On Saturday and Sunday, an uneasy truce prevailed over the campus and the surrounding streets. This period of relative calm simply obscured the deeper hostilities. With police and National Guard units hovering in the background, we met on campus to evaluate what had happened the previous week and how to shut down the campus the following week. Many activists criticized the lack of clear-cut leadership, indecisiveness, the reliance on spontaneity, and the poorly organized, anarchic demonstrations. Yet others praised the militant posture of the protest actions, suggesting that "Give Peace a Chance" (John and Yoko) marches had outlived their usefulness, suggesting that keeping the established forces of law and order off balance had tipped the scales in our direction, and arguing that our actions put the war machine on notice. During this weeklong series of protest events, we moved across a range of targets, including military contractors (TI), campus ROTC as part of the war machine, and the LBJ Library as a symbol of the LBJ war effort. We spent a great deal of time and energy on winning active-duty GIs to the antiwar cause. We understood that a military force unwilling to fight was a clear weak link in the US war effort.[95]

These April events triggered a veritable war of words in speeches, newspaper reporting, and letters to the editor. The blame game took on a fevered frenzy. The president of the university, Steven Spurr, issued a predictable statement: "What started out as a peaceful protest quite evidently degenerated into inexcusable mob action apparently involving many non-students." He decried the "senseless vandalism," singling out the broken windows at Sid Richardson Hall and the destruction of wooden doors in front of Board of Regents meeting room in the university main building.[96] In extending an olive branch to protesting students and to drive a wedge between moderate and militant factions in the antiwar movement, President Spurr suggested that "the University should always be a place of tolerance and rationality where ideas can be dealt with objectively and responsibly." He blamed "outside agitators," whom he argued "were bent on disruptive violence purely and merely to attract headlines." He singled out "campus hangers-on, drop-outs, or non-starters living in a steady diet of alienation" as the source of the disruption. Spurr appealed to faculty, students, and staff "to create an atmosphere for responsible and objective discussion."[97] The chair of the Board of Regents, Frank Irwin, did not mince his words: Those who broke windows at Sid Richardson Hall were a "goddamned bunch of thugs."[98]

In surveying popular opinion, newspaper reporters found a variety of views, ranging from outright condemnation of law-breaking to it's about time to step up the direct-action protests.[99] Editorials and letters to the editor expressed considerable angst about how a peaceful demonstration turned into a violent confrontation. A flurry of letters to the editor remarked how "the conservative citizenry, the large majority of Austin and America, are bewildered and frightened that the government they have trusted and worked for so long has led them astray."[100] Others expressed a common view: "I am against the war, but no one is listening." Arguing that "the police wanted a fight," one letter writer accused the "vultures in blue shirts" of indiscriminately attacking protesters.[101] In a typed letter addressed to the chief of police and saved in the George Carlson Papers, one UT student claimed that "both sides over-reacted." In expressing disapproval of breaking windows at LBJ Library and unauthorized seizure of main building, this letter writer complimented the police for preventing further destruction, claiming that police action broke up the protests.[102]

One editorial writer for the *Daily Texan* captured the brutal realities in the police bag of tricks: "Mace is probably the closest thing to liquid fire ever devised by man. A few drops of that infernal mist and your body feels like the core of a Bessemer Oven." He continued: "Mace compares to tear gas like a B-52 compares to a balsa glider." One can confront the ill effects of tear gas with water. "Guess what element of nature reacts to Mace like gasoline reacts to a butane torch? Water. Use water to wash yourself and it is 'burn, baby, burn.'"[103]

On a sobering note, David Powell, editor of the *Daily Texan*, worried aloud that "we've been fortunate so far there have been no deaths." "But unless heads stay cool and everyone tempers their emotions," he suggested, "the University could become the Kent State of 1972." "It's only a matter of time before someone gets killed if things keep going the way they've been going."[104] The movement leadership core was somewhat disorganized, incapable of containing the anger at the edges, and unable to prevent violent confrontations with police, rock throwing, and window breaking. Petty vandalism like graffiti and spray-painted messages about the war and student strikes appeared on walls and buildings everywhere. Self-appointed liberal leaders, like Jeff Friedman and Student Body President Dick Benson, attended rallies and demonstrations, trying in vain to prevent confrontations. They were unsuccessful.

On Monday morning (24 April) picketers passed out leaflets calling for a continuation of the student strike, announcing a mass gathering at noon on the main mall with teach-ins, targeting corporate involvement in war, US economic interests, history of us involvement in southeast Asia, and history of antiwar movement.[105] The university administration agreed to allow a rally to take place but demanded that Student Body President Benson control the microphone and that university officials approve list of speakers. About six hundred protesters ignored this order and staged a continuation rally at 3:00 p.m. on the Main Mall. Campus police did not intervene. If they interfered, a riot would have broken out.[106]

The University of Texas System police had imported an outside contingent of at least a dozen police officers from as far away as Galveston, Arlington, and Dallas to bolster their understaffed local campus police. In a memorandum to Mr. E. D. Walker, deputy chancellor for administration, dated 26 April 1972, George Carlson, director of police, estimated expenditures in excess of $15,000 in operating costs incurred by the University of Texas System Police for their special assignment during 20–28 April 1972. These costs included hotel accommodation (La Quinta Motor Inn), car rentals, and overtime pay.[107] These costs were only a partial list. E. D. Walker reported that costs to the city of Austin were in excess of $13,000 for tear gas dispensers. Sid Richardson Hall (the site of the LBJ Library) and the UT main building sustained an estimated $12,000 in physical damage due to broken windows, graffiti, and other instances of "vandalism."[108]

Continuation

We once again targeted TI for our direct action campaign on 1 May 1972. We built a protest coalition that included VVAW, Direct Action, Gay and Women's Liberation groups, and the Palestine Solidarity Committee. The key organizer, Martin Wiginton, said TI was a "symbolic target." Once again we decided on a combination of three interwoven but discrete militant tactics: first, mass leafleting in the vicinity of TI facilities; second, civil disobedience, such as blocking traffic; and third, affinity groups conducting their own hit-and-run tactics. It was agreed that affinity groups were on their own and were not to discuss publicly what they intended to do. As one undercover informant said, Wiginton insisted that we do nothing "that might endanger life."[109]

Many of us operated in affinity groups, breaking into small bands of mobile protesters to avoid arrest. We instructed protesters not to carry lethal weapons or engage in tire slashing or other destruction of property so as not to alienate ordinary people. We deliberately made the choice to pull back from wanton destruction because we saw it at this time as counterproductive to getting our message across. One inventive affinity group pushed an old car onto North Lamar, blocking traffic for quite some time.[110] In the end twenty-three persons were arrested for disrupting traffic.[111] An undercover informant alleged that hippies deliberately stalled a vehicle in traffic, resulting in a three-car pileup. Protests dropped piles of sharp objects on the highway, seeking to disrupt traffic.[112]

Undercover informants were active in attending meetings, taking notes, and reporting to their superiors. One such spy reported on an antiwar rally (with two hundred people in attendance) on the UT campus at 7:15 p.m. on 9 May to plan mass actions. Political organizations that had previously worked alone now began to collaborate. Those named as prominent leaders included Casey Donovan, Mike Alewitz, Melissa Singler, and Jim Denny of the SMC, and me and my brother Mark Murray, Molly Minus, John Houghton, Billy Pope, Steve Krinsky, Jeff Jones, and Martin Wiginton. There seemed to be a decision among the leaders to "keep the authorities as confused as possible" as to what the group would ultimately decide to do.[113]

The assembled group introduced two proposals for discussion: first, attending Democratic Party county conventions in order to radicalize participants; and second, sponsoring a protest march and candlelight procession to Camp Mabry with the aim of getting inside the gates and conducting civil disobedience. This second choice of target represented an expanded horizon for antiwar protesting. Located three miles northwest of downtown Austin,

Camp Mabry was the home to the Texas Military Department headquarters, containing the Joint Force Headquarters of the Texas Military Forces and office of the Adjutant General of Texas. It was also home to the Texas Army National Guard, Texas Air National Guard, and Texas State Guard and hosts the Texas Military Forces Museum. In order to protect political organizations from legal difficulties (including the work of agents provocateurs to instigate actions that would result in conspiracy trials), it was agreed that any actions of violence or civil disobedience would be on the part of individuals and not groups.[114]

Two days later, on 11 May, we held a mass action rally at Woolridge Park. We planned to combine a mass march with picketing the draft board, military recruiting offices, downtown banks, and the federal building. One purpose was to push our protest actions off campus and into the wider Austin community. The VVAW contingent agreed to organize mass leafleting on the UT campus on 11 and 12 May in preparation for the rally. We made an effort to deceive the police by suggesting that we were only planning a rally at the federal building.[115] On 12 May we led a march to the federal courthouse with a small group of only 125 protestors. We were able to obtain a parade permit with a 4–2 vote from city council.[116] Speaking before the city council in the application for the parade permit, John Lane, a self-declared anarchist and yippie, announced that he was getting tired of parades and declared that the "SMC did not represent the University community." This sentiment marked a crack in the façade of unity in the antiwar movement. The militant faction of the antiwar movement objected to the excessive legalism of the SMC and other more moderate antiwar groups.[117]

Battle of Flags and Slogans

Thinking backward over the years of public protests, I am struck by the significance of the symbolism displayed in various flags, banners, and posters. As the liberal wing of the antiwar movement finally came to the surface, these tentative moderates placed a great deal of emphasis on such innocuous slogans as "Give Peace a Chance," "Bring the troops home," "Mothers for peace," and "Stop the war." The appeal of these slogans was to attract a wide base of latecomers to an antiwar position. I did not disagree with the message these slogans conveyed but thought they could, and should, have gone farther. The SMC never ventured beyond their "Bring the troops home" slogan and their single-issue focus on the war in Vietnam. They were able to recruit liberals to their bland version of politics. I welcomed the liberals; it got them on our side of the fence. They often broke out into song, borrowing from John Lennon and Yoko Ono: "All we are saying is give peace a chance."

On the other hand, we hewed more closely to the Rolling Stones and "Street Fighting Man." I aligned with the militant, anti-imperialist faction of the antiwar movement. In demonstrations in 1969 and beyond, we took an anti-imperialist stance, carrying NLF and Democratic Republic of Vietnam (DRV) flags, and openly endorsed victory for the other side. Our chants reflected our politics:

Ho, Ho, Ho Chi Minh
Dare to Struggle
Dare to Win
Ho, Ho, Ho Chi Minh
The NLF is going to win

We interspersed these chants with other more provocative ones:

One, two, three, four
We don't want your fucking war
Five, six, seven, eight
Pick up the gun and smash the state

What do we want?
Revolution
When do we want it?
Now

We also identified with those whom we considered revolutionary heroes: Ho Chi Minh, Che Guevara, Fidel Castro, and more. We used their images on posters and in various publications.

In time the VVAW contingent marched under their own banners, supporting GI resistance and ending the war. By 1970 the Vietnam vets always moved to the front of planned marches and invariably provoked confrontations with the police. That was the nature of their pent-up anger and frustration. The tiny PL faction tended to stress the worker-student alliance over antiwar slogans. For all their years of effort, they hardly recruited anyone to their brand of politics. The miniscule Spartacist League (the Sparts)—all three of them—always carried their token banner: "All Southeast Asia MUST go Communist." Since they were Maoists and took the China side in the Sino-Soviet split, PL and the Sparts did not favor the victory of the NLF or DRV since they regarded the Communist leadership in Vietnam as puppets of the Soviet Union. Oh well. The purity of political lines will always find a place in a broad movement. This kind of hair-splitting was lost on 99 percent of those who participated in antiwar demonstrations.

By 1969 or so, we got clever in manufacturing an assortment of flags. We sewed them out of cloth. At first our favorites were the standard-bearers of historic protests: red flags (Communist) and black flags (anarchist). These were carried proudly in demonstrations or else draped out of windows from occupied buildings. Then we shifted to more political flags: NLF (red on top, blue on bottom, and a yellow star in the middle) and the Pathet Lao (a red-blue-red horizontal triband with a white circle in the center). We usually had to explain the Pathet Lao flag (representing the national liberation movement in Laos) since most did not know. Liberals favored the US Stars and Stripes flag. What was certain is that we never hoisted a white flag. We vowed never to surrender.

Certainly during the spring 1970 antiwar marches around the Kent State killings, liberals seemed always unprepared: some wore sandals (a great hindrance in running from the police) and failed to cover their exposed arms and legs. Astonishingly, they actually believed that they enjoyed the full range of civil liberties and that the police were there to protect their rights to assembly and free expression. After the first indiscriminate volley of tear gas and seeing peaceful protesters beaten and arrested, the liberals lost their naive attachment to those inalienable rights they learned about in grade school. There is nothing like a police club to disabuse liberals of fanciful myths about constitutional protections under the rule of law. In the mayhem of the streets, discretionary power replaced the law. I once witnessed a middle-aged man, dressed in a well-tailored suit and tie, get between a line of riot police and protesters, shouting at the cops, "This is a peaceful protest. I am a college professor." A bury cop wacked him upside the head, and down he went in a heap. He was arrested for disorderly conduct. Poetic justice?

On the other hand, we came prepared: boots, long pants, heavy shirts, and wet bandanas tied around our heads and necks to provide some protection against tear gas. Some came with gloves to pick up tear gas canisters and toss them back at the police lines. It was always important to be prepared for any eventuality. We were never sure what tactics the assembled police might employ. They were never quite ready for our improvisation.

The End of the End

The nature of political protest took a sharp turn. Unlike the lack of clear leadership and the ambivalence over strategy and tactics that occurred during May 1970, the antiwar movement learned valuable lessons about the use of mobile tactics and the merit of focusing protests on specific targets. Another current in the antiwar movement, Direct Action, worked in tandem with the militant faction. With its origins in peace group politics with religious roots, Direct Action focused on bringing the war home through grassroots nonviolent civil disobedience.

For one, Martin Wiginton expressed a clear political strategy. In an article in *The Rag* he wrote, "We do have power when we act collectively to threaten the major powers that run this country. . . . If the domestic costs become too high, either in terms of the material destruction of their property, disruption of their transportation or communications systems, rising costs to support their domestic police actions, or the sowing and acceptance of ideas that might fairly quickly lead to significant numbers of Americans deciding to break through their conditioning and start taking control of their own lives, then these decision-makers will change their war policy."[118]

In October 1972 we held a number of marches and demonstrations, including a rally at the ROTC building, a demonstration at Bergstrom Air

Force Base, and meeting with a delegation of students from Vietnam who opposed the war. We built a wide alliance of antiwar groups called the October 14th Coalition (remnants of the AMDT, Direct Action, Gay and Women's Liberation), and we sponsored a march on 14 October 1972 from the steps of the LBJ Library to the offices for the Committee to Re-Elect the President. The dwindling numbers of participants—fifty to one hundred protesters—indicated the widespread exhaustion with rallies and marches.[119]

The so-called Christmas bombing of Hanoi during a ten-day period in December 1972 marked the last gasp of the US war machine to squeeze concessions out of their Vietnamese enemies. The use of B-52 airplanes to carpet bomb the area around Hanoi was indeed a war crime. We organized a few demonstrations in the short period before the peace treaty was signed in January 1973. These events marked the end of public demonstrations against the Vietnam War. A kind of bewilderment set in, leaving us pondering what to do next, if anything.

PART 3

Organized State Repression

Chapter 6

The State Security Apparatuses and Policing

The antiwar movement in Austin was born under the bad sign of police surveillance and undercover infiltration. The various branches of the security apparatus constituted a kind of shadow state that operated under the false veneer of respect for civil liberties, the rights of free speech and assembly, and a system of jurisprudence that rested on the principle of innocent until proven guilty. Security agencies created a system of surveillance that brought countless numbers of law-abiding citizens under their scrutiny.

In retrospect, it is now clear that the repressive arms of the state security apparatus—the FBI and its secret COINTELPRO operations, military intelligence, and criminal intelligence divisions attached to local police departments—did not see themselves as bound to the constitutional niceties of civil liberties and equal protection before the law. The intelligence services, in alignment with local police forces, did not hesitate to engage in extralegal tactics. They watched us, they followed us, they sought to sow dissention in our ranks, and they sought to lure us into illegal acts that they actually planned. It truly was low-intensity warfare outside the bounds of law.

The aim of the policing agencies was to eliminate what they regarded as a threat to national security. The playing field for the bitter contest between the broad movement and the security agencies was not the one constructed in the liberal imagination that revolved around formal constitutional guarantees respecting the rights to free assembly, free speech, and free expression. The security agencies quickly dispensed with respect for civil liberties, and they engaged in a sub-rosa, extralegal reign of terror against the political left and the antiwar movement.

What gave the security apparatuses a distinct advantage was the arbitrariness of the exercise of power. Undercover informants epitomized capricious, discretionary power. It was their very ordinariness that helped disguise them, enabling them to mingle freely inside antiwar circles. They formed the enemy hidden within, reporting to the enemy without. Because they were not always reliable and because they often were not sure what was important enough to report, undercover informants were actually one of the weakest links in the security armature arrayed against the antiwar movement. Yet despite their enormous potential for suppressing dissent, the security agencies were unable to derail the antiwar movement and quell the upsurge in popular sentiment for equal protections under the law and racial justice.

The Extended Reach of the Layered Security Apparatuses

Seen through a wider lens of state security, police investigative and intelligence units, commonly known as Red Squads for their pursuit of radical political activists, can trace their origins to the search for subversives during the Gilded Age and Progressive Era. The work of these Red Squads expanded with the anti-Communist campaigns of the 1940s–1950s and the efforts to undermine the New Left in the 1960s and 1970s. The compulsive reaction of Cold War anti-Communism that endowed these investigative and intelligence policing units their raison d'etre remained in place even as the perceived threat of domestic Communism had largely receded and the Red Squads shifted their attention to the Civil Rights and the Black Power Movements, New Left organizations, and antiwar activists. The full panoply of state and federal law enforcement agencies shared this trajectory. Enjoined with the mandate of COINTELPRO, the FBI (under the leadership of J. Edgar Hoover) linked with military intelligence agencies to coordinate the active pursuit of alleged subversive individuals and organizations, while at the same time state- and local-level intelligence units synchronized similar efforts through law enforcement agencies at all governmental levels. Seeking to align their work with one another, police intelligence units at federal, state, and local levels shared information and collaborated to trap political activists in a hoped-for seamless web of surveillance.[1]

We in the Austin antiwar movement viscerally understood that security agencies were monitoring us. In retrospect, we had no idea of the extent to which state security agencies sought to coordinate their efforts or the extent to which they actively engaged in extralegal methods to disrupt our activities, including blatant violations of civil liberties. From our perspective they were not as successful as they might have imagined.

During the 1960s and through the 1970s, a range of government security agencies operated formidable domestic surveillance programs that both paralleled each other and overlapped. In time official state efforts to monitor radical political movements coalesced into a whole security complex that was organized vertically, with the national headquarters of the FBI in Washington, DC, at the apex. The regional FBI San Antonio office had jurisdictional control over Austin. The FBI coordinated their surveillance and monitoring efforts with military intelligence, the Texas DPS, the APD Criminal Intelligence Division, the Travis County Sheriff's Department, the University of Texas System security (George Carlson), and the US Secret Service. Whatever the differences between the various branches, the security apparatuses created an elaborate system to monitor political dissent and sanctioned actions by their agents that violated both the legal rights of individuals and organizations. Illegally wiretapping phones, taking surveillance photographs of political demonstrations, and using undercover informants to infiltrate political groups were commonplace practices in Austin. The visible presence of law enforcement agencies fostered the belief that Big Brother was always watching.

A great deal of scholarship has convincingly demonstrated that national security operations were considerably more extensive than was imagined at the time. According to Brian Glick in *War at Home: Covert Action Against US Activists*, the state security apparatus deployed four main methods of operation: infiltrating suspected subversive organizations and groups, conducting psychological warfare (psych-ops) from the outside, harassing known activists and political organizations through the legal system, and using extralegal force and violence as a way of disrupting and undermining political activism. The centerpiece of the state security apparatus was the FBI, and the aim of COINTELPRO was to "expose, disrupt, misdirect, discredit, or otherwise neutralize" political organizations that the FBI considered subversive or a potential threat to national security. Created in 1956 to counteract the alleged Communist infiltration of US institutions, COINTELPRO acquired new life when the FBI designated New Left organizations and the growing antiwar movement as the main threat to national security. COINTELPRO most frequently targeted left-wing organizations, including communist and socialist parties, Black Power organizations, and anti–Vietnam War groups. As Glick put it, the security police "resorted to the secret and systematic use of fraud and force to sabotage constitutionally protected political activity."[2]

The Historical Specificity of Police Surveillance in Austin

In the early years (1963–1965), as the political movement in Austin emerged and took shape, Burt Gerding was a familiar and legendary figure known to local activists. His assigned policing role was to monitor subversive activities in Austin. For a time in the mid-1960s, Gerding was a permanent fixture on the UT campus and around town. He attended virtually every political meeting and event organized by campus radicals, "always with his ironic smile, greeting everybody by name." He took great pleasure in catching people off guard, offering unsolicited comments on "information he had about them."[3]

By the time I began attending SDS meetings in fall 1967, Gerding was always lurking about in the background, observing rallies and demonstrations from a safe distance. He occasionally attended public meetings and took photographs of demonstrations. I remember on at least one occasion when Gerding tried to slip into a political meeting, the participants shouted him down and yelled at him to leave. He left. After that time in early 1968, Gerding, as I remember, was no longer a physical presence at meetings.

For the most part, security agencies were not adept or effective at gathering reliable information. Depending upon undercover informants was not a particularly productive way to find out what was happening. I found a detailed, single-spaced, nine-page report written at some time in early 1968 outlining the state of play of political organizations in Austin. The combination of exaggeration, incorrect information, and misplaced attribution demonstrates that the security apparatus did not have a good understanding of what was going on. What is striking is the lack of attention to political positions and ideological differences. The author of this report seemed clueless about what divided political organizations and tended to lump them all under the same banner—pseudo-Communist.[4]

Lt. Burt Gerding may have been the author of this report. But it seems too sophisticated for him. He seemed very skillful at identifying individuals involved in political activities. But from my reading of the Gerding Papers and from my occasional yet infrequent encounters with Gerding, I do not believe that he had the capacity to think analytically or outside the box of conventional wisdom that was rooted in 1950s anti-Communism.

This security report does not have a title, date, or any identifying marks. The author begins with the claim that groups and organizations evolved since the early 1960s and can trace their origins to two groups: the Student Peace Union and Students for Direct Action. The Student Peace Union consisted of "young intellectual liberals" advocating the abolition of nuclear weapons and promoting peace. The Students for Direct Action was an ad hoc group of students and young faculty members dedicated to the racial integration of movie theaters and restaurants near the University of Texas campus. This was the first group to hold organized demonstrations—sit-ins and picket lines—in Austin in opposition to racial segregation.

After identifying a number of organized groups, the anonymous author then proceeds to comment analytically on each in turn. The author focuses first on SDS and claims it first came into existence after a "negro" member was refused entry into a local bar. The report declared that by late 1967 SDS had approximately one hundred very active members in Austin. "This group's members have become more and more involved in all movements: draft resistance, anti-Viet-Nam War demonstrations, Black Power, Industrial Workers of the World, Spartacist, Progressive Labor, Socialist Worker [*sic*] Party, Communist Party USA, W.E.B. DuBois Club, the Hippie Movement and its involvement in hallucinatory drugs." According to the report, the members of SDS had multiple memberships and were involved in all sorts of different groups: "We do not know of a single S.D.S. member that does not have membership in some other organization." This observation does not seem particularly insightful. The report continued: "This 100 are of a very active militant nature and form the hard core of all the active organizations in the area. This group is inclined towards acts of civil disobedience." Members of SDS established the underground newspaper, *The Rag*. The goal of *The Rag* was "to attack the local and national power structure, the academic power structure and community *mores*."[5]

This security report next turned to draft resistance. "This group is dedicated to assisting and counseling young males of draft age in how to escape military service." In particular, the group "encourages desertion from the service and aid deserters in evading apprehension by military authorities. They are involved in providing an 'underground railroad' to assist draft dodgers and deserters." Wow. If this were actually the case, members of the draft resistance would be liable to charges of treason. Draft counselors were much more cautious than this report suggests. The author suggests that women members of the draft resistance planned to assault Marine recruiters in the Union Building in November 1967 by throwing pies, but that local law enforcement (FBI, APD, and campus security) appeared on the scene to prevent this action. I have serious doubts that this scenario ever took place. I was there, and I do not recall any discussion or effort to implement this plan of action. It seems like exaggerated bragging.

The report then focuses on the UTCEWV. The UTCEWV was an affiliate of SDS. The author gives a long litany of protest activities that this group allegedly organized. During 1967 this group demonstrated in opposition to President Johnson's appearance in Killeen, Texas; General Howard K. Johnson's appearance on the UT campus; Vice President H. H. Humphrey's and Dean Rusk's appearance before the Texas legislature. The author claims that this organization had fifty active members. UTCEWV was a subcommittee of SDS. While members of the UTCEWV may have participated, this organization was certainly not the prime mover behind the demonstrations listed above. SDS was the main culprit. I know. I was there.

The report refers to "Black Power" organizations. The author makes the outlandish claim that SNCC was meeting in private homes in Austin, along with representatives from PL, the Industrial Workers of the World, and CPUSA. "Informants indicate that the purpose of these meetings is to plan for riots in Houston during the summer of 1968." This claim is utterly ridiculous. Representatives of those organizations would never meet, let alone plan, anything together. It is clear that the author of this report either inadvertently relayed misinformation or deliberately made exaggerated claims to possibly please his/her superiors.

The author claims that the Industrial Workers of the World (IWW) came into existence in Austin in 1966, and that members of this organization were also active in SDS. This is possible. Activists who declared some sort of loose allegiance to the IWW were indeed active in SDS. Professing allegiance to IWW principles was mainly a way of distancing oneself from emergent Marxist–Leninist currents.

The author then investigates the Spartacists. "Their members are known to teach the use of fire bombs and small firearms in disturbances." This wild accusation was absolutely not true for Austin. The Sparts were a very small group, known for their ideological purity, their adulation of the Chinese Revolution, and their aversion to militant action. They were a nuisance—nothing more and nothing less.

The author also considers the CPUSA and its youth wing, the W. E. B. DuBois Clubs. While claiming that the Communist Party had five active members in the Austin area, the author asserts that these members were active in civil rights, student politics, and Black Power. These were aspirational goals that were never realized. "They had a major hand in the planning of the University Freedom movement last Spring [1967] and one of its members has recently been appointed to a high office in S.DS." Both George Vizard and Mariann Vizard were members of the Communist Party. George was murdered in spring 1967. Both he and Mariann played active and nonsectarian roles in SDS and *The Rag*. George and Mariann certainly strongly influenced the direction of politics in 1966 and 1967, but they did not control it.

The hippie movement was the last group considered. "The hippie [movement] is a broad movement involving many different forms of social behavior." The author continued:

> Generally, the hippies can be broken down into the following groups: those involved in sweeping social revolutionary changes; those involved in drugs and the use of drugs as an escape mechanism, and PSUEDO religious experience; those involved in psychedelic movies, art and music; and the so-called FLOWER CHILDREN which seek to promote great brotherly love and gentleness in human behavior; those that are known as the DIGGERS which is a group within the overall group that seeks to help all other members of the hippie movement when they become ill, physically or mentally, or when they have bad experiences with hallucinogenic drugs or when they have nothing to eat or no place to stay.

This analysis is ridiculous. The author demonstrates no real understanding of the growing groundswell in opposition to the Vietnam War, the rejection of the cultural straitjacket of rigid adherence to traditional gender roles, and the repudiation of state authority imposed from above. The author never once used the term "New Left."

The report concludes with a paragraph each on the PL Party and the Socialist Workers Party. The author dismisses both as inconsequential, with small membership and little influence. Actually, the SWP did have a presence in Austin, especially through their affiliates YSA and SMC. The SMC was able to mobilize participation in antiwar marches but failed on its own—without temporary alliances with other antiwar groups—to garner much attention.

The Wider Arc

In May 1968, as the New Left and antiwar movements intensified their activities across the United States, J. Edgar Hoover implemented a secret FBI "counterintelligence" program called COINTELPRO. At its core COINTELPRO was an insidious and constitutionally unlawful campaign that targeted and harassed political activists, infiltrated (and disrupted) organizations, and monitored underground newspapers that the bureau considered subversive—and especially those that had criticized Hoover or the FBI. "Our nation is undergoing an era of disruption and violence caused by various individuals generally connected with the New Left," Deputy Director Charles D. Brennan proclaimed in a memo (dated 9 May 1968) written to Domestic Intelligence Director William C. Sullivan. In proposing the formation of COINTELPRO, Brennan wrote, "The New Left has on many occasions viciously and scurrilously attacked the Director and the Bureau in an attempt to hamper our investigation of it and to drive us off the college campuses." The purpose of COINTELPRO was to "expose, disrupt, and otherwise neutralize the activities" of New Left groups. "It is hoped," the memo concluded, "that with this new program their violent and illegal activities may be reduced if not curtailed."[6]

Efforts to derail the antiwar movement through COINTELPRO used a combination of exaggerated caricature, misinformation, and outright fabrication to smear the reputations of individuals and discredit organizations. According to the findings of the 1974 Church Committee investigating bureau intelligence activities, the COINTELPRO New Left program used about fourteen different types of harassment methods, "from the simply annoying to the vicious and potentially deadly." The attacks from the bureau included sending anonymous letters, often using fictitious authors, like a fabricated person named Dillon J. O'Rourke, who was the favorite of the FBI San Antonio field office. Under the mandate of COINTELPRO, law enforcement security agents planted incriminating evidence in drug arrests, made fake phone calls to obtain information, engaged in deliberate harassment of well-known activists, and created an extensive network of paid undercover informants.[7]

While COINTELPRO received a lot of national attention, very little has been written that exposes how these dirty tricks operated on the ground in places like Austin. A few examples (drawn from FBI files) should suffice to make the point that COINTELPRO did not shy away from fabrication, fakery, and exaggeration, especially of an explicitly sexual nature. The effort to undermine the career of a woman from Houston SDS is worth recounting in detail because it illustrates in microcosm the extent to which the FBI would go. Local FBI agents in Houston began with observations on a young woman whom they alleged was active in SDS at University of Houston, was involved in "SDS-sponsored anti-American activities, [led a] promiscuous personal life, use[d] marijuana, and [displayed a] resentment of authority." According to FBI agents, she gained the attention of local school authorities who reprimanded her for wearing a miniskirt during her practice teaching course. After being told that wearing miniskirts was not allowed, she appeared in dresses well below the knee—"which were as outlandish as the mini-skirts." "She was obviously showing her rebellion against the authorities."[8]

In an internal memo (dated 8 July 1968), and framed under the heading "Counterintelligence Program, Internal Security, Disruption of the New Left," FBI headquarters in Washington, DC, authorized local agents in Houston to "prepare and mail to the Los Angeles Board of Education an anonymous letter mailed from a fictitious address. The letter should be prepared on locally purchased stationery [and] not traceable to the Bureau or the Government."[9] The FBI suggested that the following letter be forwarded from the Houston FBI office to the Los Angeles school board:

> Dear Sirs . . .
>
> It has come to my attention that [the name of the young woman redacted] who was a former resident of this apartment complex is enrooted [*sic*] to Los Angeles, California to obtain a teaching position. While I am in complete agreement of her leaving Houston, I feel it is my duty to inform you of the background of this girl as she is completely unsuitable in my estimation for teaching youngsters. She was a well-known radical and troublemaker while a student at University of Houston. She appears proud of the fact that she has been affiliated with a group calling themselves Students for a Democratic

> Society and also that she has been involved in many demonstrations against the Vietnam War and other anti-American activities. She is extremely promiscuous in her personal life as well as a user of marijuana. She has had numerous beatnik type persons spend the night in her apartment. Also during the time she was taking practice teaching I understand that she got the officials at the school upset by wearing mini-mini-skirts. She was told she would have to wear more appropriate clothes and she thereafter came to school wear ankle length dresses. Obviously she merely wanted to cause trouble rather than become educated. As you can see this girl is certainly not the proper person to be in charge of and teaching youngsters in yours or any other school system. It is suggested that you might want to thoroughly check this person before offering her a teaching position.
>
> Yours truly,
> Ann Hill
> 1549 Lombardy
> Houston, Texas

The name Ann Hill was fictitious, and the 1549 Lombardy address was a vacant unit in the apartment complex where the unnamed woman who was targeted for this dirty-trick operation had resided.[10]

In trying to disrupt SDS recruitment activities, the FBI Houston office mailed fictitious letters to parents of students at University of Houston, Rice University, San Jacinto College, and other educational institutions in the area, warning that leaders of SDS were "for the most part filthy, bearded, long-haired individuals whose reputations leave much to be desired and who obviously are utilizing current problems in the US for their own demented activities and in the process are carrying a lot of well-meaning and reputable students along with them. The SDS is far from a legitimate campus organization. The leaders advocate the elimination of all authority at the universities and subsequent chaos and control by the students."[11]

FBI COINTELPRO and Austin

One cannot understand the context of the Austin movement without looking at the implementation of state-organized and state-sponsored counterintelligence programs—notably of COINTELPRO—and their impact on local political practices. Living under the watchful eye of a vengeful Big Brother created a climate of fear. As the antiwar movement gained momentum, the political repression in the country increased dramatically, and many of us feared the possibility of a full-fledged police state. All in all, COINTELPRO was designed to crush the New Left, the antiwar movement, and all other allegedly subversive organizations.

In furthering its aim of disruption, the COINTELPRO strategy involved using anonymous letters to stir controversy. In 1967 the San Antonio FBI office (with jurisdiction over Austin) sent an anonymous letter to Frank Erwin, chair of the Board of Regents, supposedly from an irate parent trying to protect a prospective student, complaining that "free love comes to the surface on and around the UT Austin [campus]." This anonymous letter was undoubtedly the first of a series of letters sent to University administrators complaining about "radical politics" and licentious behavior at UT Austin.[12] In their internal discussions, FBI branch offices discussed and debated whether to send anonymous letters to key University of Texas officials (Harry Ransom, chancellor; Frank Erwin, chair of Board of Regents), political figures (Texas State Senator Wayne Connally, brother of Governor John Connally), and various newspaper editors around the state of Texas. The aim of these anonymous postings was to associate SDS with Communism.[13]

In June 1968 the FBI San Antonio field office expressed elation that the national headquarters had initiated COINTELPRO, arguing that a "successful counterintelligence program can help to stifle the growth of activity of the New Left which in some cases appears to border on sedition." The San Antonio office identified SDS as the prime mover behind New Left politics in Austin and estimated that its membership and sympathizers numbered around 150 individuals.[14] Of course this number was a gross underestimate of students and others attracted to SDS and New Left politics. In July 1968 the FBI announced plans under COINTELPRO to recruit "high level informants to infiltrate the New Left Movement" in Austin. In the same memorandum, the San Antonio FBI field office identified (by code names in highly redacted text) at least nine informants whose job it was to spy on the antiwar movement and other New Left organizations in Austin.[15]

Under COINTELPRO protocols FBI agents also send anonymous letters to parents of young people employed at the Oleo Strut, a GI coffeehouse located in Killeen. Motivated by what they believed to be the "depraved character and moral looseness of the New Left," they kept up a relentless campaign of counterintelligence operations.[16] In one example FBI agents anonymously informed the parents that their children were engaging in anti-war indoctrination of active-duty soldiers stationed at nearby Fort Hood. Ostensibly written by "concerned citizens," these letters complained that the young people working at the Oleo Strut were "living in a commune and attending pot parties."[17]

An example of the lengths the FBI field offices would go to vilify and destroy a targeted individual is evident in a memo dated 15 October 1968 from the special agent in charge (SAC) in San Antonio. In the memo the SAC reported that a local schoolteacher had been a member of SDS while a student at Cornell University. The SAC reviewed "credit and criminal records and selective service records" to verify the information. "If [redacted name] was a member of the SDS this would be an excellent opportunity to discredit him with the South San Antonio school district." Bureau headquarters in Washington, DC, jumped to approve the request, writing in response, "An investigation of [redacted] should be aggressively pursued to pursue his current status in regard to SDS."

Much to their dismay, the FBI learned that the teacher in question had never been a member of the SDS but had instead either turned in or destroyed his draft card while a student at Cornell. Undeterred and undaunted, FBI agents still pushed forward with the false accusation in a letter sent to the South San Antonio school system in January 1969. "I feel that we do not need this type of person in any school system," the letter writer wrote, signed by a "concerned citizen who believes in true academic freedom." In an April 1970 follow-up memo, the FBI field office verified that the school board fired the falsely accused teacher and that he subsequently moved out of Texas.[18]

In discussing how to disrupt the SDS National Council meeting held in March 1969, various FBI field offices weighed in with proposals. One involved printing one thousand leaflets to be placed clandestinely on a literature table during the meetings. The purpose of the leaflet was to drive a wedge between the PL and National Office (Chicago) factions of SDS. The substance of the leaflet alleged that the PL group was heavily infiltrated by security agencies. The FBI headquarters took this plan so seriously that they elicited comments from field offices in Cleveland, New York, and Chicago on the feasibility of this scurrilous innuendo. FBI headquarters worried aloud whether such an allegation would lead to exposure of undercover agents already implanted in PL. In the end the FBI decided not to distribute the leaflet at the National Council meeting but left open the possibility of using it at a future date.[19] On a broader terrain, non-PL members of SDS would not have been shocked by these charges because they believed that PL was operating in ways that objectively undermined the antiwar movement, whether they were influenced by security agencies or not.

A 5 July 1969 FBI COINTELPRO memo reflects particular interest in University of Texas groups such as UTCEWV, Afro-Americans for Black Liberation, and the W. E. B. Du Bois Club. In point of fact, the UTCEWU did not exist in Austin in 1969. It was SDS. This memo also contains redacted personal data about the leaders of these groups obtained from FBI sympathizers via university records, including height, weight, build, hair color, and even the names of parents and addresses. A 12 August 1969 memo suggests publishing phony articles in the local press to show the "depravity" of New Left leaders and members. The memo stated, "Letters and articles showing advocation [*sic*] of the use of narcotics and free sex are ideal to send to University officials, wealthy donors, members of the Legislature, and parents of the students who are active in New Left matters." This memo added that these phony letters should be written not directly from the FBI but pseudonymously, "in the vein of an irate parent" or "an angry taxpayer."[20]

Apparently, J. Edgar Hoover approved this type of surreptitious activity, and a bureau-sponsored campaign of harassment and slander soon got underway. The San Antonio SAC rented a post office box under the fictitious name Dillon J. O'Rourke, PO Box 382, San Antonio, 78206, for the sole purpose of sending letters to *The Daily Texan*, the student newspaper at UT. Over many months O'Rourke became possibly the most prolific letter writer in Texas, with this name appearing on numerous letters to the editor in *The Daily Texan* during this period. References to Dillon O'Rourke appear numerous times in

FBI files. This make-believe person carried the burden of fomenting exaggerated disinformation. FBI Director J. Edgar Hoover warned field offices to make sure that "all necessary steps are taken to prevent the Bureau from being identified as the source of these notes."[21]

The FBI field office in San Antonio kept busy with their "counterintelligence actions," such nefarious acts as spreading rumors that particular political activists were "narcotics agents."[22] The aim was to undermine the political influence of those rumored to be narcs. At the end of the day, the effectiveness of these measures was extremely limited. In their internal communications, the FBI admitted that, with few exceptions, they were "unaware of any tangible results" from anonymous mailings.[23] I would guess that realizing your own ineffectiveness with extralegal tactics would be dispiriting to say the least. Yet like missionaries unable to make much headway in hostile territory, these security agents regarded their failures as a sign to redouble their efforts in the vain hope of future success.

We in the antiwar movement were often naive, but we were not completely stupid. We knew that persons busted for possession or sales of drugs often agreed to become undercover informants in order to obtain reduced sentences. We always joked that our phones were tapped. We were always on the lookout for police photographers during demonstrations. Even if we did not know or even suspect individuals, we knew that undercover agents infiltrated our meetings. As we became more collectively aware, the security agencies became more desperate, gradually lifting the veil of legality to engage in counterintelligence activities outside the law.

The Organizational Matrix of the Security Apparatuses

In Austin the rogue's gallery of law enforcement agencies and agents aligned against us was formidable. The layered security apparatus consisted of many diverse branches—military intelligence, Texas DPS, UT campus security, the Criminal Intelligence Division of APD, and more—and each operated in accordance with their own rules and their own mandates, collecting different types of intelligence. Whatever cooperation developed was not organic.

The security apparatus consisted of four layers. These overlapped and intersected but largely operated under their own organizational logics, chains of command, and modes of operation. The first layer consisted of legions of detached observers hired to perform such mundane tasks as typing memos, filing reports, and making phone calls. These low-level functionaries were not particularly politically motivated. These were largely bureaucrats who monitored and recorded tapped phones, took photographs from afar at demonstrations, and provided information when asked (university registrars, landlords, campus officials, and the like). They were necessary cogs in the wheels of information gathering and surveillance.

The second layer was comprised of paid security personnel who made their presence known on occasion, largely to instill fear and to demonstrate to activists that they were indeed watched. These were FBI agents, uniformed police officers, and campus security officials. We encountered this layer of the security system at times of demonstrations, rallies, and marches, when uniformed police officers drawn from various security agencies confronted us on the streets with clubs and tear gas. The visible presence of these security agents represented the physical authority of law enforcement.

The third layer consisted of undercover police informants who were active members of political organizations and movements. They deliberately sought out leadership positions, volunteered for sensitive tasks (keeping phone lists of members), and studiously participated in political activities and debates. These undercover informants often represented Austin organizations in regional or even national conferences. They constructed believable cover stories to sever any possible connection to the security apparatus. For the most part, they gained our trust and friendship. Some of these undercover agents joined organizations in Austin after police training in special surveillance academies. Others were turned by security agents after arrests on various felony charges, agreeing to inform on political activists under threat of long prison terms. Still others agreed to work as undercover informants because of their political beliefs in opposition to militant antiwar activities.

The fourth and final layer consisted of special agents whose goal was to disrupt movement activities through their own clandestine and often illegal activities. COINTELPRO epitomized this approach. Some agents specialized in spreading false rumors about activists, sending anonymous letters to newspapers and employers and creating fake organizations. Other agents clandestinely broke into apartment buildings, opened mail, and went through discarded trash. At the extreme, some agents actively tried to encourage gullible and unsuspecting activists into conspiracies to commit illegal acts, like bombings, destruction of property, and assembling weapons caches. The aim here was to ensnare activists into illegal acts that would lead to conspiracy trials.

What becomes evident in reading the Gerding Papers is that security agencies operated as relatively autonomous organizations with their own aims and their own sources of information. For example, George Carlson, head of security for the entire UT System and a former FBI agent, relied upon a combination of undercover informants and lower-ranking university employees to supply him with information. But he conducted his work independently of other agencies, like the Criminal Intelligence Division of the APD and the FBI San Antonio field office.

What the assembled parts of the security apparatus achieved in organizational coherence and dedicated service, they lacked in truly acquiring an understanding of what was happening. Their fixation on organized national parties—Communist Party USA (CPUSA), PL, Social Workers Party (SWP), and the Spartacist League—meant that they almost always overlooked local, home grown movements not affiliated with the usual suspects.

The various security agencies gravitated back and forth along a continuum of cooperation and competition. For one, the FBI operated in a self-imposed silo. Due to its experience in monitoring the civil rights campaigns in the US during the 1950s and early 1960s, national FBI headquarters did not authorize regional offices to share information with local law enforcement agencies because they did not trust these local police departments to keep this information to themselves. The FBI learned from its mistakes in working in civil rights cases in Mississippi and Alabama that local police departments were untrustworthy partners. In Austin Gerding claimed that the FBI "either cooperated with me or they didn't get good stuff." In short, the FBI put themselves in jeopardy by not cooperating. "I got so close to some of these [FBI] agents," Gerding claimed, "they would tell me things." In his interviews with the Briscoe Center, he said that FBI agents purposefully left materials for him to read when they were out of the room.[24]

Information Gathering

Certainly by early 1968, if not before, the movement in Austin had grown too large for Burt Gerding to monitor adequately by himself and with the assistance of University of Texas Campus Police Chief Allen Hamilton. Where did the help come from, and how was it done? The APD Criminal Intelligence Division had clearly infiltrated our ranks very early. I remain forever dumbfounded and curious about this untold story. Certainly the security forces used undercover informants and spies. Now, with the advantage of hindsight, I have come to believe that there were many more informers than I would have suspected at the time. I have my own suspicions about who some of them were.

The collected files that constitute the Gerding Papers are frustrating to read. Much of the material included consists of occasional memos, handwritten notes (scribbled quickly on scraps of paper), newspaper clippings, and random leaflets. Much of the handwritten notes refer to meetings of various organizations, almost always listing names, dates, and themes. The material seems to have just been dumped indiscriminately into files without any rhyme nor reason. Many of these hastily scribbled notes are cursory notations, intended (so it seems) for recall later. It is literally impossible to identify a narrative thread here. On a larger scale, it is impossible to understand how these materials—scraps of paper, odd leaflets, and arcane notes—would have been useful to the APD Intelligence Division.

After reviewing the assorted leaflets and printed materials in the various boxes that made up the Gerding Papers, I arrived at a startling question. I know we produced a lot more written material than what Gerding saved. We produced countless numbers of leaflets, newsletters, and mimeographed broadsheets that we were constantly distributing. Production of written materials was a virtual cottage industry. What was the selection bias here? Why were some items gathered, stored, and eventually donated to the Briscoe

Collection? There appears to be no coherence, no logic, and no story behind their collection efforts. I think that what the Criminal Intelligence Division saved was largely happenstance; that is, an undercover police informant happened to lay his or her hands on a leaflet or a pamphlet and that became their method of collection. Pretty simple really. But also not a good strategy if the goal of the security forces was to piece together what the movement was doing and planning.

After reading the Gerding Papers, one of the security practices that stands out is the almost obsessive fixation on naming names. Handlers instructed police informants to record the names of those who attended meetings. To give one example, an undercover police informant reported on a GI-civilian picnic attended by approximately seventy-five persons (including "30–40 who appeared to be GIs") held in a park in Austin on 19 July 1970.[25] For obvious reasons active-duty GIs were extremely reluctant to reveal their true identities. Despite these precautions the undercover informant was able to identify three GIs by name and to provide a long list of many of the non-GIs who attended the picnic. Undercover informants displayed a kind of quiet power—"a power that comes that has always come, that always will come, from secret knowledge."[26] Perhaps unknowingly or even inadvertently, they passed along shards of information that stood in for truth.

One of the common features of security files is the use of pseudonyms and code names. The FBI preferred some combination of letters and numbers (for example, "S-100-A") to refer to an undercover informant. Burt Gerding, on the other hand, constructed names for his informants: Sally, Sam, and Leroy, for instance. While the identities of undercover informants were kept anonymous, the heads of security agencies who were the recipients of the undercover reports were always identified by name. Security agencies made extensive use of an idiosyncratic language that is difficult to decipher what they meant or intended.

At the time I did not spend an inordinate amount of time thinking about undercover informants. I had encounters with agents provocateurs (persons encouraging us to engage in illegal actions), and that was disconcerting enough. We maintained our own levels of secrecy, sometimes organizing meetings only with those whom we believed we could trust. We kept secret our plans to go outside the law. I never suspected that the security agencies would have infiltrated us to the extent they did. I was naive.

These documents produced by various security agencies reveal a degree of secrecy. But in reality what I have learned from these documents about clandestine intelligence gathering is only the tip of the iceberg. What is clear is that these documents constitute a kind of elaborate fiction, a fabricated story defined principally by the search for subversion. Security agencies were probing for indicators of subversive activities. Undercover informants were perhaps only so willing to cherry-pick what they heard and saw, always on the lookout for clues that suggested nefarious subversive intent on the part of antiwar militants.

On occasion the depth of interest was surprisingly detailed. Some undercover police reports refer to meetings attended by as few as ten people. Others mention a few names but little else. Those who collected and stored these documents sometimes inadvertently made mistakes and revealed the identities of undercover informants. In an example of clumsy recordkeeping, a memo (dated 9 June 1970) prepared by an undercover informant reported on the whereabouts of Jeff Jones, a known Austin activist who was later elected student body president at UT. This police report inadvertently identifies its author as Jack Steell. It seems that Burt Gerding did not bother to sanitize, or "clean," his papers before donating them to the Briscoe Center.[27]

Making Sense of Undercover Informants

In *The File* Timothy Gaston Ash recounts how he traveled to the eastern section of Berlin in the late 1970s in order to conduct research for his doctoral dissertation. With the fall of the Berlin Wall, Ash uncovers the files of Stasi agents who monitored his activities when he traveled for research purposes. He decides to meet with these agents to see if he can get them to reveal their motivations for spying on him. In the end he does not seem to have found convincing answers to his questions.

Similarly, in trying to figure out how the entire network of undercover informants operated in Austin, I am at a loss. There are some clues that suggest that their surveillance machine was not as well-oiled as they hoped. Both FBI memos and documents in the Gerding Papers often refer to undercover informants who "had furnished reliable information in the past." Why would they report on several occasions that an informant—say, for example, codenamed SA T-1—was "reliable"? The Criminal Intelligence Division of the APD collected what they called "Intelligence Reports"—each labeled "Memorandum for Information"—as part of their record-keeping operation, in keeping an eye on the radicals. At first, from documents that I found in the Gerding Papers starting around 1965, these intelligence reports appeared on a standardized form and were prepared in accordance with a regular formula: There were specific categories that were to be filled in to correspond with the intelligence gathered. Every intelligence report that I found in the Gerding Papers from the early years was signed by Gerding himself. What was quite intriguing about these intelligence reports is the formulaic scale to evaluate the performance of undercover informants. This formula appears at the bottom of the last page of each report. This scale was divided into two categories: "source evaluation" and "accuracy evaluation." The subcategories reveal some interesting insights. "Source evaluation" is divided into (1) completely reliable, (2) usually reliable, (3) fairly reliable, (4) not usually reliable, (5) not reliable, and (6) cannot be judged. The "accuracy evaluation" scale is divided into (1) confirmed by other sources, (2) probably true, (3) possibly true, (4) doubtfully true, (5) probable, and (6) cannot be judged.

So what do we make of these scales? What is clear is that the spying agencies had reason to remain skeptical about the accuracy and reliability of the information they received from undercover police informants working in the field. They did not really trust all their police informants, and their willingness to classify their undercover informants implies that they intuitively knew that there were unreliable sources, or at least gradations of reliability.

I dare to ask: How was reliability judged? What is the difference between, say, "usually reliable" and "fairly reliable," or "doubtfully true" and "probable"? How did the spying agencies know these differences? How were undercover police informants recruited and employed in the first place? Were some undercover informants tasked with monitoring their fellow spies? I am afraid that the answers to these questions are forever lost. These are the unknown unknowns.

I conjecture that some undercover agents were only doing their spying for money. Perhaps they were caught selling drugs and persuaded to spy in order to avoid jail time. Perhaps some of these undercover agents actually were our friends, but those who "turned" under pressure. I also suspect that undercover agents were probably prone to exaggeration. If they uncovered good stuff, perhaps they could stay on the payroll longer.

Piecing together what I know, I think that the FBI headquarters and field offices trained their own undercover operatives and drew agents from active duty police officers in local departments and from military intelligence. At the same time, the FBI also recruited informants who had no previous training or expertise. This range of undercover operatives paralleled the continuum spanning the "reliable" and "unreliable" extremes.

By mid-1968 the formulaic intelligence report form with its standardized categories had all but disappeared in the Gerding Papers. A simple unsigned "Memorandum for Information" (referencing its purpose on the first line and with a date at the top righthand corner) replaced the standardized form. Yet we know with certainty that buried deep in the archival bowels of the records of the Criminal Intelligence Division—if they were not destroyed in some house cleaning operation in later decades—are supervisory reports on the reliability and trustworthiness of undercover police informants.

Who Were the Spies?

"There is a new man on campus among the freaks and fraternity men, the athletes and esthetes, the bookish types and the bomb throwers. He is the spy. He has not come to study Russian or Chinese or to infiltrate some foreign nation. Instead, his mission is to watch the students, the faculty, and the off-campus crowds. Though such undercover activity was almost unheard of five years ago, it has now become a permanent institution on the American college scene."[28]

In reporting for the *New York Times*, Anthony Ripley informed the wider public about spying on college campuses. This practice was not new for us. But for the readers of the *New York Times* it may have seemed like a revelation, if not a shocking discovery, that such surveillance was well underway.

From reading both the FBI files and the various law enforcement collections deposited at the Briscoe Center, I know that undercover agents infiltrated our movement and were quite active in reporting up the chain of command. We knew this, of course. But we were not aware of the extent of their penetration and their abilities to win our trust and avoid arousing suspicion. Undercover informants attended meetings, recorded debates, and even became our friends. I understand how a person who might be arrested for possession of a lot of marijuana with intent to sell would be offered the opportunity to plea to a lesser charge in exchange for doing undercover police work. I also understand how young people with military or policing backgrounds could "take their turn" as undercover agents. I suppose those offered the chance to inform on antiwar activists as part of their paid employment saw this as a thrilling opportunity.

But I do believe the story is much more complicated than this. I am interested in uncovering and understanding the distinct mentality, the state of mind that allowed some individuals to easily slide into undercover work. Being an undercover police agent requires a great deal of free-wheeling bravado, a willingness to manipulate, deceive, and just plain lie to people who trust you and whom you pretend to like. I still wonder how someone working secretly as an undercover spy for the security apparatus could adjust their moods to conduct their work. Especially those informants who befriended us, how could they fake loyalty to the antiwar movement and friendship to us while simultaneously seeking to uncover secrets and to report to law enforcement agencies on what we were doing?

I am convinced beyond any reasonable doubt that the man who called himself Nicholas (name withheld) was a paid undercover police agent. Nick was a man in his early thirties who turned up in Austin around 1969 or 1970. He identified himself a military veteran. He began attending antiwar meetings and gradually ingratiated himself to some key organizers. He even shared a house with Jeff Jones for a short time.

Over time many of us became suspicious and began to refer to him as Nick the Cop, even in his presence. Why were we suspicious? Nick was vague and ambiguous about his background. He seemed to appear as if from out of nowhere in particular, with no history of activism. He said that he had lived in Mexico during the decade before he came to Austin. This claim provided a convenient yet difficult to disprove alibi explaining his occasional days- and weeks-long disappearances from town, offering only vague answers accounting for his unexplained absences. He had no visible source of income but claimed that his grandmother had established a trust fund for him and he lived off an inheritance from his deceased parents. He enrolled as a student every term yet never managed to complete his courses. He dropped out every semester, declaring to anyone who would listen that "political work was more important."

When masquerading as someone else, an undercover informant should never be sloppy. To be effective an undercover informant must become a master of deception. One must dress the part, adopt the rhetoric, pepper speaking with slogans, and build at least a modest understanding of political issues. Nick accomplished none of this. Given his awkward mannerism and his lack of a verifiable background to account for his political awareness, let alone history of political activism, he bore all the telltale signs of someone just implanted in our movement as a spy.

Nick came to every meeting of any radical persuasion and took copious notes. He always volunteered for any position that enabled him to collect mailing and phone lists, particularly on newcomers who did not suspect him of anything. He and his camera were inseparable. He owned a pistol, which he kept in a locked safe in his apartment. But most importantly he held no clearly discernable political views or coherent ideology. Nick used radical rhetoric all the time but was unable to articulate a political position on just about everything. He had no real understanding of capitalism, imperialism, Marxism, or socialism. We could not figure out where Nick stood on any issue.

Nick kept extensive records on demonstrations, groups, and individuals in a locked file cabinet. He always befriended young women and pestered them about their knowledge of key figures in the movement. He fits my profile.

In the end we came to believe that Nick was an active undercover agent who took extensive rest-and-recreation excursions to clear his head and spend his money. From observations revealed in undercover police reports in the Gerding Papers and in FBI files (and referred to in the written text by his full name), Nick D. was a constant presence at VVAW and, later, in New American Movement (NAM) meetings. Over time he began to play both a visible and vocal role in both organizations. At meetings he seemed to be constantly speaking about this and that and not making any sense. In an FBI file, VVAW member Rick Griffin, speaking openly and forthrightly, indicated that he did not trust the person whom he named explicitly as Nicholas Dykema, and that he did not want this person to have anything to do with the veteran's organization.[29]

For me the coup de grace came in early 1972, when some of us, frustrated with the lack of intensity of protest, decided to gather together only those whom we trusted in order to engage in a frank discussion of what to do next. We agreed to discuss tactical options that might have been on the other side of legality. We recruited for this meeting by word of mouth, emphasizing that we should only invite those whom we trusted. The meeting was held in secret at my house—a huge mansion with a second-floor porch that could hold a large number of people. All in all, about forty arrived, including Nick the Cop. We never found out who invited him. He brought along two long-haired, freaky guys who claimed they were affiliated with VVAW. We had never seen these two guys before. Nick vouched for them.

VVAW was the most militant GI-related antiwar group in the country. On three or four occasions, when we organized marches (always unapproved and hence illegal) from the UT campus down Guadalupe Street toward the State Capitol, VVAW activists insisted on leading the march with their banners and chants. They always directed their ire at police lines who blocked the path to the Capitol. These confrontations brought out the tear gas, the police batons, and the ensuring riot.

At the meeting we talked for a while, everyone remaining cautious and reluctant to speak forthrightly. As the meeting gathered some steam in considering what we might do that pushed the envelope of legality, one of the two self-proclaimed VVAW guys, who were decked out in military fatigues that were festooned in antiwar buttons, blurted out, "We have to step up the struggle. We can get you guns and dynamite to blow up buildings." That was enough. Only the most gullible among us would have failed to realize that these guys were agents provocateurs attempting to draw us into a conspiracy. I remember that I stood up, interrupted the proceedings, and announced, "This meeting is over." The discussion ended abruptly.

Nick was only too obvious. Only newcomers who knew no better and the most trusting among us talked with him or took him seriously. He did not seem to care that some of us were openly suspicious of him.

There were other undercover infiltrators. In his papers Burt Gerding takes great pride in recruiting Mike Simpson, a local news reporter working for KVUE TV, as an undercover informant just before the Chuck Wagon Riot in November 1969.[30] Gerding informed his "friends in the FBI" that Mike was such a good source that the bureau recruited him and paid him to supply them with information. In an investigative journalist report in the *Texas Monthly*, Simpson "acknowledged that between 1969 and 1971 he filed verbal and written reports on suspected subversive activities in and around the University of Texas at Austin."[31] At the time Simpson worked on a part-time and sometimes full-time basis with local rock music station KNOW-AM. Simpson conceded that he supplied information to the FBI in addition to reporting to intelligence units with the Texas DPS, Criminal Intelligence Division of APD, and University of Texas police. While he was a reporter for KNOW-AM, Simpson admitted that the FBI gave him money to cover his expenses for his reporting on the massive peace march in Washington, DC, in November 1969 and to pay for his trip to Cleveland in February 1970 to report on the National Student Anti-War Conference. Simpson participated in the meetings, using his cover as a reporter for the Austin TV station KVUE.[32]

Two of Simpson's former news directors said that they were unaware of his work for the FBI but acknowledged that he seemed particularly close with law enforcement agencies in Austin. Broadcasts by Simpson on KNOW-AM and KVET-TV won many statewide awards, including laurels for his coverage of the October 1968 SDS Convention in Austin, the Chuck Wagon police riot, and his reports on the protest surrounding the dedication of the LBJ Library on the UT campus in May 1971. It seems that for some individuals who were recruited as undercover informants, their work as low-level spies was only a career opportunity, opening up avenues for upward mobility in a branch of the security services. By the early 1980s, Simpson went to work for the Travis County Sheriff's Department and eventually started his own private security firm called Ranger Security. When Gerding joined Westinghouse as head of security, he hired Simpson's private security company, Ranger Security, to work with him.[33]

Undercover informants, especially those that actively participated in antiwar organizations, performed a kind of seduction. They pretended to care. They tricked us into believing that they were part of the antiwar movement. In the Gerding Papers, the name of one person—Barbara Roseman—appears with a great deal of regularity in police undercover reports. She was identified as a political activist who often assumed leadership positions in various organizations. We learned in later years from multiple sources she worked for Lt. Burt Gerding as an undercover informant.

Barbara Roseman arrived on the Austin political scene around early 1968. She said she came from Dallas with M. B., whom (as I recall) she claimed was her boyfriend. She enrolled as a student, joined a sorority, and possibly entered an ROTC program. We did not know any of these details at the time.

Barbara was an effective imposter: young and eager, friendly, personable, and outgoing. Everyone liked her. Before the start of large meetings, those in attendance elected a chair by voice acclamation. We often selected Barbara. She was the best chair for large, raucous meetings. Without obvious political views sufficient to alienate her from any particular group or political faction, and with a loud, booming voice useful for silencing disruption in meetings, she was the perfect fit for a clandestine operative spying on us.

Barbara was a clever undercover agent who managed to get herself elected or else volunteered for leadership roles. She attended and participated in gatherings organized by the SMC and served as our representative (along with her close friend, M.B., who was probably also an undercover informant) to various regional meetings. She was indeed a political gadfly, working with the Radical Alliance, SMC, CUF, and other organizations that attracted political activists.

Pat Cuney, political activist (*standing, left*), and Barbara Roseman, undercover informant (*rising to her feet, right*). Undercover police surveillance photograph. Circled numbers represent police identification with names listed on the back of the photograph. Courtesy of George Carlson Papers, camh-dob-017272, Dolph Briscoe Center for American History, University of Texas at Austin.

For instance, Barbara represented the Austin SMC—along with Jeff Jones and probably some YSA people—at a national SMC meeting in Cleveland in February 1970. She came to the meeting with Mike Simpson, the news reporter for KVUE TV who doubled as an undercover informant. Other Austin radicals who attended the SMC meeting in Cleveland suspected that Barbara was working as an undercover informant, but unfortunately these suspicions never reached a wider audience. Pat Cuney recounts how Barbara came over to her house sometime in 1971 or 1972. They chatted, and Barbara said that she had a police radio/scanner that she listened to, and that she had permission to do target practice at the police firing range. Barbara offered Pat the opportunity to accompany her. Pat declined. Perhaps this represented a fumbling attempt at recruiting Pat Cuney into undercover work for the police? Peter Van Bavel also recounts an instance where Barb engaged him in an uncomfortable discussion about guns and target practice. Again, was this a probing exercise in trying to recruit Peter to become an undercover informant?[34]

In May 1970 Barbara Roseman was elected one of five officers in the leadership of the Radical Alliance, one of many radical non-PL and non-SMC groups. The Radical Alliance was the backbone behind the election of Jeff Jones as student body president for the 1970–1971 academic year. As I think about it, Barbara Roseman reminds me of something akin to a human chameleon, a shape-shifting person possessed with the uncanny capacity to assimilate and fit comfortably into whatever circumstances in which she found herself.

Gavan Duffy told me that when he was returning on a bus from San Antonio, where he had taken a preinduction physical examination at Fort Sam Houston, he sat next to a guy who said he was dating Burt Gerding's daughter. This guy said that he actually met Barbara Roseman at Burt Gerding's house when he was there visiting Gerding's daughter. Around 1985, ten years or so after the intensity of political protest in Austin had dissipated, a person whom I knew applied for a job at Westinghouse Corporation just outside of Austin. She learned that Burt Gerding, who had retired from the APD to take a position as head of security for Westinghouse, required interviews with all possible employees. As I was told, my friend scheduled a meeting with Gerding, hoping that he would have forgotten her from her antiwar days. When she showed up for the meeting, she came face-to-face with Barbara Roseman, who was working as Gerding's personal assistant. Wow. They recognized each other. Apparently, a few weeks later, some women asked Barbara to go out for a beer. They confronted her with their suspicions about her police work, and she confessed to working as an undercover informant.

This story gets even stranger. Barbara Roseman died in Austin after a long career in the local music business. She was buried in Omaha, Nebraska. I know because I found a YouTube video recording of her burial service, presided over by her brother. In July 2023 a close relative of hers acknowledged—without any prompting on my part—that Barb worked for Gerding as an informant. Barb was very close to Gerding's son, Gary. Apparently at the invitation of Gary and Barb, this relative went to dinner at Burt and Mildred Gerding's house in Austin. This new information raises the question whether Barb was recruited to work as an undercover informant because of her possibly close relationship with Gary Gerding.

The security system operated on two intersecting principles: secrecy and chain of command. Undercover informants typically did not know the identities of other spies who had infiltrated the same groups. Information moved up the chain of command to the heads of security agencies, and instructions flowed downward, telling undercover agents what to do and how to do it. Either other informants, unaware that Barbara also worked undercover, reported on her, or she submitted reports and referred to herself in the third person. At any rate, Barbara Roseman certainly fooled me. I liked her, I trusted her, and I never suspected that she worked as an undercover informant.

This practice of deceit and subterfuge must have presented some mental discomfort for her and other undercover informants. They must have experienced some degree of cognitive dissonance, or the unsettling psychological stress associated with trying to reconcile befriending antiwar activists while simultaneously spying on them. This chameleon-like behavior must have produced divided selves and multiple personalities.

The local VVAW chapter certainly had its share of undercover agents. George Carlson, Head of Security for the UT System, maintained an extensive file on VVAW. Documents in the Carlson Papers reveal that by 1971 VVAW had sixteen chapters in Texas. The documents also include six and a half pages that list the names and addresses of over two hundred people associated with the Austin VVAW chapter. Undoubtedly, an undercover informant was able to obtain a copy of the conference registration lists of people who attended a VVAW conference in Austin.[35] By 1971 VVAW was propelled to center stage in the antiwar movement. The respect that antiwar veterans had gained provided a convenient and legitimate cover for infiltration from military intelligence, the FBI, and APD criminal intelligence. Various agents provocateurs regularly attended meetings planning for demonstrations. Their encouragement of "trashing" (breaking windows, setting fires, throwing rocks and bottles at police, and so on) found a receptive audience among the growing numbers of impatient, anarchistic, anti-intellectual, and youthful hippies who threw caution to the wind, urging us to escalate the struggle "to smash the state." It seemed that some undercover police agents floated in and out of local movements, hoping to trigger illegal actions that security agencies could target for conspiracy trials.

Lt. Burt Gerding and His Red Squad

When there is power without knowledge, then repression takes on a life of its own. In spring 1970 Burt Gerding prepared a report for Chief R. A. Miles, head of the APD, laying out the state of the New Left in Austin. What is surprising to me about this report is how inaccurate and incomplete it was. The accumulation of factual errors invariably leads to sloppy analysis. Gerding's fixation on reporting almost exclusively on the status of national organizations—CPUSA, SWP (and the YSA), PL and its worker-student alliance, the Spartacist League, Black Panther Party and Black Liberation organizations, and, later, the Weather Underground—meant that he turned a blind eye to local, homegrown movements that were more ephemeral but carried the burden of propagating the antiwar message, organizing rallies and demonstrations, and coordinating political activities. In the Gerding report, what he ignored was much more important than what he included as part of the official record. CPUSA membership never amounted to no more than three to five persons led by Marian Vizard before she took a decided detour into countercultural and feminist politics. After the breakup of SDS in summer 1968, PL was a spent force in Austin, attracting ever-dwindling numbers to its events. The Spartacists League was never more than perhaps five hardcore fanatics. Their arcane—and frankly absurd—political positions were never going to be a way to build a vibrant political movement in Austin. The Sparts were pathetically irrelevant.

After correctly assessing the declining significance of the CPUSA and PL, Gerding anointed the SWP and YSA with an oversized and exaggerated role. He erroneously attributed the bulk of organizing antiwar rallies and marches to the SWP/YSA/SMC troika. This claim is so out of touch with reality that it is ridiculous. I believe that Gerding was unable to think outside of the box of organized Marxist–Leninist parties. In seeking to identify the source of political agitation in Austin, he tried to squeeze all political expression into a traditional 1950s model of Communist outside meddling and interference. In looking for Communist puppet masters lurking in the shadows, Gerding failed to understand that political militants in Austin were capable of thinking on their own.[36]

Toward the end of his report, Gerding focuses on the Motherfuckers, a small collection of drug-dealing hippies who contributed virtually nothing to the political movement. They were flamboyant and boisterous for sure, but these self-described "outlaws in Amerika" were living on the edge of both Austin and reality. The Motherfuckers showed up for demonstrations and were always loud and intimidating. Their politics consisted of not much more than embracing a kind of libertarian-anarchist stew of anti-establishment ideas.

Under his treatment of the anarchist movement, Gerding focuses on the GWMC, a small cadre of sociology graduate students and their friends. I was involved in this effort, but it paled in comparison with broader antiwar activities and organizations with which I was aligned. The Gerding report fails to even mention any of the currents that characterized the broader antiwar movement, which by this time was larger than ever.[37]

One has to ask: Why was this report so incomplete, so filled with silences and omissions, and so erroneous in its attribution of the driving force for antiwar rallies and demonstrations? Logically speaking, there are only two possible explanations. First, Gerding was deliberately telling Chief R. A. Miles what he thought his boss (and FBI national headquarters) wanted to hear. Second, Gerding actually did not know what was happening, either through sloppy detective work or through an inability to connect the dots of militant radicalism right before his eyes. Perhaps Gerding was losing interest in his surveillance work and his job. Seen retrospectively, this report appears toward the end of his career as head of Criminal Intelligence Division. Maybe his bosses in the APD had begun to lose faith in his capabilities.

If this report is the best that the head of the Criminal Intelligence Division can produce, we political activists had little to fear from their incompetent sleuthing. This report did not help their cause of gathering information, sifting through it, and arriving at a clearheaded analysis. Yet at the end of the day, the problem for us was that these policing agents had the power of the entire state security apparatus to back them up.

To be sure, documents never reveal everything. What I have obtained from reviewing the police security files available to me constitutes only a thin layer of deeper levels of intrigue. It is truly impossible to know what they knew—or thought they knew.

Security Chief George Carlson and the Spectral Presence of Gerard Winstanley

In September 1967 I entered graduate school at UT Austin as a PhD student in the Department of Philosophy. I quickly became disillusioned with the almost antipolitical ethos of the faculty. I could care less about what Hegel borrowed from Kant, or was it the other way around? I was gravely disappointed and dissatisfied with the lack of connection between the prevailing philosophical discourse and my growing political consciousness and activism. I found that philosophy, or at least the way it was presented at UT Austin, offered only an arcane, pedantic approach to understanding social life.

In the first week of September 1969, I was eating lunch in the Chuck Wagon in the University Union with a group of friends. I was complaining that I was really tired of being a PhD student in the Philosophy Department. I said that I was unable to do any work that related to politics. Besides, in the spring term of 1969, I had been a teaching assistant for Larry Caroline. It was his last term at University of Texas since he had been fired the year before. Larry was the only breath of fresh air, but the department failed to collectively stand by him.

I proclaimed to no one in particular that perhaps I should seek admission to the Department of English, or any other department, for that matter. My friend Richard Minus said, "Why don't you enroll for courses in the Sociology Department. You can do whatever you want there." That seemed to be my kind of place. Richard had moved into sociology the year before from the PhD program in economics—which he hated. What an idea! Richard gave me the names of the courses he was taking in sociology, and later that afternoon I dropped my stupid philosophy seminars—metaphysics, the origins of continental philosophy, and deciphering Kant (with Professor John Silber)—and without much forethought I enrolled in the three seminars in the Department of Sociology that Richard had suggested.

The Department of Sociology was conventional in every sense, yet there were a handful of professors who were somewhat sympathetic to the New Left. The subject matter of what constituted sociology was sufficiently amorphous, diverse, and ill-formed that I could pursue my intellectual interests without restraint and without fear of reprisal—or so I thought, until I discovered decades later that there was a spy among us.

After I entered the PhD program in sociology, I quickly gravitated to like-minded radicals. As we used to say in Austin, I was in hog heaven. I could do whatever I wanted in the courses in which I enrolled. I did just that—whatever I wanted. I wrote papers on the power elite in America, US imperialism, and the Marxist roots of the Frankfurt School. The intellectual ferment that we created in the department provided me with a creative environment within which to learn, and to learn quickly. Together we investigated Marxist theory, critically evaluating and arguing over the relevance of the young Marx versus the old Marx. We formed study groups, and we debated revolutionary strategy and tactics handed down from the masters like Lenin, Trotsky, Mao, Luxemburg, Gramsci, Che Guevara, Ho Chi Minh, and Vo Nguyen Giap.

For the first time in academia, I was excited. My intellectual interests dovetailed with my political activism. It was a theory-and-praxis moment. My involvement in the broader antiwar movement frustrated me at times because action all too often overshadowed critical thinking about what we were doing and why. With my fellow comrades in sociology, I could debate theoretical questions like peasant revolutions, the relevance of the industrial working class as an agent for change, and how to connect the Women's Liberation Movement with racism and the war in Vietnam.

It was not long before we arrived at a kind of bore-from-within insurgent strategy. It was the "long march through the institutions" that political activists in Europe often advocated. Late in fall 1969, a number of us in sociology began talking about forming a left-wing caucus that would sponsor our own New Left education and raise some demands challenging the archaic practices that governed the administration of the department. I know it was not me, but someone—most likely Steve Krinsky—who came up with a name: Gerard Winstanley. Winstanley was a sixteenth-century "digger." Diggers were levelers, fighting against income and property inequalities in the English countryside. The diggers were sort of protosocialists, standing against the abuses of private property and the feudal strictures on the peasantry. So we radical and Marxist graduate students formed the GWMC to proselytize our views and to recruit members into our tiny cabal. This was an activist moment, where ideas translated into practice. We held several study sessions, reading and learning about diggers, levelers, and early anarchism. It drew us into thinking about Pietr Kropokin, Proudhoun, and eventually Joe Hill and the IWW, or Wobblies. We learned to appreciate novels by John Steinbeck, like *The Grapes of Wrath* and *Cannery Row*, and Ernest Hemmingway, like *For Whom the Bell Tolls*. We used seminar time in courses like political sociology and sociological theory to introduce new debates and to talk openly about contemporary politics. Within several months we built a core of around fifteen participants out of a total cohort of around sixty PhD students.

Our high point came with the weeklong student strike of May 1970. We transformed the sociology department into one vast study group, linking ourselves to a network of caucuses that had emerged and formed in other university departments. We flew the red flag along with the black flag of anarchism outside the window of the third floor of Garrison Hall. For one brief moment, we ruled, and they—the frightened faculty and the careerist graduate students—cowered, waiting for the world to once again get back to normal.

We in the GWMC produced a long (and long-winded) manifesto and an irregular newsletter. We sponsored some teach-ins and a few rallies. Not much, really. Little did any of us know that the GWMC would draw the attention of the UT security police and the FBI. For some odd reason, our efforts warranted the placement of at least one undercover informant in our midst to monitor our activities. My first inkling of this infiltration was when I discovered—five decades later—a report stored in the Gerding Papers from an undercover informant (a woman) who attended a party on 4 September 1970 at the house where I lived, sharing with three others the entire third floor. The purpose of this gathering was to introduce incoming PhD students in sociology to the GWMC and our gang of irreverent radical graduate students. This undercover informant was, by her own admission, a fellow PhD student in the Sociology Department. This person claimed that about thirty to forty people showed up for the party, and we sang anarchist songs from the IWW songbook. She named names of those in attendance, dividing these partygoers into two groups: those who "are not activists and are not involved, although they may be sympathetic to the cause," on the one side, and the hardcore political activists on the other. This spy zeroed in on Carlo, an incoming PhD student from Italy who was allegedly a Communist. She could not recall his last name; it was Ginoletti. He was a solid comrade for the next several years. He was married to the cousin of Inti Peredo, a man who accompanied Che Guevara on his ill-fated excursion in Bolivia.

Perhaps to establish her credentials as a good spy, this undercover informant in the Sociology Department declared that "Only this writer, Pat O'Day, Dr. Joseph Lopreato (Chairman of the Sociology Department) and Carlo know of these connections [with the Communist Party in Italy]." She concluded her report with a rhetorical flourish: "There was some marijuana smoked at the party—possibly belonging to Martin Murray." What makes this observation particularly ominous is that possession of marijuana was a felony in Texas at the time, and passing a joint was considered legally equivalent to selling—a serious felony. In 1968 Lee Otis Johnson, leader of SNCC in Houston and a member of the Black Panther Party, was convicted of selling marijuana for allegedly passing a joint to an undercover agent at a party. The lone testimony of this agent was sufficient to sentence Johnson to prison for thirty years. Was this undercover informant at my house party in Austin trying to set me up for a drug bust?[38]

In another report an FBI undercover agent claimed that the GWMC was launched at this "pot party" at my house on Twelfth Street. This assertion is not accurate. The GWMC was started much earlier. Even today it is a bit disconcerting to learn that someone I must have known pretty well was spying on me at a party.[39]

I discovered another shard of information placed in the Gerding Papers in a file dedicated to exposing UT faculty linkages to the New Left. The letter (dated 1971 without a day or a month) was addressed to George Carlson, head of security for the University of Texas System. He was also a former FBI agent and a contributor to the COINTELPRO program. The author of the letter begins, "Dear George [Carlson]: I am writing to you in my personal capacity and not as a police informant." This person reveals in the letter that she was at the time a student enrolled in the PhD program in sociology and had been a member of the Graduate Student Union in the department. The letter writer complains bitterly about her experience with the then Department Chair Joe Lopreato. She said that in class he was insulting and demeaning toward students, treating them like idiots and so forth. She was right. He did do that. He was often dismissive of students and their "dumb-ass" (his word) ideas. He was my faculty advisor and my mentor. I greatly appreciated him and how he forced me to clarify my ideas.

After blasting away at Lopreato, the letter writer then concentrates on me. She expressed great dismay that after only one year in the sociology PhD program, I was asked to teach a political sociology course for which, in her estimation, I was not qualified. In her view I adopted a narrow framework—Marxism—and I taught the course "incompetently" (in her words). My first teaching evaluation! I did not fare very well in her estimation. By the way, in that course on political sociology, I had the great pleasure to have invited the Frankfurt School philosopher, Herbert Marcuse, to give a lecture when he visited Austin. I still have the cassette tape upon which I recorded his presentation.

This undercover agent then goes on to say that I used my undeserved teaching position as leverage to take over the GWMC. This claim is ridiculous on the face of it. She then proceeds to talk about how we in the caucus were outmaneuvered by liberal faculty members when we demanded changes in the department. She ends this discussion with the assertion that she had already reported to George Carlson on the Winstanley Caucus. (Unfortunately, I was not able to locate her reports in the Carlson Papers.) Why would the GWMC—with perhaps a dozen active members—figure so prominently in the imagination of the security police? What real threat did we pose to national security?[40]

George Carlson donated his papers to the Briscoe Library. One separate file was entitled "Gerard Winstanley Caucus." The bulk of the file is devoted to the reproduction of the GWMC manifesto—a staccato-like broadsheet aimed at criticizing just about everything. The files also contain the report from this female undercover informant who recounts a conversation with me (see note).[41] The file also contains the names of twelve students in the Department of Sociology who identified with the GWMC Caucus.

I discovered another reference to the GWMC in the George Carlson Papers. Buried in an innocuous corner of random scraps of irrelevant information, I found a handwritten note undoubtedly from an undercover informant who referred to me, Jim Gundlach, and John Houghton as affiliated with Gerard Winstanley. The note draws a connection between the GWMC and the social theorist Seymour Martin Lipset. Contrary to the suggestion made by this police informant, Seymour Martin Lipset was not a source of inspiration for us in our critique of the role of mainstream social science inquiry in justifying the policies of the US government. Actually, theorists like Lipset were targets for our reproach. Lipset's staunch liberal views fit comfortably with the defense of the extension of the American empire to all corners of the globe. The failure of the undercover informant to come even close to an understanding of what we thought was yet another indication of the weakness of their information gathering and their inability to comprehend what was going on. If I was (in her estimation) an "incompetent" instructor, then she was a woolly-headed thinker who had a woefully inadequate understanding of sociological theory.[42]

The Carlson Papers also included a memo to Carlson referring to a missed telephone call. The name of the caller was recorded as Nancy Pfieffer. Was she the undercover informant? I believe so, but we will never know. I was unable to trace any mention of her or reference to her anywhere.[43]

The FBI Poking Through My Garbage

By the early 1970s, Austin became a kind of outlaw territory, a place where alternative lifestyle folks could do their own thing. An occasional escapee from the Weather Underground surreptitiously slipped into Austin, disappearing and living incognito among the rural communes that seemed to sprout everywhere in country hideaways outside Austin's city limits. Yet the politics of the Weather People never achieved a following in Austin. Ever vigilant, the FBI got wind of some "outlaws" in the Texas Hill Country.

Of course, I knew at the time that security agencies were watching me. One fine morning around 11:00 a.m. in May 1971, after the demonstrations at the dedication to the LBJ Library, as I was taking out the trash at my house at Twelfth Street, I crossed paths with two FBI agents plowing through my garbage can. One was on the ground, poking through discarded trash, and the other had his hand way down in the can, retrieving errant materials. I instinctively knew they were FBI agents: they were dressed (in the hot Texas sun, no less) in inexpensive dark-blue suits with matching thin ties, pressed white shirts, and, of course, those requisite white socks with black dress shoes. Along with dark glasses to hide their eyes, they looked like minor actors in an old Hollywood gangster movie. Comic figures indeed. To borrow from Timothy Garton Ash, how can one characterize their dress? "A disguise? A uniform? An identity?"[44] I suppose it was a bit of all the above.

One blurted out, "Hi, Martin, is your brother still in town?" The other inquired whether I knew the whereabouts of Linda Evans, a known Weather Underground fugitive who was on the FBI's Ten Most Wanted list at the time. I had seen her weeks before around Austin, but I would never reveal that piece of information. They requested that I come to the local FBI office and answer some questions. How utterly pathetic. I told them to call my lawyer, Cam Cunningham. The matter died, but I know that FBI agents approached others with similar requests for conversations. The poking around they did yielded miniscule results.

The Use of Surveillance Photographs

In the 1960s and early 1970s, police surveillance photography was not particularly sophisticated. The images are often grainy and out of focus. By 1971 and 1972, undercover agents were able to use telephoto lenses to photograph individuals engaged in acts deemed illegal at demonstrations, and law enforcement agencies used these photographs to arrest people after the events in question. At the Chuck Wagon Riot in November 1969, police photographers took dozens of pictures. Perhaps two hundred of these photographs can be found in the George Carlson Papers. Many of these photographs were simply random images of the sit-in inside the Chuck Wagon, while only a few captured the action in the streets outside. Perhaps a quarter to a third of the photographs identified particular persons by name with arrows and circles on the images themselves and names printed on the back. I am named in two photographs inside the Chuck Wagon as the sit-in was taking place. There is also another photograph that identifies by name Pat Cuney and Barb Roseman, who were talking with each other in animated poses. Did the police photographer realize that Barb was an undercover informant?[45]

The George Carlson Papers also include a trove of photographs from the 5 May 1970 preparation for the large-scale march and rally at the State Capitol downtown. Undercover police agents from the DPS turned these photographs over to George Carlson. These photographs were largely casual images, usually of large crowds of protesters gathering on the Main Mall, groups sitting on the grass, and long strings of people walking near the Tower. The photographers seemed to walk aimlessly around the gathering place for the march, taking random pictures. This collection of black-and-white visual images contains at least one photograph that deliberately focused on me as I was standing in a small group.[46]

The Gerding Papers contain an hour-long compilation of police surveillance films—seven in all—collected from the late 1950s to the early 1970s.[47] These short film clips, spliced together to form an incoherent whole, consist of a Ban the Bomb demonstration in the late 1950s, a dance on the UT campus in the early 1960s, and a late 1960s peace march. The film is grainy, the camera jumps incongruously from scene to scene, and there is no sound. The pièce de résistance, however, is a ten-minute film that captures various scenes from one of the May 1970 marches that rocked Austin. In watching this film, I was struck with how useless they were in genuinely capturing what was happening on the ground. I recognized four individuals in the film on the May 1970 rally and march: Jeff Jones, John Lane, Burt Gerding (the camera person lingered on his image for a full ten seconds), and a quick, passing image of me standing in a crowd at a street corner.

Police surveillance photograph, Martin Murray, in the middle of the frame, wearing eyeglasses. Courtesy of George Carlson Papers, camh-dob-017269, Dolph Briscoe Center for American History, University of Texas at Austin.

Police Surveillance in a Micro-Setting: CUF

One particular file in the Gerding Papers labeled "Pat [reports on CUF], 1970" provides a partial glimpse into how security agencies used undercover informants to spy on organizations that they deemed as potentially subversive. These files contain seven separate reports from September to November 1970 that consist of the observations of an undercover informant who successfully infiltrated the CUF, a local Afro-American community organization based in East Austin. To make sense of this spying effort, let's begin at the end. Given shards of information from other sources (including confirmation from other participants in CUF at the time), I am able to piece together a composite picture of which persons were involved with CUF. I can say that in all likelihood that the undercover informant was Barbara Roseman. From other sources I know that only three women not from East Austin were involved with CUF. Barbara Roseman was one of them. Outsiders—meaning those who were not African American and not from East Austin—had to convince the CUF leadership that they could be trusted.

In a final report (dated 6 November 1970) submitted to Burt Gerding, the undercover informant reported that she "has spent approximately six months working with the CUF. Visits to the center first numbered one per two-week period and then increased to two per week. Participation in the Political Prisoners Conference, Oct. 29–November 1 [1970] may also be included in [my] experience with CUF." The report began with the observation, "On the surface, CUF appears to be fostering a charitable operation which is well-supported by donations." Yet then, perhaps as if to shield herself from charges of ill-informed bias, she asserted, "It should be noted at the outset because contact has not been constant, this writer may possess a very limited and/or distorted view of the Community United Front, its works and its program."[48]

In painting a picture of the CUF and its political orientation, the undercover informant observed that the CUF was not a Black nationalist organization. In providing evidence to support this view, she declared that "CUF supports freeing brown and white 'political prisoners,'" and was not tied solely to "black issues and goals." As further evidence, she stated that "whites and chicanos, provided they go along with or agree with the philosophy and/or actions of CUF, are allowed to participate in the program." In offering a speculative observation, she concluded that "the political aim is revolution by the most efficient and quick techniques possible. At present, the accepted techniques are those of the Black Panther Party." From her long experience with the inner workings of the CUF, this undercover informant identified key figures as Larry Jackson, Anthony Spears, "Big Mike," Susan Gore, Janice Lawson, and Cecilia Garcia.[49]

Let's return to the beginning. The first report available in the Gerding Papers (dated 15 September 1970) consists of the observation that thirty-five Black children participated in the free breakfast program and that Larry Jackson, "Big Mike," and Susan Gore were the organizers. The undercover informant also provided a hand-drawn map of the CUF building at 1103 E. Sixth Street, outlining in detail the shape of the layout and the location of rooms. She also noted numerous posters of Huey P. Newton, "Seize the Time," and "Off the Pig" that festooned the walls.[50]

A second undercover police report compiled only two days later identified "Peter van Babel" (actually, Peter Van Bavel) as an outside participant in the breakfast program. The undercover informant also reported, "There were also three white females (including this writer), two of whom appeared to be UT students and one of whom appeared to be a faculty member or the wife of a faculty member." The undercover report also contains the license plate numbers and descriptions of automobiles parked outside.[51] In subsequent reports the undercover informant identified Cecilia Garcia, a visiting professor at UT Austin from Chile, providing her address and a description of her residence ("an apartment unit with cactus on front porch"). Once again, the report contains a list of license plate numbers from cars parked outside and the observation that Anthony Spears and Larry Jackson were in attendance, and that Roy Breaux (affiliated with the John Brown Revolutionary League in Houston and linked with People's Party II) was seen collecting money for CUF on UT campus.[52]

The next undercover police report goes a step further, offering observations from a planning meeting at which thirty-two people participated, providing a partial list of those in attendance. The undercover informant described the discussion at the meeting, focusing on the efforts to get permission to use the Chuck Wagon facilities for the breakfast program, and the status of other CUF initiatives like a free medical clinic, tutoring for elementary school children, and the political education program.[53]

Almost without exception these undercover police reports contain lists of cars parked nearby, including license plate numbers and descriptions of makes, colors, and models. Many of these typed police reports included supplementary additional pages attached at the bottom. These affixed notations suggest to me that while the main undercover spy participated in the meetings, plainclothes police in unmarked cars patrolled the area to gather further information on cars and license plate numbers.

As a participant in the 29 October Texas Conference to Free all Political Prisoners in Amerika, the undercover informant reported that she observed three or four guns (either rifles or shotguns) secreted in a back room. She also reported on a speech by Yolana Birdwell at the 1 November rally sponsored by political prisoner's conference. Birdwell allegedly declared

Community United Front organizer Larry Jackson. The "Carl Lives!" poster in the background refers to Carl Hampton, leader of People's Party II in Houston, deliberately killed by a police sniper. Courtesy of Alan Pogue, photographer.

that "the days of the rally are over," and that people should learn how to make explosives and shoot guns (as she is claiming to be doing). Birdwell allegedly argued that the police shooting death of Carl Hampton of People's Party II in Houston had illustrated the need for more militant action and for armed self-defense.[54]

Amazingly, in the final 6 November 1970 report, the undercover informant actually departed from the standard role of the observant spy who faithfully reports what took place at meetings and adopted a position of advocacy. In departing from a detached point of view, this police spy actually said that she believed that "if the Community United Front obtains many more footholds in Austin, a large amount of trouble may be in the offing." "If the Community United Front grows much bigger or gains more goals, the [Black Panther] Party might see fit to come in and take over the program (with or without Larry Jackson's participation)." "On the basis of the above-stated view," she says, "this writer would recommend that the Community United Front be stopped in any political moves it tries to make."[55] One can only imagine that offering policy recommendations to her security police handlers—especially from someone who began by apologizing for possible gaps in her knowledge and understanding of the CUF—was out of the ordinary. What could have possessed such a lowly person in the security status hierarchy to offer such bold advice on such sensitive matters? One will never know.

This undercover informant made the audacious recommendation that the university administration no longer acquiesce in allowing the breakfast program to operate on campus. "It would seem to this writer that the University has no responsibility to support a group which is politically designed to destroy a government and system which is, in part, maintained by the University." Finally, she went a step further, proposing specific methods the university might utilize in removing the program from the campus. These methods included convincing the chair of the Board of Regents, Frank Erwin, despite the distain with which he was regarded, to issue a statement condemning the presence of the CUF on the UT campus. The thinking behind this proposal was that public condemnation of the CUF from the top of the administrative hierarchy would trigger an avalanche of voices from below that would result in the university administration barring the CUF from using university facilities for its breakfast program. If a violent confrontation followed from this decision, the undercover agent vowed to personally shield the children attending the breakfast program from any harm.[56]

What is remarkable here is that this undercover informant went from functioning as a detached observer to advocating for security policy changes.

These recommendations may or may not have been followed. In time the CUF stopped using the Chuck Wagon for its breakfast program. Over the next several years, CUF projects and programs gradually unraveled, and what was left of the organization became a shell of its former vibrant self.

Police Undercover Infiltration of the SMC

With the collapse of SDS following the fiasco at the June 1969 national convention, political activists in Austin looked for an organizational focus to continue with antiwar activities. A number of key people decided on an entrance strategy, participating in the SMC in order to create an organized faction that could gain control over the political direction of the organization. Political activists like Jeff Jones, Doyle Niemann, Pat Cuney, and others (including Barbara Roseman) joined the SMC, hoping to steer the organization away from its longstanding single-issue politics captured in the slogan "Bring the Troops Home Now!" At this time the SWP controlled the YSA, an organization that in turn dominated the SMC. The non–SWP/YSA faction in SMC argued for a multifaceted politics that incorporated other causes, like support for women's liberation, the struggle of Afro-Americans, and gay rights. The traditional leadership drawn from SWP/YSA dug in their heels, trying to prevent what they considered dilution of their single focus. Meetings often resulted in bitter debate. Both sides were able to claim partial victories. Yet the entrance strategy was soon eclipsed by the tremendous outpouring in May 1970 of popular opposition to the Vietnam War following the killing of four students at Kent State.

Despite their fundamental differences regarding how to build the antiwar movement, both the SWP/YSA leadership and the entrance militants agreed that sowing dissent among active-duty GIs was a key element in the overall strategy to stop the war machine. Without the commitment of their troops and their willingness to unquestionably follow orders, the military brass could never be certain that they could rely on soldiers in the field of operations. The US military was already plagued with rising discontent, including "fragging" of officers (deliberately targeting officers with fragmentation grenades), drug usage, and refusal to obey orders. The antiwar movement sought to tap into this cauldron of dissatisfaction, transforming disorganized dissent in the military into organized resistance.

Political activists in Austin worked behind the scenes in draft counseling centers and as volunteers at the Oleo Strut, a GI coffee house in Killeen (Texas), outside Fort Hood military base. Those civilians and active-duty GIs turned the Oleo Strut into a key outpost for antiwar activities, publishing an underground newspaper called the *Fatigue Press*, organizing boycotts, establishing a legal defense office, and participating in peace marches.[57]

I participated in occasional leafleting forays to Fort Mabry and Bergstrom Air Force Base. We would gather at the entrance, shouting slogans and passing out leaflets to occupants of passing vehicles. The MPs did their best to harass us.

Political activists affiliated with the SMC did much more. To their credit the YSA and SMC understood that a weak link in the war machine was the capacity of the branches of military service to convince soldiers to fight and die for the red, white, and blue. The YSA/SMC sought to undermine the morale of the fighting troops.

With a degree of boldness, the SMC organized clandestine forays onto military bases in order to distribute antiwar leaflets and other "subversive" literature. Leafleting techniques were ingenious in their simplicity. Getting access to military bases was not as difficult as it might seem. Using some excuse at the entryway checkpoint, three people in a car would drive onto the military base after dark: one driver, one to watch for MPs, and one to jump out and distribute leaflets, pamphlets, and underground newspapers. The goal was to distribute this literature in places where direct contact with GIs was to be avoided but where GIs were likely to find these materials—in bathrooms, phone booths, and bus stops; under church doors; on top of newsstands, the counter of snack bars, and the like. Those who leafleted were instructed to stay on the base for not more than one hour in order to avoid suspicion from patrolling MPs. They were told to make sure that all leaflets were cleaned out of the car before leaving the military bases, including throwing remaining literature out of car windows.[58]

We also organized picnics in local parks that were specifically designed to draw in active-duty GIs who often came from Fort Hood to Austin on weekends. Burt Gerding almost always dispatched undercover informants to spy on the goings-on at these picnics. One undercover informant reported on a GI civilian picnic, held 19 July 1970, in a park in Austin. About seventy-five people attended, including thirty to forty active-duty GIs. The organizers of the informal picnic talked about the Oleo Strut and *Fatigue Press*. But the main focus of conversation was training in riot control. The aim of the discussion was not so much to encourage GIs to actively resist training in riot control but to "create distrust among military officials." "In this way, if a riot takes place, the officials will not be convinced that they can deploy their troops" with any degree of confidence that their orders would be obeyed. Antiwar activists argued that "distrust can be created [simply] through the holding of discussions against riot control." Undercover informants at the picnic did their best to identify active-duty GIs by name, referring to one GI who "looks Italian." They named Ann Locklear and Roy Breaux, as well as Larry Jackson and Anthony Spears from CUF, as persons in attendance. Plainclothes officers in unmarked police cars patrolled the perimeter, recording license plate numbers on cars coming from Fort Hood.[59]

A police undercover agent reported on the SMC Regional Conference that took place 19 September 1970. In this four-page report, this police informant identified 100–150 persons in attendance from seven cities in Texas, paying particular attention to active-duty GIs in attendance, giving descriptions like "blonde-brown hair, mustache thin, about 5'8" or 5'9" in height." Activists at the conference informed active-duty GIs that according to the Army Command Policy labeled AR 600-20 (one of a set of internal rules governing conduct in the military ranks), they could participate in demonstrations as long as they did not wear their uniforms. It was common practice for undercover agents to try to recover lists of names and addresses of those who attended meetings and conferences. One undercover informant managed to reproduce the names and addresses of the 127 people (including Barb Roseman, 615 W. St. Johns, #219) who attended the conference, and then turned them over to his/her security handers.[60]

On 3 October 1970, four people leafleted Lackland Air Force Base in San Antonio. As the undercover informant reported, "Those involved were Marshall Anderson, Larry Foltz, Arlene Benson, and this writer. This writer was the driver." An accumulation of clues in the police security files and elsewhere point to the identity of the undercover informant in all likelihood as Barbara Roseman. In this instance she was indeed an active participant in extralegal activities. In a detailed three-page report, this undercover informant described the leafleting of Lackland Air Force Base. Leafleting consisted of driving through the base and dropping literature from open windows of the car when no people were in sight.[61] The participants were able to place an antiwar poster in the nose of a plane. Yet when the four leafleteers were leaving the base, vigilant MPs stopped the car and questioned the occupants about why they were on the base. The driver—the police informant—lied to the MPs in order to avoid being detained for questioning. In signing off on her report to her security handlers, this informant expressed a great deal of displeasure with this experience, proclaiming in a nonsensical phrase: "Gr-r-r-r-r @#$%^&*()!"[62]

In subsequent police reports on SMC meetings, it is clear that this undercover informant played an active role in the antiwar organization. In frustration this spy informed her security superiors, "To whom it may concern: This writer probably missed many details in terms of dates and times; however, tolerance is asked because of the role played in diplomatic relations." This comment suggests to me that the undercover informant was distracted because she was actively involved in keeping the peace between factions.[63] This undercover informant had become such a trusted participant in the organization that the steering committee selected her as one of four members to represent the SMC in a fact-finding and recruiting trip to Brownsville, Edinburg, and McAllen in South Texas. "Those [who] will possibly go will be: Jim Denny, Eric Sell, Homer Garcia, and this writer."[64]

At an SMC Steering Committee meeting held on 24 October 1970, the undercover informant reported on the deteriorating situation for high school students in Austin. There were widespread reports that high school football players were encouraged by their coaches to beat up "long hairs." The informant passed along reports that some high school students had issued clandestine bomb threats at Austin High School, and that two students at Lanier High School were in possession of dynamite and were contemplating plans to blow up the school because of relentless harassment. Gaining access to the inner sanctum of SWP headquarters in Austin, the undercover informant was able to construct a detailed map of the rooms and facilities at the site. At the end of the report, she signed off: "RESPECTFULLY SUBMITTED, The water-boy." Whether or not this highly unusual ending was a sign of disrespect or of frustration, we will never know.[65]

What is clear is that undercover police agents were able to infiltrate the SMC and CUF without attracting too much attention at the time. In virtually all the undercover police reports in the Burt Gerding Papers concerned with SMC and CUF, Barbara Roseman is explicitly identified as a participant in meetings. It is not at all clear whether or not she was the only undercover informant in attendance. She may have been referring to herself. From piecing together available clues, I would suggest that she was not alone, and that undercover informants did not know the identities of other spies. Not only were these agents able to collect a lot of information, but they were also able to ascend in the hierarchy of the organization into leadership positions, entrusted with important tasks. What is not known is to the extent to which these spies were able to sow dissent by exaggerating factional differences. While undercover informants were about to infiltrate and comprise our organizations, they were never able to cripple our antiwar activities. What these police reports on the infiltration of both SMC and CUF demonstrate is that undercover agents seemed to seamlessly move from positions of observing and reporting to ones of active participation, sometimes in activities of questionable legality.

Relationality

Von Clausewitz once famously observed that in war, the strategy of one side dictates the strategy of the other. While it was certainly not obvious at the time, the strategy and tactics of the antiwar movement and the state security apparatuses evolved and changed over time, adopting and adjusting to the perceived strengths and weaknesses of the other side. When it became obvious that law enforcement agencies were tapping our phones, we stopped communicating in this way. When we became aware that law enforcement agencies were using photographs to arrest participants in the days following protest events, we began wearing face coverings and eventually staging demonstrations after dark. Law enforcement agencies massed their forces to break up demonstrations and block our intended routes for marches. In response we adopted mobile tactics that maximized flexibility, using small affinity groups to operate semi-autonomously in the sea of large protest gatherings. When we became aware of undercover informants and agents provocateurs among us, we relied on coded terms and oblique messaging to communicate planned extralegal activities.

Chapter 7

Merry Prankster, Pied Piper, and Rogue Cop

Lt. Burt Gerding and His Fantasy World of Espionage

> [Burt Gerding] is a frightening person, mostly because he is so blind to the realities of others and so narrow in his vision of the world. Combine these qualities with his passion for the use of force, including deadly force, to impose what he sees as correct behavior, and you've got a person as terrifying as any Gestapo member. He is exactly the kind of person joining militias across the country and advocating the killing of federal officials and the bombing of government institutions.
>
> —Archivist Sarah Clark, 5 April 1996

In 1950 Burt Gerding joined the APD, and three years later he became a sergeant with the forgery detail. By the early 1960s, he was promoted to the rank of lieutenant with the mandate to lead the Criminal Investigation Division. Assigned to the district around UT, he interacted frequently with the UT Police Department and UT students. During the desegregation efforts of the early 1960s, Gerding monitored demonstrations and protests aimed at racial integration of commercial establishments near the university. In his role as an APD intelligence officer, Gerding quickly expanded his surveillance activities. In consultation with the UT Police Department and the FBI, Gerding set out to monitor the activities of suspected campus radicals and New Left political activists. Through FBI agent and friend George Carlson (head of UT System security), Gerding worked with agents from the FBI's COINTELPRO. In late 1970 Austin Police Chief R. A. Miles transferred Gerding (in what amounted to a demotion) to the Vice and Narcotics Division. In this short reign between his rise to administrative prominence in the Criminal Intelligence Division and his abrupt fall from grace, Gerding left his mark on the political terrain and a lasting impression on the radical activists he encountered.

In trying to make sense of Gerding and the security apparatus in which he played a significant role, truth is the first casualty. In his transcribed interview surprisingly hidden away in the Gerding Papers held at the Dolph Briscoe Center for American History (at the University of Texas) and his signed police memos, he purports to hew closely to a faithful rendition of what happened and his role in it. Yet in his three-part transcribed interview of over one hundred pages, Gerding plays fast and loose with the truth. He spins yarns that are unbelievable on the face of it, exaggerates his role as intelligence officer, and freely admits he operated outside the law. Gerding was at one and the same time a criminal intelligence officer devoted to spying on the Austin antiwar movement, a clever huckster marketing his brand of Cold War anti-Communism, and a kind of pied piper incarnate—a cunning folkloric figure who (according to him) successfully lured unsuspecting young people to join his merry band of undercover police informants. He was also a merry prankster who delighted in having fun at the expense of those he decided to harass, and a rogue cop who operated outside the law and engaged in illegal dirty tricks directed at political activists.

The Burt Gerding Papers (8.5 linear feet in all) are stored at the Briscoe Center. Along with donated materials from other security officials (notably George Carlson, director of police, UT System, special services security division; and Allen Hamilton, University of Texas traffic and security chief), the Briscoe Center has collected a vast storehouse of documentary evidence chronicling the story of extensive police surveillance that targeted political dissent in Austin in the 1960s and 1970s. Piecing together evidence from these and other sources, it is possible to construct an account of security overreach at a time of political upheaval in America. Despite the ostensible patina of liberal democracy and respect for civil liberties, the security apparatuses overstepped the bounds of legality, engaging in extralegal practices, including systematic violation of civil liberties and individual rights, designed to crush political dissent.

The Gerding Papers contain a startling document: a three-part interview (only partially completed) with Lt. Burt Gerding conducted by Sarah Clark on 19 September 1994, continued on 10 October 1994, and resumed on 25 March 1995. This third interview is found in a separate box and under a different file name. This interview material does not receive any particular pride of place but instead is buried toward the end of his collected papers, appropriately labeled "Gerding oral history interview [cassette tapes and transcript]."[1]

The two-part interview transcript for 19 September 1994 and 10 October 1994 itself is quite lengthy: fifty-three single-spaced pages. The interview takes the form of a confessional treatise. It resembles a personal diary organized as if by a collection of random thoughts, a stream of consciousness spoken aloud and transcribed by another person. Sarah Clark poses a range of questions to Gerding, allowing him to ramble on (sometimes almost incoherently) most of the time. He is surprisingly candid, seeing no need to cloak his real and imagined exploits in a veneer of official and professional legitimacy. In reminiscing about his policing exploits, he is clearly bragging.

From this interview and from a number of written reports included in the Gerding Papers, it is possible to piece together a composite image of the man and his work as a law enforcement officer involved in criminal intelligence. For me three themes stand out: First, he was a dedicated police officer who recognized no fixed boundaries of legal propriety that restricted what he might do, or imagine he could do. He openly admits with prideful arrogance about engaging in illegal acts. Second, he possessed a rather shoddy, incomplete, and simple-minded understanding of the antiwar movement he devoted his adult life to disrupting and dismantling. He seemed to possess no interest in grasping what motivated political activists to act in ways that put them sometimes at grave risk. Third, he seems to confuse and blend fantasy and reality, making improbable claims that are impossible to verify but also impossible to believe. He comes across as a kind of pathetic figure who substituted dirty tricks for careful surveillance and intelligence-gathering work.

Burt Gerding brought the unseemly qualities of huckster, trickster, and charlatan to his job. He was an unprincipled man who delighted in abusing the official powers bestowed upon him as a police officer bound to enforce and uphold the rule of law. At every opportunity he cloaks himself in virtue, putting himself on the side of angels, justifying his unwarranted behavior as an expression of his imaginary struggle of good versus evil. Like the Leonard Zelig character in the 1983 Woody Allen film *Zelig*, Gerding locates himself at the center of the action, claiming—in his own words—"I knew everything that was going on, everywhere."[2] Similarly, like the trickster Tom Ripley in the psychological thriller *The Talented Mr. Ripley*, Gerding sometimes seemed more intent on pretending to be a competent criminal intelligence officer than actually functioning as one.[3]

While the description of the many faces of Burt Gerding may offer a glimpse into the multiple sides of his personality, it is also necessary to acknowledge that he often strayed from factual accuracy. In his three-part interview, not only did Gerding stumble over names of people and misremember dates of events, but he also concocted wild tales of his personal exploits so preposterous that they strain any semblance of credulity.

Our Nagging Nemesis

The first half of the two 1994 interviews consists of Sarah Clark allowing Burt Gerding to talk about growing up in Texas, his experience in the US Army, and his first years as a police officer in Austin. After serving for years as a lowly patrol officer in the APD, Gerding rose to the head of the Criminal Intelligence Division. At the start of his career in criminal intelligence, Gerding reveals his early friendship with an FBI agent, George Carlson, who rose to the position of head of security for the University of Texas System. One thread that runs through these interviews is Gerding's almost obsessive need to cultivate personal relationships with key figures in the FBI, in the police establishment, and at the top echelons of the university administration.

Burt Gerding wanted poster. Clandestinely posted in conspicuous places in 1967 or 1968. Courtesy of George Carlson Papers, camh-dob-017296, Dolph Briscoe Center for American History, University of Texas at Austin.

As he tells his story, one gets the distinct impression that he is a true believer in his anti-Communist crusade. He seems obsessed with the policing world of secrecy and subterfuge. He delights in recounting tales of late-night meetings with his police informants, dressing them in disguises, and driving them in his car around town after dark. He seems to really enjoy taking awestruck young undercover informants into the inner sanctum of the APD, showing them his office and files. He embraces his tasks with a kind of missionary zeal found only in religious institutions. He expresses great pleasure with disrupting the lives and frightening people in the anti-war movement. He seems totally disinterested in the legal rights of those whom he opposes. Nothing seems to get in the way of the pursuit of his mission. He expresses a willingness to break the law with impunity when it suits his purposes of spying. He is filled with bravado, self-importance, and puffery. He brags a great deal about his exploits.

In consultation with local FBI agents, Gerding used sketchy and sometimes illegal counterintelligence techniques to monitor and disrupt left-wing organizations and political activists on the UT Austin campus and beyond. In his own telling, he recounts numerous instances of employing such methods as excessive harassment (such as routine but unreasonable traffic stops), disclosure of private personal information to discredit individuals, vandalism and destruction of personal property, psychological dirty tricks (such as anonymous letters and dissemination of false and misleading information), illegal phone taps, and warrantless break-ins. Gerding claimed to have built an extensive network of undercover informants (a number of whom he claimed to get onto the FBI payroll) whom he instructed to surreptitiously attend political meetings and to spy on the activities of political activists. He targeted leftist political groups like SDS and the SMC, along with the local Black Power group known as the CUF, gathering information through the use of undercover agents with the goal of discrediting these organizations and disrupting their activities.

In carrying out his official duties as head of the Criminal Intelligence Division, Lt. Burt Gerding was at once a jolly prankster, a law-breaking vigilante, and a pathetic figure who suffered from delusions of grandeur. He seemed obsessed with his work, gleeful about making political militants and radical activists feel uncomfortable when he encountered them. He was bombastic, self-aggrandizing, and downright arrogant. At times and places, he allowed wishful thinking to replace actual facts and seemed totally uninterested in what motivated people to action. Much of his bravado consisted of the fantasy meanderings of a law enforcement officer who saw himself as outside conventional legal restraints.

Burt Gerding was obsessed with carrying out his imaginary war with the antiwar movement. I strongly suspect that he deliberately lies in these interviews, exaggerating his role in the spying business and just fashioning incidents out of whole cloth. Reviewing the transcripts of his interview, I do not think the veracity of his claims can be trusted. What is glaringly evident is Gerding's willingness to talk before thinking carefully about what he was going to say.

The aim of the Criminal Intelligence Division, with Lieutenant Gerding at the helm, was to gather information about subversive, anti-American activities and to piece this together in order to provide a coherent understanding of the antiwar movement. This enterprise involved cobbling together raw materials, resources, and tools of the trade to produce the desired outcome. Carrying out the Gerding plan depended upon knowledge of the terrain: the ideologies of organized parties, the strategies and tactics of organizations in the antiwar movement, and the pendular swings of political mood.

According to Gerding himself, he brought together a whole team of undercover informants, surveillance experts, and dirty tricks operatives. Despite the mobilization of resources, the Gerding enterprise was doomed from the start. Because he could not possibly know what he needed to know, he resorted to disruption and sowing discord. He had no interest or real understanding of the politics of the antiwar movement. In 1970 he prepared a report for Chief Miles, a five-page document included in his papers. In this document Gerding offers his assessment of movement organizations. Indeed, for someone who claims to have reliable undercover informants and to have infiltrated organizations and secretly reported on meetings, this assessment was pathetic. It was incomplete, relied on deductive tropes about Communist organizations, and was incomplete in its coverage. As our movement grew in strength and numbers, he seems to have fallen back on well-worn truisms that were no longer (if they ever were) instructive. His claims to have his finger on the pulse of the movement were only matched by his woefully inadequate ignorance of what the movement—its people and organizations—were actually doing. We were building organizations to confront the war machine, racism, misogyny, and homophobia. Gerding was trapped in old paradigms and analytic frameworks inherited from the 1950s Cold War. He was obsessed with tracing poplar protests back to one of several national "Communist" organizations—CPUSA, SWP, and PL. While these organizations had a presence in the Austin movement, their members were certainly not orchestrating or leading popular protests. By 1970 both the CPUSA and PL were spent forces in Austin, and we regarded the SWP and its offshoot sibling organizations—the Trots, as we called them—as more or less irrelevant.

Gerding seems to epitomize the banality of evil: a self-deluded, ordinary little man who believed that he could act with impunity because he operated under the official sanction of the security agencies he worked with.

Gerding the Charlatan

There are experiences that remain stubbornly resistant to understanding and synthesis. I have trouble making sense of why Gerding did what he did. Reading the text of his interviews, I come away with the distinct impression that the man was obsessed with restoring his own faith in himself as a dedicated criminal intelligence officer. To do so he embellished his accomplishments, fabricated his own exploits, and placed himself at the center of the security efforts to undermine political dissent.

The materials contained in the Burt Gerding Papers provide only a fleeting glimpse into the man and his mission. At the end of the third interview, he claims that the Austin city manager in the 1970s authorized the disposal of the security files he had collected over the years. Gerding alleges that he was only able to save three or four large boxes of materials out of a total of about fifteen. This claim may or may not be accurate. Yet Gerding's allegation suggests that he felt betrayed by the security operatives who followed in his footsteps, erasing his lifelong contribution to intelligence gathering and treating his work as no longer relevant or important.

Besides the random assortment of newspaper clippings, leaflets, and political pamphlets, the Gerding Papers contain reports from undercover informants, lists of names, and observations from Gerding himself. The veracity of these firsthand reports and political observations cannot be taken at face value. The accuracy of these materials needs to be evaluated in relation with other forms of documentation, along with the recollections of participants.

It seems clear that frequent reports (called "Memorandum for Information") from undercover informants followed a script: time and date of a political meeting, who chaired, how many people attended, and what were the topics of discussion. These reports ignore nuance and subtlety. The accuracy of the information provided cannot be verified as unvarnished truth. With the exception of the demonstrations at the Don Weedon Conoco Gas Station, the Waller Creek tree incident, and the Chuck Wagon Riot, there are virtually no police reports on particular marches, rallies, and demonstrations. The absence of these security observations is unfortunate, since we know that undercover informants certainly watched, and often participated in, raucous gatherings.

In the Gerding Papers, undercover police reports appear in isolation, surrounded by a sea of silence. Undercover informants dutifully attended political meetings and reported on discussions of planned rallies and demonstrations. Yet follow up assessments of what happened at these events are nowhere to be found. Why? I do not know. Perhaps the undercover police reports were kept in separate files and then destroyed. What is clear is that undercover informants did not always get the facts straight, sometimes identifying people by the wrong names and attributing the wrong political affiliation to individuals. In the shadowy world of espionage, truth is often the first casualty.

Recruiting Spies: Undercover Informants and Information Gathering

In describing his preferred modus operandi, Burt Gerding proclaimed, "I spent my afternoons and days a lot of times going over to the Chuck Wagon, and buying coffee and sitting down at a table." As he put it, "And the next thing you know, I'd have a tableful of people, and all of these people are interested in what I'd be doing because they knew I was doing something and they were trying—they were trying to find out from me."[4] Gerding seemed to revel in what he considered to be his uncanny capacity to charm young people. Like the Venus flytrap, he believed he could capture them with his cleverness and his charm.

In describing his recruitment strategy, Gerding claimed he was looking for students who fit a certain profile. "I was evaluating each of 'em, and the ones I was looking for were highly intelligent, Grade A-plus students, and they were bored." As he put it, "And because they're bored they're always looking for a thrill. So what better thrill to be part of an underground Movement that is subversive—and yet at the same time be safe and be a cop."[5]

Gerding fashioned himself as the pied piper, luring bored (and trusting) "kids" into his secretive world of police spying. He seemed to think that it was only necessary to get these naive youngsters to feel the thrill of being a secret agent. He seemed to have convinced himself that the lure of adventure was sufficient to recruit informants into the underworld of undercover spying.

He seems to really want to be liked and respected. It seems pretty clear that he "turned" young people who were arrested for drug possession or drug dealing into undercover agents, offering a suspended jail sentence for undercover work. He says he attracted curious onlookers from his perch in the Chuck Wagon. From September 1967 onward, I went to the Chuck Wagon almost every day, sometimes more than once. I do not recall ever seeing Burt Gerding holding forth with coffee to offer. I know he is exaggerating a great deal here.

At this time, there was a national TV program called the *Mod Squad*. The leader of this undercover police team was named Captain Greer, and he had a couple of white and Black kids working for him. As Gerding explained his recruitment strategy:

> I'd sit there [drinking coffee in the Chuck Wagon], and look 'em in the eye, and I'd say, "How would you like to be in my Mod Squad?" One of 'em, Sally, said, "Could I, really?" And I said, "You might could.

> Think about it." So she calls me up later and says, "I'll come in only if you let my friend in." And so I said, "Who is your friend?" So she tells me and so I say, "So you and your friend meet me tonight at the parking lot of such-and-such a place and we'll see about it." Now that's where I recruited Sally and Sam. And they were two of the best I had. Sam was highly intelligent. He's now a physician.

Gerding expressed a great deal of pride when he said, "They'd call me Capt'n Greer because they identified with being in the Mod Squad." He concluded, "This was just another one of my methods for recruitment and control."[6]

In order to make his undercover informants feel important, he put ski masks on them and let them ride around with him at night. He drove his undercover informants to the police station "with a paper sack over their head" and "let them look through some of my files and see how I operated and everything. So—they were really tickled because they kind of felt like they were part of the Police Department."[7] He also took "his little agents" (as he put it) out to a dump near Lake Travis and let them fire a semiautomatic rifle he had confiscated. This special treatment was meant to keep his undercover agents in line.

Gerding created a hierarchy among his undercover informants. Some he liked and trusted more than other ones. He seemed to revel vicariously in what he imagined were their exploits in disrupting the antiwar movement. He declared with a great deal of pride that "one of my best agents was a young woman whose code name was Sally." She was "the kind of kid who could get anything from anybody . . . she could get information from people without 'em knowing she was getting information from 'em." He declared that she "was obviously brilliant" and "smart enough" to keep up and "figure out what I was doing a lot of the time." She was "looking for excitement."[8]

Gerding also spoke highly of another undercover informant code-named Sam. As Gerding put it, "He was one of these guys who could get his two best friends into a fight, by merely insinuating that one of 'em said something about the other one." "So he was always getting one faction into a fight with another faction, in such a way that they never realized that it was he who instigated the whole thing. So he was very valuable to me in those ways."[9]

In his three-part interview, Gerding talks about other spies he worked with. One person code-named LeRoy volunteered to work with Gerding "because he liked to pay Machiavellian games."[10] Gerding worked with another undercover informant who initially approached the FBI "because he had been in military intelligence and was in a good position to get in with these people who he really hated." The FBI put him on their payroll. As Gerding explained, "He never actually came to me, and told me that he was an FBI informant. He just started calling me and giving me reports, and meeting me for beer and talking about all these things so he just kind of worked into me. And then I found out later that the Bureau was paying him."[11]

Gerding also bragged about recruiting Mike Simpson, a news reporter for KNOW-AM in Austin, as a trusted undercover source. Recruiting undercover informants from the mainstream news media crossed the line of propriety. Gerding saw nothing improper in enlisting Mike Simpson into his group of undercover informants. Gerding instructed Simpson to interview participants in the Chuck Wagon Riot and then turned the tapes over to the district attorney to aid in the prosecution of alleged "law breakers."[12]

Gerding established elaborate ways to communicate with his group of undercover informants. As he put it, "You never meet them at the same place twice. You set a date for a meeting. If you need a meeting in the meantime, you would go down and make a chalk mark on a telephone pole. Or if he wanted a meeting, he would go down and make a chalk mark on a telephone pole."[13]

> You got to have some way to get in touch with each other without picking up the phone and making a phone call. And you would schedule regular meetings, and you would tell them, "our next scheduled meeting will be in the H.E.B. parking lot." And then the next meeting would be in another place. Some place where you—two people sitting in a car would not be—any attention paid to 'em. Or it was such an out-of-the-way place that no one would ever come there. One of the places that I used quite frequently was—there's a private air service at Municipal Airport, Browning Air Service. And there was quite a few parking places there. But there were always quite a bit of cars parked in this lot and it was very dark and quite easy to get to and you could sit

> there and keep your eye on Airport Boulevard and see what was going on. . . . At any rate, this is how we would meet, regularly or at different times, or if we had some reason.[14]

Gerding also established lines of communication with his undercover informants via a particular pay phone. He maintained regular contact both before and after antiwar meetings that they attended.[15]

The Master Spy and His Networks of Undercover Informants: Infiltration of the Antiwar Movement

Gerding had a highly inflated sense of his own self-importance in infiltrating the antiwar movement with his police spies. He mimicked standard FBI practice of sending his local informants to big out-of-state antiwar meetings.[16] He also boasted that his coterie of undercover informants constituted "almost a quorum at every [antiwar] meeting."[17] This claim is ridiculous on the face of it. Some antiwar meetings consisted of hundreds of participants.

Gerding's claim that he functioned like a puppet master, bending decision-making for the movement to his will does not bear up under scrutiny. In his three-part interview, Gerding returned again and again to this trope of his capacity to use his undercover informants—at one point he claimed eight to ten police agents in a meeting—to divert demonstrations away from "trashing the Drag [Guadalupe Street]" and toward the ROTC building. He bragged that he told his undercover informants that "their standing orders were if it looks like they were trying to get off campus, then you immediately start saying, 'No. Let's go down to the ROTC Building [on campus].'" Gerding was so proud of his strategy of using his undercover agents to "keep these [antiwar people] from any real violence in the community."[18]

This account is, of course, pure bravado. Only a self-delusional person out of touch with reality would make a fanciful claim like this. While some adventurous militant types in the movement might have suggested trashing commercial establishments along the Drag, the overwhelming majority of us thought that this tactic was counterproductive from the perspective of building popular support for the antiwar effort. The ROTC building—a true symbol of the war machine—was a much better target. Any savvy political activist knew that. The way Gerding describes his role is a clear indication that he really did not understand the antiwar movement and its strategy and tactics. Usually without parade permits, antiwar organizations starting from SDS and onward always directed protest marches off campus in the direction of the State Capitol building. He never stopped that.

What is striking is Gerding's claim about the number of undercover informants who he instructed to attend meetings of antiwar movement groups. It seems clear that he did not always trust the judgement and accuracy of reports from his own informants. It is highly unlikely that Gerding was able to get more than a few undercover informants to attend out-of-town meetings. We in the antiwar movement would send some of our own political activists to attend these out-of-town meetings and to report back. At most only a few political activists had the time or the inclination to attend out-of-town meetings. These were not all undercover agents. For example, somewhere between six and ten of us from the Austin chapter of SDS attended the ill-fated 1969 National Conference in Chicago. Of those I know that attended this meeting, I cannot think of one who could have been an undercover informant.

On several occasions in his three-part interview Gerding boasted that he had successfully put "his people" in "high places" in the Communist Party, PL, and the Black Panthers. This claim is false on the face of it. The Communist Party and PL membership in the Austin antiwar movement was very small, and they were by themselves incapable of steering the direction of political action by themselves. With the collapse of SDS in June 1969, PL disappeared as a local presence in Austin. While an Afro-American organization called CUF existed in Austin, there was no Black Panther Party.

Relying on Racist Tropes

In his three-part interview, Gerding discusses his work as a uniformed law enforcement officer in handling demonstrations in Austin related to the racial integration of segregated facilities in Austin in the early 1960s. He talks about his delight in cultivating a personal relationship with Booker T. Bonner, an African American civil rights activist organizing protests in Austin in the early 1960s. Calling him the "father of integration [movement] in Austin," Gerding says that Bonner "would stick his neck out when no one else would."[19] He claimed that he was able to get Bonner to provide him with information about planned protests.

Gerding draws a sharp distinction between his relationship with Bonner and his assessment of a much more militant African American activist named Larry Jackson. Gerding used the occasion of a large demonstration in October 1968 at the Weedon Conoco Gas Station at Thirty-Second and Guadalupe to single out Jackson for his opprobrium. Gerding expressed his displeasure that mainstream news reporters did not blame the confrontation at the gas station on Jackson.

By 1968 Jackson had taken the lead in creating the CUF, a grassroots African American organization based in East Austin and modeled on the Black Panthers and their Free Breakfast for Children program. With a few loyal adherents, Jackson almost single-handedly kept the organization afloat. SDS and other movement organizations worked closely with the CUF.

Always on the lookout for Black militants, Gerding said that he "assigned one of my informants to get involved in the Breakfast Program—to keep an eye on it because it was potentially very militant."[20] He claimed that the CUF "extorted money" out of students when in fact they were soliciting funds around the UT campus. He alleged that he learned from one of his undercover agents that Jackson was able to obtain a new car, mobile phone for the car, and new clothes from CUF solicitation efforts. In the Gerding Papers, there are references to Barbara Roseman serving on the board of the CUF. She was an undercover informant. Chair of the Board of Regents Frank Erwin requested information on Larry Jackson. Gerding provided Erwin with a report on Jackson, outlining his possible relationship with the Communist Party. While Jackson worked with members of the local Communist Party, there is no basis in fact to suggest he was a member.

In expressing some begrudging admiration for the free breakfast program, Gerding was unable to disguise his overall contempt for what he regarded as poor Afro-Americans who took advantage of welfare "handouts." His views coincided with conservative opinions at the time. He fell in line with the illiberal and racist trope of "welfare queens." As he put it, "This [idea of self-help] is the message blacks should be getting instead of go out and get on welfare and have babies."[21]

Whether subconsciously or deliberately, it matters little; Gerding played right into the trope about interracial sexuality. He claimed that Jackson used the movement "as an excuse to have sexual relations with white girls"—"usually a different girl every night." As Gerding said, "So most of the little liberal girls were initiated into the movement in this way."[22] This rhetorical framing amounts to a racist characterization. Gerding was merely mimicking the mythical constructions that were commonplace in the ranks of the security apparatuses.

Cracks in the Security Armor

Yet there were cracks in this cloak-an-dagger world of undercover spies. If Gerding was correct when he claimed to recruit young and impressionable people to work as undercover informants, then of course he would have to deal with the possibility of these secret agents questioning themselves and his motives. He seemed quite confident that his mixture of moralism and excitement was enough to keep these youngsters in his spy ring. Gerding claimed that many of his undercover informants would go to a meeting and "get radicalized." He said that he was "constantly re-indoctrinating them and re-recruiting them" the next day following their attendance at a political meeting. As he put it, "The real problem with all these informants was, every day you'd have to reconvert 'em. They would go to a meeting at night and they'd get all fired up and ready to take on the Establishment, and to hell with this, that and the other and the next day when I'd talk to 'em, they'd be, you know, highly infuriated." He referred to this strategy as "reconversion": "I'd have to talk 'em back into the right avenue every day. . . . I'd convert them in the beginning—that they should be working for the forces of good, and not the forces of evil."[23]

Burt Gerding was enamored with his own charm and wit. He saw himself as a country preacher, converting undercover agents to the way of the Lord. Gerding tried to establish personal relationships with his undercover informants that combined trust and dependence. He needed the spies to believe they were doing the right thing. There are other documents in the Gerding Papers that provide a ranking system to judge the reliability of informants. This formal procedure suggests that some undercover informants were more committed than others, and some were more capable of following instructions.

Gerding was keenly aware of his volatile relationship with his undercover informants. As he said, "These kids could very easily go out of control because they were the type who would have gravitated to this out of curiosity, and out of the thrill involved in it." To keep them in check, he claimed that he offered them "an even greater thrill, in that they were working undercover for me, and they were able to do it—without their friends knowing it." He promised his undercover agents that when their spying days were over, he would invite all of them to a party, and he would "hand out little solid-gold pins that say 'FYB, fuck your buddy,' because they would say every day, 'Well, you know, all I'm doing is fucking my buddy here by telling on 'em and all this stuff.'" He told them, "When the day comes, you can all meet one another, and so you'll know who all was involved, and I'll hand out these little gold pins." Gerding assured his undercover informants that they would never know who the other agents were who worked alongside them. "So this was the typical day-to-day handling that went on, and recruiting never stopped."[24]

Gerding was acutely aware that his undercover spies knew that "I had other informants, and they were always trying to figure out who they were." He boasted that "to this day they do not know, because I had promised these people when I recruited 'em, 'If anyone ever finds out you have been an undercover cop, it will be because you have told them, because I will never tell, ever. So you have to tell them. Or they will never know.'"[25]

The FBI gave numbers to the undercover informants they recruited. They cross-indexed this number in a card file that listed the person's real name. As Gerding put it, "I kept no card file. Purposefully." "Everyone had a code name and never was their real name ever written down," he proclaimed. "So to this day they don't know who they are."[26]

Gerding's claim that the names of undercover informants were never revealed is of course not true. Gerding disclosed in his three-part interview that his prized informant, code-named Sally, was a member of a sorority. Barbara Roseman was a member of a sorority. There is a file in the Gerding Papers that contains a lot of printed antiwar pamphlets and flyers that originated from New York and Chicago. In the midst of these materials, I discovered two large envelopes that were mailed from New York and Chicago and addressed to Barbara Roseman. These envelopes were somehow thrown into the files and allowed to stay there. This paper trail blows her cover. It seems in all likelihood that Barbara received pamphlets from New York and Chicago and that Gerding and his office staff mistakenly included these envelopes with her name on them in his files. Barbara Roseman—the name we knew her by—was an undercover informant.

Gerding also bragged about the eventual prestigious occupation of one of his favorite undercover informants code-named Sam. I know of only one person who could fit this profile—M. B., who received his medical degree at UT San Antonio medical school. Rumors. I remember on the morning of a planned afternoon demonstration at the federal courthouse in the spring of 1972, someone reported that he saw M. B. get out a police car near the site about five hours before the scheduled protest. When confronted M. B. defended himself, claiming he was getting a light for a cigarette. We were suspicious of him anyway. Once the seeds of suspicion are sown, the taint of possibly working as an undercover informant never really disappears. The clouds of doubt followed M. B. wherever he went.

Gerding as the Center of the Action

Burt Gerding expressed great admiration for J. Edgar Hoover and the FBI. As he put it, "J. Edgar Hoover had built probably one of the most efficient organizations there ever was."[27] Yet at the time Gerding suggested that the various branches of the security apparatus did not work very well together. The interorganization dynamics among parallel security agencies were fraught with problems. Because "each law enforcement agency had their own private little turf," there was "very little cooperation." As Gerding put it, "You don't step on somebody else's jurisdiction."[28] From secondary sources it seems plausible that security agencies did guard their own private fiefdoms fairly judiciously, only reluctantly disclosing information to others. Given difficulties the agency encountered during the 1960s civil rights struggles in the South, the FBI was cautious about working with local law enforcement officials. According to Gerding the FBI issued "standing orders . . . that no agent could directly contact a student, without first getting permission from the Special Agent in Charge, which at time was in San Antonio." The result was that the FBI "had no real contact with students."[29] Actually, this claim is incorrect: there was no blanket order prohibiting FBI contact with students.[30]

As Gerding said, "I would go out—I had free rein [to recruit students]." Seeing a propitious opportunity to ingratiate himself with various security agencies, with the FBI at the apex, Gerding recruited students as undercover informants as a platform for his own ends. Gerding saw himself as a law enforcement officer with a magic touch, acting as a conveyer belt moving unpaid student informants along the value chain to paid undercover agents working for the FBI.[31] "I would work 'em in," he said, and "control them for a period of time and make sure they were in fact really good, reliable sources." Then, he said, "I would turn them over to the FBI who could pay them, and did pay them, and—quite a few of those kids went through school."[32] "So a lot of these kids actually—their education was paid for by the FBI."[33]

Gerding liked to imagine himself at the center of the action, using his ability to withhold information to compel agencies like the FBI to cooperate with him. He claimed to be more enlightened, to possess more wisdom and foresight, and to be better at gathering information than other security agencies. As Gerding tells it, informal information sharing was the way that competitive branches of the security apparatus worked together, if at all. As he bragged, "I was the primary source of information, and if they [i.e., the FBI] did not cooperate with me, then they were cut out from what was really going on because they were not allowed to go out and recruit people [students]" as undercover informants.[34] As Gerding put it, "So I made these agencies corroborate, and when they didn't corroborate I'd just shut 'em off. They'd contact me, and I'd say, 'I don't have anything.

You know, you're wasting your time. I don't have any information for you.' And they would suddenly get the impression that—hey, wait a minute, you'd better cooperate, or it's not going to work. And this included military intelligence, secret service, FBI, DPS Intelligence. Everyone that I worked with—including—the C.I.A. called me up one time and wanted information on someone."[35] Yet by law the CIA was restricted from conducting domestic intelligence gathering. If Gerding is telling the truth, he sheds a light on the illegal activities of the CIA.

Gerding saw himself as the key link in the security apparatus in Austin. He admitted that he drove around streets on the days of big demonstrations, recording license plate numbers. He forwarded this information to George Carlson and the FBI, who identified the owners of automobiles with the aim of knowing who attended demonstrations.[36] What is clear is that that the agencies that formed the security apparatuses relied upon both formal and informal means of communicating with each other.

Dirty Tricks

When Burt Gerding learned of the FBI COINTELPRO operations, he experienced what he regarded as an epiphany. He was pleased to discover that, in his words, "I had been doing counterintelligence all along, which was things that would disrupt or divert, or in some way discredit the movement." He claimed that if he found that a political antiwar activist "was particularly vulnerable, then I would use that vulnerability in clandestine ways to really keep him shook up." In his estimation the COINTELPRO effort authorized FBI agents "to use any and methods at their disposal to discredit any members of the Old Left, New Left, or any of this Movement people." What the launch of the COINTELPRO accomplished was, in effect, "sicking the dogs on 'em." As Gerding put it, "Up until then the Bureau did not have latitude to do things to these people. They could only collect information. So to me this was really turning the dogs loose."[37]

Gerding gloated that he used counterintelligence—dirty tricks—before he learned of the elaborate plans undergirding COINTELPRO. For him counterintelligence meant using the information he gathered against what he termed "the enemy." "If you find that there's something vulnerable that the enemy has, then you strike it, and your counterintelligence people do that. So I had been using counterintelligence all along, in various and sundry ways."[38]

Whether outside the boundaries of the law or not, he endorsed, and engaged in, a proactive campaign of disruption. Gerding boasted about using his repertoire of dirty tricks to frighten activists, disrupt meetings, and generally foster uncertainty. He bragged endlessly about spreading unfounded rumors, engaging in unwarranted breaking and entering into homes of known activists, flattening tires, tapping phones, photographing unsuspecting people, and disrupting meetings with fireworks.

Let us look at some of these dirty tricks in more detail. Gerding boasted that he knew that an FBI undercover informant with whom he developed a working relationship—a person who came to the FBI from military intelligence—broke into people's homes and taped marijuana cigarettes in discreet places. He did nothing to stop these kinds of dirty tricks to possibly entrap antiwar activists in criminal behavior.[39] At the time possession of marijuana was punishable with up to ten years in prison. Gerding's inaction made him complicit in a crime. It is clear that Gerding stepped over the line of legality when it suited his purposes. In this instance there was an air of deniability.

Gerding boasted about his homemade electronic bugs used to wiretap the phones of known activists. He justified his illegal wiretapping by claiming those he targeted were "members of one Communist Party or another." He said he was interested in finding out "if they were getting any orders from somewhere else or what they were saying to other places." Gerding claimed that he worked with an "electronics expert" who helped him construct a tiny telephone bug that fit into a small box that was sealed with epoxy adhesive to make the device almost indestructible. He said that he wore "climbing shoes with spikes" so that he could easily ascend telephone poles. He said he would venture out at "two, three, or four o'clock in the morning, by myself, I wanted to make sure nobody knew about it." He claimed that he installed these telephone bugs before they were illegal.[40]

According to Gerding these telephone bugs transmitted a distance of about three to five miles, and "you could sit anywhere within the 3–5 mile circle" and listen to conversations. These electronic bugs only operated when the unsuspecting targets of the clandestine surveillance operation picked up the phone to make or receive a call. Gerding took great pleasure in announcing that these transmitters "used the power of the telephone company to power itself." He affixed adhesive decals that said "Bell System" so that repair people would not remove them. Gerding's standard modus operandi was to install an antenna and radio receiver for tape recording in the trunk of a car he obtained from the police pound. He left the car parked close to where his targets lived. He changed the tapes every day or two. He said he "shared information with the FBI" but never told them it came from illegal electronic bugs.[41]

Gerding insisted that almost every night he drove around with his undercover informants outfitted with black ski masks, "check[ing] out at least twenty or thirty of these people's residence to keep tabs [on them] and where they were or what they were doing." He claimed that "a lot of times" on nights when regularly scheduled meetings were held, "I would park my car several blocks away, sneak up to the front porch and detonate a [large] M-80 firecracker." As he put it,

> When the thing would go off, these people would just completely freak. They never even once thought it was anything but a gunshot. It never entered their mind it might be a firecracker. So they would immediately panic. Some of 'em would run out the back, some of 'em would hide under beds. And after a while somebody would peek out the front door, and then the next thing you know three or four of 'em would peek out the front door, and then they would all come out and search the house for bullet holes—when all the time this was nothing but a firecracker. Well, what this accomplished was one—it broke up their meetings. Two, it made them all more paranoid, and scared the hell out of 'em. And three, I found it real amusing.[42]

Gerding boasted that "this was the type of counterintelligence stuff I was doing."[43] What I find insightful is the extent to which Burt Gerding—a law enforcement officer with a sworn obligation to protect the public—found it amusing to set off firecrackers to disrupt meetings. He fashioned himself as a kind of merry prankster, turning police surveillance into "fun." He became a rogue cop with an outlaw mentality.

Gerding seemed enamored with the use of explosive devices as "a sort of practical joke." He claimed that "my best of all success with M-80 [firecrackers] was when SDS was having a fund-raiser at the University YMCA."[44] He also bragged that he brought along his undercover informants Sally and Sam to set off M-80s at the home of a John Birch Society member. This story seems so ludicrous that it is almost beyond belief. As head of Criminal Intelligence Division, his job was to collect information on so-called fringe political organizations regarding possible wrongdoing and illegalities. Exploding firecrackers outside a meeting of the John Birch Society had nothing to do with gathering information.

Along with an undercover informant code-named LeRoy, a person whom he referred to as "my friend," Gerding "decided it would be fun if some of these people would have flat tires when they were attending a meeting." Leroy would use an ice pick to puncture "at least two tires on each car." With two flats and only one spare, political activists "had to spend a lot of time jacking their car and get one tire fixed and then go down [to the filling station to] get the other one fixed." "This is kind of—pretty much a lot of the things that happened."[45] This wanton destruction of private property and petty harassment did little to advance the mission of the Criminal Intelligence Division in collecting information.

Gerding bragged that he unlawfully forged documents as part of a "sting operation" to sow mistrust against an activist member of the Communist Party. Gerding identified this person as Paul Pipkin, declaring that he left Austin and never came back.[46] In addition, Gerding expressed great satisfaction at orchestrating the dismissal of an activist from a teaching position, for no other reason than he belonged to the SWP.[47]

Gerding proclaimed that "one case I am most proud of" was that of university professor Larry Caroline "who was a real threat. He was sharp. . . . He was controversial. At any rate, he was a real danger, in that he had prestige, and he could really get these people worked up." As he recalled:

> One of my informants spent a lot of time with him so I pretty much knew what he was gonna do and when he was gonna do it, and where he was going to be and what be doing. Leroy [undercover informant] had gotten him so many times [punctured tires] so that he finally went

> out and bought puncture-proof tires and put 'em on his car, which are very expensive. . . . From my informant that was with him, Larry thought it was members of the PLP that was doing it, and—or one of the Trots [Trotskyists], or somebody else in the movement that was doing it.[48]

Gerding claimed that along with his undercover informant LeRoy broke into Larry Caroline's home and moved furniture around as a way to sow paranoia. After applying various other kinds of illegal harassment, Gerding claimed that Caroline "suddenly decided it was time for him to leave Austin and go to California." Gerding bragged that "it was this type of counterintelligence where we were able to get rid of a person who was really a strong potential—not potential but a strong leader—and keep them off balance."[49] Claims of success like this one might sound good because they seem credible. Larry and Dina Carolina actually moved to Philadelphia of their own volition so that Dina could attend medical school at the Medical College of Philadelphia. She became a well-known and successful physician.

Perhaps a person consulting the Gerding Papers might be enticed into believing these stories that Gerding recounted about Larry Caroline. I contacted Dina and Larry Caroline by telephone and email. Dina Caroline said that "almost 100 percent" of Gerding's allegations were false. According to Gerding, political activists like Larry Caroline secured their places of residence and the SDS office with a Master 210 lock that undercover informants easily bypassed with their own keys. This apocryphal story is totally fabricated out of thin air. SDS did not have an office, and no one I knew had Master Locks on their doors. Dina Caroline said that they never locked their house, and friends came by frequently when they were not there.

Gerding was totally cavalier about engaging in harassment practices that had nothing to do with police surveillance work. He claimed that he was able to get the student body president and hippie named Jeff Jones to believe that his house was bugged with listening devices. As Gerding put it, "I saw an opportunity to just kinda have some fun."[50] This offhanded comment provides a window into understanding Gerding's motivations and intentions. What does "having fun" have to do with serious criminal intelligence work?

Nothing. He abused his official authority to play a side game designed to freak out Jeff Jones. In communication with me, Jeff Jones disputed these "facts," claiming nothing of this sort ever happened. It seems that Gerding engaged in make-believe. He was the consummate fabulist. Whether he believed his own falsehoods is a matter of speculation. The alleged harassment of Jeff Jones—whether it took place or not—strongly suggests that Gerding saw himself as a prankster with a badge. He seemed to believe that he had license to do whatever he wanted.

Burt Gerding was not averse to fantasizing about the discretionary use of arbitrary police violence. In responding to what he interpreted as a threat from Communist Party member Bob Speck in 1967 to "kill him," Gerding boasted that at "any time I wanted I could just wipe him out."[51] Why would a police officer say what he said, let alone imagine it? In fantasizing about his own omnipotent power to do deliberate harm to political dissenters, Gerding expressed his utter contempt for the rule of law.

Gerding seemed overly fixated on the November 1969 Chuck Wagon imbroglio, trying to lay the blame for the police riot on nonstudents. "The Yippies and street people took over the Chuck Wagon," as he put it, "and students couldn't get in there."[52] This claim is totally inaccurate. Gerding correctly identified the precipitating event: Undercover police entered the Chuck Wagon and arrested a runaway girl nicknamed Sunshine. He claimed—in exaggerated and overly hyperbolic language—that "street people" surrounded the police car used to take "little Sunshine" away, breaking its windows, slashing its tires, and jumping on its roof. This pathetic excuse was Gerding's explanation for the police riot: If this response to the arrest of the young runaway started the confrontation, then irresponsible agitators hurt innocent people the next day when they threw bottles and rocks into the crowd. In Gerding's view, the police were innocent victims just doing their job and rioters were simply lawbreakers.

Of course what Gerding completely overlooked in his story was how plainclothes police entered the Chuck Wagon without announcing who they were and forcibly removed Sunshine, and how on the day of the riot, out-of-control police indiscriminately beat people in the crowd, arresting anyone they could apprehend. Yes, I do believe that innocent people were injured by indiscriminately thrown rocks and bottles. Yes, we had irresponsible people in our midst. Gerding seeks to put the blame for the police riot on "evil people," thereby ignoring the indiscriminate use of police force.

Gerding used the occasion of the Chuck Wagon Riot to condemn the mainstream media, particularly the *Austin American-Statesman*, for "printing things they know are lies, for manufacturing lies." As proof of his claim, Gerding referred to a photograph printed in the *Austin American-Statesman* showing a riot-clad policeman with a raised nightstick about to club a cowering protester. He claimed that the carefully cropped photograph failed to show the broader view in which protesters were attempting to free Lori Hansel from the grasp of police after she was caught sticking a knife in a police car tire.[53] Gerding had it wrong: Lori Hansel was not caught trying to flatten the tire of a police van. It was someone else—Pam Stubblefield.

All Power to His Imagination: Gerding and His Fantasy World of Espionage

In imagining himself as the center of the spying universe, Gerding claimed that "I had people calling me all the time. I had people from the Far Right that would call me and give me a little tidbit of information. I had people from the Far Left who would call me and tell me something about the Far Right, and I was also keeping up with the Far Right, the John Birch Society, at the time."[54] In placing himself at the center of information gathering, Gerding seemed to want to be wanted. His need to feel important and significant seemed to dwarf his police work. As a "spymaster" he seemed to think he was in a position to orchestrate everything.

In perhaps his most farcical boast, Gerding claimed that he "knew everything that was going on, everywhere."[55] This preposterous assertion was, of course, far from accurate. In the formative years at a time when the Austin SDS chapter was experiencing its early growth pangs, Gerding was able to maintain at least a partial understanding of political activism because of his hands-on, direct observation of movement activities. He could easily name the early leadership of SDS. He attended meetings, took photographs, and was a physical presence at rallies and demonstrations. He bragged about engaging key activists in conversations. He surprised people by calling them out by their first names. I know this to be true, because Gerding did this to me.

Over time this somewhat cozy but always uncomfortable relationship between Gerding and New Left activists gradually came to a close. His early fixation—obsession, really—on identifying Communists and the efforts of organized Communist Parties to infiltrate the Civil Rights Movement and the growing antiwar movement blinded him to really comprehending the root causes for political dissent. In holding to his belief rooted in Cold War ideology that the Communist threat was an external, outside malevolent force trying to hoodwink alienated youth, he failed to see how growing political consciousness was a relatively autonomous occurrence, growing in tandem with organized left-wing parties but never subservient to their ideology or directives. The antiwar movement expanded and fractured that it was impossible for Gerding to know everything by himself.

Whether he misremembered or he deliberately lied, Gerding often misrepresented the facts. For example, he claimed that a Houston-based African American activist named Lee Otis Johnson was involved in a shootout with Houston police.[56] This allegation is false. Houston police did kill an African American activist named Carl Hampton, the leader of an organization called Peoples Party II, in a deliberate assassination that was far from a shootout. Three political activists originally from Austin were involved in this organization.

In one of his most outrageous and preposterous allegations, Gerding claimed that "Jeff [Shero] and Alice [Embree] left here [Austin] to join the Weathermen."[57] They actually went to New York to help start the underground newspaper called *The Rat*. Yet he persisted in recounting this preposterous lie: "But the last I saw of them was when they left here to become members of the Weather Underground."[58] If that were the case, why did the FBI not apprehend Alice Embree when she returned to Austin in 1970, participating openly in the Women's Liberation Movement and with *The Rag*?

Gerding also alleged that Bob Pardun was "a big Communist Party organizer from [the] beginning." This statement is totally fallacious. When he lived in Austin, Bob Pardon was rather inactive in the antiwar movement. Gerding also claimed successes that were patently false. He bragged that

"Bergstrom [Air Force Base] is the only [military] base in the US that was not leafletted. And of course this was a sense of pride to me."[59] This statement is astoundingly inaccurate. I picketed and passed out leaflets at Bergstrom on at least three separate occasions.

At other times in his interview, Gerding displayed a remarkably unsophisticated view of politics on the ground. For example, he referred to the Spartacists as "an elite Trotskyite group."[60] In fact, the Spartacists were a small, insignificant faction with little national presence and few adherents in Austin. Their most popular slogan, written on bedsheets and carried in protest marches, was "All Southeast Asia must go Communist."

Gerding often displayed contempt for the movement and its goals. In commenting on the protests directed at the university administration for cutting down trees at Waller Creek in 1969, Gerding suggested that "I could recognize these people were looking for any kind of cause."[61] As a way of discrediting protest marches, he said that protestors "always had several women carrying children or babies in their arms, and the reason that they were there, in the front ranks, was to keep the police from using tear gas . . . because the police would not use tear gas against innocent children."[62] I cannot count the times I remember uniformed police using tear gas indiscriminately on crowds. Cops firing tear gas canisters never surveyed the crowds, being careful not to bring harm to women and their babies. Women carrying babies at front of demonstrations—a rather rare occurrence of it ever happened—were not immune from police abuse.

Gerding also claimed credit for monitoring protest activities at the May 1971 demonstrations protesting the dedication of the LBJ Library. "So I went down and rented about six citizen-band walkie-talkies," he alleged. "And I gave 'em to my people [his informants], and had them scatter 'em out among their crowd, because the police had communications and they didn't. So they're here talking to one another and I'm sitting here in the L.B.J. Library with a monitor, listening to every word they say. . . . They were using radios that I provided 'em."[63] There is something incongruous with this story. Was he working on a special assignment? All evidence points to the fact that Gerding had left the APD well before this event took place. Why would he simply make up a story like this?

As an ideal, gathering information as part of criminal intelligence is a practice linked with three principles: It is secretive and clandestine, it is fact-based, and it is comprehensive. While Gerding's police work was conducted largely behind the backs of political activists whom he spied upon, the results were not particularly rooted in accurate factual accounts and were certainly not comprehensive. Because undercover informants were not particularly well-versed in the language and practices of the antiwar movement, their reports often substituted clichés for nuance and completely overlooked the political strategies that guided movement actions. The undercover police reports that Gerding collected were far from comprehensive.

Gerding's sleuthing work amounted to a tangled skein of commitment to an elusive cause and a penchant for making his own rules. He largely operated as a Lone Ranger, seemingly without much supervision from his superiors in the APD.

The Downfall of Lt. Burt Gerding

Poor Burt. He spun the wheel of fortune and lost. He suffered a humiliating defeat. In his 27 March 1995 interview with Sarah Clark, Gerding claimed that he decided to leave the Criminal Intelligence Division and retire from the APD because he was "burned out." He used the phrased "burned out" five times in the interview. "It was everything," he said. "You know, I was just burned out. I had done this for so long and it was just getting out of hand, and my home life was causing me problems and because of the hours I was working."[64]

At this point the story that Gerding tells in his interview gets a little messy. Gerding claimed that he submitted his resignation on the day of the "tree incident" (protests at Waller Creek) in late October 1969. After some mind-gazing, he then seemed to suggest that he resigned in 1971.

Neither of these dates are accurate. In mid- to late1970, Chief Miles of the APD relieved Lieutenant Gerding of his duties as head of Criminal Intelligence Division and transferred him to the Vice and Narcotics Division. Gerding began his APD career In Vice And Narcotics, and he absolutely hated it. As he put it, "So I suddenly get transferred to Vice and Narcotics. I didn't have to wonder why, I knew exactly why." Gerding fell back into a conspiracy: this transfer "tells me how much they had my phone line bugged, because I used to say if they ever wanted to get rid of me, all they had to do was put me in Vice and Narcotics."[65] Accusing fellow law enforcement officers with tapping his phone is a serious, albeit unsubstantiated, charge. Gerding saw this demotion as a personal blow, an affront to his own sense of self and to how much he had contributed to his security mission. He left the APD soon thereafter.

But Gerding conveniently only recounted part of the story. In mid- to late 1970, he became personally enmeshed in an internal imbroglio in the APD involving the issuance of traffic tickets to a fellow officer named Donald Primrose. Apparently Gerding was too quick to go to the mainstream press to report on this internal matter. Perhaps it violated the unspoken rule that what happens with the police, stays with the police. As a result of this apparent indiscretion, Chief Miles was left with little choice but to punish Gerding by demoting him.[66] It also seems likely that Chief Miles was not satisfied with the work that Gerding did in collecting and evaluating information on political activists.

So all in all, Gerding's ignominious career as an anti-Communist crusader lasted less than six years. It was a meteoric rise and a rapid, dishonorable collapse. Cast adrift from his comfortable position, the embittered Gerding casually remarked in his interview, "No matter what I did, it was ineffective." He saw himself as part of a thin blue line that separated honest people from the anti-American riffraff. "I thought, no matter what I do—and all I have done in the past amounts to nothing," he conceded. "So put yourself in the position of someone who has devoted his life to crime fighting, and all of a sudden they pull the rug out from under you and change the rules in the middle of the game."[67]

It is interesting to note that Gerding regarded his spy work against individuals and organization expressing their constitutional rights in opposition to the war in Vietnam as genuine crime-fighting. What crimes did he uncover? What criminals were ever prosecuted under his watch? What crimes did he commit under the guise of intelligence gathering?

Certainly by the mid-1970s, voters in Austin elected slates of progressive people to the Austin City Council and to the office of mayor. According to Gerding, the new city manager seized police records. As he put it, "These records I have turned over to you [at the Briscoe Center] are only a very small part of the records that I collected." Gerding claimed that he only managed to save three or four boxes out of fifteen—the "City Manager burned the rest."[68] This is a pity; perhaps in a hasty effort to cleanse the police department of its shameful record of wrongdoing, the city manager deprived us of our capacity to hold these rogue cops accountable for their illegal actions.

Within a year or so, Gerding took a job as manager of Administrative Services at Westinghouse Corporation in Round Rock, outside of Austin. His duties consisted primarily of hiring and firing employees and managing security. He saw one of his main responsibilities as protecting the company from union organizing efforts. Gerding admitted that he spied on union organizers in violation of the National Labor Relations Board. True to form, Gerding acknowledged that he operated outside the law: "All of this was a violation of the law—I know now."[69] What a liar. Gerding knew all along that he violated the spirit if not the letter of the law to carry out his vindictive effort to break the New Left and the antiwar movement. He failed. After a long illness, Gerding died in March 2013. Someone replaced him as head of the Criminal Intelligence Division. We never knew who that person was.

The Work of Criminal Intelligence

As an ideal the work of criminal intelligence is framed as coherent and unchanging: monitor "subversives" in the antiwar movement in order to ensure that they do no harm. Yet this startlingly fixed view was out of touch with the everyday, lived experience of antiwar activists. Our world was incoherent and unfixed. Our strategies and tactics were unbounded and constantly shifting. There was a gap in the space between these two conceptions. Law enforcement agencies—and Gerding with his ideal notion of his work in the Red Squad—filled in the gap with cynicism, hypocrisy, and fantasy, closing the fissures with a kind of double vision. The security apparatuses were at once capable of seeing what they wanted to see and not capable of seeing what they wanted to ignore—that is, paying lip service to respect to the law and respecting the civil rights of antiwar activists while at the same time violating the law to accomplish what they regarded as the greater good. This free-floating imaginary world of surveillance and monitoring offered comfort against the nagging reality that the misadventure in Vietnam became known to ever widening circles of people and that the conformist popular culture of the 1950s had come unglued.[70]

Borrowing from Hegel, it might be said that history is an unfolding narrative in which particular times that appear secure and coherent unknowingly incorporate the seeds of their own undoing. The University of Texas campus in the 1950s and early 1960s was a remarkably stable place. Institutions like college football, the exaggerated role of fraternities and sororities, and a paternalistic campus administrative hierarchy established a kind of ideological straitjacket that reinforced conformity and looked down upon any expressions of deviation from compliance with the acceptable normative order of things. Until it began to unravel in the early 1960s, the practice of racial segregation was deeply enmeshed with both the city of Austin and the UT administrations. Holding tight to the traditions of the Old South operated as an article of faith, creating the temporary illusion of durability. Racial inequities in hiring, the agonizingly slow pace of racial integration of the student body and athletic teams, and the resistance of commercial business owners to allowing for the racial integration of their facilities represented the final rear-guard actions to maintain this sense of continuity with the past. The combination of the rise of the civil rights struggle and the birth of a fledgling antiwar movement in Austin were the subversive forces that began to systematically erode the pillars upon which this conventional normative order maintained its grip over social life.

It is clear that from the start Lt. Burt Gerding, as head of the Criminal Intelligence Division of the APD, was intently focused on monitoring agitation and protests around civil rights. Like other security agents around the country, he was obsessed with finding outside Communist influence in the Civil Rights Movement. In the mid-1960s the focus of attention for the Criminal Intelligence Division shifted from monitoring civil rights protests to spying on those political activists that clustered around the New Left. Gerding himself was clear about his mission and the identity of his adversaries:

"They were a bunch of dope-smoking Communists, out to overthrow the country."[71] His main goal was to spy on these Communists and undermine their goals—by whatever means necessary.

On the whole the security apparatuses saw their principal task as maintaining a semblance of order by monitoring dissent and isolating dissenters. Despite the rhetoric of confidence in the eventual success of their mission, the goals of the various security agencies aligned against the civil rights struggle and the antiwar movement were fundamentally unstable, held together by the willful embrace of hypocrisy. When the deficits of this hypocrisy gradually replaced the benefits, the deliberate attachment to shaky foundational principles began to come unglued. Gerding's approach was premised on what Fintan O'Toole in another context called the "unknown known": the self-serving balancing act for knowing and not knowing at the same time.[72] Gerding remained confident with what he thought he knew: Dissent and subversion were outside forces rooted in an alien Communist ideology that was anathema to the American way of life. He willingly dispensed with acquiring any genuine understanding as to why the antiwar movement continued to grow and grow, eventually challenging the cherished values of postwar America: faith in free enterprise, rigid gender roles, and the inherent goodness of US foreign policy in the fight against godless Communism. This is what he did not know and did not want to know.

Gerding was able to maintain this self-deception, or useful fiction, for only so long. What reveals his loss of faith in his own self-deception can be found in his own words, contained in his three-part interview with Sarah Clark. When Gerding begins to brag about his trickster exploits, using powerful firecrackers to frighten those attending protest meetings, flattening tires, and illegally breaking into private homes, then it becomes clear that he has abandoned all hope of maintaining the kind of political conformity and quietude that he longed for. His cynicism reveals his hypocrisy. The two sides of the known/unknown couplet—the knowing and the not knowing—began to unravel. Gerding had lost confidence in what he thought he knew, and he was incapable of knowing what he did not know. Faith in the basic precepts of the American way of life worked to the extent it remained as an unspoken and yet integral element of his unseemly contract with hypocrisy. To lay bare the immorality of the war in Vietnam revealed the grim realities of US imperialism that had remained obscured by the rhetoric of the goodness of America. To expose (as the Women's Liberation Movement did) the inherent misogyny in both institutions and personal relations undermined confidence in conventional gender roles. The rise of the Black Power movement was a telling sign of the failures of the Civil Rights Movement to achieve the goals of racial equality. The center could not hold. All that was solid melted into air.

At the start Gerding took refuge in the embrace of absolute conviction in an unfounded belief. In the end his actions belied the durability of his original certitudes. When Gerding left the APD in late 1970, he had become an angry and embittered man, disillusioned with the institutional scaffolding that had sustained him and disappointed in the security apparatus that he had worked so diligently to create. By his own admission, he felt unappreciated and betrayed by the APD. Stripped of purpose, he became a lost soul.

Chapter 8

My Twin and I and the FBI

While I had not bothered to look into getting my own FBI files chronicling various policing agencies spying on me in the late 1960s and early 1970s, my twin brother used a FOIA request in 2017 to obtain his FBI files. He was able to get three separate caches of files that originated from three different sites. The files were packaged together in distinct bundles. They were labeled 100-HQ-460860; SC-0100-0049B: SC; and OM-0100-0098B: OM. Each bundle ranged in size from fifteen to twenty-five pages. All in all, the national FBI headquarters in Washington, DC, coordinated efforts with three regional FBI offices (San Francisco, Omaha, and San Antonio) to construct files on my brother and me. There was a lot of material crammed into these pages. These files form a kind of time capsule, hidden relics from the past preserved in aspic.

Reading these files is truly surreal. What was strange is that these FBI reports treated my twin and me like bookends, toggling back and forth between undercover reports on him and on me. We are twins, so I guess it is not surprising that reports in the FBI files paired us as mirror images, dancing in tandem in a choreographed ballet of "subversive activities" (in the words of the various reports). FBI agents crafted both my brother and I as dangerous radicals that were genuinely threats to national security. We appear as almost indistinguishable lawbreakers in the drama the FBI created in order to try to make sense of political activities that their undercover informants were incapable of truly grasping or understanding in any comprehensive way.

As I peered into the world of police informants spying on the two of us, I encountered reports that treated us as if we were so far outside the conventional mainstream that we required watching. Scrutinizing what undercover informants said about my brother and me from a vantage point fifty years later is uncanny. My twin and I are, of course, those persons referred to in the documents. Yet at the same time, the caricatured figures in the files bear little resemblance to the real persons that we were. The police reports linked both of us with particular meetings and protest events. I remember little about what role I played or what I said publicly at those meetings. I remember a great deal more about the protest events in which we participated. Yet in many ways I have relied upon these FBI files as memory aids to help me to recall events and people.

On Reading These FBI Files

In these FBI reports, security agents constructed my twin brother as a kind of secret double, a doppelgänger—a folkloric figure from the late eighteenth century often portrayed as an evil twin or a scheming Other who operates through destabilizing one's own equilibrium.[1] The doppelgänger functioned in FBI reports as my alternative identity, never identical but not quite separate. In my brother's FBI files, I become the backup, whereas in fact I was active full-time in the antiwar movement in Austin and my twin visited three times over compressed periods of time, attending meetings with me and participating (along with me) in protest events.

Security handlers considered undercover informants their key source of on-the-ground information. The embedded spies submitted irregular reports. The police undercover informants who reported up the chain of command to their security superiors operated on the principle that surface appearances are not to be trusted and that deeper truths lay hidden beneath them. The role of undercover informants was to use their toolbox of deception and subterfuge to uncover the real intentions of militant and subversive radicals. These undercover informants were, in fact, quite inept and clumsy.

Cobbled together, the FBI reports that my brother and I obtained through FOIA weave a narrative with a cast of characters—"subversives"—and a plot line that focuses on "militant radicals" who were bound and determined to disrupt the established order by breaking the law. This story is relatively seamless and closed. It is a fanciful fairy tale framed as good versus evil: FBI agents and their undercover informants—the "good guys" only doing their jobs—battling against subversives (the "bad guys") bent on destruction and mayhem. Of course, what is missing from this story are accounts of illegal phone tapping, home break-ins and planting of eavesdropping devices, sowing of false rumors, beating of imprisoned antiwar protestors, and assassinations of political activists (Fred Hampton, Black Panthers, Chicago, 1969; Carl Hampton, Peoples Party II, Houston, 1970; and more).

One of the broad conclusions that I have reached after reading the files is just how uninformed the FBI agents actually were. They focused very narrowly on individuals and alleged subversion. They completely ignore the collective dimensions. For me, making sense of these group dynamics would be the starting point for understanding what was happening. Within their own cocoóned hierarchies and their outdated Cold War ideological fixations, the FBI agents seemed ill at ease and uncomfortable, unsure of how to pinpoint subversive persons except to use undercover informants to listen in at public or semipublic meetings. Like all security agencies that begin to see that they cannot patch the widening cracks in the wall, the state apparatuses charged with law enforcement reverted to extralegal tactics, sometimes with deadly consequences. As the antiwar movement grew in size and influence, the state security apparatuses reverted to expanded repression, ranging from using the legal system to shut down protests avenues to the use of conspiracy laws to target groups and individuals.

Reading the FBI reports is an eerie experience that at once triggers memories of a time and place that I have not thought about for decades. It provokes feelings of dread with the shocking revelation that unknown persons—police and undercover informers—were watching me up close and personal, actually monitoring my comings and goings, and even recording snippets of conversations. After reading these files, I felt that the FBI, as a huge security bureaucracy with tentacles reaching everywhere, had not only violated my personal space (and had invaded my privacy) but also shown complete disregard for my civil liberties of free assembly and free speech.

Obtaining My Own FBI Files, Finally, After Four Years of Trying

The stockpile of FBI records I obtain in March 2025 proved to be a godsend. Upon reading these FBI files, three features stand out. First, there is the consistency of inconsistency. The way the files are presented seems quite haphazard. The display of documents does not conform to a clear organizational logic. The files follow no easily recognizable patterns. The files are often out of sequential order and contain no thematic essence. Second, the FBI agents who prepared the files never provided any indication as to why their undercover informants paid any attention to me. Why were they so focused on me? To be sure, many of the FBI files contain lists of other files organized by numbers and names of people I knew. So I was not alone in their quest for information. The FBI also assigned a specific file number—100-SA-10848—in which they stored information related just to me. They also collected information on me in two other file collections: 100-SF-72168 and 100-HQ-474899. What cuts against the grain of the consistency-of-inconsistency trope is a curious regularity: Certain undercover agents, with various code names, seem to have been assigned to regularly report on me. The same undercover agents reported on me and my attendance at numerous meetings over a long period of time. Third, the level and intensity of the surveillance on me seemed so exaggerated. Why did the FBI pursue such an extensive inquiry on me?

These files contain a surveillance photograph of me from an October 1969 demonstration hoisting an IWW banner with the message "Worker Control." There is also a Department of Motor Vehicles photograph of me from 17 January 1972. I must say, I did look frightful with long hair, a bushy beard, and large glasses.[2]

What is clear from the FBI files is that the San Antonio Field Office was keenly aware of the growing presence of SDS in the Texas-Oklahoma region very early on. The FBI reported on a regional meeting of SDS held outside of Dallas in late January–early February 1969. Around fifteen activists were invited to attend this meeting that included representatives from Austin, Dallas, Houston, Arlington, Rice University, Oklahoma, and North Texas (Denton). This confidential FBI memo was distributed to FBI Headquarters, OSI, the 112th Military Intelligence Group, NISO, and the Secret Service (San Antonio and Austin), and included in thirteen separate files (including my own). The first purpose of the caucus was to schedule the National Council meeting of SDS in Austin in March 1969. The second was to replace the regional travelers in the Texas-Oklahoma region with regional committees, including three division leaders in Austin: one for the University of Texas, another for local high schools, and a third to focus on the GI movement.[3]

After declaring that both my twin and I were engaged in "subversive activities," FBI headquarters authorized efforts to identify my immediate relatives.[4] My mother was a trusting person. Hence, it is perhaps not surprising that she fell for an old FBI trick. On two occasions (24 April 1972 and 27 October 1972), FBI Special Agent James Gaskins of the FBI—using the suitable pretext that he was an old friend trying to get in touch with me, reached my mother by phone. Believing what this FBI agent told her, my mother answered his questions truthfully. Unsuspecting of any chicanery, my mother spilled the beans on me, so to speak. She provided my address, my phone number, my employment status at University of Texas, and even declared that I had lived in Austin for the past five years with the "exception of summers when he returns to the San Francisco area."[5]

I have already said FBI special agents approached my father at his place of work to inquire about me, but he refused to divulge any information. The FBI also contacted my high school guidance counsellor, the registrar at University of Texas, and others to collect personal information on me. FBI agents also searched the files of the Walnut Creek Police Department, the San Francisco Police Department, and the Contra Costa Sheriff's Office (Martinez) in vain for a criminal record. Besides listing my social security number, they also obtained descriptive data from the records of the Sacramento Department of Motor Vehicles when I renewed my driver's license on 25 October 1972.[6] Another FBI agent identified my 1961 Ford pickup truck with Texas license plate number BLZ 311. Another special agent of the FBI contacted the office of a journal named *Socialist Revolution* with which I was affiliated to obtain information about my whereabouts in the San Francisco Bay Area. I was only one of many—perhaps hundreds—of antiwar political activists about whom the FBI sought to unearth personal information regarding addresses, phone numbers, employment status, and more. For what purpose?

The FBI files reveal a striking pattern of surveillance directed at me. These files contain at least ten separate reports on my activities between 1968 and 1972. It seems that two particular FBI undercover informants—codenamed SA-10-1 and SA-10-4—reported on me. What illustrates their commitment to surreptitiously collect information is the independent reports of two undercover agents who both attended a meeting of ten persons. I doubt they knew that the other was a spy. Why did the FBI handlers expend the time of two agents to report on such a small meeting?

One undercover informant reported that I attended various meetings in connection with the "proposed establishment of another [underground] GI newspaper at Bergstrom Air Force base" in Austin.[7] The attached report from the undercover informant claimed that I attended a "general rap session" at the house I shared with Bobby Nelson and Martin Wiginton to discuss the formation of a social organization and the creation of an underground newspaper to be mailed to military personnel at Bergstrom Air Force Base "in an effort to establish closer ties with the military." The police spy also reported that those in attendance at the meeting discussed how to recruit Austin high school students "to the socialist cause." These students were identified as having been "instrumental in the past in causing disorders at various high schools."[8]

Another police informant supplied the San Antonio FBI office with the names of thirty-five individuals (including me) who were involved in a "COUNTER INAUGURAL DEMONSTRATION" on 20 January 1973. The speakers included a Catholic priest from the Catholic Student Center, a representative from the Gay Liberation Movement, an active-duty GI from Fort Hood, a student from Huston-Tillotson College (a historically African

American University in Houston), and a local high school student.[9] What do we learn from this report? First, we were able to assemble a wide range of groups to participate. Second, the undercover informant was sufficiently integrated into the antiwar movement as to be able to identify by name so many individuals.

In an information report classified under the heading "Bobby Nelson has traveled to Cuba and is interested in Racial Situations," an FBI undercover informant who attended a meeting at my house on 20 December 1972, made some strange claims. First, "The other professor [from UT Austin] is Martin Murray. His wife or girl friend is named Carol." Wrong on two counts. I was a graduate student, and I never had a girlfriend named Carol. Second, "Nicholas Dykema is suspected of being an informant for some law enforcement agency because he has no source of income and yet is able to travel and live without any problems." Yes, we did suspect that Nick worked for a law enforcement agency. He was also present at this meeting. Second, "Martin Wiginton and Bobby Nelson seem to have a lot of money. This is based upon the fact that they have served meals to a group of 15 to 25 individuals on every occasion that a meeting has been held at their residence. They also maintain a plentiful supply of good liquor and wine." Wrong. They did not have a lot of money.[10]

Surprisingly, the FBI files revealed the identities of the special agents who observed me on 14 October 1972 (James King and James Holmes), and on 20 January 1973 (Howard Riley and Philip Craig Cagnoni). The report also listed eight "confidential sources" under the codenames SA T-1 to SA T-8 who were "furnishing valuable information on a continuing basis relative to revolutionary activities."[11] The FBI tracking and surveillance on me culminated in a lengthy twenty-page report prepared by FBI Agent Howard Riley from the San Antonio Field Office and submitted to FBI headquarters on 22 February 1973. The confidential report was titled "MARTIN JULIUS MURAY—SECURITY MATTER—REVOLUTIONARY ACTIVITIES." In a way this report left no stone unturned. It represented a summary of sorts, beginning with a great deal of personal information taken from my driver's license and other sources, including my date of birth, my employment status as a teaching assistant at UT Austin, the organizations with which I was affiliated, my parent's names and their address, my social security number, names of the universities I attended, my degrees, the number of hours of study I had completed, my Austin home address, and my health status. FBI agents contacted the APD and the Texas DPS to inquire about any arrest records for me.

In a separate section labeled "activities in revolutionary-type organizations," the report identified over seventy events or meetings in which I was a participant, starting with 1969 and ending with 1973. The report identified eight different undercover agents as "confidential sources" who issued reports on me. Two undercover informants—codenamed SA T-3 and SA T-4—figured prominently over the years in compiling these regular sightings of me. Given clarity and precision of these observations, there is absolutely no doubt that I must have known these individuals and probably considered them friends and fellow activists.

These FBI reports began on 10 January 1969 with an observation from an undercover informant (codenamed SA T-3) that I had manned a literature table organized by the NLEP during spring registration. Two undercover informants (SA T-3 and SA T-4) reported that I was present at a NLEP meeting attended by ten people on 25 January 1969. Think carefully about this. The ten people in attendance certainly included two undercover spies. The FBI seems to have expended a lot of resources on monitoring my activities. Over the next several months, the undercover informants codenamed SA T-3 and SA T-4 issued reports on my activities on average once a week, and sometimes as many as two to three times a week. The topics included preparations for the SDS National Council meeting to be held in Austin, legal defense for those arrested at the antiracist demonstration at the Don Weedon Conoco Gas Station (May 1968), dismissal of charges against me for solicitation of funds under the auspices of NLEP, and a meeting to create a Stop the Draft Committee with the aim of harassing the local board of the Selective Service System. An undercover FBI agent remarked that on 29 January 1969 I was observed "selling subversive literature." Still another FBI undercover agent reported that I spoke at a rally on 13 March 1969 in support of "Afro-Americans for Black Liberation." Undercover agent (code named SA T-8) noted that on 11 November 1969 I was one of ten speakers at a rally

Martin Murray, looking skyward at circling helicopter, antiwar march, fall 1969. Courtesy of Alan Pogue, photographer.

that preceded the "take over" of the Chuck Wagon. This same agent claimed that I participated in a demonstration that was "antimilitary in nature" at the Oleo Strut coffee house in Killeen on 20 May 1972. Agent SA T-4 reported (on 18 December 1970) that I taught a course on political sociology that "concerned itself with Marxist theory." Another FBI agent reported that on 4 February 1971 I formed the Ad Hoc Committee for Socialist Ecology.[12] This attribution is indeed incorrect.

An undercover informant codenamed SA T-6 seemed to have buttressed the work of agent SA T-4 as another spy assigned to monitor my activities. This use of additional undercover work coincided with preparations for the May Day demonstrations planned for 3–5 May 1971 in Washington, DC. Agent SA T-7 reported (7 May 1971) that approximately ten people traveled from Austin to participate in the May Days demonstrations. This ill-informed spy was way off: Around 250 people from Austin participated.

Agents SA T-4 and SA T-6 went into overdrive to report on my participation in the demonstrations (22 May 1971) to disrupt the dedication of the LBJ

Library at the edge of the UT campus. Agent SA T-6 seemed to have carefully tracked my movements on that day. All in all, no less than three different undercover informants reported on my activities concerning demonstrations at the dedication of the LBJ Library.[13] In the following months, an undercover informant codenamed SA T-8 seemed to provide additional monitoring work for the FBI. This new spy focused on my participation in the NAM, formed in Davenport, Iowa, in November 1971. Curiously enough, this security agent—named Weldon Kidd, Intelligence Section, the Texas Department of Public Security—reported on 12 February 1973 that I referred to the "United States as an outmoded and irrational system."[14] These reports submitted by undercover informants go on and on with a kind of dull regularity. Now, in retrospect, I am left with an uncanny feeling realizing that I was constantly being watched.

An undercover informant reported that Martin Wiginton and I took the lead in planning demonstrations in April 1973 at the LBJ Ranch and Bergstrom Air Force Base to protest the appearance of President Thieu from South Vietnam.[15] The FBI files also contain an essay I wrote entitled "Why We Are Still There," exposing US business interest in Vietnam.[16] The collection of FBI files classified as SA 100-10848 ended with an inordinate amount of material on the NAM. These files consist of an array of handwritten notes prepared by undercover informants who attended meetings, a collection of policy statements, and a list of NAM members (fifty-five in total), with addresses and phone numbers, and each assigned an FBI file number. These reports are uninteresting and not helpful in understanding the workings of spying agencies.

In the end, after reading these FBI files, I have come to the conclusion that FBI agents were seemingly rummaging around everywhere, looking for clues of subversive activities. Using a suitable pretext, a special agent of the FBI visited the offices of the journal *Socialist Revolution* on Sanchez Street, San Francisco, to inquire about my whereabouts.[17] Using the justification that I was involved in "revolutionary activities," FBI agents searched the records of the San Francisco Police Department, Walnut Creek Police Department, Selective Service, and the Contra Costa Sheriff's Department looking for any criminal record that I might have had. FBI agents concluded that they were unable to uncover any "additional derogatory information" on me.[18] These FBI files classified as 100-SF-72168 contain a copy of my driver's license and two photographs of me.[19] An FBI memo lists at least fourteen confidential sources (codenamed SF T-1 to SF T-14) who provided information on activists (including me) who were associated with the journal *Socialist Revolution.*[20]

FBI Documents as Archive

I remain to this day very curious about the organizational structure of the security apparatuses. How did the APD Red Squad under Burt Gerding and the local FBI actually recruit spies? How much were they paid? Did they all adopt code names? In my brother's FBI files, undercover informants were referred to in letters and numbers like S-1, S-2, S-3, and so on. I know from my sleuthing that using numbers and letters was a common FBI practice for identifying undercover informants. Did the undercover agents know their fellow spies? Did they meet with their police handlers in person? Were some undercover informants tasked with one particular type of spying, while others were hired to do other kinds of secret activities? What was the difference between undercover informants who started in the law enforcement agencies or military intelligence before they were recruited to infiltrate the antiwar movement, as opposed to those recruited without any prior experience? Did the teams organizing the security apparatus divide informants into subcategories? Were some undercover informants recruited because they were compromised, facing jail time for drug possession or other crimes?

On the broader terrain of interpersonal relationships, why would these undercover informants spy on people who, in turn, regarded them as trustworthy friends, and treated them as committed comrades-in-arms? In this schizophrenic charade, I can only imagine the kinds of personal suppression of feelings that undercover informants must have undergone to do their dirty work. What kind of faux "true identity" did these undercover spies have to adopt to justify to themselves how they reported on people who trusted them, and even liked them?

The Paper Trail: Chaos Without Order

While there is a great deal of overlapping text in all three FBI bundles that my brother obtained from his FOIA request, there are some differences in each. What this slight discrepancy suggests to me is that different FBI offices were piecing together reports that they received from different sources and then subsequently added a little new information of their own. My twin and I appear almost as if we were one person but with two detached bodies (e.g., "Mark Murray, brother of Martin Murray," appears numerous times, as if a mantra). On every page of these documents, there were handwritten notations, circled names, and underlined words. In short, it is clear that there were at least a dozen security agents at various levels of the security bureaucracy poring over information related to my twin and me. The files appeared as a long litany of memos and reports. As the files circulated among various FBI branches and offices, the same identical memos appear again and again. With so many disconnected and repetitive overlapping pieces, this format makes for disconcerting reading. A great deal of repetition breaks the temporal sequence.

All of this attention directed at my twin and me raised some questions for me: Why did the various security agencies identify us as persons of interest? Who compiled these documents? What was the chain of command? What was the relationship between different law enforcement agencies, ranging from the Criminal Intelligence Division of the local APD, UT Campus Security, the FBI (regional offices and national headquarters), and military intelligence? What sorts of information were privileged over the rest? What documentation did they fail to divulge?

These FBI documents are like a time machine, a vehicle to transport me back to the past. The way that the FBI agents compiled these files is interesting. FBI chroniclers make no effort to produce a coherent storyline. As the files circulated from one office to another in search of additional collaborating information, they pile up like a big car wreck on a foggy highway. Each separate vignette careens back and forth, appearing over and over as the files bounce around FBI offices, occasionally bumping into the Secret Service, with elliptical references to local police forces.

In my brother's FBI files, it is clear that undercover police informants were responsible for gathering information. Where there more than one? An undercover agent code-named SA T-3 reported that Mark Murray attended a meeting on 17 May 1971 attended by twenty-five persons at 2831 Pearl Street to discuss plans for the disruption of the LBJ Library dedication on 22 May. Another undercover report from an agent code-named SA T-1 substantiated the information provided by the other agent.[21] I suspect that there were at least two, if not more, undercover informants at that meeting. All of this raises a nagging question for me: Did the FBI also collect records on the other twenty-four persons in attendance at this meeting? Surely my brother (a visitor) and I were in all likelihood not the only two persons of interest. I can only imagine twenty-five documents—one for each person in attendance—stored in some dark vault somewhere, reconstructing what happened at this meeting and who attended.

The Archival Me

If a tree falls in the forest and there is no one there to hear it, does it make a sound? If FBI agents and their string of undercover informants decide not to write down all the information they obtained from spying, does this mean that what was not recorded was therefore not significant? Think of this process in this way: A tree falling in the forest without anyone to hear it still ends up in a pile of rubble on the ground. In other words, just because undercover agents did not report on meetings cannot be interpreted to mean those events were unimportant or insignificant. I would venture a guess that FBI officers did not, and could not, require their undercover informants to attend every meeting. More importantly, plans for demonstrations and extralegal activities often took place informally, in bars and backyard barbeques and all sorts of places outside the range of the prying eyes and ears of the spies. We were not unaware; we knew that the FBI listened in on phone conversations and surreptitiously took photographs. Sometimes, one could hardly carry out a conversation on the phone with so many clicking noises and errant sounds. (When making a phone call from home, I often started by saying, "Hey, Burt [Gerding], how are you?")

On 24 April 1973, the San Antonio Field Office contacted FBI headquarters to reveal that a computerized telephone number file quarterly composite for the fourth quarter of 1972 indicated a number of suspicious calls to my phone (number 512-477-2839). We knew that our phones were tapped, but this memo confirms our suspicions that the FBI collected locations of incoming calls. Again, interestingly enough, the FBI files reveal their undercover source, William Hamilton, security officer, Southwestern Bell Telephone Company. He was a former FBI special agent.[22]

What is striking is how these FBI documents construct—in words and innuendo—my twin and me as larger-than-life cartoon characters rather than actual persons with disparate interests, sensibilities, and motivations. We participated in organized efforts to end the war in Southeast Asia and to combat racism and sexism. All this was irrelevant. Police documents reduced us to "subversives" (words in the report), "agitators," and lawbreakers. It is strange to imagine, from the vantage point of today, that my twin and I were constructed as such one-dimensional stick figures collapsed into the single-minded intentionality of "subversion."

In a strange and uncanny way, archival death takes places when the reporting breaks off and dries up. What can one interpret from the recurrent silence about me after, say, 1973? That I was cured of the radical politics disease, and hence no longer a threat? My whole personhood—the one who enjoyed country music, played basketball, and enjoyed friends—is totally irrelevant. In both the FBI and security police reports, I am a ghostly presence, and nothing about my brother and me is important except uncovering our subversive inclinations. This juxtaposition between real and imagined selves feels uncomfortably surreal.

We knew that undercover informants for many security agencies had infiltrated our movement, but we carried on nonchalantly, somehow not giving it much thought. After reading these FBI files over and over, I acquired a distinct impression of how undercover informants went about their business of gaining access to what they considered the truth—or perhaps more to the point, what they constructed as the truth. Their spying amounted to what by analogy might be understood as something akin to a surreptitious interrogation. Those who have experienced a police interrogation know that it involves repetition. Over and over, the interrogator asks the same questions, looking to ferret out small discrepancies that hint at unspoken truths hidden away. The security agencies always began with the same assumption: Subversive radicals were hiding something. Undercover police informants follow the same tactics, asking themselves the same questions about how and why unsuspecting participants in meetings were hiding truths. Police undercover informants were attracted to any signs of subversion, illegal intent, or unpatriotic thinking. Bounded by these obsessions, they surely missed the real reasons for these kinds of "subversive politics." Police informants never turned the gaze on themselves and their handlers, inquiring about their own illegal tactics in supporting an unjust and undeclared war seven thousand miles away in a far-off land.

In the Burt Gerding Papers, one document contains a rather lengthy (twenty-page) typescript (with handwritten notes) describing organizations that were active in Austin in 1971. The author of the document referred to Student Nonviolent Coordinating Committee as the "Student Non-Violence Cooperating Committee." Oh well. Sloppiness happens. Yet this error is so egregious that it suggests inattention and incompetence. The author also seemed disinterested in different politics and political strategies. For example, he (and I do believe it was George Carlson, head of security for the University of Texas System, who authored the piece) makes no effort to understand the differing ideologies and motivations of different political groups.[23]

If the security agencies had a more complete understanding of the different political orientations of militant organizations, they might not have seemed so clueless and ill-informed. We who operated on the terrain of everyday politics understood the subtle nuances that separated one organization from another. We knew that the SMC never ventured beyond approved rallies and marches organized around the single issue of Bring the Troops Home. First in SDS and then in all the other political organizations that stepped into the void after the June 1969 collapse, we were not averse to calling for what were deemed unlawful rallies and marches, for engaging in building take-overs, and for participation in disruption. We were never single-issued about anything. By 1970–1971 we carried NLF flags and openly supported the victory of the Vietnamese revolution. SMC would never do that. So there was no reason for us to mingle with the folks with whom we did not share the same orientation.

This example leads me to the conclusion that the FBI, COINTELPRO, and other security agencies were only narrowly interested in Communist infiltration of the New Left and the capacity of the student movement to disrupt business as usual. Curiously, it almost seems that information gathering took on a life of its own; collecting pamphlets, listening to phone conversations, and producing undercover reports on meetings acquired its own momentum. The security agencies seemed disinterested in understanding the root causes of dissent and the strategic and tactical differences between different organizations.

Text and Context, Silences and Gaps

The silences and elisions are just as significant as the reported information in the FBI files. The FBI reports seek to string together disparate data points to compile a composite montage of subversion. From their point of view, it must have been frustrating to have only an incomplete picture, something less than a full accounting, of what those "subversives" upon whom they were spying were actually doing. It was impossible for informants to fully comprehend our thinking and to monitor all our actions. I believe that this lack of information gave rise to one-dimensional stereotypes and caricatures of radicals, subversives, and countercultural hippies. It was a matter of course for law enforcement agencies to lump protestors into simplified categories like pot-heads, dopers, Communists, anarchists, subversives, and lawbreakers.

The FBI files reveal only shards of information that were taken out of context. By focusing on individuals, the policing agencies seem to have lost touch with the wider dynamics of protest and agitation. Individuals were replaceable parts. What was the endgame here? Did the FBI have embryonic plans for massive roundups of subversives?

Thinking about these files from the benefit of hindsight, I have reached the conclusion that undercover informants and their FBI handlers were interested not only in what we were doing but also in what we might do, and what we were thinking about possibly doing. What is missing in these FBI files is what they intended to do.

In truth, there were considerable silences and gaps in the FBI story. FBI headquarters in February 1973 approved the destruction of sixty-four of the eighty-seven files they had collected on me.[24] I wonder what was contained in those files that I will never be able to see. This is the unknown unknown. After reading these FBI files, I am perplexed as much by what was seemingly completely overlooked as by what was included. Why were some activities and some meetings referenced in the report and yet others not mentioned? I know that both my twin and I were involved in other meetings, like planning for protests and demonstrations, that were just as significant as those that undercover informants brought to light.

Logically speaking, there are two explanations for this oversight. On the one hand, FBI informants and other undercover agents were not particularly attentive, missing key pieces in the "subversive" puzzle. These gaps raise questions about their competence. On the other hand, and this explanation is much more uncanny, the informants knew about—and reported on—other activities my twin and I engaged in, but these files were never released to us, or were destroyed. I believe both explanations contain grains of truth. Yet I am aware that requesting FBI files under the terms of FOIA do not always produce the full picture of what they have. Perhaps the reason why this lack of transparency can be explained by the desire of the FBI to cover the identities of their informants. Even covering over names in reports cannot guarantee that my twin and I could not accurately ascertain the identities of those individuals who were assigned to spy on us.

Years later I still have an eerie feeling about the ability of spies to be among us. At least five undercover agents—with the SA code names—submitted reports on my brother at various times and places.[25] Yet he was only a visitor, remaining in Austin for very short periods of time. Why did they seemingly zero in on him?

After carefully reading these FBI files, what strikes me is the limited grounds whereby undercover agents obtained information deemed worthy to pass onto their superiors. The points of contact between us and them were almost exclusively semipublic meetings. Undercover police informants, after befriending us and gaining our trust, were able to attend meetings without arousing too much suspicion. What is surprising about the FBI reporting on my brother is that there is little concrete evidence about what we actually did. The undercover reports add up to really not much more than guilt by association. Mark and I attended meetings that planned protests, and police informants reported on our presence. That was about the extent of it.

FBI reports do not conform to the standard protocols of storytelling. Like the investigation of someone's tax returns, the reported information only yields a partial story—a small truth in a wider world of circulating polysemic truths. The information reported in the FBI files only contains a sliver of what my twin and I were involved in over the course of many years. I guess I take some solace in knowing that FBI agents did not know everything and were only able to learn a little part of our planning and acting. I was certainly involved in a lot more plotting and scheming to build the antiwar movement than they ever discovered. I witnessed my brother on several occasions do something that was a violation of the law. Thankfully, the police could not be everywhere.

The FBI collected and accumulated their information in distinct silos. This way of storehousing information actually limited their capacity to understand what was going on. In the entire basket of memos and reports, my twin and I appear together frequently, but there are no mention of any other "subversive" persons. We did not act by ourselves outside of our groups. It is if we operated as lone rangers, without compatriots and accomplices. Separated from the group, we were framed as atomistic individuals, as if to suggest our thinking and actions were developed independently of the groups into which we were thoroughly embedded. The FBI constructed us as if we were suspicious persons in isolation, Leibnizian monads, dynamic substances bouncing randomly off each other but with no true causal relation with other like substances. This approach is bound to produce limitations to knowledge.

Truth and Non-Truth

The FBI memos that my brother obtained brings back memories of those turbulent times. Reading the text reveals a sort of half-hearted story that FBI agents were piecing together so that they might make sense of what was happening and why. One undercover report refers to my brother Mark as a participant in antiwar demonstrations in Austin, 5–6 May 1970, that erupted into a "confrontation with Austin PD involving arrests and use of tear gas."[26] Burt Gerding advised the FBI San Antonio office that "a source" (in this instance, an undercover police informant) suggested that Mark Murray "stated that he considered himself a student-riot type leader." This undercover informant stated that my brother "did not want to become involved in any confrontation inasmuch as it could lead to his arrest for crossing of state lines to participate in a riot."[27] Finally, they produced something concrete. Interestingly enough, an interpretive thread appears: This undercover police informant reported to his/her superiors that my brother "intimated that he was possibly wanted in Omaha or the State of Nebraska on other charges."[28] Wow. Why the hyperbole? Falling prey to the power of the imagination, this undercover informant reached the conclusion that my brother had a warrant out for his arrest in Nebraska. This supposition had no basis in fact, but it did trigger the FBI to inquire with the police in Omaha about outstanding arrest warrants issued against my brother. These undercover police reports triggered an information gathering exercise that spiraled ever outward. On 6 May 1970, FBI headquarters initiated a security probe involving FBI field offices in Omaha, New York, San Francisco, and San Antonio to search for information on the two of us. The FBI in the Omaha office searched arrest records and credit checks with regard to my brother. These efforts turned up no damning evidence of wrongdoing.[29]

This alleged arrest warrant in Omaha vignette reveals in microcosm the nature of the relationship between us and them. Think of it: One cryptic, offhanded remark made by one undercover informant derived from a casual conversation at the end of a meeting is not much more than hearsay or speculation. Since there was never an arrest warrant issued for my brother in Omaha, there is no reason that he would have suggested such a thing. The undercover informant either misinterpreted what my brother said or else deliberately concocted a story. Whatever the case, it triggered a firestorm of FBI activity, provoking a flurry of memos up and down the chain of command, where the FBI office in Omaha was alerted to this possibility of wrongdoing and was required to check its veracity.

This frantic approach is akin to looking for a needle in a haystack. What sticks with me is the extent to which police informants were willing, in all likelihood, to take liberties with the truth and to employ poetic license to conjure the possible. Yet their approach also suggests to me that they were shooting wildly in the dark, not sure what to do or where to look. Memos passed back and forth between FBI field offices in Omaha, New York, San Antonio, and San Francisco, checking for any records concerning Mark Murray or Martin Murray.

What surprised me was how extensive the surveillance net was. Despite the huge gaps in the information they managed to obtain, the FBI reports are more detailed than I would have imagined. For my brother, the FBI field offices from San Antonio (with jurisdiction over Austin), Omaha, Nebraska (where he lived), Sacramento, California (where he moved), and San Francisco compiled and shared information. In tracking down the pasts of my twin and me, the national FBI headquarters instructed the San Francisco field office to send agents to interview officials at St. Mary's College High School in Berkeley—the high school we both attended from 1963 to 1967—to inquire about our student days there.

Local FBI agents immediately jumped to the task, promising to "obtain background information from St. Mary's College High School, and determine if subject [Mark Murray] has been involved in any New Left activities at Berkeley." In a subsequent memo, FBI agents reported that their interview with Mary Woodson, the registrar at St. Mary's High School, revealed that "both brothers were excellent students and that neither gave any trouble to the administration at the high school."[30]

In addition, the San Francisco FBI Field Office reported on 30 November 1970 that one of their agents interviewed Brother Cassian Frye, "Dean of Studies" (no such position existed) at St. Mary's College High School to obtain information about the two of us. The dean reported that Mark Murray was a "hard-working student." Yet on one occasion, in a conversation the dean revealed that my brother "said something to him which indicated that the Subject may have somewhat liberal leanings." For the dean this admission was a bit shocking. He reported that he "was quite surprised to hear the Subject talk that way," also claiming that he had "no recollection of anything about the Subject to indicate that he was part of the New Left movement or that he was in any way militant."[31] What is quite distressing to me is that a person in a position of authority at St. Mary's College High School would venture an opinion such as this, or for that matter, any opinion at all, to FBI agents who randomly showed up at his office. It is also important to remember that we graduated from High School in 1963—about seven years earlier.

FBI reports include the names of our father and mother and their home address (1120 Blvd. Way) in Walnut Creek, California. Furthermore, they correctly referred to my father's place of work (McDonnell Nursery) and his occupation as "nurseryman."[32] Years later my father offhandedly said that two FBI agents approached him at his place of work, asking about my brother and me. He said he refused to talk with them.

Surprisingly, one FBI report also mentions what agents refer to as an autobiography (dated September 1966), in which my brother stated he had "traveled to Mexico with Amigos Anonymous, a student-worker group that does community development work in Latin American countries."[33] This report is only partially accurate. Amigos Anonymous originated in the San Francisco Bay Area, recruiting students to do community development in Central Mexico, not in Latin America. All of this information gathering begs the question: What "autobiography" might they be referring to? My brother did go to Central Mexico under the auspices of Amigos Anonymous in June–July 1966. He most certainly wrote about this experience in the formal application for CO status with our local draft board in Martinez, California. Did FBI agents approach the Martinez local draft board to gather information on the draft status of my brother? This scenario seems, in all likelihood, to be a distinct possibility. Yet the FBI records reveal no such effort to seek information at the local draft board in Martinez.

The FBI was not finished yet. The Omaha field office reported my brother's local address (5920 N. Thirty-Third Avenue, Omaha) and his selective service number (4-31-45-250). The Omaha FBI office contacted Lt. Charles Blankenship (Omaha Police Department), Julie Pool (Douglas County Sherriff's Office), Leah Mace (Omaha Credit Bureau), Pat Larsen (Omaha School District), Mary Jean Taylor (supervisor, Omaha Census

Bureau), and Hilda Hass (Omaha Board of Education) for information on Mark or Martin Murray. This search turned up nothing.[34]

FBI reports list Mark's educational history, mistaking a summer course in which he enrolled at Columbia University in North Carolina, and not correctly as in New York City.[35] After correcting for their mistake, the New York FBI Field Office included another report on Mark Murray, indicating that he had attended summer session in 1965 at Columbia University ("a student in good standing"). A search of the Credit Bureau of New York, the Special Services Division, and the Bureau of Criminal Identification for New York City revealed nothing of importance. Their efforts yielded a fairly complete profile. The FBI field office in Sacramento even identified his four roommates at his place of residence (on L Street) and listed his phone number.

In addition, the FBI field office in San Antonio promised to consult with the Houston office to do a background check on Martin Murray.[36] A 20 October 1970 report included in this string of memos indicated that the Berkeley Police Department had no incriminating records on me.[37] FBI agents reported that I graduated from USF in 1967, received a master's degree from UT Austin in 1970, and "attended UTAT during the school years 1967–1968, 1968–1969, ad 1969–1970."[38] All in all, FBI agents followed a vaporous trail of evidence of suspected wrongdoing, again only to end up with nothing.

Reading against the grain, the FBI seemed intent on uncovering the roots of our deviant behavior. I suspect that the FBI was hoping to discover "trouble-making behavior" in our youth, thereby fitting into the convenient narrative trope that antiwar agitation was not much different than antisocial juvenile delinquency. Curiously, they actually thought that becoming radical was tantamount to a personality disorder, a character flaw, and with enough sleuthing they might discover its pernicious source. They wanted to know: From where did the temptations (to turn "subversive") originate?

In referring to my brother, the director of the FBI issued a memo on 17 February 1971 instructing field officers, "in view of statements allegedly made by Murray in May, 1970," to "remain alert for any indications of subversive activity on his part." "If any such information is received,

Police surveillance photograph of Mark Murray (twin brother of Martin Murray, *right*) at a political rally. Courtesy of George Carlson Papers, camh-dob-017278, Dolph Briscoe Center for American History, University of Texas at Austin.

immediately reopen this matter, complete a complete security investigation and submit results in a summary report. Consideration at that time should also be given to subject's inclusion on the Security Index."[39] The Security Index was a secret list of American citizens who were targeted for detention in a national emergency under the Subversive Activities Control Act.[40] This memo concluded on a strange note: "remain alert as to any indication that Murray may be receptive to an interview."[41] How can one interpret this move? Does this suggestion mean to imply that FBI thought that if interviewed, we might confess to subversive thoughts and actions? Weighing in against the tide, the Omaha FBI field office cautioned against pursuing an interview with Mark Murray, declaring "interview of the subject is not warranted due to his status as a [final year medical] student and the fact that unfavorable publicity might occur."[42]

Sometimes the streams of information seem disconnected. Yet it is interesting how the net of information gathering brings in other people. In a memo dated 31 August 1973, the FBI field office in Sacramento reported that Bobby Nelson, an attorney from Austin (and member of the National Lawyers Guild) had contacted my brother by phone. This phone conversation represented guilt by association. In this memo security agents reported that Bobby Nelson has "had contact with individuals involved in revolutionary or subversive activity and who [i.e., Bobby Nelson] is being investigated in relation to the WEATHFUG program." The identities of the five distinct sources of information consisted of designations SA T-1, SA T-2, SA T-3, SA T-4, and SA T-5.[43] These cryptic number-letter combinations are codes to protect the confidential identities of undercover informants. The way the FBI report was written suggests that their security agents were relying on intercepted phone calls and on deeply embedded informants, the true identities of whom they were keen to protect.

At the end of the day, I am convinced that undercover informants were concerned less with uncovering the truth than they were seeking to tell a story that conformed to what they imagined their superiors wanted to hear. The low-level informants at the bottom of the information-gathering hierarchy were only valuable employees to the extent that they could deliver what was considered by their superiors to be reliable. I can only imagine how informants who were embedded in social networks and associations with those upon whom they were spying must have been somewhat conflicted about their subterfuge and double-dealing. Seeing this situation from the perspective of the undercover agents, it makes sense that they would inflate the numbers of people who attended meetings, exaggerate the threats that political activists posed, and just name names for the sake of seeming to know who the key players were.

May Days Demonstrations, May 1971

I remember well the slogan for the May Days demonstrations for the 3rd to the 5th of May 1971, in Washington, DC: "If the government won't stop the war, we'll stop the government." This rhetorical provocation amounted to a call to arms, actually setting up an inevitable confrontation between the mass of protestors and the assembled forces of repression. Because the slogan projected an impossible goal, our actions were doomed from the start to fall well short. Even if we were able to disrupt the normal operations of Washington, DC, government for a period of time, we could not do so indefinitely. Did we succeed or did we fail? Actually, we did neither.

I strongly identified with the "stop the government" maxim. Like so many others, I had grown tired of the liberal sentiments that stressed working within the system. The most militant factions of the antiwar movement had broken definitively with the mainstream liberal canon of focusing on bringing incremental change through electing the "right people" and policy reforms. We really disliked the liberals with their holier-than-thou attitudes and reformist gradualism. We saw their willingness to compromise as a kind of collaboration with a structurally flawed system. I thought that the plea to "Give Peace a Chance" was platitudinous nonsense. Those who managed the war machine were not responsive to moral appeals. "Get clean for Gene" was the liberal mantra that accompanied recruiting antiwar activists to participate in the effort to elect Eugene McCarthy in the 1972 presidential election. I was so tired of that constant liberal claptrap.

The FBI San Antonio field office obtained information "from a source who supplied reliable information in the past." This undercover informant reported that my brother, along with others (and that included me), traveled to Washington, DC, "on or about April 30, 1971," with the intention to participate in "planned violent demonstrations" during the first week of May 1971 to "shut down the government." We were never quiet about our intentions. So it is no surprise that the FBI reported that the "demonstrations included the blocking of streets and highways, the destruction of personal and government property and physical obstruction to prevent government employees from reporting to work."[44] This is an accurate assessment of our aspirational goals to shut down Washington, DC.

It is here where the reports of undercover police agents get more precise. An undercover police informant with the code name SA T-1 reported on a 25 April 1971 meeting of the AMDT that was held to finalize travel arrangements to Washington and to strategize over "first day techniques." A second informant—given the code name SA T-2—took a wider view. He/she reported that the AMDT was an active participant in the May Days demonstration 3–5 March 1971 coordinated by the PCPJ based in Washington, DC. The PCPJ consisted of over one hundred organizations committed to using "massive civil disobedience to combat racism, power, repression and war." SA T-2 expressed the view that the AMDT "was one of the more militant and violence-prone organizations participating in the PCPJ demonstrations in May 1971."[45] This claim amounted to hyperbolic excess. Looking backward, I am quite pleased and proud that the FBI ranked us so highly in their list of subversive organizations. I would characterize our motives as militant disruption, but I would not attach the "violence-prone" label. "Violence" is one of those portmanteau categories that is so broad that it becomes somewhat meaningless as a label. "Violence-prone" suggests an inherent characteristic that is subversive in its intent.

A police informant reported that my brother participated in a second meeting attended by approximately thirty people at another location in Austin, at which time he volunteered to be part of a medical squad participating in the 1971 May Days demonstrations. Since my brother was in medical school at the time, this assertion is undoubtedly accurate. Agent SA T-4 confirmed that my brother went to Washington, DC. Agent SA T-2 provided information that my brother participated in efforts on 3 May 1971 to shut down traffic in the general vicinity of Scott Circle. It seems that undercover agents were swarming all over the place before, during, and after the May Days demonstrations.[46]

My brother and I drove to Washington, DC, in a caravan but in separate vehicles. AMDT broke into small cells of around three to five persons each. My brother and I were linked with different affinity groups. These so-called affinity groups operated semiautonomously without central command. It would be impossible for undercover informants to know what each cell planned to do and what they actually did during the three days of street protests unless these spies participated in disruption along with us. In retrospect, I suspect that the woman who offered her family Volkswagen van and volunteered to drive a group of us to the May Days demonstrations may have been an undercover informant. She showed up at planning meetings a week or so before we departed. She did not seem to have clear direction in her political orientation. After we returned from Washington, DC, she just disappeared from sight. Unfortunately, I have forgotten her name. I will always wonder about her.

Dedication of LBJ Library, May 1971

We returned from the Washington, DC, May Days demonstrations buoyed with our success. While we did not stop the government, we certainly disrupted normal governmental activities for three days. Our motley crew of returning protesters rebranded ourselves as the Armadillo May Day Collective. We were a loose affiliation of anarchists, anarcho-syndicalists, Wobblies (Industrial Workers of the World), crypto-Communists, disgruntled Vietnam veterans (loosely grouped under the banner of VVAW), troublemakers, and excitement seekers.

We decided to make use of similar militant tactics to disrupt and possibly shut down the dedication of the LBJ Library on 22 May 1971. Agents SA T-1 and SA T-4 collaborated to confirm our planning, reporting on a meeting held in Austin with twenty-five people in attendance. Still another undercover agent—code-named SA T-5—attended an early evening rally in Eastwood Park on 19 May where approximately 150 people gathered to finalize plans for the upcoming demonstration at the LBJ Library dedication. Agent SA T-2 corroborated this police report by his/her fellow undercover agent.[47] I am left wondering if the undercover agents knew each other's identities and roles as informants.

Why were there no FBI and security police reports on the actual demonstrations organized to shut down the LBJ Library dedication and what happened in its immediate aftermath? What I remain curious about is why the security files never contained assessment reports that provided evaluations of what happened at events and demonstrations. For me these gaps amount to inexplicable silences.

It is here where undercover police reports get even more bizarre. Like *Alice in Wonderland*, is it possible to conjure the spectral presence of people even when they were not there? There is a curious anomaly in the FBI files that I just cannot explain. The FBI report of Harold Riley, San Antonio Office, issued in 28 November 1973 and entitled "Security Matter. Revolutionary Activities," contains a collection of observations constructed by undercover informants regarding my twin brother. The FBI files contain references to a police report (dated 22 April 1972) compiled by an FBI undercover informant who provided observations on a meeting attended by approximately five to seven hundred persons two days earlier on 20 April, the purpose of which was to finalize plans to shut down the University of Texas campus in the coming days. The undercover informant (code-named SA T-2) claimed that at the conclusion of the meeting, "MARK MURRAY and two others talked about taking individual action." This vague yet ominous phrase about "individual action" is left open to interpretation. About two weeks later, on 9 May 1972, an FBI undercover informant codenamed SA T-4 reported that "50 to 150 individuals, including MARK MURRAY met on the University of Texas, Austin campus, to discuss possible plans for reaction to US escalation of the war in Southeast Asia."[48]

These two reports from undercover informants seemed to follow the predictable script of reporting on individuals that they considered to be subversives and troublemakers. What completely messes up the neatness of this story is that at the time my twin brother was in Sacramento, not Austin. This false sighting is where faulty intelligence crosses from the absurd and nonsensical to the surreal and ludicrous. My brother was not in Austin any time after May 1971. What accounts for this egregious error of conjuring the spectral presence of my absent brother out of thin air? Perhaps these two different undercover informants, in their enthusiasm to report on subversive activities, just fabricated my brother's presence. Perhaps these undercover informants confused us, believing that I was not really me but actually my twin brother? Who knows why this instance of mistaken identity occurred.

Careening Down the Hill

After my brother obtained his medical degree at Creighton University in 1971, he moved to Sacramento to accept a residency at a hospital there. On 1 January 1974, an FBI agent, pretending to be an old friend from Texas, called my twin's employer at his medical residency in Sacramento to find out if he actually worked there.[49] Ever vigilant, FBI agents included an official photograph and identification documents, taken from his security check at his place of employment in Sacramento. FBI reports included all this personal information in their ongoing investigation of him. With his long hair and droopy mustache, he certainly looks the part of a 1960s hippie.[50] In addition, another FBI memo contained information that listed my brother's address and a picture of his driver's license. This FBI memo also contained information that he was the registered owner of a 1972 Chevrolet sedan bearing a particular California license plate number. The interest in my brother continued into 1974. The Sacramento County Sheriff's Department recorded my brother's fingerprints as part of his application for a license to practice medicine in California. An FBI memo reproduced this information.[51] If the FBI was focusing on this kind of mundane information, I suspect that my twin did not receive his complete and unadulterated reports. I would suspect that FBI informants compiled long lists of known associates and organizational affiliations that pertained to my brother.

Within the secret files of the various security state apparatuses, there must be instructions and training about how to spy and how to identify which persons are deemed suspicious enough to watch. I suspect that for the six weeks or so in total that my brother spent in Austin, the security agencies devoted an inordinate amount of time and energy doing surveillance on him. In hindsight all this effort might seem frivolous and excessive. Yet if the antiwar movement had gained considerably more strength and threatened the state apparatus, this information may have proven useful for mass incarceration of militants.

Curious Anomalies: Imbalance Between FBI Reporting and the Rhetoric of Repression

What I find intriguing is that as the sheer number of concrete reports on particular activities (and the temporal distance between them) dissipated, the rhetorical attention to subversion escalated. The delayed response between the frenzied attention devoted to my brother in two concentrated periods of time—May 1970 and May 1971—when he was visiting with me in Austin and the internal FBI discussions about how to package this information is striking. On 23 November 1973, the San Antonio FBI office circulated information about my brother to the main Secret Service offices in Washington, DC, Sacramento, New York, and San Francisco concerning his participation in the 1971 May Days demonstrations (3–5 May) in Washington, DC. In November 1973 FBI national headquarters opened an investigation on my twin brother under the heading "Security Matter-Revolutionary Activities." On 23 November 1973, Clarence Kelly, director of the Secret Service, formally listed Mark Francis Murray as "potentially dangerous as to background, emotional instability or activity in groups engaged in activities inimical to the US."[52] This memo circled among Secret Service offices in Sacramento, San Antonio, and Austin. Look at the dates here. The Secret Service memo was almost a year and half after the last reported surveillance on my brother.[53]

There is more. Under a section ominously titled "Predilection," the San Antonio field office, making use of an undercover informant "who had provided reliable information in the past," concluded that Mark Murray, along with me, "participated in planned violent demonstrations during the first week of May, 1971 to shut down the government." Demonstration plans "included the blocking of streets and highways, destruction of personal and government property, and physical obstruction to prevent government employees from reporting for work." As a consequence of these findings, the FBI (in conjunction with the US Secret Service) opened an investigation on 28 November 1973 to determine whether my brother's activities around the May Days demonstrations "could involve violation of Title 18, US Code 2383 (Rebellion or Insurrection) and Article 2384 (Seditious Conspiracy)."[54] Again, look at the dates here. The FBI considered charging my brother with serious crimes two and a half years after the events in question. Now, of course, whatever they were saying about my brother they were also saying about me.

Why such a time lag? I think there may be several reasons for these temporal gaps. First, I think that the FBI, the Secret Service, and other intelligence agencies were chasing after events and people from the late 1960s onward. It seems that their own cumbersome bureaucratic procedures ensured a time lag between events and their own internal decision-making process outlining how they should respond. Their efforts to infiltrate the Weather Underground and to arrest key figures never produced concrete results. Prosecutors opened perhaps two hundred conspiracy trials around the country, many of which consisted of undercover police informants urging and abetting unsuspecting "radicals" to conspire to break the law. Most of these trials ended in acquittal. Second, I think that perhaps the intelligence services were trying to wrap up their clumsy investigations of "subversive activities" with a degree of bravado, trying to cement into official intelligence reports that their own extralegal actions in pursuit of subversives was justified due to the threat to national security.

At the end of the day, my twin and I were only walk-on actors with few speaking lines in this great watershed moment in US history. We were only two out of tens of thousands of antiwar activists whom security agencies were able to capture in this information dragnet starting in the mid-1960s and continuing through the next decade. These efforts amounted to the early warning signs of a police state.

PART 4

The Demise of Popular Protest

Postscript

Denouement

The Demise of Popular Protest and the Eclipse of the Antiwar Movement

It is easy to see the beginning of things, and harder to see the ends.
—Joan Didion, *Slouching Towards Bethlehem*

The number of active participants in antiwar activities declined significantly after April–May 1972. What we called movement fatigue took its toll. As the United States active military participation in the war in Vietnam came to a close with the signing of the January 1973 Paris Peace Accords, mass protest actions dried up. Without the familiar script of staging mass demonstrations and marches, political activists looked around to find a place for themselves.

Bitter and often rancorous debate about how to revive a political movement that seemed inexorably bent on mindlessly escalating trashing (i.e., wanton destruction of property) to an art form produced a cascading number of casualties. Those long-term political activists who called for a multipronged strategy of low-profile political organizing and coalition building came under fire from frustrated militants who refused to abandon the confrontational politics to which they had grown so accustomed. These hardcore militants who wanted to bring more protesters into the streets accused their doubters and skeptics of talking about the revolution but being unwilling to make the revolution. They accused those who did not follow them into the streets of failing to understand the urgency of the moment. Shrill moral appeals of this sort backfired. Demanding that people take to the streets did not succeed in winning very many converts from those not already committed to this position.

Many veterans of the Austin antiwar movement who had participated for years in organizing demonstrations and public rallies showed little tolerance for what they regarded as the shrill rhetorical harangues from some diehards that questioned their commitment. They no longer participated in events, making concerted efforts to develop and improve their personal relationships and to build small-scale, manageable collectives (such as food co-ops, communal living arrangements, and forms of entertainment). Women's collectives, in particular, proliferated. Frustrated with the male-dominated organizations and the prevailing male chauvinistic approach to political action, many women turned their attention to sisterhood, abandoning the male-dominated movement to what they regarded as its own self-destructive impulses.

At the same time, some of the best and brightest movement activists gravitated toward existing Marxist–Leninist parties, as well as toward inchoate preparty formations that mimicked the organizational formats of the Old Left. I understood the desire to find a political organization to replace the emptiness. Joining a political organization provided a lodestar pointing a clear pathway forward. The fissures that divided the personal from the political widened. It was a time for self-reflection. Some of my good friends were incapable of analyzing themselves, and many became disillusioned and sometimes self-destructive with drugs and alcohol. Others turned inward, seeking more stable personal relationships and reliable sources of income. Still others looked to start careers in lucrative fields unrelated to political activism.

Alternative Pathways: The NAM

The NAM originated in the political space between the left-leaning liberal wing of the Democratic Party and its reformist electoral strategy and the hydra-headed array of Marxist–Leninist party formations that proliferated in the early 1970s. The sectarian factionalism of these tiny groups swept so many dedicated activists into their orbit. Each of these pre-party formations spent an inordinate amount of time and energy furiously debating and identifying the vanguard of the revolution and how they might connect with it. Messianic zeal and self-righteous rhetoric seemed to consume the minds of some of the best political activists across the country.

Perhaps eight to ten of us from Austin traveled to Davenport, Iowa, in November 1971 to attend the launch of the NAM. Seeking to create a successor organization that could mimic the early years of SDS, the founders of NAM envisioned a socialist and feminist political organization firmly rooted in the principles of the New Left and free from the bitter sectarian infighting that characterized the proliferating Marxist-Leninist sects. By calling for an end to US imperialism and the capitalist system, the NAM shared the broad political orientation of the New Communist Movement (as the various Marxist-Leninist party formations came to be collectively known) but repudiated the single-minded focus on building a "vanguard party." NAM provided an ideological home and organizational base for those not drawn into sectarian politics. The commitment to a socialist vision was sufficiently vague and appropriately general to appeal to political activists from across a wide spectrum of ideological currents.

The organization consisted of a loose assemblage of local chapters, which devoted their energies to forming Marxist study groups, debating contemporary issues, supporting local labor actions, and working in local communities to raise political awareness. According to authoritative estimates, total membership of the organization never exceeded 1,500 at any point in its existence. In the main, chapters were located in large metropolitan areas and on college campuses with a history of political activism. At the time when NAM merged with the Democratic Socialist Organizing Committee to form the Democratic Socialists of America in 1982, it claimed a membership of 2,500.[1]

In Austin a core of committed activists turned to NAM as a national organization that offered a home for socialists who were not attracted to Marxist–Leninist parties. NAM incorporated many of the lessons of the antiwar movement, declaring that, for instance, "racism is a key foundation stone of modern US capitalism," and identifying "sexism as a characteristic of social relations in capitalist society."[2]

By 1973 the movement in Austin was so hydra-headed that it was impossible to identify a central core or center. Women's Liberation, Gay Liberation, and Black Power organizations constituted their own relatively autonomous focal points of protest and direct action. Anarchist affinity groups shared food and money. Collective living arrangements were the norm. In short, an embryonic alternative society was gradually being born in the midst of our critique of conventional institutions and traditional norms and values.

This alternative vision, of course, did not last. The US military defeat in Vietnam in May 1975 took the heavy wind out of the sails of the antiwar movement. Nationally, in major cities the hard core of what remained of the New Left went headfirst into Marxist–Leninist parties, each with their own ideological purity tests and their own identification of who constituted the vanguard of the revolution. Was it the conventional working class, needing to break the shackles imposed by the charlatan faux-leadership of the trade union movement? Was it African Americans, trapped in ghettos and oppressed by racism? Or was it none of the above, at a time when national liberation movements around the world seemed to portend the downfall of American imperialism? These ideological battles were a lot of sound and fury, signifying nothing.

Flying Too Close to the Sun

Too many of us suffered from some degree of hubris or unwarranted overconfidence and fell victim to the fate of Icarus. In so many ways, we believed that because we were right, we were invincible. Like Icarus, were we so consumed with exaggerated pride and the belief in our own righteousness that we failed to heed sage advice? The danger of flying too close to the sun has always haunted me. I know friends who, metaphorically speaking, rolled the dice one too many times, convinced they could not lose. Yet in so many ways, we did lose: friendships gone awry over stupid political disputes, attaching ourselves to impossible utopian dreams that never materialized, adopting political positions that proved to be sectarian and divisive, or sabotaging possible careers through poor choices.

The urgency of the moment—the war in Vietnam raging out of control, racial injustice dividing the country, women remaining as virtual second-class citizens—called on us to act, and to act decisively. In Austin, if we had always obeyed the law, we would never have marched off campus (whether on sidewalks or in the streets). We would have never sold literature (and *The Rag* in particular). We would have never disrupted official speeches by invited war propagandists. We would have never staged sit-ins and building occupations. We would have never entered the Chuck Wagon without valid identification. And we would have never held unauthorized rallies on the Main Mall. If we had followed the rules and obeyed official regulations, we would have contributed to our own oppression. We deliberately broke the law and violated official regulations, and we were prepared to suffer the consequences. Then and now, I have no regret about trying to toss tear gas canisters back from where they came, about marching in the streets without a permit, about charging into police lines, and about invading the Texas State Capitol rotunda. Through a combination of sheer numbers and our commitment, we had the power to disrupt, and we did so—sometimes dramatically.

I now understand, in retrospect, that our use of militant, disruptive tactics after May 1970 had a Clausewitzean quality, directing pressure on the US war machine to disengage from Southeast Asia by making the war at home more painful than bringing the troops home. We took the position—and Martin Wiginton spearheaded this thinking—that the attritional pressure of protest events like 1971 May Days civil disobedience and disruption in Washington, DC, would gradually wear down the war machine until the architects and functionaries of imperialism decided that it was no longer worth the cost of remaining in Vietnam. We, of course, did not subscribe to the ideology of the Weather Underground, who believed that an orchestrated campaign of targeted bombing would garner popular support for their cause. We believed then, and know now, that the Weather Underground was a bunch of adventurist fanatics that through their actions alienated wide swaths of people who could have been won over to the antiwar movement.

Our choice of disruptive tactics was emphatically political, even though a great deal of confusion originated out of frustration with the sense that we were not doing enough and that we were ineffectual. At root we knew that the antiwar movement could not be beaten, suppressed, or eradicated. We also understood that we maintained the capacity to disrupt the status quo when we wanted.

Curiously, police surveillance and infiltration engendered both a retreat from popular politics and rising militancy. On the one hand, the security forces contributed to a climate of fear and anxiety, sowing suspicion and distrust. As a consequence, many activists from the early years of popular protest pulled away for political involvement. On the other hand, most antiwar activists responded to security repression by expanding the repertoire of protest tools, including nighttime marches, wearing bandanas across our faces as disguises, and the occasional destruction of property.

How did the security forces use infiltrators to disrupt the antiwar movement by sowing dissent, fueling suspicions and distrust, and engineering divisions? This is a story that needs to be told. Were our divisions and faction fighting real, or were they orchestrated by the security operatives?

The police were often pretty vicious during demonstrations. The list of incidents of police brutality is long. I remember that political activists, particularly in the 1967–1969 period, faced an uncertain reception in the local jail. The police jailers purposely looked the other way, encouraging inmates to assault political activists. At demonstrations police officers routinely beat people with clubs and used Mace indiscriminately. I could list many more examples of police brutality, but the story is frightfully familiar.

Insular Worlds: Looking Backward in Time

We were part of a movement that was far greater and more hydra-headed than we admitted or understood at the time. We created and inhabited an insular world, cut off from the mainstream, with our own vocabulary, our own narrow controversies and discussions, and our own measure of success. "Smoking weed," "Don't bogart that joint," and "skinny-dippin'!" were popular countercultural signals. Our shared language was at once arcane and obscurantist: Trotskyists meant one thing, while Trotskyites was something altogether different. "One Step Forward, Two Steps Back" was not a Texas line dance but a passage from Lenin. The Mobe and the Mob were shorthand terms for two different organizations.

We learned about anarchism, syndicalism, anarcho-syndicalism, and Marxist Leninism. We honored the memories of Joe Hill and the Wobblies, Rosa Luxemburg, Che Guevara, and James Connolly. We debated the merits of democratic centralism and the vanguard party. In short, we cared a lot about old ideas and arcane political debates from earlier decades that no one else paid any attention to. There were times when success meant not getting arrested and staying out of jail, or pushing through police lines, or breaking as many windows as we could.

We lived in our own insulated sociocultural world, a historically specific dreamtime that did not exist before and will never exist again. We made choices, every day and every hour, that produced the people we were. Choosing this path, and not another, cut off possibilities that were never realized. Could the big antiwar ship have been steered in a different direction? Yes, but that is beside the point.

In the broad arc of history, I neither sought nor achieved notoriety as a leading figure in New Left politics. I was a dedicated, committed activist in a local setting. Of course, there were the dilettante activists who floated in and out of radical politics, as if on a whim, seeking a kind of amusement. There were plenty of others who sought the political limelight and were often successful. I maintained no respect for this type of political activist.

There were also those whose flame burned bright in my early years in Austin SDS. Perhaps because of sheer exhaustion with the effort or through debilitating disillusionment, many of those I knew at the beginning were not there at the end. All sorts of less apparent activities not directly related to the street politics of visible protest lured countless numbers into their ambit: experimental schools, unconventional lifestyle choices, women's self-help collectives, and building alternative institutions like radical legal services, farming co-operatives, and more. I truly respected these choices. The social world of street-level political activism was not for everyone, nor should it ever have been that way.

What motivates me to look back in time? In part, I just want to keep in touch with who I once was. As an antiwar activist in the Lone Star State in my mid- to late 20s, I was flush with the possibilities of actually making a difference. I believed in reason and reasonable argument. I believed in progress and improvement in the human condition. That was the person I was: youthful, optimistic, committed, resolute, and convinced of the truthfulness of my beliefs. I had no reason, then, to look backward, only forward.

Now with the benefit of hindsight, I can say that I recognize that person whom I once was. Now I am less sanguine and more willing to be less confident about the future. Looking backward I can say that I know that all of us in the antiwar movement, as a messy collective mass, did make it more difficult for the war machine to operate with impunity. We did make a difference.

In my mind, I often return to that uncomfortable feeling: If I knew then what I know now, would I have done anything differently? I am not sure. Besides, there is no way of reasonably answering that question. Yes, I do believe that we collectively could have staged bigger and more militant demonstrations against the war and racial injustice. I am not convinced that we left much of an institutional legacy. In retrospect, we tried to achieve the impossible, and we came up short.

As a general rule, journalistic writing is from the vantage point of looking inward, seeking to uncover and expose someone else's point of view or mindset. In contrast, I write from the perspective of looking outward, trying to discern whether what I thought and felt during my years of participating in the antiwar movement was appropriate for the times. Selective memory is the inevitable outcome of both the passage of time and perhaps even the unconscious desire to shape the past to conform to what we want to believe in the present. In constructing this account that focuses on my personal biography, I feel a little like a relic frozen in the past, an artifact from another time that has faded into obscurity. The cruelty of the inevitable passage of time is that the arrow points only forward, leaving everything behind as fading memory.

In a real way, memory pushes against disappearance and oblivion, using the powers of recollection to ensure the survival of remembered traces of the past. We struggle against failing memory and those very real impulses to consciously or unconsciously misremember past events for whatever reasons. Forgetting provides us with a way of pushing aside uncomfortable events and exchanges in our past. Yet it is only my memories and the available shards of evidence left behind in archival collections, newspaper accounts, personal conversations, and FBI records that enable me to attach my personal biography with my history.

Lessons

In recounting his epic journey that lasted for eight months across the length and breadth of Latin America, Ernesto "Che" Guevara reflected on what he had learned: "This is not a story of heroic feats [nor a tale of stunning victories and great successes]. It is a glimpse of [multiple] lives running parallel for a time, with similar hopes and convergent dreams."[3]

In an uncanny way, I find a remarkable coincidence in Che's commentaries that dovetail with my own thoughts. Looking backward, can I say, as Che put it, that our vision was "never quite complete, or that it was too transient or not always well-informed?" Or was it too narrow, too biased, and too utopian? Maybe. "Were we too uncompromising in our judgments," unwilling to accept anything less that our optimal objectives?[4] Perhaps so. I simply cannot say for certain.

The realization that the changes we worked for and hoped for were not going to happen came in incremental stages. For me the song "Working for the Clampdown" (The Clash, 1979) symbolized our failures to reach our objectives. When once we were on the offensive in the 1960s and early 1970s, the song for me provided a grim recognition that by the late 1970s we were on the defensive.

What did we learn from close to a decade of fever-pitch political activism? I learned that the thin veneer of liberal tolerance only concealed a deeper and enduring state impulse to clamp down on dissent, preserve the sanctity of private property, and maintain the commitment to free enterprise. In the United States, political power has always aligned with the maintenance of corporate capitalism both at home and abroad. The rule of law can protect us, but only so much. I also learned that combatting inequalities of whatever kind and supporting social justice are values not shared by everyone. I also learned that persons faced with stark choices can take a personal stand that is not particularly popular and willingly relinquish the rewards that come with political conformity. Burning draft cards, refusing induction, marching against the war and racism in the face of superior repressive force, and challenging the rampant sexism in organizations and institutions were difficult choices, but they represented commitment and resolve. These ideas gave me hope at the time, and they still give me hope today.

Acknowledgments

My twin brother Mark actually got me started on this journey. In 2017 he used the FOIA to obtain three tranches of FBI files, which he passed along to me. Once I decided to write this personal account of my years in the antiwar movement in Austin (1967–1973), I returned to the FBI files collected on my brother only to find that I figured more prominently in the records kept on him than I remembered.

I never imagined that I would embark on this voyage into the past. Once I started, I found I could not stop. In Austin in the late 1960s, we inherited a perfect storm: the war in Vietnam was accelerating out of control; racism (both institutional and interpersonal) was a daily fact of life in Austin; the conformist ideologies of post-World War II America were disintegrating; sexual freedom loosened the ties that governed the traditional image of family life; and the Women's Liberation Movement, along with the Gay and Lesbian Liberation Movements, were being born. The story I tell is not a saccharine walk down memory lane. We who built and directed the antiwar movement in Austin stumbled along as best we could, making errors of judgment and hurting each other too much of the time.

As this writing project unfolded, I began to communicate regularly with fellow activist Alice Embree. She is strongly committed to preserving the historical record of activism in Austin during the long 1960s and 1970s. She has tirelessly supported my writing project. Both Alice and Steve Krinsky read the manuscript and offered really insightful suggestions for corrections and additions. I am truly grateful. I also began email correspondence with Pat Cuney, Lori Hansel, Jeff Jones, Doyle Niemann, Bill Meacham, Gavin Duffy, Marianne Vizard, Sharon Shelton, Steve Krinsky, John Houghton, and Billy Pope. Besides these folks listed above, I want to acknowledge the inspiration I received during my years in Austin from the following comrades: Martin Wiginton, Bobby Nelson, Gary Fitzgerald, David Dye, Victoria Foe, Gretchen MacBryde, Connie Lanham, Paul Turner, Carlo Gineletti, Nancy Folbre, Brady Coleman, Jim Simons, Cam Cunningham, Jim Gundlach,

Carol Gundlach, Rene Ochoa, Richard Minus, and many more. I want to single out Beth Livezey, a lawyer from a law firm in Los Angeles called Bar Sinister. She was an absolute joy with whom to work when the Austin Law Commune was born. I visited her in Los Angeles, and she introduced me to Tom Hayden and Jane Fonda, who lived nearby in Venice Beach.

Well after the Austin dust had settled, I connected with David MacBryde on three separate occasions in Berlin. He was a dear comrade—full of ideas and as energized as ever. Peter Megaw, who was a high school student at Austin High School with whom we collaborated for Stop the Draft Week in 1970, contacted me out of the blue and provided me with some materials from that period. Besides Peter, I would also like to acknowledge that Steve Krinsky, Alice Embree, and David Hamilton provided me with materials that were useful in constructing this book.

I visited Austin for a week in March 2023, and again in April 2024, to consult with records kept at the Dolph Briscoe Center for American History. I want to acknowledge and thank John Houghton (an old friend from sociology days) and Karen Houghton for accommodating me at their home for part of my time in Austin. I want to thank Alice Embree and Lori Hansel for putting together a meaningful social gathering at Shoal Creek Inn in March 2023. About fifteen people turned up, many of whom I knew quite well during my time in Austin. Thank you, Billy Pope, Sharon Shelton, Alice Embree, Lori Hansel, Bill Meacham, David Hamilton [Pratt], Throne Dryer, Pat Cuney, Judy Mahler, Bill Gordon, Peter van Bavel, and more. Many of these same folks came together for a similar get-together at Scholz Beer Garden in April 2024.

I really enjoyed my long conversations with Billy Pope. We lived together in a big house on Twelfth Street for three years. This event at Shoal Creek spun off into a nice evening listening to the Melancholy Ramblers. I was pleased to see band member Brady Coleman, my old lawyer friend during the turbulent late 1960s and early 1970s. The music was great, and it brought back plenty of memories of drinking beer and carrying on at the Split Rail, Scholz Garden, and Lake Austin Inn.

I want to thank the staff at the Dolph Briscoe Center for American History, University of Texas, for their assistance. I worked with Aryn

Glazer and Caitlin Brenner for over two years by email when I submitted requests for files. The director, Don Carleton, was very generous with his time. I want to thank Olaia Chvite Amgo and Patrick Young, Michigan Design, for graphic design.

I would like to acknowledge the wonderful support I received from the University of North Texas Press. I really want to thank Ron Chrisman (Director), Joe Alderman (Marketing Coordinator), Amy Maddox (Managing Editor), and Alexandra Cosmann (Administrative Coordinator), who were wonderful to work with. Ron believed in this project from the start, and I am forever appreciative. I also want to thank the two outside reviewers, Alice Embree and Gregg Michel, for very helpful comments on an earlier draft of this manuscript.

I would like to acknowledge the work of the Sorenson Law Firm, LLC (Peter Sorenson, senior attorney), which did the heavy lifting on my four years of FOIA requests to the FBI and NARA.

Anne Pitcher, my wife, insisted that I needed a larger thread to hold my personal story together. She was correct. Because of her influence and insistence, I created two parallel stories: one about my autobiographical self, and the other about exposing the extralegal operations of the security apparatuses watching us, infiltrating our organizations, and seeking to disrupt our efforts. Despite attracting the suspicion of the state security apparatuses, our only transgression was to stand up for a more decent and just world.

I am quite sorry that my parents, Robert and Margaret Murray, did not live long enough to read this book. FBI reports mentioned them by name, and many of the stories I recount here I entertained them with in late-night conversations in their living room in my childhood home in Walnut Creek. My brothers Mark (who figures prominently in this book), Dennis (no longer with us), Greg, and Thomas will share my pleasure with tackling the war machine. My three grown children—Jeremy, Andrew, and Alida—do not know what I was involved in during the 1960s and 1970s. I hope this book makes them realize I did not sit on the sidelines and watch the war machine go by, destroying so many innocent lives around the world.

DARE TO STRUGGLE, DARE TO WIN.

TEXAS FOREVER!

Appendix 1
Timeline: The Protest Cycle in Austin

17–18 April 1965

SDS organized a vigil at LBJ ranch, on the outskirts of Stonewall, Texas

Spring 1965

Picketing against businesses on Guadalupe for refusal to serve African American customers

23 April 1967

A free speech demonstration in which six people (Alice Embree, Tom Smith, John Lefeber, Dave Mahler, Dick Reavis, and Gary Thiher) were charged with violating university policy and threatened with disciplinary probation. Five of the six were SDS members. John Lefeber was a member of Young Democrats.

24 April 1967

Demonstration against visit of Vice President Hubert Humphrey to Austin

16 June 1967

Demonstration against visit of President Lyndon Johnson to Austin

14 October 1967

Larry Caroline gave an antiwar speech at the State Capitol building, and his words about the need for a "new American revolution" sparked a firestorm of controversy that led to his eventual dismissal. (He said, "You can't change things one at a time. The whole bloody mess has to go. What we need is a new American revolution.")

14–18 November 1967

SDS-sponsored weeklong "sit-in" protesting presence of Marine recruiters in University Union Building

<u>30 November 1967</u>
Disruption of speech by General Harold K. Johnson at UT campus

<u>April 1968</u>
SDS protest in the shadow of the University Tower against fraternity-sorority Round-Up event

<u>21–30 April 1968</u>
SDS-sponsored Ten Days of Protest and Resistance, ten consecutive days of a mix of protest activities

<u>3 May 1968</u>
Mass rally and pickets at Don Weedon Conoco Gas Station to protest racism, leading to confrontation with police and forty arrests on various charges, including assault on a police officer, resisting arrest, and disorderly conduct

<u>18–20 October 1968</u>
SDS Texas-Oklahoma Regional Meeting in Austin

<u>12–14 December 1968</u>
Legal Defense for Political Dissidents Conference, Wimberley, Texas

<u>February 1969</u>
African Americans for Black Liberation (AABL)–sponsored occupation of building on UT campus in support of creation of Black Studies Department

SDS organized four consecutive days in support of AABL demands

<u>28 February 1969</u>
Disciplinary hearing regarding NLEP selling literature on campus (Martin Murray, defendant)

<u>Week of 16 March 1969</u>
Stop the Draft Week, targeting high schools (William B. Travis on Monday, A. N. McCallum on Tuesday, Stephen F. Austin on Wednesday, and John H. Reagan on Thursday)

<u>28–29 March 1969</u>
Clampdown at the SDS National Council Meeting in Austin

<u>June 1969</u>
Ill-fated SDS National Convention, Chicago, leading to the break-up of SDS. An estimated six to ten Austin SDS members attended

<u>15 October 1969</u>
Moratorium to End the war in Vietnam rally and protest march in Austin with estimated ten thousand participants

<u>October 1969</u>
Students for Strikers demonstrated in solidarity with the Economy Furniture strikers

<u>21–23 October 1969</u>
The Waller Creek incident, signaling the start of environmental consciousness; twenty-seven arrested

<u>10 November 1969</u>
Chuck Wagon Riot; twenty-one arrested on conspiracy charges

<u>15 November 1969</u>
Large moratorium march and rally in Austin in solidarity with nationwide protests; close to ten thousand participants

<u>April 1970</u>
Political activist Jeff Jones elected student body president on a student power and antiwar platform

<u>23 April 1970</u>
Anti-Creeping Meatball Coalition, an anti-ROTC demonstration with water pistols; participants arrested after the fact via police photographs

<u>1–7 May 1970</u>
Series of rallies and marches around invasion of Cambodia and then amplified by the killings at Kent State followed by Jackson State

<u>11 June 1970</u>
Protest at Jester Dormitory around Texas Boys State Convention

<u>1 October 1970</u>
Women protesting fraternity portrayal of women in frat promotion of attendance at a football game

30 October 1970

Arson attack on University of Texas Law School

31 October 1970 (Halloween)

March to State Capitol to coincide with National Peace Action Council nationwide protests; yet another confrontation with police

1 December 1970

Broad-based church-affiliated direct-action group sponsored an anti–war tax march and rally at the IRS and the downtown headquarters office of Southwestern Bell Telephone

5 December 1970

Direct action protest on field of Texas-Arkansas football game

10 February 1971

Massive rally and protest march against US military incursion into Laos

19–20 February 1971

VVAW-sponsored rallies against Navy recruiters on UT campus

April 1971

Local Women's Liberation groups sponsored an International Women's Day with meetings and a rally

Women affiliated with WITCH arrested for stenciling "Free Food Today" on outside wall of a supermarket

4 April 1971

Rally in memory of the legacy of Martin Luther King Jr.

12–17 April 1971

Organized telephone call-in to Bergstrom Air Force Base and picketing at the main gate, a tax refusal demonstration at Southwestern Bell Telephone Company to call for nonpayment of taxes; Austin Veterans for Peace sponsored the picketing at Bergstrom Air Force Base on 15 April

18 April 1971

GI-civilian solidarity march to State Capitol building; confrontations with police

19–23 April 1971

VVAW protests in Washington, DC, called Operation Dewey Canyon III; Austin contingent led by Terry Dubose

24 April 1971

Huge antiwar march of over a half million people in Washington, DC, sponsored by NPAC with Austin contingent

3–5 May 1971

May Days demonstrations in Washington, DC, organized by PCPJ; "If the government won't stop the war, we will stop the government"

AMDT contingent of 250 from Texas and Oklahoma

Austin parallel activities

1 May: Leafleting on campus to support People's Peace Treaty

2 May: Leafleting of churches in the morning and large commercial stores in the afternoon in support of People's Peace Treaty

3 May: Rally in support of minimum family income at Austin State Capitol

Austin Veterans for Peace, Direct Action, and May Day Tribe sponsored rally at Capitol rotunda

4 May: March around Travis County Jail in support of demand to free all political prisoners

5 May: "No Business as Usual"—call for a strike at businesses and schools

Guerrilla theater downtown at Selective Service and then at the J. J. Pickle Federal Building

A group called High School Direct Action endorsed People's Peace Treaty

An estimated seventy-five high school students gathered at the State Capitol and marched down Congress Avenue passing out leaflets

Specters of Death—nine people with faces painted and wrapped in gray-blue robes—led the march

20 May 1971

WITCH demonstrations downtown and at LBJ Library

<u>22 May 1971</u>

AMDT and the LBJ Library dedication demonstration

<u>October 1971</u>

Demonstration of around four to five thousand protesters to shut down the federal courthouse downtown

<u>13 April 1972</u>

Leaflets at Texas Instruments after bombing of Hanoi

<u>17 April 1972</u>

Leafleting at Bergstrom Air Force Base and rally at federal building following Haiphong mining, gathering with Bergstrom GIs at Pease Park

<u>20 April 1972</u>

March to federal building

<u>21 April 1972</u>

Student strike, march down Guadalupe to the State Capitol

Women's Action seized the UT radio-television building

Nighttime march on ROTC building and LBJ Library (breaking windows), occupation of main building

<u>21–22 April 1972</u>

National Guard occupation of campus

<u>24 April 1972</u>

Student strike continues

<u>25 April 1972</u>

All-night vigil at ROTC with Direct Action playing a leading role

<u>29 April 1972</u>

SMC-sponsored march to State Capitol and rally

<u>1 May 1972</u>

Disruption of traffic on Lamar in front of Texas Instruments; thirty-one arrested for disrupting traffic

3 May 1972
Moratorium Day; picketing at Texas Instruments

8 May 1972
Haiphong ports mined; teach-ins, meetings, and rallies

11 May 1972
Woolridge Park rally

12 May 1972
Leafleting at Texas Instruments on Route 183

13 May 1972
SMC-sponsored march to State Capitol

14 May 1972
Candlelight vigil with three to four hundred participants drawn from various Church-affiliated and nonaligned peace groups, a march converging from five collection areas; “Give Peace a Chance” sentiments and reading of war dead

14 October 1972
October 14th Coalition march from LBJ Library to offices of the Committee for the Re-Election of the President

Appendix 2

"'SEATO Myth' Poor Excuse for Viet War Involvement"

Designed by Patrick Young, Michigan Design

In My Opinion

'SEATO Myth' Poor Excuse For Viet War Involvement

By Martin Murray
SDS Member

In reference to Gen. Paul Harkins' pro-Vietnam address to a Catholic social fraternity, I would like to make a few comments.

Because of space limitations, I will address myself to only one of the misleading and fallacious statements which were attributed to Gen. Harkins in The Daily Texan report.

Otherwise, I could address myself to all the historically unfounded misrepresentations which have continued to mesmerize and dupe a great many Americans about the justice, legality, and sanity of this war.

"Another condition," he said, "was a reason for the United States involvement," and I quote from The Daily Texan, "was the agreement the United States made in the Southeast Asia Treaty Organization."

Firstly, a few points specifically with regard to SEATO must be mentioned:

- The members of the original SEATO treaty (or Manila Treaty), signed in September, 1954, are Australia, New Zealand, Pakistan, the Philippines, Thailand, United Kingdom, United States, and France. Neither "South" Vietnam nor any Vietnam for that matter, signed this agreement in 1954.
- However, the significant point is that South Vietnam could not and cannot sign this agreement. In July of that year, 1954, two months before the SEATO treaty, the United States in the Geneva Agreements "took note" of the "unity, independence and territorial integrity" of the whole of Vietnam. as one country, and "took note" of "free general elections by secret ballot . . . to be held in July, 1956." Nowhere in its declaration in the Geneva Accords did the United States speak of a "South" or "North" Vietnam.
- Also in the Geneva Accords the United States "declared" that it would "refrain from the threat or use of force to disturb them" (the provisions). (A report from the Chatham House Study Group, "Collective Defense in South East Asia," pages 181-188). Thus, the United States seems to be pledged to avoid all armed conflict in the Vietnams.
- The so-called "free territory under the jurisdiction of the State of Vietnam" (meaning the territory of Vietnam south of the Seventeenth Parallel) was mentioned in an additional protocol of the SEATO treaty for the purposes of Article IV.

In this Article the eight signatories agreed to report any "aggression by means of armed attack" upon this so-called "free territory," to "meet the common danger in accordance with its constitutional processes" (which cannot be stretched so far as to allow sending 525,000 troops, or any troops for that matter, to "South" Vietnam), and to "consult immediately in order to agree (emphasis on "agree") on the measures which should be taken for common defence in cases other than "armed attack." Thus, neither the SEATO treaty nor its additional protocol constituted a commitment by the United States (or any other SEATO signatory) to any government or state of so-called "South" Vietnam. Any such obvious commitment would have directly violated the Geneva Agreements (George Kahim, John Lewis, "The United States in Vietnam," page 62-63.)

Further Point

These above points are strong enough to expose the over-simplifications and half-truths in General Harkins' manipulation of the SEATO treaty as a friendly "excuse" or moral "justification" for United States' involvement in Vietnam.

Yet there is a more convincing one still to come: the United States was involved in Vietnam with military personnel and equipment four years before the SEATO treaty even existed.

In August of 1950 President Truman dispatched a 35-member American military assistance group (MAAG) to Vietnam to act as "advisors" to the French and their puppet, Bao Dai, on the use of American equipment. (Theodore Draper, "The Abuse of Power," pages 25-6.)

In fact, from June 1950, to May, 1954, when the French were defeated at Dien Bien Phu, the United States provided $2.6 billion worth of military and economic aid to the French and Bao Dai. This amounted to no less than 80 per cent of the total cost of the French war effort ("Congressional Record," Feb. 21, 1966, Senate, page 3410.)

Nuclear Warheads

A month before the Geneva conference began in 1954, United States government officials had contemplated the use of American pilots, flying American planes (but with French insignia), to drop nuclear warheads on the Viet Minh in order to save the French from sure defeat. Large-scale land invasions for the Haiphong area were also discussed ("Operation Vulture," "Congressional Record," April 6 and 14, 1954, pages 4402-4977.)

President Dwight D. Eisenhower and then Secretary of State, John Foster Dulles, were desperately afraid that American intervention by itself, particularly with ground forces that might follow an air attack, would place the United States under a stigma of colonialism (Robert Shaplen, "The Lost Revolution," page 95.)

Dulles' solution was the creation of SEATO a few months later, which he hoped would give legal international sanction and justification to United States' intervention in Indochina. (Robert Shaplen, "The Lost Revolution," page 95.)

Thus, it seems to me that Gen. Harkins, as well as other government "officials," should not try to pawn off misrepresentations and half-truths upon the American public. They would do better to find other "excuses" than this SEATO myth to justify the deaths of so many Americans and Asians.

A Note on Sources

At the start, let me confess that what I write is not intended primarily as a scholarly treatise that rests upon a mountain of checked (and cross-checked) source materials in order to ensure its balance and objectivity, and its accuracy and veracity. This account is not a full-blown effort to uncover the history of the political turmoil in Austin, 1967–1973. At root it is my story.

When I first started thinking about undertaking this autobiographical project, I combed through old boxes and stored objects that miraculously remained in my possession. These boxes contained an archive of sorts—old photographs, a film (without sound) from May demonstrations of 1970, scattered newspaper accounts, and some pamphlets. These items proved invaluable in not only filling in gaps but also triggering new memories of old events.

In constructing this story, I have relied upon a variety of different sources of information. First, I have recounted events and organizations from memory. Now of course, memory is always faulty and selective. Sometimes memories are recollections of previous memories that are in turn detached from the original events. My memories are embedded in what Raymond Williams called "structures of feeling." This "irreducible quality of lived social experience" is peculiar to me as an individual, and is not captured in archival records, contemporaneous observations, or newspaper accounts.[1] I kept several boxes of old newspaper accounts, broadsheets that we produced, pamphlets I wrote, leaflets that we distributed, and materials related to my application for CO status. I used these memory aides to assist me with bringing back recollections of times that had faded somewhat into obscurity.

To compensate for my own memory failures, for omissions, and for elisions, I turned to published accounts—autobiographical recollections and scholarly examinations of the Austin political movement—to balance my personal recollections. In short, I sought corroborating accounts that would supplement the deficiencies of my memory. Several published accounts were my second source of information. I know that in writing this account I am subject to experience bias: I see things from my point of view with limited access to all sources of information. My approach is not the only one that one could have adopted.

There are several other written accounts that focus on Austin during the same historical period. Notably, Doug Rossinow's *The Politics of Authenticity* offers an historical account of the movement in Austin from its origins to its demise.[2] Despite my criticisms of his basic premise and his limited sources of evidence, Doug Rossinow provides what I consider a fairly accurate chronology up until around 1970–1971. His detailed accounts of people and events certainly triggered both my imagination and my memory. Yet I would argue strongly that he is incorrect at some key junctures, particularly in interpreting events in Austin after the June 1969 collapse of SDS.

Similarly, Alice Embree's *Voice Lessons* is an autobiographical account of a personal journey through those tumultuous times.[3] Alice offers a wonderfully personal and poignant account of her experiences in the movement, spanning early years in Austin SDS, the creation of *The Rag* underground newspaper, a period in New York working on *The Rat* underground newspaper, her temporary retreat into a communal alternative lifestyle experience in rural Arkansas, and her return to Austin in 1971. She carefully reconstructed her personal story through the interiors of her life. This distinction between stressing personal experience, intentionality, and meaning—as opposed to focusing on social action and public events—has deep and enduring methodological roots. Many of the events in which I participated were not part of Alice's world. Similarly, her deep immersion in early feminist politics in Austin were not part of my experience. Alice's voice comes from the heart. She captures, better than anyone else, the interior motivations and feelings that gave our movement its rock-solid foundation in our desire to create a better world without war, racism, sexism, and all the other divisive forces that divide humanity. Her autobiographical memoir truly *humanizes* our collective journey.

These books offer different angles of vision. Without a doubt, both Rossinow (as outside observer) and Embree (as inside participant) interpret events and processes somewhat differently than I. That is fine. No one has a claim to full and accurate truth. We are all constrained by our singular angles of vision. For me there is no privileged vantage point—only differences in epistemological orientation.

The third source of information I have relied on consists of printed materials donated to the Dolph Briscoe Center for American History at the University of Texas and stored in their vast archives. During the COVID years, the Briscoe Center was closed to researchers. For two to three years, I was able to obtain materials through email requests. I carefully scoured the records of three police/security officials who donated their papers to the Briscoe Center: Lt. Burt Gerding, head of the Criminal Intelligence Division, APD; Allen Hamilton, chief of security, University of Texas at Austin campus; and George Carlson, head of security for the University of Texas System and retired FBI agent. Each in their own way, these papers yielded important pieces of information about surveillance of key individuals and political organizations, information gathering and the reliance on undercover informants, and the use of disruptive tactics to keep the movement off balance. Unlike FBI files that often follow a formulaic script in gathering information and reporting on surveillance, the papers of Gerding, Hamilton, and Carlson are more freewheeling and open-ended, allowing for sorts of materials like newspaper clippings, political pamphlets, leaflets, and completely irrelevant items to appear in a kind of random distribution. I used the newspaper articles and leaflets to buttress my own recollections of events.

A word of caution is in order. These archived papers (Gerding, Hamilton, and Carlson) contain a great deal of information, most of which is irrelevant, trivial, and inconsequential. These files do not constitute the archival record of heads of agencies or the inner workings of security bureaucracies. The documents in these files consist in large measure of remnants, residues, and remainders—documents that somehow stayed in the personal possession of these three law enforcement officials. They do not comprise, or were ever intended to comprise, an accurate and complete historical record of policing activities. These documents reveal shards of information that are so fragmented and discontinuous that they cannot be pieced together to tell a coherent story.

Yet these documents provide a window through which to make sense of how the security apparatuses functioned and what they wanted to know.

The fourth and final source of information consists of records of the FBI. I began with three separate collections of documents that my twin brother was able to obtain from the FBI through FOIA requests he submitted in 2017. Under my own request for FBI files under FOIA, I was able to obtain large batches of files from the FBI, but most of it was not particularly detailed and was mostly irrelevant. For the most part, this material did not yield the kind of information about myself I was seeking. I worked with this material the best I could, weaving it (along with the other sources I used) into my narrative account of my time in Austin during the turbulent years of political protest.

Through the tireless efforts of Peter Sorenson, I was able to obtain multiple caches of files in March 2025 related to me, Bobby Nelson, Martin Wiginton, the LBJ Library dedication protests, and more. These files amounted to close to two thousand pages of new materials. I incorporated this new FBI material into my story as best as I could as the book writing project was winding down.

In trying to recover FBI records about myself, I worked first with Ralph Simpson, a lawyer from Detroit. In time I enlisted the support of Peter Sorenson, a lawyer specializing in FOIA requests. At the end of the day, through a painstakingly lengthy legal battle, I was able to obtain FBI files that the agency had originally said were unable to be located or had been destroyed.

Endnotes

Notes for the Preface

1. For an excellent, in-depth account of early SDS in Austin, see Alice Embree, *Voice Lessons* (Austin: Briscoe Center for American History / University of Texas Press, 2021).
2. See Embree, *Voice Lessons*; Robert Pardun, *Prairie Radical: A Journey Through the Sixties* (Los Gatos, CA: Shire Press, 2001); and Todd Gitlin, *The Sixties: Years of Hope, Days of Rage* (New York: Bantam Books, 1987).
3. Simon Schama, *Dead Certainties* (*Unwarranted Speculations*) (New York: Albert Knopf, 1991), 320.
4. See Winthrop Jordan, *Tumult and Silence at Second Creek: An Inquiry into a Civil War Slave Conspiracy* (Baton Rouge: Louisiana State University Press, 1993), 5–6.
5. John Lennon, "Give Peace a Chance" (Apple, 1969).

Notes for the Introduction

1. C. Wright Mills, *The Sociological Imagination* (New York: Oxford University Press, 1959).
2. Tom Hayden quoted in Louis Menand, "Change Your Life: The Lessons of the New Left," *New Yorker*, 22 March 2021, p. 46.
3. For a solid analysis of this tension, see John Moretta, "Political Hippies and Hip Politicos: Counterculture Alliance and Cultural Radicalism in 1960s Austin, Texas," *Southwestern Historical Quarterly* 123, no. 3 (2020): 266–91.
4. Timothy Garton Ash, *The File: A Personal History* (New York: Random House, 1997), 23.
5. See, for example, Terry Anderson, *The Sixties*, 5th ed. (New York: Routledge, 2017); Terry Anderson, *The Movement and the Sixties: Protest in America from Greensboro to Wounded Knee* (New York:

Oxford University Press, 1996); Gitlin, *The Sixties*; and Kirkpatrick Sale, *SDS* (New York: Random House, 1973).

6. Kenneth Heineman, *The Peace Movement at American State Universities in the Vietnam Era* (New York: New York University Press, 1992).
7. See, for example, Donald Summerlin, "Peach State Protest: The Anti-Vietnam War Movement in Georgia, 1964–1974," *Journal of the Georgia Association of Historians* 26 (2005): 1–16; Nicole Thompson, "Utah, the Anti-Vietnam War Movement, and the University of Utah," *Utah Historical Quarterly* 78, no. 2 (2010): 154–74; Nora Sutton, "'Have You Bought Enough Vietnam?' The Vietnam Antiwar Movement at West Virginia University, 1967–1970," *West Virginia History* [NS] 13, no. 1 (2019): 27–56; and Jeffrey Drobney, "Generation in Revolt: Student Dissent and Political Repression at West Virginia University," *West Virginia History* 54 (1995): 105–22.
8. Douglas Rossinow, *The Politics of Authenticity: Liberalism, Christianity, and the New Left in America* (New York: Columbia University Press, 1998).
9. Moretta, "Political Hippies and Hip Politicos," 266–91.
10. Sarah Eppler Janda, *Prairie Power: Student Activism, Counterculture, and Backlash in Oklahoma, 1962–1972* (Norman: University of Oklahoma Press, 2018). For a cogent review, see Gregg Michel, Review of Sarah Eppler Janda, *Prairie Power: Student Activism, Counterculture, and Backlash in Oklahoma, 1962–1972*, *Journal of American History* 105, no. 4 (2019): 1094–95.
11. John Ernst and Yvonne Baldwin, "The Not So Silent Minority: Louisville's Antiwar Movement, 1966–1975," *Journal of Southern History* 73, no. 1 (2007): 105–42.
12. Robbie Lieberman, *Prairie Power: Voices of 1960s Midwestern Student Protest* (Columbia: University of Missouri Press, 2004).
13. Matthew Levin, *Cold War University: Madison and the New Left in the Sixties* (Madison: University of Wisconsin Press, 2013).
14. Tom Bates, *Rads: The 1970 Bombing of the Army Mathematics Research Center of the University of Wisconsin and Its Aftermath* (New York: HarperCollins, 1992).

15. Garton Ash, *The File*, 12.
16. Garton Ash, *The File*, 249.
17. Garton Ash, *The File*, 12 (source of quotation).
18. Katherine Verdery, *My Life as a Spy: Investigations in a Secret Police File* (Durham, NC: Duke University Press, 2018).
19. Verdery, *My Life as a Spy*, 12–14.
20. Verdery, *My Life as a Spy*, 27.
21. Verdery, *My Life as a Spy*, 7.
22. Garton Ash, *The File*, 17.
23. Verdery, *My Life as a Spy*, 184.
24. Verdery, *My Life as a Spy*, 28.
25. Verdery, *My Life as a Spy*, 28.
26. Verdery, *My Life as a Spy*, 29.
27. Verdery, *My Life as a Spy*, 185.
28. Mike Dennis, *The Stasi: Myth and Reality* (London: Pearson/Longman, 2003), xii.
29. See, for example, Pat Watters and Stephen Cillers, eds., *Investigating the FBI* (Garden City, NY: Doubleday, 1973); Nelson Blackstock, *COINTELPRO: The FBI's Secret War on Political Freedom* (New York: Monad Press, 1975); and Frank Donner, *The Age of Surveillance: The Aims and Methods of America's Political Intelligence System* (New York: Knopf, 1980).
30. Richard K. Betts, *Enemies of Intelligence: Knowledge and Power in American National Security* (New York: Columbia University Press, 2009); David J. Garrow, *The FBI and Martin Luther King, Jr.: From "Solo" to Memphis* (New York: W. W. Norton, 1981); Kenneth O'Reilly, *Hoover and the Un-Americans: The FBI, HUAC, and the Red Menace* (Philadelphia: Temple University Press, 1983); Ward Churchill and Jim Vander Wall, *Agents of Repression: The FBI's Secret Wars Against the Black Panther Party and the American Indian Movement* (Boston: South End Press, 1990); Kenneth O'Reilly, *"Racial Matters": The FBI's Secret File on Black America, 1960–1972* (New York: Free Press, 1989); James Kirkpatrick Davis, *Assault on the Left: The FBI and the Sixties Antiwar Movement* (Westport, CT: Praeger, 1997);

Seth Rosenfeld, *Subversives: The FBI's War on Student Radicals, and Reagan's Rise to Power* (New York: Farrar, Straus, and Giroux, 2012); and David Cunningham, *There's Something Happening Here: The New Left, the Klan, and FBI Counterintelligence* (Berkeley: University of California Press, 2004).

31. Tim Weiner, *Enemies: A History of the FBI* (New York: Random House, 2013); Betty Medsger, *The Burglary: The Discovery of J. Edgar Hoover's Secret FBI* (New York: Vintage, 2014); Curt Gentry, *J. Edgar Hoover: The Man and the Secrets* (New York: Norton, 2001); and Rosenfeld, *Subversives*.
32. Frank J. Donner, *Protectors of Privilege: Red Squads and Police Repression in Urban America* (Berkeley: University of California Press, 1990).
33. Seth Kershner, "'A Constant Surveillance': The New York State Police and the Student Peace Movement, 1965–1973," *Global Sixties* 16, no. 1 (2023): 22–52; and Edward Escobar, "The Dialectics of Repression: The Los Angeles Police Department and the Chicano Movement, 1968–1971," *Journal of American History* 79, no. 4 (1993): 1483–514.
34. Johanna Fernández, *The Young Lords: A Radical History* (Chapel Hill: University of North Carolina Press, 2020).
35. Gregg Michel, *Spying on Students: The FBI, Red Squads, and Student Activists in the 1960s South* (Baton Rouge: LSU Press, 2024).
36. See Gary T. Marx, "Thoughts on a Neglected Category of Social Movement Participant: The Agent Provocateur and the Informant," *American Journal of Sociology* 80, no. 2 (1974): 402–42.
37. Michel, *Spying on Students*, 115–55, 156–88; and Gregg Michel, "Surveilling the Memphis Movement: Police Spying in Memphis, 1968–1976," *Journal of Southern History* 87, no. 4 (2021): 673–710.
38. Gregg Michel, *Struggle for a Better South: The Southern Student Organizing Committee, 1964–1969* (New York: Palgrave Macmillan, 2004).
39. Gregg Michel, "Government Repression of the Southern New Left," in *Rebellion in Black and White: Southern Student Activism*

in the 1960s, ed. Robert Cohen and David J. Snyder (Baltimore: Johns Hopkins University Press, 2012), 235–52 (esp. 236–37; quotations from 239, 240).

Notes for Chapter 1

1. Luke Stewart, "'Hell, They're Your Problem, Not Ours': Draft Dodgers, Military Deserters and Canada–United States Relations in the Vietnam War Era," *Études Canadiennes / Canadian Studies* 85 (2018): 67–96; and Renée Kasinsky, *Refugees from Militarism: Draft-Age Americans in Canada* (New Brunswick: Transaction Books, 1976).
2. Michael Foley, *Confronting the War Machine: Draft Resistance During the Vietnam War* (Chapel Hill: University of North Carolina Press, 2003).
3. Local Board Memorandum No. 107, issued July 6, 1970, by director, Selective Service System, Curtis W. Tarr.
4. Sherry Gershon Gottlieb, *Hell No, We Won't Go! Resisting the Draft During the Vietnam War* (New York: Penguin Books, 1991).
5. George Flynn, *The Draft, 1940–1973* (Lawrence: University Press of Kansas, 1993), 179; and John Hagan, *Northern Passage: American Vietnam War Resisters in Canada* (Cambridge, MA: Harvard University Press, 2001).
6. Bill Raley, "How Conscientious Objectors Killed the Draft: The Collapse of the Selective Service During the Vietnam War," *Cleveland State Law Review* 68 (2019): 151–76.
7. Amy Rutenberg, *Rough Draft: Cold War Military Manpower Policy and the Origins of Vietnam-Era Draft Resistance* (Ithaca, NY: Cornell University Press, 2019).
8. Flynn, *The Draft*, 171.
9. Lawrence Baskir and William Strauss, *Chance or Circumstance: The Draft, the War, and the Vietnam Generation* (New York: Knopf, 1978), 51.
10. "Draft Induction," *San Francisco Examiner*, 21 March 1971.

Notes for Chapter 2

1. Memo, director of FBI to SAC, San Antonio, Re: Counterintelligence Program, May 28, 1969, Freedom of Information and Privacy Acts, Subject: (COINTELPRO), New Left San Antonio 100-449698-45, *FBI Records: The Vault*, https://vault.fbi.gov/cointel-pro/new-left/cointel-pro-new-left-san-antonio-part-01-of-01/view. I refer to this publicly available cache of documents in subsequent footnotes simply as FBI COINTELPRO Records. See also Embree, *Voice Lessons*, 31–79, esp. 38–39, 62. Bob Pardun provides an excellent description an analysis of "early SDS" in Austin and the first shouts of political protest. See Robert Pardun, *Prairie Radical*, 91–112, 135–37.
2. For the observations of one of the participants, see Embree, *Voice Lessons*, 70–75.
3. Photographs, Box 3T1b [SRH12230027229] Photographs, UT Traffic and Security Chief Allen R. Hamilton Records, circa 1950s–1960s, Dolph Briscoe Center for American History, University of Texas at Austin (hereafter cited as DBCAH).
4. Thorne Dreyer, "The Spies of Texas: Newfound Files Detail How UT-Austin Police Tracked the Lives of Sixties Dissidents," *Texas Observer*, 17 November 2006.
5. Dreyer, "Spies of Texas."
6. Dreyer, "Spies of Texas."
7. These ideas and examples are taken from Dreyer, "Spies of Texas."
8. Dreyer, "Spies of Texas."
9. See Ward Churchill and Jim Van Der Wall, *The COINTELPRO Papers: Secrets from the FBI's Secret Wars against Domestic Dissent* (Boston: South End Press, 1990).
10. Report on New Left Activity at University of Texas at Austin, 5 July 1968, FBI COINTELPRO Records.
11. Memorandum for Information, 15 November 1967, Box 4Zf354, "UT Student Political Groups Observations and Memos 1967–1968," Burt Gerding Papers, 1959–1980, 1994 (hereafter cited as Gerding Papers), DBCAH.

12. See Memo, FBI Headquarters, New left Activity, University of Texas at Austin, 5 July 1968, FBI COINTELPRO Records. 2006.
13. The Oleo Strut was only one of many antiwar coffee houses located near military bases around the United States. In what amounted to paranoia, J. Edgar Hoover had identified GI coffeehouses as primary targets in the FBI's broader effort to destroy the New Left. In cooperation with local and state law enforcement officers, FBI agents infiltrated coffeehouses seeking evidence of illegal drug use and other criminal activities to justify arrests of coffeehouse staff and soldiers. See David Parsons, *Dangerous Grounds: Antiwar Coffeehouses and Military Dissent in the Vietnam Era* (Chapel Hill: University of North Carolina Press, 2017), 88–110. The spread of coffee houses was only the tip of the iceberg of GI resistance to the Vietnam War. See Richard Moser, *The New Winter Soldiers: GI and Veteran Dissent During the Vietnam Era* (New Brunswick: Rutgers University Press, 1996).
14. Douglas Rossinow, *Politics of Authenticity*, 218–19.
15. Kathy Stevenson, "Walkout Staged as General Speaks," *Dallas Morning News*, 1 December 1967.
16. Stevenson, "Walkout Staged as General Speaks."
17. In *Politics of Authenticity*, Doug Rossinow completely overlooked our choice of disruptive tactics (218–19).
18. Curtis Wilke, "Silber's Odyssey in Search of Truth," *Boston Globe*, 27 September 2012.
19. Nat Henderson and Derro Evans, "Caroline Issues Aired at Forum," *Austin American–Statesman*, 17 May 1968.
20. Derro Evans, "Caroline: No Statement from Council on Contract," *Austin American-Statesman*, 8 October 1968.
21. FBI, Confidential Memo, San Antonio Office to FBI Headquarters, "Ten Days of Protest and Resistance, 21–30 April 1968," 10 April 1968, File 22-cv-2593, Section 3, FBI Records, National Archives Records Administration, Kansas City, MO (hereafter cited as FBI Records).
22. FBI, Confidential Memo, "Ten Days of Protest and Resistance."
23. Intelligence report provided by Lt. B. Gerding, 11 July 1968, Box 4Zf351, "Folder SDS 1968–69," Gerding Papers.

24. Intelligence report provided by Gerding, 11 July 1968.
25. Austin Police Department, Intelligence Report, "Subject: Significant Projected Plans of the New Left, 9 October 1968," Box 4Zf355, "Police Reports on Austin Political Groups, 1968–1970; undated," Gerding Papers.
26. SAC, San Antonio, to director of the FBI, memo, "Attachment: Regional Conference, Leaflet, Announcing 18–20 October Meeting in Austin," 11 October 1968, File 22-cv-2593. Section 13, FBI Records.
27. FBI Internal Memo: Internal Security–SDS; Sedition, 24 January 1969, Attachment: Report from DL–T-3, 1 November 1968, File 22-cv-2593. Section 6, FBI Records.
28. FBI Internal Memo: Internal Security–SDS; Sedition, 24 January 1969, Attachment: Texas-Oklahoma Regional Office Special Mailing, 21 October 1968, File 22-cv-2593, Section 6, FBI Records. See also "SDS Convention Members Veto Massive Rally Proposal," *Daily Texan*, 20 October 1968.
29. For an excellent analysis of the antiwar movement in Oklahoma, see Janda, *Prairie Power*. See also Freedom of Information and Privacy Acts, Subject: (COINTELPRO) New Left-Oklahoma City, FBI (pp. 1–75), FBI COINTELPRO Records.
30. SAC, San Antonio, to director of the FBI, memo, 12 October 1968, File 22-cv-2593, Section 13, FBI Records.
31. SAC, San Antonio, to director of the FBI, memo, 30 October 1968, File 22-cv-2593, Section 13, FBI Records.
32. "'No Contest' Plea of Five Students," *Austin American-Statesman*, 3 March 1969.
33. Lyke Thompson, "AALA Members to Seek Classroom Time for Talks?" *Daily Texan*, 14 October 1969.
34. Confidential: Memorandum for Information, 28 January 1969, Box 4Zf354, "UT SDS Observation Report and Memos, 1967–1969," Gerding Papers.
35. Memorandum for Information, "Re: NLEP, 29 January 1969," Box 4Zf354, "UT SDS Observation Report and Memorandum, 1967–1969," Gerding Papers.

36. Memorandum for Information, "New Left Education Project Selling Literature, 29 January 1969," Box 4Zf354, "UT SDS Observation Report and Memos, 1967–1969," Gerding Papers.
37. Martin Murray, principal author, "New Left Education Project," Box 4Zf351, "SDS, Civil Rights and Anti-War Movement, Student Pamphlets, Hand-Outs, and Notes, 1968–1969, Undated," Gerding Papers.
38. Memorandum for Information, 29 February 1969, Box 4Zf354, "UT SDS Observation Report and Memos, 1967–1969," Gerding Papers.
39. Memorandum for Information, 28 February 1969, Box 4Zf354, "UT SDS Observation Report and Memos, 1967–1969," Gerding Papers.
40. Handwritten memo labeled "SDS Meeting," 20 February 1969, Box 4Zf351, "SDS, 1968–1969," Gerding Papers.
41. My memory of these events is assisted by reference to several undated newspaper accounts that I have in my possession. See Memorandum for Information, "RE: SDS and New Left Education Project," 21 April 1969, Box 4Zf354, "UT SDS Observation Report and Memos, 1967–1969," Gerding Papers.
42. "RE: SDS and New Left Education Project," 21 April 1969.
43. "RE: SDS and New Left Education Project," 21 April 1969.
44. FBI Reports, File 100-SA-10848.
45. Dick Reavis, "SDS: From Students to Seniors," in *No Apologies: Texas Radical Celebrate the '60s*, ed. Daryl Janes (Austin: Eakin Press, 1992), 102–7 (quotation from p. 103).
46. Greg Calvert and Carol Neiman, *A Disrupted History: The New Left and the New Capitalism* (New York: Random House, 1971).
47. SA Emil Schroeder, Chicago Office, United Stated Department of Justice, "Gregory Alan Calvert, Security Matter - Miscellaneous," August 9, 1967, NW# 657361, FBI Records.
48. SA Spurgeon Peterson, St. Louis Field Office, United States Department of Justice, "Gregory Alan Calvert, Sedition," July 1, 1968, NW# 657361, FBI Records.

49. Subject: Greg Calvert, August 1967 and September 1972, 400 pages, Records of the Department of Justice, Entry UD-WW 4233, Box Number 371, File 146-23-4137, Record Group 60, FBI Records.
50. Memorandum for Information, "SDS Meeting," 17 December 1968, Box 4Zf354, "UT SDS Observation Report and Memos, 1967–1969," Gerding Papers.
51. SAC, San Antonio, to Director FBI, Attn: Assistant to the Director, C.D. DeLoach, 7 November 1968, File 22-cv-2593, Section 13, FBI Records.
52. Dale Brumfield, "The Facts Were Immaterial," *Austin Chronicle,* 7 June 2013.
53. Memorandum for Information, notes from SDS meeting 20 March 1969, Box 4Zf354, "UT SDS Observation report and memos 1967–1969," Gerding Papers.
54. Brumfield, "Facts Were Immaterial."
55. SAC, San Antonio, to Director of FBI, memo "COINTELPRO–New Left," 17 March 1969, File 22-cv-2593, Section 13, FBI Records.
56. Andy Yemma, "SDS Schedules Rally to Protest Board Ruling," *Daily Texan,* 18 March 1969.
57. Donna Dickerson, "Stand on SDS," *Daily Texan*, 18 March 1969; and Barbara Barnard, "Erwin Studies Plea on SDS Convention," *Austin American-Statesman,* 19 March 1969.
58. Austin Police Department, Intelligence Report, "Subject: Students for a Democratic Society National Council Meeting," 27 March 1968, Box 4Zf355, "Police Reports on Austin Political Groups; 1968–1970," Gerding Papers.
59. Confidential: Memorandum for Information (police report prepared by Burt Gerding), 1 April 1969, Box 4Zf354, "UT SDS Observation Report and Memos 1967–1969," Gerding Papers (hereafter cited as Gerding Report, 1 April 1969.)
60. SAC, San Antonio to Director of FBI, memo, COINTELPRO, 10 June 1969, File 22-cv-2593, Section 13, FBI Records.

61. Memorandum for Information, "Notes from SDS Meeting," 20 March 1969, Box 4Zf354, "UT SDS Observation Report and Memos 1967–1969," Gerding Papers.
62. Memorandum for Information, "Notes from SDS Meeting," 20 March 1969.
63. Burt Gerding Memorandum, 27 March 1969, Box 4Zf354, "UT SDS Observation Report and Memos 1967–1969," Gerding Papers.
64. Memorandum for Information, "Notes from SDS Meeting," 20 March 1969.
65. Gerding Report, 1 April 1969.
66. Years later, well after the total collapse of the Weather Underground, I had several occasions to talk with Bernadine Dohrn. I found her likeable, introspective, and a bit sad, really.
67. Memo, FBI, "Students for a Democratic Society, National Council Meeting, 27 March 1969," 15 April 1969, File 100-SA-10834, FBI Records.
68. Memorandum, SAC, San Antonio, to Director, FBI, regarding National Council Meeting, 15 March 1969.
69. Gerding Report, 1 April 1969.
70. Gerding Report, 1 April 1969.
71. Burt Gerding Memorandum, 27 March 1969, Box 4Zf354, "UT SDS Observation Report and Memos 1967–1969," Gerding Papers.
72. Gerding Report, 1 April 1969.
73. Burt Gerding interview with Sarah Clark, 27 March 1995, p. 86, Box2X209b, "Transcripts," Gerding Papers.
74. Gerding Report, 1 April 1969.
75. There is extensive literature, but see Rhodri Jeffreys-Jones, *The FBI: A History* (New Haven: Yale University Press, 2008).
76. Herbert Marcuse, "Repressive Tolerance," in Robert Paul Wolff, Barrington Moore Jr., and Herbert Marcuse (eds.), *A Critique of Pure Tolerance* (Boston: Beacon Press, 1969), pp. 95–137.
77. Confidential Memo, undated, Box 4Zf353, "Speech Material, UT (speeches, police reports, notes, clippings, memos, police policy) 1972–1973, undated," Gerding Papers.

Notes for Chapter 3

1. Gitlin, *The Sixties*, 292–327 and 328–48. Gitlin was a leader of the early SDS. His book is filled with justifiable criticism about the post-SDS movement and the turn to sectarianism and mindless destruction of property. But he fails to comprehend how the post-SDS movement developed a sophisticated critique of US imperialism, racism, sexism, and homophobia, despite its faults.
2. See Moretta, "Political Hippies and Hip Politicos."
3. Austin Police Department, Intelligence Report, prepared by Lt. Burt Gerding, August 1968, Box 4Zf353, "Reports on SMC; SDS; and other student groups; 1968–1968; undated," Gerding Papers.
4. Sharon Lowry, "Union Board Oks CUF Dining Request," *Daily Texan*, 8 October 1970.
5. Various newspaper clippings and leaflets are available in Box 3W15b, "Community United Front, 1970," George Carlson Papers, 1967–1973 (hereafter cited as Carlson Papers), DBCAH.
6. Thorne Dreyer, "The Spies of Texas," *Texas Observer*, 4 January 2009. See also John Schultz, *The Conspiracy Trial of the Chicago 7*, 2nd ed. (Chicago: University of Chicago Press, 2009); and Kit Bakke, *Protest on Trial: The Seattle 7 Conspiracy* (Pullman: Washington State University Press, 2018).
7. For the source of some of this information, see Beverly Burr, "History of Student Activism at the University of Texas at Austin (1960–1988)," unpublished paper, spring 1988.
8. *The Economy Furniture Strike* is a feature-length documentary film about a local labor dispute that resulted in the political mobilization of Mexican Americans in Austin / Travis County. Paradigm Shift Media and the Austin Community College's Center for Public Policy and Political Studies produced the film, which was directed by Jackie McCardell Jr. It was hosted and narrated by Emmy award-winning journalist Dan Rather and is available at https://www.austincc.edu/cppps/economyfstrike/index.html.
9. Stanley Karnow, *Vietnam: A History* (New York: Viking Press, 1983), 599.

10. Aaron Fountain, "The war in the Schools: San Francisco Bay Area High Schools and the Anti–Vietnam War Movement, 1965–1973," *California History* 92, no. 2 (2015): 22–41 (esp. 33).
11. Sarah Thelan, "Mobilizing a Majority: Nixon's 'Silent Majority' Speech and the Domestic Debate over Vietnam," *Journal of American Studies* 51, no. 3 (2017): 887–914.
12. Ruth Doyle, "Moratorium Day Encompasses UT, Capitol," *Daily Texan*, 16 October 1969.
13. Doyle, "Moratorium Day."
14. "Washington in 1969 Hosted Largest Antiwar Protest in US History," *Stars and Stripes* (Washington, DC), 15 August 2019.
15. Memorandum for Information (confidential), RE: Student Mobilization Committee (SMC), 20 October 1969, Box 4Zf353, "Reports on SMC," Gerding Papers.
16. For a wider historical view of Waller Creek, see Katherine Leah Pace, "Forgetting Waller Creek: An Environmental History of Race, Parks, and Planning in Downtown Austin, Texas," *Journal of Southern History* 87, no. 4 (2021): 603–44.
17. Memorandum for Information, undercover police report, 21 October 1969, Box 3W15b, "Trees Incident 1969," Carlson Papers.
18. Lyke Thompson, "Saplings Removed from Creek Area," *Austin American-Statesman*, 23 October 1969; and "Protesters Plead 'Nolo Contendere' to Creek Charges," *Daily Texan*, 5 November 1969.
19. "Creek Construction to Resume Today," *Daily Texan*, 28 October 1969 (Tuesday).
20. Robert Carter, "Construction Site Blocked by Protesters," *Daily Texan*, 22 October 1969 (Wednesday).
21. Editorial, "Erwin's Actions Irresponsible," *Daily Texan*, 24 October 1969; "Tree Fight Ignites Opposition Group," *Daily Texan*, 24 October 1969; and "The Trees of Texas are upon you," *Daily Texan*, 26 October 1969.
22. Anne Mundy (staff photographer), "Tale of Tree Protesters," *Austin American*, 23 October 1969.
23. Rick Fish, "Ladders, Nets Used by the Police," *Austin American*, 23 October 1969. See also Kristin Phillips, communications coordinator,

Office of Sustainability, "The Battle for Waller Creek's Trees," *University of Texas*, 22 October 2019, https://sustainability.utexas.edu/news/battle-waller-creeks-trees.

24. See also Memorandum for Information, 31 October 1969, Box 4Zf353, "9-5-69–3-8-70," Folder "Notes, Memos, Clippings on Student Political Groups, 1968–1970 and undated," Gerding Papers. Includes Waller Creek Incident and Chuck Wagon..
25. Mundy, "Tale of Tree Protesters."
26. Larry Grisham, "Administrators vs. Trees at the University of Texas," *Daily Crimson* (Harvard University), 3 December 1969.
27. Mundy, "Tale of Tree Protesters"; and Leslie Donovan and Bill Cryer, "26 Arrested at Work Site," *Austin American-Statesman*, 23 October 1969.
28. Memorandum for Information (confidential), 23 October 1969, Box 3W15b, "Trees Incident 1969," Carlson Papers.
29. Beth Doyle, "Cut Timber Barricades Main Door," *Daily Texan*, 23 October 1969; and Roland Nethaway, "Trees Fall at UT Despite Protestors," *Austin American*, 23 October 1969.
30. For the source of some of this information, see Burr, "History of Student Activism." See also Jim Morris, "Students Sympathize with Tree Protesters," *Daily Texan*, 23 October 1969.
31. Robert Carter, "New Trees Planted Along the Waller Basin," *Daily Texan*, 26 October 1969.
32. "Protesters Plead '*Nolo Contendere*'"; and "Nine Want Trials in Waller Cases," *Daily Texan*, 5 December 1969.
33. Memorandum for Information [Confidential] Re: Tree Incident [no date], Box 3W15b, "Trees Incident 1969," Carlson Papers.
34. "Protesters Plead 'Nolo Contendere.'"
35. Memorandum for Information [Confidential] Re: Tree Incident.
36. Memorandum for Information [Confidential] Re: Tree Incident.
37. See David Hamilton, "The 1969 Chuck Wagon Riot," *Rag Blog*, 17 February 2011, https://theragblog.blogspot.com/2011/02/david-p-hamilton-1969-chuck-wagon-riot.html.

38. For the source of this information, see Hamilton, "1969 Chuck Wagon Riot."
39. Austin Police Department, "Supplementary Offense Report," 6 November 1969, Box 3W15b, "Chuck Wagon Incident, 1969–1970," Carlson Papers.
40. Robert Wallace, "Letters to the Editor: Actions Deplored," *Austin American-Statesman*, 20 [?] November 1969. See also leaflet distributed 10 November 1969, "Mass Meeting–11:00AM–Main Mall [undated]," Box 3W15b, "Chuck Wagon Incident, 1969–1970," Carlson Papers.
41. John Bryant, "Runaway Sunshine Sent to Girlstown," *Austin Statesman*, November 1969. Thanks to Alice Embree for drawing my attention to this investigative reporting piece. See also Robert Wallace, "Letters to the Editor: Actions Deplored," *Austin Statesman*, November 1969; "Mass Meeting–11:00AM–Main Mall [undated]"; and Austin Police Department, "Supplementary Offense Report," 6 November 1969, Box 3W15b, "Chuck Wagon Incident, 1969–1970," Carlson Papers. In a personal communication, David Hamilton [Pratt] confirmed that protesters hurled bottles at police.
42. Bryant, "Runaway Sunshine Sent to Girlstown." See also Austin Police Department, "Supplementary Offense Report," 6 November 1969; and Austin Police Department, "General Offense Report," 6 November 1969, Box 3W15b, "Chuck Wagon Incident, 1969–1970," Carlson Papers.
43. Bryant, "Runaway Sunshine Sent to Girlstown."
44. I have borrowed this phrase from David Hamilton (Pratt).
45. Lynn Flocke, "Chuck Wagon Violence Follows Union Decision," *Austin American-Statesman*, 11 November 1969.
46. "Police Battle Crowd at UT: 4-5 Arrested," *Houston Post*, 11 November 1969.
47. "Union Board Statement," *Daily Texan*, November 1969, in Box 3W15b, "Chuck Wagon Incident, 1969–1970," Carlson Papers.
48. In a private communication, David Hamilton (Pratt) supplied this information to me.

49. Burt Gerding, interview with Sarah Clark, partial transcript, 1994, Box 4Zf353, Gerding Papers.
50. "Chuck Wagon Cleared as Violence Erupts," *Austin Statesman*, 11 November 1969.
51. Flocke, "Chuck Wagon Violence Follows Union Decision."
52. Karen Elliott, "Mace Used on Protesters," *Austin American-Statesman*, 11 November 1969; and "Chuck Wagon Cleared as Violence Erupts," *Austin Statesman*, 11 November 1969.
53. "Police Battle Crowd at UT: 4-5 Arrested."
54. Lynn Taylor, "UT Campus—No Longer Exempt," *Austin American-Statesman*, 11 November 1969.
55. Thanks to Pat Cuney for pointing this out to me. In a personal email communication (10 September 2022), she wrote, "I was standing outside after the cops chased us out of the Chuckwagon. I was on the loading dock driveway, along Guadalupe, about 2 or 3 people deep in the crowd facing the line of cops [who were blocking the driveway]. I watched the police arrest people protesting around their van at the back of the Student Union, and it was clear they were looking for individuals. They did not arrest people who were giving them the most problems up close, but [purposefully] moved into the crowd. I watched one cop speak quietly to another and point into the crowd near me. The two cops and one or two more then linked arms in a V-formation and plunged into the crowd, [which knocked] me and several other people aside. They reached Paul Spencer who was just standing there, a couple of people behind me. They grabbed Paul and dragged him back out of the crowd, threw him down, and handcuffed him." In a response to David Pratt's *Rag Blog*, Alan Locklear observed, "I can testify as to the violence of that police 'phalanx' or flying wedge that got Paul. I was standing in the crowd just behind the front line of people and one or two people in front of Paul. I watched a cop point into the crowd while whispering to a fellow officer. Then, after a brief confab, about 5 officers formed up very quickly and plunged into the crowd right between me and the person next to me. I (and several other people)

were shoved roughly aside as the cops bore in on Paul. They reached him, grabbed him and hauled him back out into the cop circle and cuffed him. At no time, did he do anything remotely like 'rioting' or misbehaving in any way. He was just standing there, maybe shouting (as everyone else was doing)."

56. Flocke, "Chuck Wagon Violence Follows Union Decision."
57. Staff Reporter, "Police battle crowd at UT: 4–5 Arrested," *Houston Post*, 11 November 1969.
58. Lynn Taylor, "UT Campus—No Longer Exempt," *Austin-American Statesman*, 11 November 1969.
59. Flocke, "Chuck Wagon Violence Follows Union Decision."
60. Photographs, Chuck Wagon incident, 11 November 1969, Box 3W15d [SRH1230030510], Photographs, Carlson Papers.
61. Flocke, "Chuck Wagon Violence Follows Union Decision."
62. "FBI Denies 'Hold' on 4 in Jail," *Austin American-Statesman*, 11 November 1969.
63. Captain J. C. Fann, "General Police Report," 10 November 1969, Box 3W15b, "Chuck Wagon Incident, 1969–1970, Carlson Papers.
64. Fann, "General Police Report."
65. Thomas Johnson, "Union Board Actions Supported," *Daily Texan,* November 1969.
66. Lyke Thompson, "Regents Overturn Union Board Decision," *Daily Texan*, 10 November 1970.
67. "Eight Arrested at Protest," *Austin Statesman*, 11 November 1969. Paul Spencer, Albert Cambio, James Sparks, and Scott Miller were charged with aggravated assault on a police officer. Bill Tamminga, Michael Koch, Bill Meacham, and Jay McGee were charged with disorderly conduct. Sparks, Miller, Cambio, and Spencer were also charged with disorderly conduct. In a "Memorandum of Information" [marked confidential], 25 November 1969, a police undercover informant alleged that besides the original twenty-one indictments, more were expected. More indictments did not materialize; Box 3W15b "Chuck Wagon Incident, 1969–1970," Carlson Papers.

68. "Citizens of Austin Your Freedoms Are at Stake." Notice issued by Chuck wagon Defense Committee, Box 3W15b, "Chuck Wagon Incident, 1969–1970," Carlson Papers.
69. "Taken from Non-students," *Daily Texan*, 11 November 1969.
70. Photographs, Chuck Wagon incident, 11 November 1969, Box 3W15d [SRH1230030510], Photographs, Carlson Papers.
71. Interview Report—University of Texas at Austin, 12 November 1969, Box 3W15b, "Report on Demonstration at ROTC Parade, 1969," Carlson Papers.
72. "Malpractice Suit Filed," *Daily Texan*, 14 October 1970. I have taken the circumstances surrounding this event from the contemporaneous newspaper report.
73. Email correspondence with Bill Meacham, 22 April 2023. Bill remembers the events somewhat differently than how they were reported in 1970. I reproduce his words with his permission.
74. "Sixteenth Person Arrested," *Daily Texan*, 5 December 1969.
75. "Chuck Wagon Suspect Yields," *Daily Texan,* 5 December 1969; and "FBI Charges Two Suspects in Chuck Wagon Incidents," *Daily Texan*, 4 December 1969. Thanks to Mariann Wizard-Vasquez for this firsthand information.
76. Craig Bird, "Assembly to Aid Students Charged in Union Protest," *Daily Texan,* 5 December 1969.
77. "Chuck Wagon Defendants Take Offensive Today," LEAFLET distributed 6 January 1970, Box 3W15b, "Chuck Wagon Incident, 1969–1970," Carlson Papers. See also Kelle Snyder, "Suit Names DA Smith," *Daily Texan*, 7 January 1970.
78. Statement printed in *Austin American-Statesman*, 6 January 1970, Box 3B37, Addition, Carlson Papers.
79. Lyke Thompson, "Plea Issue for Witnesses," *Daily Texan*, 22 February 1970, Box 3W15b, "Chuck Wagon Incident, 1969–1970," Carlson Papers. See also Burt Gerding, interview with Sarah Clark, 27 March 1995, Box 2X209b, "Transcripts," Gerding Papers.
80. Cliff Avery and Eric Liebrock, "Discussions Delay Union Riot Hearing," *Daily Texan*, 7 January 1970.

81. Thanks to David Hamilton (Pratt) for supplying this information in a personal communication.
82. Lyke Thompson, "Union Probe Concluded," *Daily Texan*, 6 March 1970.
83. "Special Report on the Chuck Wagon," 5 March 1970, Box 3W15b, "Chuck Wagon Incident, 1969–1970," Carlson Papers.
84. Ed Smith, "Disclosure of Facts Urged in UT Affair," *Austin American*, 6 February 1970.
85. Jim Hicks, "Aiding Students: Job of Campus Police Force," *Daily Texan*, 16 November 1969, Box 3W15b, "Chuck Wagon Incident, 1969–1970," Carlson Papers.
86. "Statement by [President Norman] Hackerman," (no date), Box 3W15b, "Chuck Wagon Incident, 1969–1970," Carlson Papers.
87. Thompson, "Union Probe Concluded"; and Lyke Thompson, "Texan Interview: The Chuck Wagon Case," *Daily Texan,* 20 November 1969.
88. Thorne Dreyer, "Movement Gets Legal Aid in Texas," Liberation News Service, 1969.
89. SAC, San Antonio, to FBI Director, and SACS Dallas, Chicago, and New York, "Urgent," 20 June 1970, File 100-SA-10834, vol. 1, FBI Records.
90. SA James King, to SAC, San Antonio, 27 September 1973, File 100-SA-11837, vol. 1, FBI Records.
91. "Sodomy Victim to Sue," *Daily Texan*, 18 October 1970.

Notes for Chapter 4

1. Memo, San Antonio FBI, "March and Rally, 11 January 1970," 14 January 1970, File 100-SA-10834, vol. 1, FBI Records. See also Chris Meredith, "March Moves to Sidewalks," *Austin American*, 12 January 1970.
2. Austin Police Department Intelligence report, "Background and Updating of Proposed Student Strike" (signed by Lt. Burt Gerding), 4 May 1970, Box Zf353, "3-17-70 - 6-23-70 Including YSA report (notes, memos, clippings on student political groups), 1970," Gerding Papers.

3. Special thanks to Peter Megaw for helping out with the sequence of events. He saved the comic book that was distributed to high school students, and he sent me a copy.
4. We learned of these legal restrictions from the experience of Austin high school students. According to Peter Megaw, an Austin High School student, “We got busted by the principal and he took our leaflets and had them destroyed.” The Austin students contacted the head of the American Civil Liberties Union (ACLU). The ACLU lawyer successfully argued that the sidewalk was public property and that the High School principal had no legal jurisdiction there. Because the school had destroyed the leaflets, they were forced to reprint them at no costs.
5. Phil Skoda, “Anti Draft Campaign Continues,” *Austin American*, 18 March 1970.
6. Peter Megaw recounted a story to me that years later one of the leaders of the prowar students came up to him on the UT campus (with hair to his shoulders and no sign of the “shit-kicker” cowboy boots he once sported in high school). This person sheepishly told Peter that the demonstration at Austin High School ultimately changed his views on the war and his perceptions of the power structure in America.
7. Jeff Brown and Haverly Parker, “2 Draft Protests Held,” *Daily Texan*, 20 March 1970.
8. Phil Skoda, “Anti Draft Campaign Continues,” *Austin American*, 18 March 1970.
9. Soeur Queens, *Soeur Queens Songbook: Songs of Sisterhood* (Fly by Night Print Collective, 1970).
10. Austin Police Department Intelligence Report, “‘The Roach’ Subversive Publication for Travis-Crockett High Schools,” 11 October 1968, Box 4Zf355, “Police reports on Austin political groups; 1968–1970, undated,” Gerding Papers.
11. Austin Police Department Intelligence Report, “The Roach,” 11 October 1968.
12. SA Howard Riley, to SAC, San Antonio, 15 May 1970, File 100-SA-10848, FBI Records.

13. Steve Krinsky told me recently that "Beware the Creeping Meatball" was a satirical campaign by 1960s radio host Jean Shepard. The Yippies popularized the term. Steve introduced it to us.
14. "Meatball Coalition: Protesters Disrupt ROTC Inspection," *Daily Texan*, 24 April 1970.
15. Leslie Taylor, "Protesters Disrupt ROTC Inspection," *Austin Statesman*, 24 April 1970.
16. Janice Haag, "Hertz Wants Student Activity," *Daily Texan*, 25 April 1970.
17. Interview Report 6-5-70, University of Texas at Austin, Box 3W15b, "Report on Demonstration at ROTC Parade, 1969," Carlson Papers.
18. I would like to thank fellow disrupter Sharon Shelton for remembering this event.
19. Interview Report 6-5-70.
20. Assorted newspaper clippings, Box 3W15b, "Teaching Assistants Association, 1970," Carlson Papers.
21. "Meatball Coalition: Protesters Disrupt ROTC Inspection," *Daily Texan*, 24 April 1970.
22. Mike Lacy, "Protest Costs Jobs," *Daily Texan*, 31 July 1970; "Demands of TAs Rejected; Jordan Justifies Dismissals," *Daily Texan*, 9 October 1970; and Dotty Griffith, "TA Files Protest," *Daily Texan*, 8 October 1970.
23. Handwritten undercover police report, 5 May 1970, Box 3W15c, "May 4–8, 1970. Demonstrations," Carlson Papers.
24. Handwritten undercover police report, 5 May 1970.
25. Lyke Thompson, "Demonstrators Tear Gassed," *Daily Texan*, 6 May 1970; Cliff Avery, "May Violence—the March," *Daily Texan*, 6 May 1970; and "Smith Talks to Press," *Daily Texan*, 6 May 1970.
26. "Reports 3-17-70 and 6-23-70 Including YSA report [notes, memos, clippings on student political groups], 1970," Box Zf353, Gerding Papers. Gerding was still around in May 1970.
27. Thompson, "Demonstrators Tear Gassed"; Avery, "May Violence"; and "Smith Talks to Press."
28. Handwritten undercover police report, 5 May 1970.
29. Handwritten undercover police report, 5 May 1970.

30. Handwritten undercover police report, 5 May 1970.
31. Handwritten undercover police report, 5 May 1970.
32. "Reports 3-17-70 and 6-23-70 Including YSA report [notes, memos, clippings on student political groups], 1970," Box Zf353, Gerding Papers.
33. Handwritten undercover police report, 5 May 1970; and Handwritten undercover police report, Frank Irwin, 7 May 1970, Box 3W15c, "May 4–8, 1970. Demonstrations," Carlson Papers.
34. Ann Hagy, "Jones Attacks ROTC during Tech-in," *Daily Texan*, 7 May 1970.
35. For the source of some information, see Beverly Burr, "History of Student Activism at the University of Texas at Austin (1960–1988)," unpublished paper, spring 1988.
36. Handwritten undercover police report, 8 May 1970, Box 3W15c, "May 4–8, 1970, Demonstrations," Carlson Papers.
37. Rowland Nethaway, "Parade Order Pleases LaRue," *Austin American-Statesman*, 9 May 1970; and "Roberts Thinks Parade Law Unconstitutional," *Austin American-Statesman*, 9 May 1970.
38. Memorandum for Information, 8 May 1970, Box 3W15d, "Photographs for George Carlson, May 6-8, 1970, [from] Texas Department of Public Safety, Confidential, Intelligence," Carlson Papers.
39. Handwritten undercover police report, 8 May 1970.
40. "Austin's March Peaceful," *Austin American-Statesman*, 9 May 1970.
41. "Austin's March Peaceful."
42. "Arson Try Suspect Convicted," *Austin American-Statesman*, 30 September 1970.
43. Henry Fessi, "Letters to Editor: Décor at UT," *Austin-American Statesman*, 10 September 1970.
44. For the source of some information, see Burr, "History of Student Activism."
45. William Bellamy, "With Boys to Fight SDS," *San Antonio Light*, 11 June 1969.
46. "Boys Staters Confront Protest Groups at Jester," *Daily Texan*, 12 June 1970; and Don Fairchild, "Yippies, Outreach Members Peacefully Meet Boys Staters," *Austin American-Statesman*, 12 June 1970.

47. "Law School Bush Burned by a Bomb," *Daily Texan*, 18 October 1970.
48. "Police Study Motives Around Bomb Threats," *Daily Texan,* 15 October 1970.
49. "Bust UCLA," *Daily Texan,* 1 October 1970; "200 Attend Lib Conference," *Daily Texan*, 27 September 1970. See assorted papers in Box 3W15b, "Women's Liberation Front," Carlson Papers.
50. John Owen, "State AFL-CIO Tells Co-Op Workers to Unionize," *Daily Texan*, 3 September 1970.
51. Rossinow, *Politics of Authenticity*, 244–45.
52. Another objection to working for Democratic Party candidates in local electoral campaigns was that the candidates were sometimes clever enough to use political activists as free labor and then reject their radical ideas as soon as the campaign was victorious.
53. Memorandum, "National Peace Action Coalition March," Box 3W15c, "October 31, 1970 March," Carlson Papers.
54. "Antiwar Group to Protest Tax," *Daily Texan*, 2 December 1970; and "Group Protests at Game, Rallies," *Daily Texan*, 6 December 1970.
55. Rick Codina, "200 Join Peace Rally," *Daily Texan,* 11 February 1971.
56. Selected newspaper clippings available in Box 3W15c, "SDS Navy Protest, February 19, 1971," Carlson Papers.
57. "SDS Protests Navy Program," *Daily Texan*, 19 February 1971.
58. Miles Hawthorne, "Rally Urges US Victory," *Austin Statesman*, 21 March 1971.

Notes for Chapter 5

1. Assorted leaflets and documents available in Box 3W15b, "Vietnam Veterans Against the War, Texas area," Carlson Papers.
2. Armadillo May Day Tribe, "An Invitation to Live" (1971), Box 3W15b, "Vietnam Veterans Against the War, Texas area," Carlson Papers.
3. In a personal communication, Alice Embree recounted fifty years later that she was told by a medical person preparing us for the May Days demonstrations that projectile vomiting was an indication of a concussion. Just to learn about what might happen to us was a clear indication of our seriousness and dedication.

4. Memo (Urgent), SAC, San Antonio, to FBI Director, Domestic Intelligence Division, SAC, Little Rock, Dallas, Houston, 20 April 1971, File 100-SA-10834, vol. 2, FBI Records.
5. Don Fisher and Larry Springer, "GIs count Dirty Cadence of in Austin Antiwar March," *Austin Statesman*, 19 April 1971.
6. A song performed by Julie Paul (drummer for Hootenanny Hoots) and Chuck Joyce at Lake Austin Inn, April 1971. Special thanks to Alice Embree for bringing the lyrics to my attention.
7. Lawrence Roberts, *Mayday 1971: A White House at War, a Revolt in the Streets, and the Untold History of America's Biggest Mass Arrest* (Boston: Houghton Mifflin Harcourt, 2021), 126.
8. Andrew Hunt, *The Turning: A History of Vietnam Veterans Against the War* (New York: New York University Press, 1999).
9. Terry Dubose, "Vietnam Veterans Against the War," in Janes, *No Apologies*, 148–58.
10. Dick Nelson, "Washington, 24 April, 1971," *The New Hampshire* (University of New Hampshire), 30 April 1971.
11. The Austin chapter of the Student Mobilization Committee (SMC)—affiliated with the Young Socialist Alliance—sent seventy-five persons to DC for the NPAC single-issue peace march. The SMC refused to join umbrella groups affiliated with the multi-issue PCPJ, and their supporters departed from Washington, DC, the day the May Day events started.
12. In movement circles the NPAC became known as the Mobe and the PCPJ as the Mob.
13. See Robert Smith, "The Mayday Tribe: 'Creativeness, Joy and Life Against Bureaucracy and Grim Death,'" *New York Times*, 3 May 1971.
14. Armadillo May Day Tribe, "An Invitation to Live" (distributed pamphlet, 1971).
15. May Day Tribe, *May Day Tactical Manual* (Washington, DC,: nd).
16. L. A. Kauffman, *Direct Action: Protest and the Reinvention of American Radicalism* (New York: Verso Books, 2017), 1. See also Lucy Barber, *Marching on Washington* (Berkeley: University of California Press, 2002); and Roberts, *Mayday 1971*, 1–20.

17. Roberts, *Mayday 1971*, 237.
18. Memo (Urgent), SAC, San Antonio, to FBI Director, Domestic Intelligence Division, SAC, Little Rock, Dallas, Houston, 20 April 1971, File 100-SA-10834, vol. 2, FBI Records.
19. FBI San Antonio, Confidential Memo, 25 April 1971, File 100-SA-10834, vol, 2, FBI Records.
20. See Martin J. Murray, "Building Fires on the Prairie," in *Radical Sociologists and the Movement: Experiences, Lessons, and Legacies*, ed. Martin Oppenheimer, Martin Murray, and Rhonda Levine (Philadelphia: Temple University Press, 1992), 92–110.
21. Roberts, *Mayday 1971*, 190–91; Kaufman, *Direct Action*, 20–40; and Smith, "Mayday Tribe."
22. Roberts, *Mayday 1971*, 266.
23. Roberts, *Mayday 1971*, 268.
24. Roberts, *Mayday 1971*, 298–99.
25. Roberts, *Mayday 1971*, 224, 305–7.
26. David Bolt and Ken Ringle, "Arrestees Mainly Under 25," *Washington Post*, 5 May 1971.
27. Editorial, "Mayday Arrests Are Evaluated," *San Francisco Chronicle*, 7 July 1971.
28. May Day leaflet, Available in Box 2-G23A, "Anti-war Demonstrations, Spring 1971," UT News and Information Service Records, 1928–1997, DBCAH.
29. Nicolaus von Hoffman, "Washington: On the Ropes," *Washington Post*, 6 May 1971.
30. Roberts, *Mayday 1971*, 71–72.
31. FBI Field Office, Indianapolis, Indiana, Confidential Memorandum, 3 May 1971, File 22-cv-2593, Section 6, FBI Records.
32. Memorandum from FBI Director to the San Antonio field office, subject "Demonstrations sponsored by People's Coalition for Peace and Justice (PCPJ), 26 April 1971," File 22-cv-2593, Section 6, FBI Records.
33. Personal correspondence with Pat Cuney, 28 November 2023.

34. Memo (Urgent), SAC, San Antonio, to FBI Director, Domestic Intelligence Division, SAC, Little Rock, Dallas, Houston, 20 April 1971, File 100-SA-10834, vol. 2, FBI Records.
35. Memo (Urgent), SAC, San Antonio, to FBI Director, 20 April 1971.
36. United States Department of Justice, FBI San Antonio field office Memorandum, 9 June 1971, File 22-cv-2593, Section 6, FBI Records.
37. San Antonio field office Memorandum, 9 June 1971.
38. Will Wilson, Assistant Attorney General, Criminal Division, Department of Justice, memorandum to Director of FBI, 23 April 1971, File 22-cv-2593, Section 6, FBI Records. See also San Antonio field office to Director of FBI, confidential memorandum, 29 June 1971, File 22-cv-2593, FBI Records.
39. Wilson, memo to the Director of the FBI (undated—possibly mid-June 1971), File 22-cv-2593, Section 6, FBI Records.
40. US Government Memorandum, from A. Rosen, Department of Justice, to Mr. Sullivan, FBI Headquarters, regarding May Days demonstrations and antiriot laws, 30 April 1971, File 22-cv-2593, Section 6, FBI Records.
41. Memorandum from A. Rosen, to Mr. Sullivan, 30 April 1971.
42. Wilson, memo to the Director of the FBI (undated—possibly mid-June 1971), File 22-cv-2593, Section 6, FBI Records.
43. Director, FBI, to SAC, San Antonio, 15 June 1971, File 22-cv-2593, Section 6, FBI Records.
44. FBI Memo, interview by Agents Tom Chapoton and James King, 7 July 1971, File 22-cv-2593, Section 6 FBI Records.
45. SAC, San Antonio, to FBI Director, Memorandum, Subject: Armadillo May Day Tribe, 29 June 1971, File 22-cv-2593, Section 6, FBI Records.
46. SAC, San Antonio, to FBI Director, Memorandum, Subject: Armadillo May Day Tribe, 29 June 1971.
47. SAC, San Antonio, to FBI Director, Memorandum, Subject: Armadillo May Day Tribe, 29 June 1971.
48. SAC, San Antonio, to FBI Director, Memorandum, Subject: Armadillo May Day Tribe, 29 June 1971.

49. Director, FBI, to SAC, San Antonio, 24 June1971, File 22-cv-2593, Section 6, FBI Records.
50. San Antonio, Memorandum, to Director, FBI, Teletype marked Urgent, 23 June 1971, File 22-cv-2593, Section 6, FBI Records.
51. SAC, San Antonio, Memorandum, to Director, FBI, 15 June 1971; and SAC, San Antonio, Memorandum to Director, FBI, 4 June 1971, File 22-cv-2593, Section 6, FBI Records.
52. FBI Memo, David Phillips and James King, FBI agents, SA-44-1783, 15 June 1971, File 22-cv-2593, Section 6, FBI Records.
53. FBI Memo, Phillips and King, FBI agents, SA-44-1783, 15 June 1971.
54. SAC, San Antonio, Memorandum to Director, FBI, Airtel, 16 June 1971, File 22-cv-2593, Section 6, FBI Records.
55. SAC, San Antonio, Memorandum to Director, FBI, Airtel, 16 June 1971.
56. "Grrrrand Jury," *The Rag*, 14 June 1971.
57. SA James King, to FBI San Antonio Field Office, 24 November 1971, File 100-SA-10834, vol. 2, FBI Records.
58. SA James King, Memo, FBI Report, San Antonio, 9 December 1971, File 100-SA-10834, vol. 2, FBI Records.
59. Director, US Secret Service, US Treasury Department, J. Edgar Hoover (signed), 9 December 1971, File 100-SA-10834, vol. 2, FBI Records.
60. Available in Box 2-G23A, "Anti-war Demonstrations, Spring 1971," UT News Records.
61. Rossinow, *Politics of Authenticity*, 239, mentions the LBJ Library dedication protests, but he gives the entirely false impression these demonstrations were not organized. Again, Martin Wiginton was the prime mover, and he was always very well organized.
62. Larry Springer, "Trouble Pledged for Library Day," *Austin American-Statesman*, 21 May 1971.
63. Rick Fish, Mike Cox, and Jay Brakefield, "'Witch' Women Nabbed in the City," *Austin American-Statesman*, 21 May 1971.
64. Memo, San Antonio Field Office to Director, Washington Field Office (WFO), Houston, Dallas, El Paso, and Oklahoma City, "Urgent," 20 May 1971, File 100-WFO-54190, FBI Records.

65. Memo, San Antonio Field Office to Director, Washington Field Office (WFO), 20 May 1971.
66. Memo, San Antonio Field Office to Director, WFO, 20 May 1971.
67. Larry BeSaw, "Disruption Forbidden by Judge," *Austin American-Statesman*, 22 May 1971.
68. "Notables on Parade," *Austin American-Statesman*, 23 May 1971.
69. BeSaw, "Disruption Forbidden by Judge."
70. Direct Action was a pacifist group advocating nonviolent civil disobedience. The group had connections with Catholic Student Center, and its members sponsored food co-ops and yoga meditation. Working with Direct Action represented the merger of counterculture and politics.
71. Kaye Northcott and Jay Brakefield, "And a Good Time was Had by Most," *Texas Observer*, 4 June 1971, pp. 4–5.
72. Undercover informant report, delivered to SA James King, San Antonio FBI, 27 April 1972, File 100-SA-10834, vol. 2, FBI Records..
73. "Guardsmen Take Over Maryland U," *Austin Statesman*, 21 April 1972.
74. "Study of a Demonstration," *Daily Texan*, 14 April 1972.
75. "Activists Set Plans," *Daily Texan*, 26 April 1972.
76. "Campus Strike," *Austin American*, 21 April 1972.
77. Bertha Lopez and Cliff Avery, "Marchers Dramatize Strike," *Daily Texan*, 21 April 1972.
78. Lopez and Avery, "Marchers Dramatize Strike."
79. Lopez and Avery, "Marchers Dramatize Strike."
80. Memorandum for Information, "Re: Antiwar Demonstration," 21 April 1972.
81. Speakers included one of the eight arrested the day before at protest rally in front of the Post Office, an "unknown homosexual," and Steve Russell representing the *Rag* staff. See Memorandum for Information, "Re: Antiwar Demonstration," 21 April 1972, Box 3W15c, "Anti-war Demonstration, April 1972," Carlson Papers.
82. Memorandum for Information, "Re: Antiwar Demonstration," 21 April 1972.
83. Lopez and Avery, "Marchers Dramatize Strike."

84. Memorandum for Information, "Re: Antiwar Demonstration," 21 April 1972.
85. Marigny Lanier, "Gas Used to Clear Streets," *Daily Texan*, 22 April 1972.
86. Lanier, "Gas Used to Clear Streets"; and Jim Gee, "Women Protesters Get KUT Air Time," *Daily Texan*, 22 April 1972.
87. Lanier, "Gas Used to Clear Streets".
88. San Antonio Field Office to Director, Justice Department, "Attention: Domestic Intelligence Division," 2 May 1972, File 100-SA-10834, vol. 2, FBI Records.
89. Tom Kleinworth, "Mace Empties the Main Building," *Daily Texan*, 22 April 1972.
90. San Antonio Field Office to Director, Justice Department, "Attention: Domestic Intelligence Division," 2 May 1972.
91. Kleinworth, "Mace Empties the Main Building."
92. Karen Justice, "New Campus Strike Planned; UT Quiet after Outburst," *Daily Texan*, 24 April 1972.
93. Kleinworth, "Mace Empties the Main Building"; Rob Taylor, "Madness in Austin," *Dallas Times Herald*, 26 April 1972; and Dotty Griffin, "Police Staying Calm," *Daily Texan*, 22 April 1972.
94. "25 Protestors Arrested," *Daily Texan*, 22 April 1972. Nicholas D., whom many suspected (rightly or wrongly, and without concrete proof) to be a police informant, assumed the role as spokesperson for VVAW.
95. Karen Justice, "New Campus Strike Planned; UT Quiet after Outburst," *Daily Texan*, 24 April 1972.
96. Griffin, "Police Staying Calm."
97. "Tolerance Requested," *Daily Texan*, 24 April 1972.
98. Steve Wisch, "Irwin, Royal Favor Barnes," *Daily Texan*, 24 April 1972.
99. Marigny Lanier, "War Protests Draw Varied Responses," *Daily Texan*, 24 April 1972.
100. Pat Kelly, "No VC Flag," *Daily Texan*, 24 April 1972.
101. Ridge Hammons, "Maced on a March," *Daily Texan*, 24 April 1972.
102. Eric Hagatitte, letter to chief of police, 24 April 1972, Box 3W15c, "Anti-war Demonstration, April 1972," Carlson Papers.

103. S. L. D. Renfrow, "Brother, Can You Spare Some Mace," *Daily Texan*, 22 April 1972.
104. David Powell, "Editorial: It's Time for Peace," *Daily Texan*, 22 April 1972.
105. Karen Justice, "New Campus Strike Planned; UT Quiet after Outburst," *Daily Texan*, 24 April 1972; and Rob Taylor, "Madness in Austin," *Dallas Times Herald*, 26 April 1972.
106. Bill Bray, "3 P.M. Rally Unapproved by Duncan," *Daily Texan*, 25 April 1972.
107. George Carlson, Director of Police, memorandum, to Mr. E. D. Walker, Deputy for Administration, 26 April 1972, Box 3W15c, "Anti-war Demonstration, April 1972," Carlson Papers; and Allen Hamilton, Memorandum, to George Carlson, Director of Police, 26 April 1972, Box 3W15c, "Anti-war Demonstration, April 1972," Carlson Papers.
108. E. D. Walker, Deputy Chancellor for Administration, UT, to Honorable John Peace, Chair of Board of Regents, 3 May 1972, Box 3W15c, "Anti-war Demonstration, April 1972," Carlson Papers.
109. Typewritten report from FBI undercover informant, 26 April 1972, File 100-SA-10834, vol. 2, FBI Records.
110. "Mayday Action Set," *Daily Texan*, 1 May 1972.
111. San Antonio Field Office to Director, Justice Department, "Attention: Domestic Intelligence Division," 2 May 1972, File 100-SA-10834, vol. 2, FBI Records.
112. Typed reports from Undercover Informant, 24 April 1972 and 1 May 1972, File 100-SA-10834, vol. 2, FBI Records.
113. This "naming" is indeed surreal. A confidential source who allegedly "provided reliable information in the past," identified my twin brother Mark as a leader. He was not in Austin at this time but living in Sacramento. SAC, San Antonio, to Director FBI, "Revolutionary Activities," File 100-SA-10834, vol. 2, FBI Records.
114. Memoradum for Information, 9 May 1972, Box 3W15c, "Anti-war Demonstration, April 1972," Carlson Papers.
115. Memorandum for Information, 11 May 1972, Box 3W15c, "Anti-war Demonstration, April 1972," Carlson Papers.
116. Mary Moody, "March on, City Tells Protesters," *Austin Statesman*, 14 May 1972, Box 2-G23A, "Anti-war Demonstrations, Spring 1972, Fall 1972," UT News Records.
117. Moody, "March on, City Tells Protesters."
118. Martin Wiginton, "Why We Must Take Action on May Day," *The Rag*, May 1972, File 100-SA-10834, vol. 2, FBI Records.
119. SAC, San Antonio, to Director, FBI, Domestic Intelligence, 14 October 1972, File 100-SA-10834, vol. 2, FBI Records.

Notes for Chapter 6

1. I have borrowed these ideas from Gregg Michel, "Surveilling the Memphis Movement."
2. Brian Glick, *War at Home: Covert Action Against US Activists* (Cambridge, MA: South End Books, 1999).
3. Thorne Dreyer, "The Spies of Texas: Newfound Files Detail how UT-Austin Police Tracked the Lives of Sixties Dissidents," *Texas Observer*, 17 November 2006.
4. Security Report (untitled and undated), Box 3W15b, "'Leftist' Campus Organizations," Carlson Papers.
5. Security Report (untitled and undated).
6. Quotations from Dale Brumfield, "The Facts Were Immaterial," *Austin Chronicle*, 7 June 2013.
7. Brumfield, "Facts Were Immaterial."
8. SAC, Houston, to Director of FBI, 8 July 1968 memo; and SAC, Houston, to Director of FBI, "Counterintelligence Program, Internal Security, Disruption of the New Left," 25 June 1968, File 22- cv-2593, Section 12, FBI Records.
9. SAC, Houston, to Director of FBI, 8 July 1968 memo; and SAC, Houston, to Director of FBI, "Counterintelligence Program," 25 June 1968.
10. SAC, Houston, to Director of FBI, "Counterintelligence Program," 25 June 1968.
11. SAC, Houston, to Director of FBI, Memo, 16 October 1968, File 22- cv-2593, Section 12, FBI Records.
12. Brumfield, "Facts Were Immaterial."
13. For one of many instances, see SAC, San Antonio, to Director of the FBI, memo, 16 September 1968.
14. Memorandum, SAC, San Antonio, to Director FBI, 28 May 1968, FBI COINTELPRO Records.
15. Memorandum, SAC, San Antonio, to Director FBI, 5 July 1968, FBI COINTELPRO Records.
16. SAC, San Antonio, to Director of the FBI, memo, 24 December 1968, File 22- cv-2593, Section 12, FBI Records.

17. Brumfield, "Facts Were Immaterial."
18. Brumfield, "Facts Were Immaterial."
19. SAC, Cleveland, to FBI Director, memo, 24 March 1969, File 22- cv-2593, Section 12, FBI Records.
20. Brumfield, "Facts Were Immaterial."
21. Brumfield, "Facts Were Immaterial."
22. SAC, San Antonio, to Director of the FBI, memo, 24 December 1968, File 22- cv-2593, Section 12, FBI Records.
23. SAC, San Antonio, to Director of the FBI, memo, 24 December 1968.
24. Interview by Sarah Clark, 19 September 1994, Box 4Zf353, "Gerding Oral History Interview Transcript [partial], 1994," p. 48, Gerding Papers.
25. Memorandum for Information, 19 July 1970, Box 4Zf353, "3-17-70 - 6-23-70 Including YSA report [notes, memos, clippings on student political groups], 1970," Gerding Papers.
26. Garton Ash, *The File*, 242–43.
27. Memorandum for Information, 9 June 1970, Box 4Zf353, "3-17-70 - 6-23-70 Including YSA report [notes, memos, clippings on student political groups], 1970," Gerding Papers.
28. Anthony Ripley, "Big Man on Campus: Police Undercover Agent," *New York Times*, 29 March 1971.
29. Typed report from undercover informant, 16 February 1973, File 100-SA-10848, FBI Reports.
30. Interview by Sarah Clark, 19 September 1994.
31. Quotation from Larry Springer, "I Led Two Lives," *Texas Monthly*, August 1976.
32. Interview by Clark, 19 September 1994. See also Larry Springer, "I Led Two Lives," *Texas Monthly*, August 1976.
33. Interview by Clark, 19 September 1994. See also Springer, "I Led Two Lives."
34. Pat Cuney (email correspondence 27 May 2022, and personal communication in Austin on 30 March 2023) and Peter van Bavel (email correspondence 21 March 2023, and personal communication in Austin 30 March 2023) are the sources for this information.

35. See "List of Names. VVAW Conference, Austin [n.d.]," Box 3W15b, "Vietnam Veterans Against the War, Texas Area," Carlson Papers.
36. Austin Police Department Intelligence Report [Confidential], Burt Gerding to Chief R. A. Miles, "Subject: Summer 1970 Situation," 22 June 1970, Box 4Zf355, "Police Reports on Austin Political Groups; 1968–1970; Undated," Gerding Papers.
37. Gerding to Miles, "Summer 1970 Situation."
38. Undercover informant report: "Gerrard [*sic*] Winstanley Memorial Caucus—4 September 1970," Box 4Zf350, "UT Austin student political activities: 1959–1976, 1994," Gerding Papers.
39. SAC, San Antonio, to Acting Director, FBI, "Re: Martin Julius Murray," 28 February 1973, File 100-SA-10848, FBI Records.
40. Undercover informant report: "Gerrard [*sic*] Winstanley Memorial Caucus."
41. "A conversation was held with Martin Murray on Monday Feb. 1 concerning the nature of the proposed aims of the GWMC as related to the attached 'manifesto.' According to Murray, the meeting on Feb. 3, 1971, will be designed to discuss the issues raised in the 'manifesto.' It will also serve as an arena for discussion of concrete action. Murray said that a list of 'concrete propositions' was in the process of being constructed. Murray does not think dialogue between professors and graduate students will take place. Nor does he think that any demands that graduate students make on the department will be enacted. Rather, he envisions the establishment of a 'counter institutional' model by graduate students. The model would include a radical sociological journal, a radical research center, a group of courses operated by graduate students & advising for coursework conducted by graduate students. This writer [undercover police informant] advised Murray that graduate students do not have the power to institute all that was included in the above model. Murray said that graduate students would 'take power.' As support, he mentioned the growth of the GWMC." Memo, "Gerard Winstanley Memorial Caucus," undercover informant and also fellow PhD graduate student, Department of Sociology,

2 February 1971, Box 3W15b, "Gerard Winstanley Caucus, 1970, 1971, undated," Carlson Papers.

42. Hand-written note, unsigned and dated 25 November 1970, Box 3B37, "Addition," Carlson Papers.
43. Telephone memo, undated, with reference to Nancy Pfieffer, Box 3B37, "Addition," Carlson Papers.
44. Garton Ash, *The File*, 187.
45. Photo, Box 3W15d, "Photographs, Chuck Wagon incident, 11 November 1969," Carlson Papers.
46. Photo, Box 3W15d, "Photographs. For George Carlson, May 6–8, 1970, [from] Texas Department of Public Safety, Confidential, Intelligence," Carlson Papers.
47. Police Surveillance Reels, Box 3Y190.1, "Police Surveillance Reels," Gerding Papers.
48. "A View of the Community United Front, 6 November 1970," Pat [reports on Community United Front], 1970, Box 4Zf350, "UT Austin Student Political Activities: 1959–1976, 1994," Gerding Papers.
49. "View of the Community United Front, 6 November 1970."
50. "Undercover Police Report on Community United Front—15 September 1970," Pat [reports on Community United Front], 1970," Box 4Zf350, "UT Austin Student Political Activities: 1959–1976, 1994," Gerding Papers.
51. "Undercover Police Report on Community United Front—17 September 1970," Pat [reports on Community United Front], 1970, Box 4Zf350, "UT Austin Student Political Activities: 1959–1976, 1994," Gerding Papers.
52. "Undercover Police Reports on Community United Front—22 and 24 September 1970," Pat [reports on Community United Front], 1970, Box 4Zf350, "UT Austin Student Political Activities: 1959–1976, 1994," Gerding Papers.
53. "Undercover Police Report on Community United Front—5 October 1970," Pat [reports on Community United Front], 1970, Box 4Zf350, "UT Austin Student Political Activities: 1959–1976, 1994," Gerding Papers.

54. "Undercover police report on 29 October—Texas Conference to free all Political Prisoners in Amerika," Pat [reports on Community United Front], 1970, Box 4Zf350, "UT Austin Student Political Activities: 1959–1976, 1994," Gerding Papers.
55. "View of the Community United Front, 6 November 1970."
56. "View of the Community United Front, 6 November 1970."
57. Parsons, *Dangerous Grounds*, 45–48.
58. "Undercover police Report, Saturday—12 September 1970," Sal [reports on Young Socialist Alliance and the Student Mobilization Committee], 1970, Box 4Zf350, "UT Austin Student Political Activities: 1959–1976, 1994," Gerding Papers.
59. "Undercover police report on GI Civilian Picnic—19 July 1970," Sal [reports on Young Socialists Alliance and the Student Mobilization Committee], 1970, Box 4Zf350, "UT Austin Student Political Activities: 1959–1976, 1994," Gerding Papers.
60. "Undercover police report on SMC Regional Conference and Regional Antiwar Conference, 19 September 1970," Sal [reports on Young Socialists Alliance and the Student Mobilization Committee], 1970, Box 4Zf350, "UT Austin Student Political Activities: 1959–1976, 1994," Gerding Papers.
61. "Police Report Student Mobilization Committee—3 October 1970," Sal [reports on Young Socialists Alliance and the Student Mobilization Committee], 1970, Box 4Zf350, "UT Austin Student Political Activities: 1959–1976, 1994," Gerding Papers.
62. "Editorial Comment on the events of the evening of Oct. 3," Sal [reports on Young Socialists Alliance and the Student Mobilization Committee], 1970, Box 4Zf350, "UT Austin Student Political Activities: 1959–1976, 1994," Gerding Papers.
63. "Student Mobilization Committee—6 October 1970," Sal [Reports on Young Socialists Alliance and the Student Mobilization Committee], 1970, Box 4Zf350, "UT Austin Student Political Activities: 1959–1976, 1994," Gerding Papers.
64. "Student Mobilization Committee—Steering Committee—14 October 1970," Sal [reports on Young Socialists Alliance and the Student

Mobilization Committee], 1970, Box 4Zf350, "UT Austin Student Political Activities: 1959–1976, 1994," Gerding Papers.

65. "Student Mobilization Committee—Steering Committee—24 October 1970," Sal [reports on Young Socialists Alliance and the Student Mobilization Committee], 1970, Box 4Zf350, "UT Austin Student Political Activities: 1959–1976, 1994," Gerding Papers.

Notes for Chapter 7

Epilogue Email notes from the archivist Sarah Clark, 5 April 1996, stored in Holding Record for the Gerding Papers, DBCAH, https://storymaps.arcgis.com/stories/c6d790bef28148b79b11902a8acea71e.

1. Three interviews conducted by Sarah Clark (19 September 1994, 10 October 1994, and 27 March 1995) for the Briscoe Center, Box 4Zf353, "Gerding Oral History Interview Transcript [partial], 1994" and Box 2X209b, "Transcripts, Interview with Sarah Clark, Gerding Papers. References to this three-part interview are hereafter cited as Interview 1, Interview 2, and Interview 3, followed by page numbers.
2. Interview 3, p. 83.
3. Patricia Highsmith, *The Talented Mr. Ripley* (New York: Coward-McCann, 1955). Many may be more familiar with the 1999 movie of the same name starring Matt Damon and directed by Anthony Minghella.
4. Interview 2, pp. 30, 42.
5. Interview 2, pp. 43–45.
6. Interview 2, p. 45.
7. Interview 3, p. 73.
8. Interview 2, p. 45; Interview 3, p. 73.
9. Interview 2, p. 45.
10. Interview 2, p. 42.
11. Interview 2, pp. 41–42.
12. Interview 1, p. 26.
13. Interview 2, p. 34.
14. Interview 2, p. 33.
15. Interview 2, pp. 33–34.

16. Interview 2, p. 31.
17. Interview 1, pp. 27–28, 26; Interview 2, p. 42.
18. Interview 1, pp. 27–28.
19. Interview 1, p. 27.
20. Interview 3, p. 95.
21. Interview 3, p. 96.
22. Interview 1, p. 21.
23. Interview 2, p. 45.
24. Interview 2, p. 45.
25. Interview 2, p. 42.
26. Interview 2, p. 42.
27. Interview 2, p. 30.
28. Interview 2, pp. 41–42.
29. Interview 2, p. 30.
30. Special thanks to Gregg Michel for point this situation out to me.
31. Interview 1, p. 26; Interview 2, pp. 43–45.
32. Interview 2, p. 30.
33. Interview 3, p. 73.
34. Interview 2, pp. 30–31.
35. Interview 2, pp. 41–42.
36. Interview 3, p. 77.
37. Interview 2, p. 32.
38. Interview 2, p. 32.
39. Interview 2, pp. 30–31.
40. Interview 3, pp. 113–15.
41. Interview 3, pp. 113–15.
42. Interview 2, pp. 32–33.
43. Interview 2, pp. 32–33.
44. Interview 2, p. 47.
45. Interview 2, p. 32.
46. Interview 2, pp. 33–34; Interview 3, p. 72.
47. Interview 2, p. 38.
48. Interview 2, pp. 39–40.
49. Interview 2, pp. 40–41.

50. Interview 3, p. 92.
51. Interview 1, p. 28.
52. Interview 3, p. 104.
53. Interview 3, p. 111.
54. Interview 2, p. 47.
55. Interview 3, p. 84.
56. Interview 3, p. 99.
57. Interview 3, p. 84.
58. Interview 3, p. 85.
59. Interview 3, p. 84.
60. Interview 3, pp. 84–85.
61. Interview 3, p. 114.
62. Interview 3, p. 112.
63. Interview 3, p. 91.
64. Interview 3, p. 119.
65. Interview 3, pp. 116–17, 118.
66. "Officer Is Moved in Primrose Affair," *Austin American-Statesman*, 2 October 1970.
67. Interview 3, pp. 116–17, 118.
68. Interview 3, p. 117.
69. Interview 3, p. 119.
70. This idea is borrowed, loosely, from Fintan O'Toole, *We Don't Know Ourselves: A Personal History of Modern Ireland* (New York: Liveright / W. W. Norton, 2022), 169–71, 422–23.
71. Interview 3, p. 86.
72. O'Toole, *We Don't Know Ourselves*, 168.

Notes for Chapter 8

1. For the source of this idea, see Verdery, *My Life as a Spy*, 4.
2. File 100-SA-10848, FBI Records.
3. FBI, Confidential Memo, San Antonio Field Office, 3 February 1969, File 100-SA-10848, FBI Records.

4. SAC, San Francisco (1007268), Acting Director, FBI, Martin Julius Murray, Revolutionary Activities, 14 November 1972, File 100-SA-10848, FBI Records.
5. Acting Director, FBI, SAC, San Francisco, 10072168, 31 October 1972, File 100-SA-10848, FBI Records.
6. Acting Director, FBI, SAC, San Francisco, 10072168, 31 October 1972, File 100-SA-10848, FBI Records.
7. SAC, San Antonio, to Acting Director of FBI, 29 December 1972, File 100-SA-10848, FBI Records.
8. Transcribed report from undercover informant, 8 December 1972, File 100-SA-10848, FBI Records.
9. Memo from SA Howard Riley, to SAC, San Antonio (100-13608), 26 January 1973, File 100-SA-10848, FBI Records.
10. Information report [undercover informant], dictated to Howard Riley, FBI, San Antonio Office, 6 February 1973, File 100-SA-10848, FBI Records.
11. Report prepared by SA Howard Riley for FBI office, San Antonio, under heading "Martin Julius Muray aka Martin Murray," and containing two separate photographs of me, 22 February 1973, File 100-SA-10848, FBI Records. What follows in the text is derived from this confidential report.
12. Information report [undercover informant], Dictated to Howard Riley, FBI, San Antonio Office, 6 February 1973, File 100-SA-10848, FBI Records.
13. Information report [undercover informant], Dictated to Howard Riley, FBI, San Antonio Office, 6 February 1973, File 100-SA-10848, FBI Records.
14. Information Report [undercover informant] to Riley, 6 February 1973.
15. Typed report from undercover informant, 4 April 1973, File 100-SA-10848, FBI Records.
16. "Why We Are Still There," by Martin Murray, May 1973, NAM (Berkeley, CA), File 100-SA-10848, FBI Records.
17. Memo, FBI San Francisco Office, 31 October 1972, File 100-HQ-474899, FBI Records.

18. Memo, FBI San Francisco Office, 31 October 1972.
19. Memo, Special Agent James Gaskins, FBI, Sacramento, 30 August 1972, File 100-HQ-474899, FBI Records.
20. Memorandum, SAC, San Francisco, to FBI Director, "Subject: 'Socialist Revolution' IS—New Left," 13 January 1972, File 100-HQ-474899, FBI Records.
21. Howard Riley, San Antonio FBI Office, "Security Matter—Revolutionary Activities, Report from SA T-2 (4/27/71)," 28 November 1973, SC-0100-0049B: SC, Mark Murray (Declassified 13 July 2017), FBI Records.
22. Memorandum, San Antonio Field Office, to FBI Headquarters, "Regarding computerized telephone number file—entry and search request," 24 April 1973, File 100-SA-10848, FBI Records.
23. "Report on Political Groups, 1971," (unsigned and undated), Box 4Zf353, "Speech Material, UT [speeches, police reports, notes, clippings, memos, police policy] 1972–1973," Gerding Papers.
24. Special Agent FBI Howard Riley, to SAC San Antonio, "Re: Martin Julius Murray," 22 February 1973, File 100-SA-10848, FBI Records.
25. Howard Riley, San Antonio FBI Office, "Security Matter—Revolutionary Activities, 28 November 1973, Sacramento Letter to the Bureau," 31 August 1973, SC-0100-0049B: SC, FBI Files
26. San Antonio (100-11808) [FBI] to Director [FBI] and Omaha, "Urgent 5/5/70," OM –0100-0098B: OM, FBI Files.
27. Director, FBI, to SAC, San Antonio (New), 4 June 1970, OM –0100-0098B: OM, FBI Files.
28. SAC, Omaha, to Director of FBI, Memorandum, 29 September 1970, SC-0100-0049B: SC, FBI Files.
29. David Hayes, SAC, Omaha, Memorandum, 6 May 1970, OM –0100-0098B: OM, FBI Files.
30. SAC, San Francisco, to Director of FBI, Memorandum, 9 November 1970, SC-0100-0049B, FBI Files.
31. SAC, Omaha, to Director of FBI, Memorandum, 29 September 1970, SC-0100-0049B; and Dwyane Eskridge, SF—100-67807, Report on 30 November 1970, OM –0100-0098B: OM, FBI Files.

32. SAC, San Francisco, to Director of FBI, Memorandum, 9 November 1970, SC-0100-0049B, FBI Files.
33. SAC, Omaha, to Director of FBI, Memorandum, 29 September 1970.
34. SAC, Omaha, to Director, FBI, Memo, 29 September 1970.
35. SAC, Omaha, to Director, FBI, Memo, 29 September 1970.
36. SAC, Omaha, to Director of FBI, Memo, 29 September 1970.
37. SAC, San Francisco, to Director of FBI, Memorandum, 9 November 1970, SC-0100-0049B: SC, FBI Files.
38. SAC, San Antonio, to Director of FBI, Memorandum, 2 November 1970, SC-0100-0049B: SC, FBI Files.
39. SAC, Omaha, to Director of FBI, Memorandum, 17 February 1971, SC-0100-0049B: SC, FBI Files.
40. John Crewdson, "F.B.I. Reported to have Listed Citizens to Detain during Crisis," *New York Times*, 3 August 1975.
41. SAC, Omaha, to Director of FBI, Memorandum, 17 February 1971, SC-0100-0049B: SC, FBI Files.
42. SAC, Omaha, to Director of FBI, Memorandum, 29 January 1971, SC-0100-0049B: SC, FBI Files.
43. Communication between Sacramento FBI field office, and San Antonio field office, 26 November 1973, SC-0100-0049B: SC, FBI Files.
44. Howard Riley, San Antonio field office, to Director of FBI, Memo, 28 November 1973, SC-0100-0049B: SC, FBI Files.
45. Riley to Director of FBI, Memo, 28 November 1973.
46. Riley to Director of FBI, Memo, 28 November 1973.
47. Riley to Director of FBI, Memo, 28 November 1973.
48. Riley to Director of FBI, Memo, 28 November 1973.
49. Carl Larsen, FBI, to SAC, Sacramento, 30 January 1974, SC-0100-0049B: SC, FBI Files.
50. Report, 5 February 1974, SC-0100-0049B: SC, FBI Files.
51. Larsen, FBI, to SAC, Sacramento, 30 January 1974.
52. Director, US Secret Service, Memo, 28 November 1973, SC-0100-0049B: SC, FBI Files.

53. Riley to Director of FBI, Memo, 28 November 1973.
54. Riley to Director of FBI, memo, 28 November 1973.

Notes for the Postscript

1. Stephen Atkins, *Encyclopedia of Modern American Extremists and Extremist Groups* (Westport, CT: Greenwood Press, 2002), pp. 222.
2. New American Movement pamphlet, Box 3W15b, "New American Movement, 1973," Carlson Papers.
3. Ernesto "Che" Guevara, *The Motorcycle Diaries: Notes on a Latin American Journey* (New York: Verso, 1996), 31.
4. Guevara, *Motorcycle Diaries*, 31.

Notes for a Note on Sources

1. Raymond Williams, "Structures of Feeling," in *Marxism and Literature* (Oxford: Oxford University Press, 1977), 132, 162–64.
2. Rossinow, *Politics of Authenticity*.
3. Embree, *Voice Lessons*.

Bibliography

Archives and Collections

Federal Bureau of Investigation (FBI) Files

FBI Records: The Vault. https://vault.fbi.gov/.

FBI Records. Records of the Department of Justice, Washington DC. Obtained via FOIA request.

FBI Records. Records of the Department of Justice, Washington DC. Obtained via FOIA request from National Archives Records Administration (NARA), Kansas City, MO.

Dolph Briscoe Center for American History, University of Texas at Austin.

Burt Gerding Papers, 1959–1980, 1994

George Carlson Papers, 1967–1973

Prints and Photographs Collection

UT News and Information Service Records, 1928–1997

UT Traffic and Security Chief Allen R. Hamilton Records, circa 1950s–1960s

Labadie Collection, University of Michigan, Ann Arbor.

Newspaper Sources

Austin American-Statesman

Austin American

Austin Chronicle

Austin Statesman

Boston Globe

Daily Crimson (Harvard University)

Daily Texan (UT Austin)

Dallas Morning News

Dallas Times Herald

Houston Post

The New Hampshire (University of New Hampshire)

New York Times

San Antonio Light

San Francisco Chronicle
San Francisco Examiner
Stars and Stripes (Washington, DC)
Texas Observer
Washington Post

Secondary Sources

Anderson, Terry. *The Movement and the Sixties: Protest in America from Greensboro to Wounded Knee*. New York: Oxford University Press, 1996.

Anderson, Terry. *The Sixties*. 5th ed. New York: Routledge, 2017.

Atkins, Stephen. *Encyclopedia of Modern American Extremists and Extremist Groups*. Westport, CT: Greenwood Press, 2002.

Bakke, Kit. *Protest on Trial: The Seattle 7 Conspiracy*. Pullman: Washington State University Press, 2018.

Barber, Lucy. *Marching on Washington*. Berkeley: University of California Press, 2002.

Baskir, Lawrence, and William Strauss. *Chance or Circumstance: The Draft, the War, and the Vietnam Generation*. New York: Knopf, 1978.

Bates, Tom. *Rads: The 1970 Bombing of the Army Mathematics Research Center of the University of Wisconsin and Its Aftermath*. New York: HarperCollins, 1992.

Betts, Richard K. *Enemies of Intelligence: Knowledge and Power in American National Security*. New York: Columbia University Press, 2009.

Blackstock, Nelson. *COINTELPRO: The FBI's Secret War on Political Freedom*. New York: Monad Press, 1975.

Calvert, Greg, and Carol Neiman. *A Disrupted History: The New Left and the New Capitalism*. New York: Random House, 1971.

Churchill, Ward, and Jim Vander Wall. *Agents of Repression: The FBI's Secret Wars Against the Black Panther Party and the American Indian Movement*. Boston: South End Press, 1990.

Churchill, Ward, and Jim Vander Wall. *The COINTELPRO Papers: Documents from the FBI's Secret Wars Against Domestic Dissent*. Boston: South End Press, 1990.

Cunningham, David. *There's Something Happening Here: The New Left, the Klan, and FBI Counterintelligence*. Berkeley: University of California Press, 2004.

Davis, James Kirkpatrick. *Assault on the Left: The FBI and the Sixties Antiwar Movement.* Westport, CT: Praeger, 1997.

Dennis, Mike. *The Stasi: Myth and Reality*. London: Pearson/Longman, 2003.

Didion, Joan. *Slouching Towards Bethlehem*, in *We Tell ourselves Stories in Order to Live: Collected Nonfiction.* New York: Alfred Knopf, 2006.

Donner, Frank. *The Age of Surveillance: The Aims and Methods of America's Political Intelligence System*. New York: Knopf, 1980.

Donner, Frank J. *Protectors of Privilege: Red Squads and Police Repression in Urban America*. Berkeley: University of California Press, 1990.

Dreyer, Thorne. "The Spies of Texas." *Texas Observer*, 4 January 2009.

Dreyer, Thorne. "The Spies of Texas: Newfound Files Detail How UT-Austin Police Tracked the Lives of Sixties Dissidents." *Texas Observer*, 17 November 2006.

Drobney, Jeffrey. "Generation in Revolt: Student Dissent and Political Repression at West Virginia University." *West Virginia History* 54 (1995): 105–22.

Dubose, Terry. "Vietnam Veterans Against the War." In Janes, *No Apologies*.

Embree, Alice. *Voice Lessons*. Austin,: Briscoe Center for American History / University of Texas Press, 2021.

Ernst, John, and Yvonne Baldwin. "The Not So Silent Minority: Louisville's Antiwar Movement, 1966–1975." *Journal of Southern History* 73, no. 1 (2007): 105–42.

Escobar, Edward. "The Dialectics of Repression: The Los Angeles Police Department and the Chicano Movement, 1968–1971." *Journal of American History* 79, no. 4 (1993): 1483–514.

Fernández, Johanna. *The Young Lords: A Radical History*. Chapel Hill: University of North Carolina Press, 2020.

Flynn, George. *The Draft, 1940–1973*. Lawrence: University Press of Kansas, 1993.

Foley, Michael. *Confronting the War Machine: Draft Resistance During the Vietnam War*. Chapel Hill: University of North Carolina Press, 2003.

Fountain, Aaron. "The war in the Schools: San Francisco Bay Area High Schools and the Anti–Vietnam War Movement, 1965–1973." *California History* 92, no. 2 (2015): 22–41.

Garrow, David J. *The FBI and Martin Luther King, Jr.: From "Solo" to Memphis*. New York: W. W. Norton, 1981.

Garton Ash, Timothy. *The File: A Personal History*. New York: Random House, 1997.

Gentry, Curt. *J. Edgar Hoover: The Man and the Secrets*. New York: Norton, 2001.

Gitlin, Todd. *The Sixties: Years of Hope, Days of Rage*. New York: Bantam Books, 1987.

Glick, Brian. *War at Home: Covert Action Against US Activists*. Cambridge, MA: South End Books, 1999.

Gottlieb, Sherry Gershon. *Hell No, We Won't Go! Resisting the Draft During the Vietnam War*. New York: Penguin Books, 1991.

Guevara, Ernesto "Che." *The Motorcycle Diaries: Notes on a Latin American Journey*. New York: Verso, 1996.

Hagan, John. *Northern Passage: American Vietnam War Resisters in Canada*. Cambridge, MA: Harvard University Press, 2001.

Heineman, Kenneth. *The Peace Movement at American State Universities in the Vietnam Era*. New York: New York University Press, 1992

Highsmith, Patricia. *The Talented Mr. Ripley*. New York: Coward-McCann, 1955.

Hunt, Andrew. *The Turning: A History of Vietnam Veterans Against the War*. New York: New York University Press, 1999.

Janes, Daryl, ed. *No Apologies: Texas Radicals Celebrate the '60s*. Austin: Eakin Press, 1992.

Janda, Sarah Eppler. *Prairie Power: Student Activism, Counterculture, and Backlash in Oklahoma, 1962–1972*. Norman: University of Oklahoma Press, 2018.

Jeffreys-Jones, Rhodri. *The FBI: A History*. New Haven: Yale University Press, 2008.

Jordan, Winthrop. *Tumult and Silence at Second Creek: An Inquiry into a Civil War Slave Conspiracy*. Baton Rouge: Louisiana State University, 1993.

Karnow, Stanley. *Vietnam: A History*. New York: Viking Press, 1983.

Kasinsky, Renée. *Refugees from Militarism: Draft-Age Americans in Canada*. New Brunswick: Transaction Books, 1976.

Kauffman, L. A. *Direct Action: Protest and the Reinvention of American Radicalism*. New York: Verso Books, 2017.

Kershner, Seth. "'A Constant Surveillance': The New York State Police and the Student Peace Movement, 1965–1973." *Global Sixties* 16, no. 1 (2023): 22–52.

Levin, Matthew. *Cold War University: Madison and the New Left in the Sixties*. Madison: University of Wisconsin Press, 2013.

Lieberman, Robbie. *Prairie Power: Voices of 1960s Midwestern Student Protest*. Columbia: University of Missouri Press, 2004.

Marcuse, Herbert. "Repressive Tolerance." In *A Critique of Pure Tolerance*, edited by Robert Paul Wolff, Barrington Moore Jr., and Herbert Marcuse. Boston: Beacon Press, 1969.

Marx, Gary T. "Thoughts on a Neglected Category of Social Movement Participant: The Agent Provocateur and the Informant." *American Journal of Sociology* 80, no. 2 (1974): 402–42.

McCardell, Jackie, Jr., dir. *The Economy Furniture Strike*. Austin: ACC Center for Public Policy and Political Studies and Paradigm Shift Multimedia, 2010.

Medsger, Betty. *The Burglary: The Discovery of J. Edgar Hoover's Secret FBI*. New York: Vintage, 2014.

Menand, Louis. "Change Your Life: The Lessons of the New Left." *New Yorker*, 22 March 2021, pp. 46–53.

Michel, Gregg. "Government Repression of the Southern New Left." In *Rebellion in Black and White: Southern Student Activism in the 1960s*, edited by Robert Cohen and David J. Snyder. Baltimore: Johns Hopkins University Press, 2012.

Michel, Gregg. Review of Sarah Eppler Janda, *Prairie Power: Student Activism, Counterculture, and Backlash in Oklahoma, 1962–1972*. *Journal of American History* 105, no. 4 (2019): 1094–95.

Michel, Gregg. *Spying on Students: The FBI, Red Squads, and Student Activists in the 1960s South.* Baton Rouge: LSU Press, 2024.

Michel, Gregg. "Surveilling the Memphis Movement: Police Spying in Memphis, 1968–1976." *Journal of Southern History* 87, no. 4 (2021): 673–710.

Michel, Gregg. *Struggle for a Better South: The Southern Student Organizing Committee, 1964–1969.* New York: Palgrave Macmillan, 2004.

Mills, C. Wright. *The Sociological Imagination.* New York: Oxford University Press, 1959.

Moretta, John. "Political Hippies and Hip Politicos: Counterculture Alliance and Cultural Radicalism in 1960s Austin, Texas." *Southwestern Historical Quarterly* 123, no. 3 (2020): 266–91.

Moser, Richard. *The New Winter Soldiers: GI and Veteran Dissent During the Vietnam Era.* New Brunswick: Rutgers University Press, 1996.

Murray, Martin J. "Building Fires on the Prairie." In *Radical Sociologists and the Movement: Experiences, Lessons, and Legacies*, edited by Martin Oppenheimer, Martin Murray, and Rhonda Levine. Philadelphia: Temple University Press, 1992.

O'Reilly, Kenneth. *Hoover and the Un-Americans: The FBI, HUAC, and the Red Menace.* Philadelphia: Temple University Press, 1983.

O'Reilly, Kenneth. *"Racial Matters": The FBI's Secret File on Black America, 1960–1972.* New York: Free Press, 1989.

O'Toole, Fintan. *We Don't Know Ourselves: A Personal History of Modern Ireland.* New York: Liveright / W. W. Norton, 2022.

Pace, Katherine Leah. "Forgetting Waller Creek: An Environmental History of Race, Parks, and Planning in Downtown Austin, Texas." *Journal of Southern History* 87, no. 4 (2021): 603–44.

Pardun, Robert. *Prairie Radical: A Journey Through the Sixties* Los Gatos, CA: Shire Press, 2001.

Parsons, David. *Dangerous Grounds: Antiwar Coffeehouses and Military Dissent in the Vietnam Era.* Chapel Hill: University of North Carolina Press, 2017.

Raley, Bill. "How Conscientious Objectors Killed the Draft: The Collapse of the Selective Service During the Vietnam War." *Cleveland State Law Review* 68 (2019): 151–76.

Reavis, Dick. "SDS: From Students to Seniors." In Janes, *No Apologies*.

Roberts, Lawrence. *Mayday 1971: A White House at War, a Revolt in the Streets, and the Untold History of America's Biggest Mass Arrest*. Boston: Houghton Mifflin Harcourt, 2021.

Robinson, Tim. *Listening to the Wind: The Connemara Trilogy: Part 1*. London: Penguin, 2007.

Rosenfeld, Seth. *Subversives: The FBI's War on Student Radicals, and Reagan's Rise to Power*. New York: Farrar, Straus, and Giroux, 2012.

Rossinow, Douglas. *The Politics of Authenticity: Liberalism, Christianity, and the New Left in America*. New York: Columbia University Press, 1999.

Rutenberg, Amy. *Rough Draft: Cold War Military Manpower Policy and the Origins of Vietnam-Era Draft Resistance*. Ithaca, NY: Cornell University Press, 2019.

Sale, Kirkpatrick. *SDS*. New York: Random House, 1973.

Schama, Simon. *Dead Certainties (Unwarranted Speculations)*. New York: Albert Knopf, 1991.

Schultz, John. *The Conspiracy Trial of the Chicago 7*. 2nd ed. Chicago: University of Chicago Press, 2009.

Soeur Queens. *Soeur Queens Songbook: Songs of Sisterhood*. Fly by Night Print Collective, 1970.

Springer, Larry. "I Led Two Lives." *Texas Monthly*, August 1976.

Stewart, Luke. "'Hell, They're Your Problem, Not Ours': Draft Dodgers, Military Deserters and Canada–United States Relations in the Vietnam War Era." *Études Canadiennes / Canadian Studies* 85 (2018): 67–96.

Summerlin, Donald. "Peach State Protest: The Anti-Vietnam War Movement in Georgia, 1964–1974." *Journal of the Georgia Association of Historians* 26 (2005): 1–16.

Sutton, Nora. "'Have You Bought Enough Vietnam?' The Vietnam Antiwar Movement at West Virginia University, 1967–1970." *West Virginia History* [NS] 13, no. 1 (2019): 27–56.

Thelan, Sarah. "Mobilizing a Majority: Nixon's 'Silent Majority' Speech and the Domestic Debate over Vietnam." *Journal of American Studies* 51, no. 3 (2017): 887–914.

Thompson, Nicole. "Utah, the Anti-Vietnam War Movement, and the University of Utah." *Utah Historical Quarterly* 78, no. 2 (2010): 154–74.

Verdery, Katherine. *My Life as a Spy: Investigations in a Secret Police File* (Durham, NC: Duke University Press, 2018).

Watters, Pat, and Stephen Cillers, eds. *Investigating the FBI.* Garden City, NY: Doubleday, 1973.

Weiner, Tim. *Enemies: A History of the FBI.* New York: Random House, 2013.

Williams, Raymond. "Structures of Feeling." In *Marxism and Literature.* Oxford: Oxford University Press, 1977.

Index

A

B

C

F

G

H

I

J

K

L

M

N

O

V

W

Y